THE THEOLOGY OF HUGH OF ST. VICTOR

In the context of the early twelfth-century urbanization of Paris, Hugh of St. Victor developed a pioneering program of intellectual and moral practices focused on reforming the soul. Boyd Taylor Coolman identifies the signature theme of spiritual re-formation as the unifying motif to Hugh's theology, and analyzes the symbolic and aesthetic dimensions of re-formation conceived as "soul-construction," in the manner of gothic cathedrals being built at the time.

This study places Hugh of St. Victor within the context of the profound religious, economic, and political changes occurring in the early twelfth century. Drawing on the majority of Hugh's writings, it reveals links between various aspects of his theology – exegesis and spirituality, theology and cultivation of virtue – and highlights the practical nature of his reforming program, aimed at both restoring the beauty of the soul and re-forming the human person into a dwelling place for the presence of God.

BOYD TAYLOR COOLMAN is Assistant Professor of Theology at Boston College. He is the author of *Knowing God by Experience* (2004).

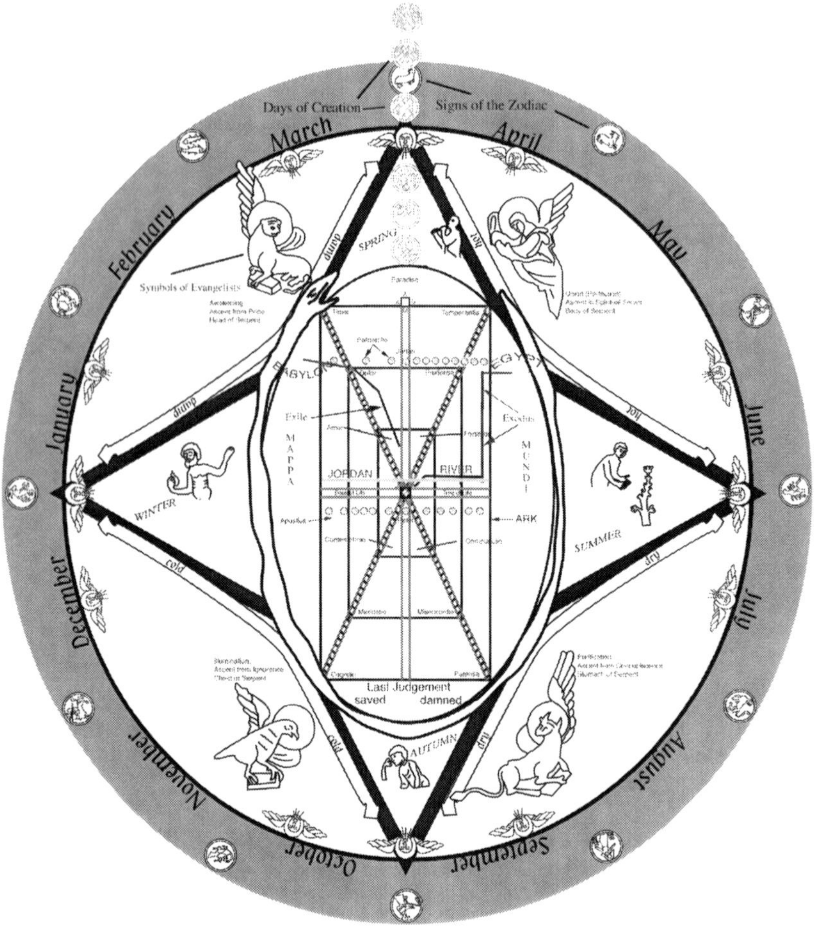

Illustration 1: A modern rendering of Hugh of St. Victor's symbolic representation of Noah's Ark. Design by Grover A. Zinn. Graphics by Sarah Nelson, Grover A. Zinn and Andrew Zinn. © Grover A. Zinn.

THE THEOLOGY OF HUGH OF ST. VICTOR

An Interpretation

BOYD TAYLOR COOLMAN

Boston College

CAMBRIDGE
UNIVERSITY PRESS

CAMBRIDGE UNIVERSITY PRESS
Cambridge, New York, Melbourne, Madrid, Cape Town,
Singapore, São Paulo, Delhi, Mexico City

Cambridge University Press
The Edinburgh Building, Cambridge CB2 8RU, UK

Published in the United States of America by Cambridge University Press, New York

www.cambridge.org
Information on this title: www.cambridge.org/9781107612259

First published 2010
First paperback edition 2013

A catalogue record for this publication is available from the British Library

Library of Congress Cataloguing in Publication data
Coolman, Boyd Taylor, 1966–
The theology of Hugh of St. Victor : an interpretation / Boyd Taylor Coolman.
p. cm.
ISBN 978-0-521-88625-3 (hardback)
1. Hugh, of Saint-Victor, 1096?–1141. 2. Theology–History–Middle
Ages, 600–1500. I. Title.
BX4705.H786C66 2010
2309.2092–dc22
2010001508

ISBN 978-0-521-88625-3 Hardback
ISBN 978-1-107-61225-9 Paperback

Contents

Acknowledgments

As a rule, academic book writing is a solitary business, even as an author shares the company of a host of textual voices, in this case both medieval and modern. Happily, however, this present book is something of an exception to that rule. Over the past decade or so, I have had the pleasure of participating in what might be called, fittingly enough, a Victorine *collatio*, a gathering of Victorine scholars who coalesced around the corpus of Hugh of St. Victor, much as their twelfth-century counterparts encircled Hugh himself at the Abbey of St.-Victor in Paris. The on-going collaboration and extended conversation on matters Victorine with Grover Zinn, Michael Signer (of blessed memory), Hugh Feiss, Dale Coulter, Deborah Goodwin, Franklin Harkins, Paul Rorem, and others, has been for me an immensely fertile and sustaining community of scholarship and – dare I say it – of faith. It is a pleasure here to acknowledge the vital role of these contemporary "Victorini" as a group in the production of this book, but also profusely to thank several of them individually for their labors: Dale Coulter, Hugh Feiss, and Paul Rorem each read and commented at length upon the entire manuscript, providing both insightful criticism and reassuring encouragement. The cliché notwithstanding, the flaws and deficiencies that remain in the book are due to incorrigible stubbornness.

Grateful acknowledgment should also be made of Christopher Beeley, Mark Burrows, Marshall Crossnoe, Deborah Goodwin, and Constant Mews, who read and commented on the initial proposal or early parts of the manuscript.

I wish also to thank my Undergraduate Research Fellows, Jeffery Peloquin and Scott Molony, for their labors on the notes and bibliography, as well as Boston College for the stipends to fund their efforts. Thanks as well to Boston College for the semester-long sabbatical during which much of this book was written. The members of the doctoral seminar, "The Theology of Hugh of St. Victor" at Boston College, provided clarifying and stimulating engagement with the idea at the heart of this book.

A particular note of thanks goes to Kate Brett, at Cambridge University Press, for her enthusiastic receptivity to the idea for such a book on Hugh of St. Victor at the outset.

May the anonymous reviewer at Cambridge University Press, who provided such insightful suggestions for its improvement, "not lose his reward."

May the young Cameron Harrington, who kept me company in the early morning hours during the fall semester in which I completed the manuscript, someday write his own book.

Finally, as always, but more than ever, I am deeply grateful to Holly Taylor Coolman for her sacrifices that made this book possible and for her patient endurance of its production.

Abbreviations

Adnot. in reg.	Adnotationes elucidatoriae in libros regum
APS-V	*L'Abbaye parisienne de Saint-Victor au moyen-âge. Communications présentées au XIIIe colloque d'humanisme médiévale de Paris (1986–88).* Ed. Jean Longère. Bibliotheca Victorina 1. Turnhout, 1991.
Archa Noe	*De archa Noe*
Arrha	*De arrha anime*
Assumpt.	*Pro assumptione Virginis*
BM Virg.	*De beatae Mariae virginitate*
Cant. BM	*Super canticum Mariae*
CCCM	*Corpus Christianorum, continuatio medievalis.* Turnhout, 1964
Chronicon	*Chronicon vel De tribus maximis cirumstantiis gestorum*
CSMV	*Hugh of St. Victor: Selected Spiritual Writings*, trans. by a Religious of The Community of St. Mary the Virgin, intr. by Aelred Squire. Classics of the Contemplative Life. London: Faber and Faber, 1962.
Didasc.	*Didascalicon*
Eulogium	*De amore sponsi ad sponsam/Eulogium sponsi ad sponsam*
Grammatica	*De grammatica*
In Eccl.	*In salomonis Ecclesiastes*
In hierarchiam	*Commentaria in hierarchiam coelestem s. dionysii areopagitae*
In Pent.	*Adnotationes elucidatoriae in Pentateuchon*
Inst.	*De institutione novitiorum*
Lament.	*Adnotatiunculae elucidatoriae in threnos Jeremiae*
Laude	*De laude caritatis*
Libellus	*Libellus de formatione arche*
Meditatione	*De meditatione*

Misc.	*Miscellanea*
OHSV I	*L'Oeuvre de Hugues de Saint-Victor I: De institutione novitiorum; De virtute orandi; De laude caritatis; De arrha animae.* Vol. I. Latin text by H. B. Feiss and P. Sicard. Translation (French) by D. Poirel, H. Rochais, and P. Sicard. Introductions, notes, and appendices by D. Poirel. Sous la règle de Saint Augustin. Turnhout, 1997.
OHSV II	*L'Oeuvre de Hugues de Saint-Victor, II: Super Canticum Mariae; Pro Assumptione Virginis; De beate Mariae virginitate; Egredietur virga-Maria porta.* Vol. II. Latin text, introductions, notes, and appendices by Bernadette Jollès. Sous la règle de Saint Augustin. Turnhout, 2000.
Quid vere	*Quid vere diligendum sit*
Quinque sept.	*De quinque septenis*
PL	*Patrologiae cursus completus sive bibliotheca universalis, integra, uniformis, commode oeconomica omnium ss. Partum, doctorum scriptorumque ecclesiasticorum qui ab aevo apostolico ad innocentii III tempora floruerunt … series [Latina].* Ed. J.-P. Migne. 221 vols. Paris, 1844–64.
Practica	*Practica geometriae*
RTAM	*Recherches de Théologie Ancienne et Médiévale*
Sacr.	*De sacramentis christianae fidei*
Sapientia	*De sapientia Christi*
SC	*Sources Chrétiennes.* Paris: Les éditions du Cerf, 1949
Script.	*De scripturis et scriptoribus sacris*
Sententiae	*Sententiae de divinitate*
Septem donis	*De septem donis Spiritus Sancti*
Tribus diebus	*De tribus diebus*
Vanitate	*De vanitate mundi*
Verbo	*De Verbo Dei*
Virtute orandi	*De virtute orandi*

INTRODUCTION

A theology of re-formation

"be reformed in the newness of your mind"
Rom. 12:2 (Douay Rheims)

INTRODUCTION: RE-FORMATION IN HISTORICAL CONTEXT

To visitors from the countryside, like the recently arrived young Hugh and his name-sake uncle,[1] Paris in 1120 offered a novel spectacle. Signs of emergent urbanization were readily apparent: Merchants, artisans, clerics, lawyers, and students went about their business,[2] as did doctors, bakers, butchers, cooks and tavern keepers.[3] Others were weaving and sewing fabrics of various kinds into "clothes, blankets, saddles, carpets, curtains, napkins, nets, ropes, hats, and baskets," forging metals and casting tools and implements, and cultivating gardens and rose-hedges, orchards and fields.[4] There was also the sensory evidence of building. Soon to be designated a royal capital by Louis VI,[5] Paris was under construction.

[1] Robert-Henri Bautier, "Les Origines et les premiers developpements de l'abbaye Saint-Victor de Paris," in *L'abbaye parisienne de Saint-Victor au moyen-âge*, ed. Jean Longère (hereafter *APS-V*), Bibliotheca Victorina 1 (Turnhout: Brepols, 1991), 35.

[2] M.-D. Chenu, "Civilisation urbaine et théologie. L'École de Saint-Victor au XIIe siècle," *Annales: Economies, sociétés, civilisations* 29 (1974), 1253–63.

[3] See Hugh of St. Victor, *Didascalicon*, 2.21–26. Critical text: *Didascalicon de studio legendi: A Critical Text*, ed. Charles Henry Buttimer, The Catholic University of America Studies in Medieval and Renaissance Latin 10 (Washington, D.C.: Catholic University of America Press, 1939). English translation: *The Didascalicon of Hugh of St. Victor: A Medieval Guide to the Arts*, trans. and ed. Jerome Taylor, Records of Western Civilization: Sources and Studies 64 (New York: Columbia University Press, 1961 and 1991). Cited as *Didasc.*, followed by book and chapter, Buttimer's page and lines, and Taylor's page when his translation is used. Taylor's introduction and notes cited as *The Didascalicon of Hugh of St. Victor.*

[4] *Didasc.*, 2.21–26 (Buttimer 39.29–44.28; Taylor 75–79). Chenu ("Civilisation urbaine," 1257) notes how urbanization brought with it a proliferation of new trades and new commercial and economic activities, which in turn required a new valuation and estimation of their rightful place among human affairs. The specialized trades, the manual arts of the towns, were no longer "servile," their practitioner was now deemed an *artifex*.

[5] Louis VI settled in Paris *c.* 1130. Margot Fassler, *Gothic Song: Victorine Sequences and Augustinian Reform in Twelfth-Century Paris* (Cambridge: Cambridge University Press, 1993), 197, writes: "Late

Craftsmen, working "with mattocks and hatchets, the file and beam, the saw and auger, planes, vises, the trowel and the level," were "smoothing, hewing, cutting, filing, carving, joining, daubing in every sort of material – clay, stone, wood, bone, gravel, lime, gypsum, and other materials …"[6] Throughout the city, foundations were being laid, structures erected, paint and color applied for adornment – all according to increasingly elaborate architectural plans.[7] Edifices of all types, some newly constructed, others under renovation, were rising throughout the city. Perhaps most conspicuous of all was the construction of churches.[8] Already under way in the eleventh century,[9] ecclesial construction was intensifying in the early twelfth century; in the following decades it would soon tower majestically in the gothic style of St.-Denis and Notre-Dame in Paris, and also the cathedral at Chartres.[10]

For the denizens of Paris, the sheer fact of city life seems to have shaped their consciousness, their thought-forms, even their worldviews in myriad ways. In the mid twentieth century, M.-D. Chenu, and before him Georges Duby, showed how in the early twelfth century "urban civilization … penetrated all the way into the tissue of reflection, of methods, of aspirations, of contemplations." This is variously manifest.

eleventh century Paris was one of several important northern French cathedral towns; by the closing decades of the twelfth century, it had become a small, but significantly more cosmopolitan, city of major significance, overshadowing its neighbors in importance. This change in the city's fortunes occurred, in part at least, because the Capetian kings of France, first Louis VI and then his son, Louis VII, made Paris a true royal capital at the very time that the French throne was being strengthened and its power consolidated."

6 *Didasc.*, 2.22 (Buttimer 40.28f.; Taylor 76).

7 See Chenu, "Civilisation urbaine," 1257–58. Among the various trades emerging in this new context, Chenu singles out the *architectes*, and with them all the related trades, fabrication, construction, carpentry, tools, ornamentation. The traditional classification of arts and trades is here exceeded. The question of architecture was thus treated separately. It is not merely the builders of cathedrals that the theologians are considering, but also the builders of human dwellings.

8 Giles Constable, "Renewal and Reform in Religious Life: Concepts and Realities," in *Renaissance and Renewal in the Twelfth Century*, eds. Robert L. Benson and Giles Constable with Carol D. Lanham, Medieval Academy Reprints for Teaching 26 (Cambridge, Mass.: Harvard University Press, 1982), 44: "An important aspect of the reform movement was the rebuilding and repair of the ecclesiastical buildings that had been neglected or destroyed …"

9 Around 1000, Ralph Glaber wrote of his world "clothed everywhere in a white garment of churches" (*PL* 142.651D).

10 See William W. Clark, "Context, Continuity, and the Creation of National Memory in Paris, 1130–1160: A Critical Commentary," *Gesta* 45 (2006), 161–75; Dominique Poirel, "Symbolice et anagogice: l'école de Saint-Victor et la naissance du style gothique," in *L'Abbé Suger, le manifeste gothique de Saint-Denis et la pensée victorine, colloque organisé à la Fondation Singer-Polignac le mardi 21 november 2000 par Rencontres médiévales européennes*, ed. Dominique Poirl, Rencontres médiévales européennes 1 (Turnhout: Brepols, 2001), 141–70; and Patrice Sicard, "L'Urbanisme de la Cité de Dieu: constructions et architectures dans la pensée théologique du XIIe siècle," in *L'Abbé Suger, le manifeste gothique de Saint-Denis et la pensée victorine*, 109–40.

In contrast to the forms of Benedictine monasticism, for example, new forms of religious life sprang up, especially the orders of canons regular, which reflected urban life.[11] Where traditional thinkers like Rupert of Duetz and Bernard of Clairvaux saw in the city the image of "the world" in all its fallenness, for the new forms of religious life, like the canons regular, the image of the city became paradigmatic of ideal human community.

Shortly after Hugh arrived at the Abbey of St.-Victor in Paris,[12] construction began on the new abbey and monastic buildings,[13] about the same time as the nearby monastery of Ste-Geneviève and the chapel of St.-Aignan.[14] The daily awareness of the gradual building of new and elaborate ecclesial structures seems to have given the image of construction a new theological significance.[15] Here was a religious ethos in which stone, wood, metal, and glass gave invisible forms structured and striking visibility, through the careful application of well-ordered practices and organized processes, in the service of both aesthetic pleasure and divine–human encounter – "the beauty of a city," Hugh will aver, "consists in the sublimity of its edifices."[16] Yet, it was a world of form, structure, and order applied not only to the construction of walls and buildings, but also to spiritual disciplines, practices of common life, educational programs, and theological systems. This link between thought and life, between material and intellectual culture, is the point of departure for the "readings of texts and the understanding of doctrines"[17] of Hugh of St. Victor pursued in this study.

Stated simply, this study argues that Hugh conceives of Christian existence in this life as aiming at the construction of a dwelling place, an *aedificatio* for the presence of God within human persons, through their reformation (*reformatio*) in the image of God, accomplished

[11] Chenu, "Civilisation urbaine," 1254–55: "The multiplication of communities of canons regular is of a piece with the changes which were affecting the social and economic milieu ...: the transition from rural stability to the mobility of mercantile fortunes, to the feverishness of towns, to the multiplication of human relations. Thus the foundation [at St. Victor], in the neighborhood of the city, and with its open school, presents itself as a novelty."

[12] The abbey of St.-Victor was founded in Paris by William of Champeaux in 1108 and housed an Augustinian order of regular canons. For the most recent study of the early history of the abbey see Bautier, "Origines," 23–52.

[13] Construction began during the tenure of Bishop Gilbert (1117–23) (Fassler, *Gothic Song*, 244, n. 11). Unfortunately, nothing of the twelfth-century church of St.-Victor remains today. "All surviving parts of the church were destroyed during the Revolution and its aftermath" (245).

[14] Bautier, "Origines," 35–36. [15] Chenu, "Civilisation urbaine," 1258.

[16] *Adnotatiunculae elucidatoriae in threnos Jeremiae* (*PL* 175.255B–322B), at 267C: "Decor civitatis in sublimitate aedificiorum." (Hereafter, *Lament*.)

[17] Chenu, "Civilisation urbaine," 1254.

through ordered practices.[18] While *prima facie* not a startling claim, it nonetheless captures a crucial feature of his theology with both breadth and precision. Many of Hugh's works can be located along the arc of his reforming program; much of what Hugh says within individual works relates to this goal. Toward that end, Hugh advocates specific practices that are both theological and ecclesial-communal. They are theological, in that they emerge explicitly in the context of this divine–human relationship and facilitate the construction of this *templum Dei*; they are ecclesial-communal, in that, while they engage persons individually and comprehensively (physically, intellectually, and morally), they are enacted in the context of the ecclesial and canonical community at the Abbey of St.-Victor in early twelfth-century Paris, and in their execution help to constitute that community. Together, this goal and these practices govern much in Hugh's theology and give it a distinctively practical cast.

This study does not pretend to be a comprehensive overview of Hugh's theology, though it does draw from nearly all of his numerous writings and hopes to offer insight into the whole of it; it is not a study of any particular doctrine, though it touches on many theological themes and tries to organize them within a single overarching frame; it is not a general overview of Hugh's theology,[19] though it does seek to elucidate what might be termed his signature thought-structure.[20] In short, at the heart of Hugh's theology and at the center of the community at St.-Victor stand "reforming practices."

[18] A similar observation is made by Patrice Sicard, *Diagrammes médiévaux et exégèse visuelle: Le Libellus de formatione arche de Hugues de Saint-Victor* (Paris/Turnhout: Brepols, 1993), 210ff. Sicard stresses the theme of interior construction, though not with the connection to form and re-form as here.

[19] For an excellent introduction to Hugh of St. Victor and an overview of his writings, see Paul E. Rorem, *Hugh of St. Victor* (Oxford: Oxford University Press, 2009).

[20] Hugh's corpus is large and diverse. On dating and sequences, see Damien van den Eynde, *Essai sur la succession et la date des écrits de Hugues de Saint-Victor*, Spicilegium Pontificii Athenaei Antoniani 13 (Rome: Pontificium Athenaeum Antonianum, 1960); Roger Baron, "Notes biographiques," and Dominique Poirel, *Livre de la nature et débat trinitaire au XIIe siècle: le "De tribus diebus" de Hugues de Saint-Victor*, Bibliotheca Victorina 14 (Turnhout: Brepols, 2002), 131–54. As Rorem notes, Hugh "taught not only all of theology in its broad sense (biblical, doctrinal, practical, philosophical) but also history and grammar, geometry and geography" (*Hugh of St. Victor*, 3). The challenge that any interpreter of his theology faces from the start is how to organize and present it. In fact, Hugh's theology is susceptible to various, complementary interpretations and presentations. For his part, Rorem's organizing principle of "pedagogy" is quite useful and illuminating. That Hugh's concept of pedagogy can be conceived of as "formation," or more precisely "reformation," is the thesis of the present approach.

REFORM IN HISTORICAL CONTEXT

Neither the theme of reform, nor the practices that facilitate it, have been extensively or systematically explored in scholarship devoted to Hugh of St. Victor. Broadly speaking, Hugh's interest in *reformatio* should be seen within the grand trajectory of pre-modern, Western Christian reform traditions, first noted by Gerhart Ladner's groundbreaking work, *The Idea of Reform* (1954) and R. Javelet's *Image et ressemblance*, and emphasized more recently by Ellen Charry's *By the Renewing of Your Minds* (1997).[21] Ladner's work demonstrated the centrality and distinctiveness of the notion of reform in pre-modern Christian tradition. John Van Engen observes that, "since re-forming … is what Christian man was supposed to be about, such movements of renewal become virtually the theme of medieval Christian civilization." According to Van Engen, Ladner was the first to find " 'reform' and variations on equivalent Latin words to be central" in early and medieval Latin Christianity. Ladner's analysis helped to distinguish reform from other kinds of renewal initiatives in the Middle Ages, including revolution, rebellion, and re-birth/renaissance.[22] For him, "reform" was a mode of renewal "peculiar to Christianity, taught first by the Apostle Paul in the New Testament, worked out by the Fathers of the church East and West, and then rendered influential in innumerable ways through a thousand years of medieval civilization."[23] Though Ladner's study did not reach as far as Hugh, our Victorine stands squarely in the tradition he identified.[24] For her part, Charry brought Ladner's thesis forward in relation to later figures such as Thomas Aquinas, Julian of

[21] Gerhart H. Ladner, *The Idea of Reform: Its Impact on Christian Thought and Action in the Age of the Fathers* (Cambridge, Mass.: Harvard University Press, 1954); Robert Javelet, *Image et ressemblance au douzième siècle: de saint Anselme à Alain de Lille*, 2 vols. (Paris: Editions Letouzey et Ané, 1967); Ellen Charry, *By the Renewing of Your Minds* (New York: Oxford University Press, 1997).

[22] See John H. Van Engen, "Images and Ideas: The Achievements of Gerhart Burian Ladner, with a Bibliography of his Published Works," *Viator* 20 (1989), 101–4.

[23] Ibid., 103: "The heart of Ladner's insight is this: Reform, as taught in the Christian scriptures and Fathers, means fundamentally personal renewal based upon man's original creation in the image and likeness of God. This renewal entails a change of mind and heart, graced by sacramental ministrations, that moves men and women ever closer to the likeness of God. The movement, the action implicit in the reforming, has been made possible by the incarnation, God become flesh, the second Adam, who represented perfectly what image-likeness is in all its fullness."

[24] This study hopes to continue Ladner's methodology, which, in Van Engen's words, followed "the principle of speaking about issues and movements in medieval civilization by way of the language contemporaries employed" (ibid., 96; 101, n. 35) and sought "to grasp how this fundamental notion [of reform] worked itself out in a variety of contexts. For this it is better not to concoct any grand scheme – Ladner himself generally refrained from doing that – but to review a series of trenchant observations about aspects of medieval civilization" (ibid., 103–4).

Norwich, and John Calvin, restating and extending Ladner's basic thesis under the rubric of pre-modern "sapiential theology," experience-rich, morally engaged, speculative *and* practical. As will be borne out below, Hugh's theology of reformation is deeply sapiential in similar ways.

More narrowly, Hugh's literary output occurred in Paris at the Abbey of St.-Victor, roughly between 1118 and 1141. Viewing his theology from the perspective of *reformatio* allows his thought to be linked more fully than is often the case to its twelfth-century milieu, where profound economic, political, cultural, and religious changes were producing the so-called "twelfth-century renaissance."[25] Hugh's Paris was in many ways at the center of these dramatic changes in twelfth-century Europe.[26] A "massive economic transformation" was under way, as agricultural production increased along with the population, as trade expanded northward from the Mediterranean Sea and southward from the North Sea, as a money-based economy emerged, as commerce flourished in emerging urban centers, as – broadly speaking – commercialization took hold. Coupled with growing urbanization, this development enabled cities like Paris to support, not only an emerging middle class of merchants and townspeople, but also thriving communities of scholars and students.[27] Charismatic masters appeared in these urban centers – possessing either a wide and developed literary culture, a profound grasp of Aristotelian logic, a technical knowledge of law (Roman or canon), or all of these – drawing students from all over Europe to their classrooms.[28] Relative peace, especially in France, facilitated the formation of strong, well-organized, and stable governments, creating demand for educated, literate bureaucrats to administrate a government based increasingly on written laws and records. The Capetian kings of France, Louis VI, "the Fat" (1108–37), and his son, Louis VII (1137–80), made Paris a true royal capital at the very time the French throne was being strengthened and its power consolidated.[29] Political stability encouraged freedom of movement for many like Hugh himself,[30] who traversed a great distance from his

[25] Recent works, e.g., Robert Norman Swanson, *The Twelfth-Century Renaissance* (New York: St. Martin's, 1999), 3–6, have stressed the highly regional nature of the so-called "twelfth-century Renaissance."

[26] See note 5 above.

[27] See C. Stephen Jaeger, *The Envy of Angels: Cathedral Schools and Social Ideals in Medieval Europe* (Philadelphia: University of Pennsylvania Press, 1994), 239–68. Jaeger notes that "the student population of Paris swelled from whatever the cathedral of Notre Dame could accommodate by itself in 1100 (certainly not more than about 100 students) to 2000–3000 by 1140" (239).

[28] See Swanson, *Twelfth-Century Renaissance*, 1–39.

[29] Fassler, *Gothic Song*, 197.

[30] Swanson, *Twelfth-Century Renaissance*, 9.

birthplace to join the newly chartered chapter of Augustinian canons at the Abbey of St.-Victor in Paris.[31]

Shaping and shaped by these dramatic changes were various monastic, ecclesial, and personal initiatives of reform,[32] "one of the central facts of the history of the eleventh century because of its many wide and deep ramifications."[33] In this period, "the terms most frequently used for religious change were *reformare* and *reformatio*."[34] Prevalent in the literature emanating from various quarters in the early twelfth century, the theme of reform has been well documented,[35] but is usefully rehearsed. Toward the end of the eleventh century, Pope Gregory VII implemented sweeping reforms directed at bishops and cathedral canons, a movement that runs parallel to profound Cistercian reforms of monastic institutions, advocating stricter observance of the *Rule of St. Benedict*.

> There was a common concern at that time, and especially in the period from about 1100 to 1160, with the nature of religious life and the ideal of personal perfection. A set of values as well as a way of life, embodied in various institutions, was at the heart of the movement of reform, which can be seen as an effort to monasticize first the clergy, by imposing on them a standard of life previously reserved for monks, and then the entire world.[36]

Gregory VII "applied *reformare* to the church as a whole," reflecting "a new perception – that institutional change was possible,"[37] and "a new

[31] On what is known of Hugh's origins, see Rorem, *Hugh of St. Victor*, 9–11, and the earlier literature, including: E. Croydon, "Notes on the Life of Hugh of St. Victor," *Journal of Theological Studies* 40 (1939), 232–53; Jerome Taylor, *The Origin and Early Life of Hugh of St. Victor: An Evaluation of the Tradition*, Texts and Studies in the History of Medieval Education 5 (Notre Dame, Ind.: Medieval Institute, 1957); Roger Baron, "Notes biographiques sur Hugues de Saint-Victor," *Revue d'histoire ecclésiastique* 51 (1956), 930; Dominique Poirel, "*Hugo Saxo*. Les origines germaniques de la pensée d'Hugues de Saint-Victor," *Francia. Forschungen zur westeuropäischen Geschichte* 33.1 (2006), 163–69.

[32] See Constable, "Renewal and Reform," 37–67 and Giles Constable, *The Reformation of the Twelfth Century* (Cambridge: Cambridge University Press, 1996). "The terms *renovatio*, *reformatio*, *transformatio*, *reversio*, *recreatio*, and *reflectio* were applied by many writers in the twelfth century to the conversion or *transitus* of the soul from the state of dissimilarity into which it had fallen as a result of sin into the state of similarity or grace in which it had been created" (Constable, *Reformation*, 45).

[33] David Luscombe and Jonathan Riley-Smith, "Introduction," in *The New Cambridge Medieval History, vol.* IV *c.1024–c.1198*, eds. David Luscombe and Jonathan Riley-Smith (Cambridge: Cambridge University Press, 2004), 5.

[34] Constable, *Reformation*, 3.

[35] See Fassler, *Gothic Song*, 187–240, and the literature she cites. Fassler observes: "Throughout twelfth-century Europe, calls to reform stirred a wide range of people: not only monks and canons, but bishops, popes and the laity as well. Ideals of reform, their sources and their translation into both new and renewed modes of religious life, are subjects central to understanding the period" (187).

[36] Constable, *Reformation*, 6.

[37] Constable, "Renewal and Reform," 38.

historical outlook, which emphasized the mutability of all terrestrial institutions."[38] Innovative here was Gregory VII's attempt to reform the whole church, not just individuals. "For the first time in Church history more than personal, more than monastic, and more than even imperial renewal, indeed a structural reform of the Church as a whole had to be envisaged."[39]

Situated as a kind of hybrid of clerical and monastic reform was the canonical movement. The canons regular, or Augustinian (Austin) canons, were distinguished from their secular counterparts by their common life of shared property and their submission to the so-called *Rule of St. Augustine*. At the same time, in certain respects, they forged an identity in contrast to traditional monasticism. The canons regular "fell in between these two branches [clerical and monastic reform] and looked to both for inspiration."[40] On one hand, they participated in the "monasticization" of the clergy; on the other hand, they strove to "promote the goals of the Gregorian reform movement."[41] Central to the canon's *raison d'être* and perhaps his most distinguishing characteristic was, in the words of Carolyn Bynum, a "sense of a responsibility to edify his fellow men both by what he says and by what he does," that is, *verbo et exemplo*.[42] Behind this central feature of canonical life lay, at least in part, newly emerging conceptions of the *vita apostolica*, characterized by a shift away from the monastic ideal of common property and shared communal life to a pastoral or evangelical ideal, "combining a stress on individual perfection with pastoral activity (e.g., preaching and teaching)."[43] Bynum thus sums up the distinctive ideals of the canonical movement, as exemplified at St.-Victor, under three heads: (1) a conviction that the mixed life (contemplation and active service) is superior to the contemplative life; (2) a new emphasis on preaching; and (3) a new emphasis on sacraments and history.[44] These interests are readily apparent in Hugh's theology.

Of particular relevance to Hugh's theology is the way in which the ideal of reform came increasingly to entail an attempt, not to return to

[38] I. S. Robinson, "Reform and the Church, 1073–1122," in Luscombe and Riley-Smith, *The New Cambridge Medieval History, vol. IV*, 275.

[39] Van Engen, "Images and Ideas," 104–5. See also John Howe, "The Nobility's Reform of the Church," *American Historical Review* 93.2 (1988), 317–39.

[40] Fassler, *Gothic Song*, 187–240. [41] Ibid., 189.

[42] Carolyn Walker Bynum, "The Spirituality of Regular Canons in the Twelfth Century," in *Jesus as Mother: Studies in the Spirituality of the High Middle Ages* (Berkeley: University of California Press, 1982), 22–58. Bynum observes that "canonical authors see canons as teachers and learners, whereas monastic authors see monks only as learners," 36.

[43] Constable, "Renewal and Reform," 54–55.

[44] Bynum, "Spirituality of Regular Canons," 33–34.

an earlier, traditional form of religious life, but to establish new and better forms. The emerging ideal, "applied to religious and secular institutions in the eleventh and twelfth centuries," was not merely change, but change "for the better" (*in melius*),[45] a forward-looking change,[46] as the prefix "re" increasingly came to mean "new."[47] Originating apparently with Augustine, and emerging as distinctively Western (Ladner's thesis),[48] this ideal of reform "for the better" had an affinity with canonical reformers,[49] including Hugh, in whose writings it appears repeatedly. Part of a "developmental mentality,"[50] both Southern and Constable have noted an optimism animating twelfth-century reform, a forward-looking posture that sensed "a new stage in God's plan for the reformation and recreation of men."[51] In a biblical idiom, the goal was not of "reforming the Garden of Eden on earth but of transforming men into paradisiacal flowers."[52]

Scholars have noted the special importance of reform for the canons regular in twelfth-century reforming initiatives. In the opening decades of twelfth-century Paris, powerful currents of both royal and ecclesiastical resistance, arrayed against reform initiatives directed at the cathedral canons of Notre-Dame, plunged the newly founded community of canons regular at the Abbey of St.-Victor into a maelstrom of conflict and intrigue.[53] The community of canons regular was initially established

45 See Ladner (*Idea of Reform*, 43, 47, 156–59) for the importance of this sense of reform in earlier Christian tradition.

46 Constable, *Reformation*, 3: Reform "could refer either to restoration and revival, in a backwards-looking sense, or to re-birth and re-formation, as a forwards-looking change."

47 Constable, "Renewal and Reform," 40.

48 Van Engen, "Images and Ideas," 103: Ladner saw different emphases between Eastern and Western versions of this theme. "In the Eastern church the key term is *apokatastasis*, a total renewal which brings about a return to the original paradisiac state." "In the West, beginning with Tertullian and then especially through Augustine, the key term is reform and especially *reformatio in melius*. Through the incarnation, the perfection and grace of the God-man, fallen man is enabled so to 'reform for the better' as to surpass in the end his original paradisiac state and to reach a new state of recreation. This is the goal, and it was this personal reform that animated notions of renewal throughout Western medieval culture."

49 Ibid., 104: "In the West … Augustine's understanding of 'reform for the better' went hand in hand with his emphasis upon building a 'city of God' different from the city of man. … Augustine's circle of friends and clerics sharing a common Christian life provided a potent image of a monastic vanguard, the model later for canons regular in the eleventh and twelfth centuries and for Dominicans in the thirteenth."

50 Luscombe and Riley-Smith, "Introduction," 2.

51 Constable, "Renewal and Reform," 62.

52 Ibid., 63. "The concept of renewal and reform that started as an effort to recreate conditions that had existed in the distant – and often mythical – past came increasingly to be based on principles of nature and reason and to accept forms of religious life that had never existed in the past and could be justified only as part of God's emerging plan for the present and the future" (66).

53 For a helpful overview of these developments see Fassler, *Gothic Song*, 187–210. For general discussions of various aspects of Victorine thought and life in the twelfth century, see Carolyn Walker Bynum, *Docere Verbo et Exemplo: An Aspect of Twelfth-Century Spirituality* (Missoula:

in 1108, when William of Champeaux, a prominent cathedral canon and leading master in the cathedral school, left Notre-Dame to establish a new mode of religious life at Paris. William, and the students who joined him, located themselves on the site of an abandoned hermitage dedicated to St. Victor just outside the city walls on the left bank of the Seine. "William's decision to leave the cathedral, contrary to the story Abelard tells, may have been motivated by a deep commitment to reform, not only to pursue a reformed clerical life, but also to promote the cause of reform at Notre Dame itself." For her part, Fassler observes that "the circumstances of [St.-Victor's] foundation suggest that the abbey was created not only as a haven for Parisian canons who yearned for the common life, but also as an example for the secular canons at the cathedral. Thus, although St.-Victor was a royal abbey from the time of its official foundation … the house nevertheless served immediately to promote conversion to a particular mode of religious life." This interest in effecting reform is evident even in the choice of the abbey's location: "It was precisely in such locations that reformers … established new houses of canons regular: far enough from the city to have land and solitude, yet near enough to make their presence strongly felt within it."[54]

The importance of reform for the Abbey of St.-Victor is thus manifest. Its reason for being was the cause of reform, both of those canons who lived within it, and of the cathedral clergy throughout the diocese and beyond. The Victorines were in the vanguard of twelfth-century reform initiatives in Paris. As Fassler has described, the decade or so between the founding of St.-Victor and Hugh's arrival there witnessed subtle maneuvering and even open conflict in the struggle between various parties arrayed for and against reform in Paris. Hugh's career at St.-Victor coincides to a great extent with the period of triumph for the reform party, of which St.-Victor was a part, in their attempts to bring canonical reform to the chapter at the cathedral of Notre-Dame.[55]

In the first half of the twelfth century, then, the diversity and ubiquity of the theme of reform, the various images used to describe it, and the wide range of objects to which it could be applied suggest that by Hugh's time *reformare* was a fundamental concept and framework by which to

Scholars Press, 1979); Bynum, "Spirituality of Regular Canons" in *Jesus as Mother*, 22–58; and Jean Châtillon, *Le mouvement canonial au moyen âge: réforme de l'église, spiritualité et culture*, Bibliotheca Victorina 3 (Paris/Turnhout: Brepols, 1992).

54 Fassler, *Gothic Song*, 201.

55 Ibid., 206: "After 1123, however, when Stephen of Senlis [a reform-minded cleric] became Bishop of Paris, there would have been no barrier to writing new works for the cathedral liturgy as well. It was during this same time that Hugh of St. Victor wrote his first great works of scriptural

conceive of the nature of the Christian life. Indeed, as already noted above, reform movements had become "virtually the theme of medieval Christian civilization."[56] By the early decades of the twelfth century, *reformare* could well have seeped deeply into the conscious and even the subconscious of many. If so, it would not be surprising to see *reformare* shaping theological discourse, not only in explicit, but also in implicit, subtle, and pervasive ways.[57] While scholarly attention has been directed at the institutional, religious, and sociological aspects of twelfth-century life, as a theological theme reform has not been widely appreciated. When it is, hitherto-unappreciated links between thought and historical context become apparent.

Along with a constellation of related terms and concepts, *reformare* is a leitmotif running through Hugh's *oeuvre*. More precisely, his theology reflects many of these larger reform movements. He, too, is interested in patterns of thought and behavior that effect reformation; he, too, is interested in exemplary individuals whose form of life is worthy of transformative imitation; he, too, is interested in reform for the better (*in melius*). His thought, accordingly, might seem rather obviously characterized as a theology of reformation.[58] Yet, Fassler rightly notes that, while "the importance of reform to Hugh has long been recognized," "his

exegesis and developed his vision of the church in the *Moral Ark of Noah* and the slightly later *Mystical Ark of Noah*." For an extended discussion, see ibid., 203–6.

56 Van Engen, "Images and Ideas," 104.

57 See, for example, Maur Standaert, "La doctrine de l'image chez saint Bernard," *Ephemerides Theologiae Lovanienses* 23 (1947), 70–129, who interprets the theology of Bernard of Clairvaux in terms of formation, deformation, and reformation, as will be done below with respect to Hugh.

58 For Hugh's theology generally, in addition to Rorem, see Roger Baron, *Science et sagesse chez Hugues de Saint-Victor* (Paris: Lethielleux, 1957), Patrice Sicard, *Hugues de Saint-Victor et son école: introduction, choix de texte, traduction et commentaries,* Témoins de Notre Histoire (Tournhout: Brepols, 1991), and the numerous articles by Grover A. Zinn, Jr., including "History and Contemplation: The Dimensions of the Restoration of Man in Two Treatises on Noah's Ark by Hugh of St. Victor," unpublished doctoral dissertation, Duke University, 1969; "Hugh of St. Victor and the Ark of Noah: A New Look," *Church History* 40 (1971), 261–72; "Mandala Symbolism and Use in the Mysticism of Hugh of St. Victor," *History of Religions* 12 (1973), 317–41; "Book and Word: The Victorine Background of Bonaventure's Use of Symbols," in *S. Bonaventura 1274–1974*, ed. Jacques Guy Bougerol (Rome: Grottaferrata, 1974), II:143–69; "Hugh of St. Victor and the Art of Memory," *Viator* 5 (1974), 211–34; "*Historia fundamentum est*: The Role of History in the Contemplative Life According to Hugh of St. Victor," in *Contemporary Reflections on the Medieval Christian Tradition: Essays in Honor of Ray C. Petry*, ed. George H. Shriver (Durham, NC: Duke University Press, 1974), 135–58; "*De gradibus ascensionum*: The Stage of Contemplative Ascent in Two Treatises on Noah's Ark by Hugh of St. Victor," in *Studies in Medieval Culture*, ed. J. R. Sommerfeldt (Kalamazoo, Mich.: Medieval Institute, 1975): V:61–79; "Personification Allegory and Visions of Light in Richard of St. Victor's Teaching on Contemplation," *University of Toronto Quarterly* 46 (1977), 190–214; "History and Interpretation: 'Hebrew Truth,' Judaism, and the Victorine Exegetical Tradition," in *Jews and Christians: Exploring the Past, Present, and Future*, ed. James H. Charlesworth (New York: Herder & Herder, 1990), 100–23; "Suger, Theology, and

writings are not usually interpreted with reform of the clergy as a major goal."[59] Extrapolating from and expanding Fassler's observation, this study seeks to describe Hugh's theology precisely in terms and from the perspective of *reformatio*, not only that of the clergy, but reform taken more broadly, to encompass the whole Christian community and the Christian existence lived within it.

RESTORATION THROUGH *REFORMATIO* IN HUGH'S THEOLOGY

Scholars have noted not only the ubiquity of the theme of reform in twelfth-century spiritual and theological writings,[60] but also the diversity of meanings and nuances given to it.[61] This study, accordingly, will forego *a priori* definitions of reformation in Hugh's thought. Rather, it will attend closely to the meaning of *reformare*, along with related terms and themes, as they arise in his works.[62]

At the outset, the theme of reformation must be related to that of restoration (*restauratio*), so prominent in Hugh's writings. Indeed, restoration is often held up as Hugh's central theme and signature theological principle. For him, restoration is the theological counter-point to creation, and with it, pivoting on the primordial Fall, constitutes a fundamental

the Pseudo-Dionysian Tradition," in *Abbot Suger and Saint-Denis: A Symposium*, ed. Paula Lieber (New York: Harry N. Abrams, 1986, 33–40); "Hugh of St. Victor, Isaiah's Vision and *De Arca Noe*," in *The Church and the Arts: Papers read at the 1990 Summer Meeting and the 1991 Winter Meeting of the Ecclesiastical History Society*, ed. Diana Wood (Oxford: Blackwell, 1992), 99–116; "Texts Within Texts: The Song of Songs in the Exegesis of Gregory the Great and Hugh of St. Victor," *Studia Patristica* 25 (Leuven, 1993), 209–15; "The Influence of Augustine's *De doctrina christiana* upon the Writings of Hugh of St. Victor," in *Reading and Wisdom: The* De doctrina christiana *of Augustine in the Middle Ages* (Notre Dame: University of Notre Dame Press, 1995), 48–60; "Hugh of St. Victor's *De scripturis et scriptoribus sacris* as an *Accessus* Treatise for the Study of the Bible," *Traditio* 52 (1997), 11–34; "Exile, the Abbey of St-Victor at Paris, and Hugh of Saint Victor," in *Medieval Paradigms: Essays in honor of Jeremy du Quesnay Adams* (New York: Palgrave Macmillan, 2005), 11:83–111; "*Vestigia victorina*: Victorine Influence on the Spiritual Life in the Middle Ages with Special Reference to Hugh of Saint-Victor's *De Institutione novitiorum*," unpublished paper, 2009.

59 Fassler, *Gothic Song*, 212, n. 10. Fassler adds that an unpublished dissertation at Harvard by Thomas Declan McGonigle (1977), "who stresses the importance of reform in Hugh's description of 'contemplative ascent' (296)," is an exception.

60 For the bibliography on the history of reform, see Ladner and the literature in his wake, as charted by Philip H. Stump in "The Influence of Gerhard Ladner's *The Idea of Reform*," in *Reform and Renewal in the Middle Ages and the Renaissance: Studies in Honor of Louis Pascoe, S.J.*, Studies in the History of Christian Thought 96 (Leiden: Brill, 2000), 3–17.

61 Fassler, *Gothic Song*, 206: "The meaning of the word 'reform' had become so blurred and general by the mid-twelfth century as almost to defy definition."

62 I wish to acknowledge the seminal importance for this study of Grover Zinn's early article "Mandala Symbolism." In that article, Zinn gestures at many of the themes that the present study traces out in much greater detail.

conceptual framework of his theology. Hugh situates this notion programmatically at the beginning of perhaps his most famous theological work, *De sacramentis*: "The subject matter of all the Divine Scriptures is the work of man's restoration. For there are two works in which all that has been done is contained. The first is the work of foundation; the second is the work of restoration." Hugh defines these works as follows: The "works of creation" (*opera conditionis*) pertain to the creation of the world and all its elements, accomplished in six days; the "works of restoration" (*opera restaurationis*) are the Incarnation of the Word and all the Word's sacraments, accomplished over the six ages of salvation history.[63]

But what precisely Hugh means by "restoration" is not often specified. Commentators have tended to assume casually that the meaning of restoration is self-evident. When it is discussed, it is rather vaguely characterized as a general recovery of what was lost in the Fall. So far as it goes, this is true. For his part, Hugh describes *restauratio* in various ways – for example, as a return to spiritual health, a return to right relationship with God, or even a return to perfection.[64] Embracing all of these, yet reducible to none, and standing at the center of Hugh's concept of restoration – so this study argues – is the notion of reformation (*reformatio*). This begins to be evident in the remark that Hugh appends to the passage just quoted: "The work of foundation is that whereby those things, which were not, came into being. The work of restoration is that whereby those things, which had come to nothing, were made *better* (*melius*)" (emphasis added). Later, in the same work Hugh elaborates:

> Therefore true faith rests in two: Creator and Redeemer ... If you believe in the Creator you know also that you were made; if you confess the Redeemer you know that you were repaired (*reparatus es*) ... In what was his He made you; in what was yours he remade you (*In suo te fecit, in tuo te refecit*).[65]

Here (1) restoration is a repairing that is also in some sense a refashioning or a remaking; (2) its ultimate result exceeds in some way the original

[63] *De sacramentis christianae fidei*, 1. Prol.2 (*PL* 176.183A–B; Deferrari 3). English translation: Hugh of Saint Victor, *On the Sacraments of the Christian Faith (De sacramentis)*, trans. R. J. Deferrari, Medieval Academy of America 58 (Cambridge, Mass.: Crimson Printing Company, 1951). (Hereafter as *De sacramentis*; abbreviated as *Sacr.*, followed by Book Part, and Section numbers, and cited with *PL* reference followed by page number in Deferrari's translation). Nearly the same description is found in *De scripturis et scriptoribus sacris* 2 (*PL* 175.11B). See also *De vanitate mundi* 2 (*PL* 176.703–20) at 716B–C. (Hereafter abbreviated as *Script.* and *Vanitate* respectively.)

[64] In the middle of the last century, Dionysius Lasić, *Hugonis de S. Victore theologia perfectiva: eius fundamentum philosophicum ac theologicum*, Studia Antoniana 7 (Rome: Romae Pontifium Athenaeum Antonianum, 1956), emphasized this point, and since then others have sounded the refrain.

[65] *Sacr.*, 1.10.8 (*PL* 176.341A; Deferrari 79).

state of creation. This second issue will be taken up below. Noteworthy at present is that restoration begins to receive content in these references to "repairing" and "remaking." Hugh's *Sententiae de divinitatis*[66] or "Opinions on Divinity" reflects this: "The work of restoration is to refashion (*restituere*) that which had been laid waste (*perierat*)"[67] that "it might build up again (*erigeret*) what had fallen into ruin (*iacentem*)."[68] Slightly later in the *De sacramentis*, Hugh is explicit. Employing a familiar biblical image, he defines restoration as a reformation that exceeds an original condition: "at the wedding feast, Jesus turned water into wine, in order to demonstrate the state of reformation for the better (*reformationis statum in melius*) and [to be] a sacrament of restoration."[69]

Throughout, Hugh's corpus reveals the importance of reformation. In his *Commentary* on *The Celestial Hierarchy* of Dionysius,[70] for example, he incorporates this theme into the Dionysian light aesthetic: "Gazing upon the beauty of the Father we are refashioned (*restituimur*), that is, reformed (*reformamur*) again, that is, converted to it ..."[71] In *De sacramentis*, he observes how it was necessary that "first [the human person] be justified from fault in order to be reconciled, afterward that he be liberated from wretchedness in order to be reformed (*reformaretur*)."[72] In his *Didascalicon*, Hugh describes the process of restoration as that by which "the divine likeness is repaired (*reparetur*) within us, a likeness which to us is a form (*forma*) but to God is his nature." In this way, Hugh continues, "the more we are conformed (*conformamur*) to the divine nature, the more do we possess Wisdom, for then there begins to shine forth again in us what has forever existed in the divine Idea or Pattern."[73] Restore, refashion, repair – all these terms constellate for Hugh around a fundamental idea, summed up in the term, *reformare*.

This study contends, accordingly, that in crucial ways, which have not received sufficient scholarly attention, Hugh's theology is a "theology of reformation": the divine intent in human salvation is realized when "a person is fully and perfectly *reformed* in the image of God,"[74] when the water

[66] Critical edition by A. M. Piazzoni, "Ugo di San Vittore 'auctor' delle *Sententiae de divinitate*," *Studi Medievali*, 3rd series, 23.2 (1982), 861–955. Cited as *Sententiae*; all translations are mine.

[67] *Sententiae* (Piazzoni, 920.234). [68] *Sententiae* (Piazzoni, 920.239).

[69] *Sacr.*, 1.1.15 (*PL* 176.199A; Deferrari 20).

[70] *Commentaria in hierarchiam coelestem s. dionysii areopagitae* (*PL* 175.923–1154). Cited as *In hierarchiam*; all translations are mine. See the discussion in Rorem, *Hugh of St. Victor*, 167–76.

[71] *In hierarchiam* (*PL* 175.942B–C). [72] *Sacr.*, 2.1.12 (*PL* 176.412A; Deferrari 249).

[73] *Didasc.*, 2.1 (Buttimer 23.17–20; Taylor 61).

[74] *De quinque septenis* (Baron 118.268–69). Critical edition: *Six opuscules spirituels*, with Introduction, critical text, French translation, and notes by Roger Baron, *Sources Chrétiennes* 155 (Paris: Editions

of creation is reformed "for the better" into the wine of restoration.[75] As will be argued below, *reformatio* gives content and texture to the general theme of *restauratio*, affording it a theological "center of gravity," which controls and organizes its other dimensions.

RE-FORMATION

A fuller, more precise sense of *reformatio*, as Hugh conceives of it, appears if its prefix is set off from its root, so that the thrust of both parts is more readily apparent. "Re-form" suggests both the importance of the notion of form (*forma*), as well as the sense of something to be done a second time.

To begin, the prefix "re-" is crucial for Hugh. It is a fixture in his works, which are littered (as seen above) with words like "renew," "repair," and "refashion." An obvious implication, to be sure, is that of recovery of something lost, and Hugh's Augustinian sense of the sin-ravaged state of human nature is a neglected aspect of his theology.[76] Though certainly conveying the idea of recovery, for Hugh "re-" also entails the notion of going beyond a lost ideal state to the attainment of something better.[77] His conception of creation contains an assumption (vaguely Irenaean) that the Edenic state was not complete, but rather was divinely intended and mandated to develop further, as Hugh says in one place, from a state of mere being (*esse*), to a fuller state of beautiful being (*pulchrum esse*). Or, as he puts it later in the same work, the ultimate goal was that human

du Cerf, 1969). Cited as *Quinque sept.*, followed by page and line numbers. All translations are mine, though I have benefited from the unpublished translation of Hugh Feiss, OSB.

75 In this, Hugh adopts key aspects of the primitive Christian experience of salvation as radical transformation in believers. See Rom. 12:2; 1 Cor. 2:16; 2 Cor. 3:18; Gal. 3:5; Eph. 4:23; Col. 3:10; 1 Pet. 1:22). Luke Timothy Johnson notes: "the overwhelming testimony of the New Testament to the early Christian experience of salvation is that it changes humans themselves both individually and communally" (*The Creed: What Christians Believe and Why It Matters* [New York: Doubleday, 2003], 149). Moreover, Hugh's "*in melius*" seems to reflect the New Testament conviction that "salvation was not merely a rescue or even a restoration. It was an elevation. Paul declares that 'the free gift is not like the trespass' (Rom. 5:15), and argues 'how much greater' is the effect of Jesus' work on all humans than the effect of Adam's disobedience on his descendants" (Rom. 5:12–21) (*The Creed*, 150).

76 Years ago, Grover Zinn (and earlier Jean Châtillon) stressed the important role the Fall plays in Hugh's theology, stressing that "his theology is incomprehensible without a clear understanding of his teaching on this point" (*History and Contemplation*, 197).

77 See Hugh's *De scripturis et scriptoribus sacris* (*PL* 175.9–28; hereafter cited as *Script.*), moreover, where Hugh speaks of the gradual "renovation" (*innovatio*), the making new of the human race, occurring through the grace of Christ over time, from the point of Christ's resurrection to the end of the age (*Script.*, 17 [*PL* 175.24C]). A partial translation is in Denys Turner, *Eros and Allegory: Medieval Exegesis of the Song of Songs* (Kalamazoo, Mich.: Cistercian Publications, 1995), 265–74. See Zinn, "Hugh of St. Victor's *De scripturis et scriptoribus sacris*."

persons "might pass beyond that which they had been made, to that for which they had been made."[78] Hugh's sense of "re-form" does indeed look backward to what was lost in the Fall; but more importantly it strains forward to what even pre-lapsarian creation lacked, but was destined to achieve. In *De archa Noe*, speaking of the "full and perfect knowledge of his Maker" enjoyed by pre-lapsarian man, Hugh immediately qualifies such fullness in this way: "full you must understand, after that fullness which he received at his creation, not after that which he was to receive hereafter, when his obedience was fulfilled,"[79] that is, in the next life. In *De sacramentis*, Hugh expresses the matter thus:

> Therefore, since man's life here can not be without change, against that change which engenders failing is opposed another change which produces progress so that, since it can not stand so as always to be the same, it moves and always moves forward so as to be better (*in melius*).[80]

This phrase, "*in melius*" (or its cognates), moreover, recurs in Hugh's writings, even where the word *reformare* is not present. At one point, he writes: "Therefore, He Himself cannot be better. But all that He has made can be better, at least if He Himself, who has the power, should so wish. And He Himself can make better what He has made ... by promoting what has been made well to something better ..."[81] As noted above, this reflects a broader twelfth-century theme. As for his contemporaries, so for Hugh, re-formation is, quite literally, change "for the better" (*in melius*).

Yet, the core idea, giving essential content to the term's meaning, is that of the root word, "form" (*forma*) – ubiquitous in Hugh's writings and fundamental to his thought. Careful attention to his use of the term exposes otherwise implicit but nonetheless central features of his theology. Typically, *forma* for Hugh retains a generally Christianized neoplatonic set of meanings, wherein it first denotes the "ideas" or essences eternally existing in the divine mind, and then secondarily refers to these forms as

78 *Sacr.*, 1.6.1 (*PL* 176.264C; Deferrari 94–95).

79 *De archa Noe morali* 1.1 (Sicard 4.34–35; CSMV 46). Critical text: *Hugonis de Sancto Victore: De archa Noe, Libellus de formatione arche*, ed. Patrice Sicard, CCCM 176 (Turnhout: Brepols, 2001). English translation: *Hugh of St. Victor: Selected Spiritual Writings*, trans. by a Religious of The Community of St. Mary the Virgin, intr. by Aelred Squire, Classics of the Contemplative Life (London: Faber and Faber, 1962). Cited hereafter as *Archa Noe*, book and chapter, followed by page and line number in Sicard's edition, and by CSMV and page. Except where noted, all translations are CSMV's. On the ark treatises, see Sicard, *Diagrammes*; Conrad Rudolph, *"First, I Find the Center Point": Reading the Text of Hugh of Saint Victor's* The Mystic Ark, Transactions of the American Philosophical Society 94, pt. 4 (Philadelphia: American Philosophical Society, 2004).

80 *Sacr.*, 1.9.3 (*PL* 176.321A; Deferrari 158).

81 *Sacr.*, 1.2.22 (*PL* 176.216B; Deferrari 40).

imparted upon receptive "matter" in order to make something to be what it is. For Hugh, squarely situated in a platonic cosmos, where "the essence of the real and our knowledge of it consists in *form*,"[82] all created reality participates in form.[83] In one of his earliest and most important works, the *Didascalicon*, Hugh lays out a program of education in the liberal arts and then in reading Scripture, which program is central to the divine work of restoring or reforming fallen human nature. With help from Boethius, Hugh casts this restoration in terms of *forma*:

> This, then, is what the arts are concerned with, this is what they intend, namely, to restore (*reparetur*) within us the divine likeness, a likeness which to us is a form (*forma*), but to God is his nature. The more we are conformed (*conformamur*) to the divine nature, the more do we possess Wisdom, for then there begins to shine forth again in us what has forever existed in the divine Idea or Pattern (*ratione*).[84]

Here, the repair of human nature involves restored participation in the *forma* of divine Wisdom, a participation construed in terms of the form/matter paradigm. For Hugh, salvation entails receiving again the form of Wisdom – in short, re-formation.

REASONING SCRIPTURALLY ABOUT *FORMA*

The *Didascalicon*'s philosophical language of *forma*, with its connection both to the divine "ideas" in God and to created things that in some way participate in these, should be duly noted. To appreciate fully Hugh's notion of re-formation, though, we must attend carefully to an apparent development in his thought in this regard. First, a glance at context. Hugh of St. Victor's Paris was not only the site of ecclesial reform movements; it was also at the center of an early twelfth-century theological milieu embracing (uneasily) hermeneutically sophisticated approaches to scriptural exegesis, daringly speculative experiments with expressing the whole of Christian truth claims, an infatuation with dialectical modes of thought, and a reinvigorated interest in neoplatonic philosophy. This was an eclectic intellectual climate, a fertile *mélange* fusing, on the one hand, neoplatonic essentialism – eternal, unchanging, abstract forms

[82] Louis Duprè, *Passage to Modernity: An Essay in the Hermeneutics of Nature and Culture* (New Haven: Yale University Press, 1993), 18.

[83] Zinn, "*Historia fundamentum est*," 148: "As H. Köster pointed out Hugh's philosophical thought world is decidedly not that of later university scholastics for whom a dialectic of nature/supernature or nature/grace is the controlling principle."

[84] *Didasc.*, 2.1 (Buttimer 23.17–20; Taylor 61).

descending and impressing themselves upon receptive matter and upon the minds that could perceive them – and, on the other hand, an increasing biblical temporalism, a heightened awareness of the dynamic, open-ended, unfolding narrative of history and of the significance of concrete, contingent particulars in definite times and places.

It is not surprising, accordingly, that shortly after writing the *Didascalicon* Hugh devoted his attention to a symbolic interpretation of Noah's Ark. (See the frontispiece opposite the title page.) Scholars continue to debate whether Hugh actually physically produced this symbolic representation of this biblical boat; but he certainly produced texts that offer an elaborate description and spiritual interpretation of it (and there have been several modern attempts to reproduce it, based on Hugh's detailed description).

As a kind of master symbol (or mandala),[85] this biblical boat became in Hugh's hands an organizing structure, a "symbolic construct" (to use Grover Zinn's apt phrase),[86] with which to think theologically about nearly everything: God, creation, Christ, church, salvation history, and the moral-religious life of the soul. Beginning with Noah's literal ark, Hugh expanded it symbolically to include the "ark" of the church in its journey through history toward its eschatological goal, and the "ark" of the individual soul in its progress in the spiritual life. In short, the visual representation of Noah's ark was an artistic representation and symbolic synthesis of all reality.

Much can (and will) be said of this ark-symbol in due course. At present, our concern is not its numerous details, but Hugh's overarching intent for it, which was not simply to organize in a visually pleasing way all the theological "data" of interest to him, but also through it, as an object of extended, theological meditation, "to initiate transformation"[87] in his students.[88] "I have said these things about the figure of our Ark, so that if it please anyone to gaze inwardly upon the elegance of the Lord's house … he might at the same time rouse his affection (*affectus*) with this exemplar (*exemplar*)."[89] That is, Hugh meant the ark to be understood tropologically or morally, not in the narrow, modern, but in the fuller, medieval sense of that which pertains to the whole spiritual life of the believer.

85 See Zinn, "Mandala Use and Symbolism." 86 Ibid., 318.

87 Fassler, *Gothic Song*, 218.

88 See *Archa Noe*, 1.1 (Sicard 3–5.1–63; CSMV 45–47).

89 *Libellus de formatione arche*, 11 (Sicard 162.119–21; Weiss 70). To be cited as *Libellus* from Sicard's edition (see note 79 above) by chapter, page and lines, and Jessica Weiss' translation of the *PL* text in *The Medieval Craft of Memory: An Anthology of Texts and Pictures*, eds. Mary Carruthers and Jan W. Ziolkowski (Philadelphia: University of Pennsylvania Press, 2002), 45–70.

Interpreted thus, the ark symbolizes what the exegete himself should do or become. After constructing the various symbolic dimensions of the ark at great length, Hugh puts this moral imperative thus:

Now therefore, enter your own inmost heart, and make a dwelling place for God. Make Him a temple, make Him a house, make Him a palace, make Him an ark of the covenant, make Him an ark of the flood; no matter what you call it, it is all one house of God.[90]

The exegete is to apply this biblical symbolic structure to himself, to build a similar structure within the heart. In many ways, this statement is a lapidary summary of Hugh's entire theological endeavor. Everything else contributes in one way or another to this moral or spiritual "construction project."

At first glance, we seem here to be worlds away from the *Didascalicon*'s neoplatonic framework of form and matter, and, to be sure, this is a different world. But there is also a crucial point of continuity. Early in his discussion of Noah's ark, after noting all the different symbolic dimensions of the ark-symbol, Hugh observes:

Yet, there is in a certain sense only one ark everywhere, for there is a singular likeness in all, and that which is not different in properties ought not to be different in name. The form (*forma*) is one, though the matter is different.[91]

Hugh here appropriates the *Didascalicon*'s philosophical ontology within this scriptural framework. He recasts the platonic form/matter ontology in terms of a biblical structure. The biblical ark-symbol is now the *forma* that is to be applied to the "matter" of the human person in order to restore it. A crucial conviction in the argument elaborated below is that Hugh scholarship has not made enough of the fact that Hugh explicitly describes the ark-symbol as a *forma*. "I have depicted [the ark] ... in a form that you can see (*in forma visibili*)."[92] In short, for Hugh of St. Victor, restoration – the overarching theme of his soteriology – is best construed as re-formation in precisely this sense, namely, that of a re-structuring of the person. And this re-forming or re-structuring is conceived of in terms of a scriptural structure.

For Hugh, then, the scriptural (concrete, particular, historical, textured) and the philosophical (abstract, universal, eternal, formal) fuse

[90] *Archa Noe*, 1.3 (Sicard 9.10–13; CSMV 51). See the list of scriptural builders in *Archa Noe*, 4.1 (Sicard 87.35–40; CSMV 123).

[91] *Archa Noe*, 1.3 (Sicard 17.242–45; CSMV 60).

[92] *Archa Noe*, 1.3 (Sicard 10.43; CSMV 52). If Hugh in fact constructed an actual diagram or symbol, it has not survived.

in the ark-symbol. In his symbolic representation, the ark is a *forma* that is constructed according to the (scandalously particular) dimensions and concrete shape of a historical boat. The abstract essence is particularized, scripturally, historically, concretely; yet this very concrete historical reality is also construed abstractly, given essential, formal density and significance. Not only that. The impersonal, abstract structure is made to house a personal divine presence that acts in salvation history. It is indwelt by God like a *paterfamilias* and ultimately as the soul's Bridegroom.

Furthermore, for Hugh the ark-symbol is, *pace* much modern interpretation, more than a hermeneutic device. Hugh is interested in using this symbol less as a complex sign to point to something else and more as an engine for the soul's re-formation and re-integration. The act of meditating on the unity-generating symbol produces – better, re-constructs – the same integrating *forma* in the soul. The true significance of the symbol is only secondarily a tool for generating understanding or for "thinking with" in order to understand something better. There is a hermeneutic benefit, but only after the soul has been conformed to the symbolic *forma*. So formed, the soul can indeed interpret reality symbolically (wholistically, synthetically, aesthetically, even sacramentally), but only because the soul has itself first been "symbolized," re-constructed in conformity with the symbol. Hugh's overarching concern is not a hermeneutics of a sign but the trans-formation of the soul. The *forma* is to be built there, constructed through various practices laboriously, gradually, orderly, moving systematically from foundation to decoration.

At the same time, Hugh's comments indicate that the ark-symbol is just one way of conceiving this reformation project; that is, a variety of biblical structures – temple, palace, house – might appropriately depict it. Hugh's primary concern is not the ark *per se*, but rather the re-structuring of the soul, conceived of scripturally. This is a fundamental principle in his thought, of which the ark-symbol is a particularly successful example. Call it an architectural or structural intuition, which is not confined to the ark treatises, but is evident throughout Hugh's corpus. While Hugh's structural intuition appears variously in his many works, it is often manifest as a simple architectural form, in which a foundation is laid, upon which is built an edifice, which is then beautifully adorned. In the *Commentary* on the *Celestial Hierarchy* of Pseudo-Dionysius, he compares the hierarchical mediation of divine providence to the architectural activity of building a spiritual edifice in created souls: "providence lays a foundation, builds up the edifice, and brings it to completion," all of which he finds signified visibly in the geometric instruments used for measuring and building.[93]

An early instance occurs in the *Didascalicon*, in his description of the multi-sense structure of Scripture:[94] Upon the foundation of the literal sense is constructed an edifice of doctrine through allegorical interpretation, which is then decorated and adorned with the beauty of the tropological or moral meaning. This tripartite architectural structure – foundation, superstructure, adornment – is a kind of master-form for Hugh, and recurs frequently.[95] Ultimately, he conceives not only Scripture, but the church and the soul too, as constructed or constructible entities. Indeed, "the image of construction recurs throughout Hugh's works,"[96] reflecting Hugh's predilection for "constructing the buildings of the mind."[97] When Hugh himself observes that "that can be called art which takes shape in some material medium and is brought out in it through manipulation of that material, as is the case in architecture,"[98] he gestures obliquely at his own entire program of re-formation and at its architectural-structural expression and execution.[99] In short, Hugh reasons in this way, by adopting a fundamental scriptural image or notion – in this case, an architectural structure – and applying it widely as a basic way of practicing theology.

THE CHRISTOLOGICAL FORM OF WISDOM

In the *Didascalicon*, participation in wisdom is ultimately participation in the second divine Person, to whom Hugh consistently appropriates wisdom as primary attribute.[100] Noteworthy, accordingly, in his symbolic construction of Noah's ark is Hugh's placement, as the architectural and structural center, of a pillar in the shape of a cube, representing the

[93] *In hierarchiam* 10 (*PL* 175.1146B): "'Geometrica' autem et 'tectonica vasa,' id est instrumenta mensurandi et aedificandi, dicunt significare 'fundativum, et aedificativum, et perfectivum, et quaecunque sunt alia providentiae reducentis, et convertentis secundorum.' Providentia enim primorum, et superiorum, quae secunda, et inferiora in melius convertit, et reducit, spiritale in eis aedificium fundat, et aedificat, et perficit. Cujus operis signa sunt vasa geometrica, et tectonica secundum corporalem speciem in visione formata."

[94] *Didasc.*, 6.2 (Buttimer 113.15–21; Taylor 135).

[95] Derived from Gregory the Great, but given original application by Hugh.

[96] Rorem, *Hugh of St. Victor*, 48.

[97] Mary Carruthers, *The Craft of Thought: Meditation, Rhetoric, and the Making of Images, 400–1200* (Cambridge: Cambridge University Press, 1998), 24.

[98] *Didasc.*, 2.1 (Buttimer 24.7f.; Taylor 62).

[99] See the insightful overview of this characteristic of Hugh's thought, with attention to important patristic precedents, in Sicard, *Diagrammes*, 211–29.

[100] See Poirel, *Livre de la nature*.

Incarnate Christ. Situated thus, Christ gives shape and structure to the remaining "arks." When Hugh says that in all these arks the "*forma* is one," though the material differs, the common *forma* of all these constructed entities – ark, church, Scripture, soul – is ultimately Christ. From this Christological center the same *forma* recurs in new instances of the same structural shape, manifesting itself in Noah's literal ark, but also in the nature of the church, the nature of Scripture, and, eventually, the nature of the soul. Later in the ark treatise Hugh is explicit: Christ Himself is the Wisdom that is building a house in the human heart.[101] In this way, the process of re-formation is concurrently "Christo-formation," "churchification," and "scripturalization," receiving this *forma* of the "ark of wisdom" within. Accordingly, the *forma* that Hugh both espies in God's works and strives to instill in the soul is ultimately the singular *Forma sapientiae*, the form of wisdom. "The *forma* is one, though the *materia* differs."

THE DIMENSIONS OF RE-FORMATION

Hugh's construal of restoration to "the form of the Good" as a re-forming of the person, through conformity to a scriptural symbol, entails a certain transposition of the dimensions of *forma* into his structural framework. It must be noted that the sources of Christianized neoplatonism that Hugh inherits from antiquity, namely, a hybrid of Augustinian and Boethian (and perhaps Dionysian[102]) versions, tend to construe the salvific restoration of human nature in terms of ascent. In one way or another, they all envision fallen humans returning "upward" to union with or participation in the Good that is God. In this light, the virtual absence of ascent language in Hugh's ark treatises is remarkable. Virtual, because there is a kind of ascent for Hugh, but it is the ascent involved in erecting a structure or edifice *within* the soul. And, significantly, it is this edifice constructed in the heart that God *descends* to indwell, so that the heart becomes a *templum Dei*, a dwelling place for the divine. In this way, Hugh's scriptural ark-*forma* has harnessed or even disciplined the neoplatonic dynamism of ascent "out of" or "above" time and place so that this ascending energy is bent toward and made to converge, like a flying

[101] *Archa Noe*, 4.1 (Sicard 88.58–64; CSMV 123): "He is Himself the wisdom whereof it is said, 'Wisdom hath builded her house,' and in another place the selfsame wisdom shows where and out of what material the house has been made, saying, 'I, wisdom, dwell in counsel and am present in reasonable thoughts …' it is clear, therefore, that wisdom builds herself a house in the heart of man out of reasonable thoughts."

[102] But see Rorem's hesitations in *Hugh of St. Victor*, 167–76.

buttress, within time and history at the Christological apex of the ark of the soul. In this way, ascent becomes not flight or escape, but house-construction within the soul.

If this is so, if neoplatonic ascent is now scriptural construction, if the soul's participation in the form of the Good is now the soul's reception of the "form of the ark," if the locus or site of the divine–human relation is now the soul re-constructed in its integrity to house the divine presence, then we might well expect to see the attributes or characteristics of *forma* taken up into Hugh's scriptural framework. In fact, three such features are readily apparent. These are, moreover, not confined to the ark treatises, but are apparent across his corpus. Stepping back to observe his thought more generally, it is apparent that Hugh consistently expresses his theology in terms of structures, with these three crucial features.

First, he applies the metaphysical form–matter paradigm widely, extending the notion of "form" to any organizing structure or pattern and that of "matter" to anything receptive of such disposition. Hugh will speak, to give just a few examples, of the *forma* of words, of sacraments, of bodies. Even God has, or rather is, *forma*, though Hugh also affirms that God transcends all form. But here Hugh innovates further by construing all form–matter relationships as graduated and dynamic, rather than instantaneous and static. For him, all of created reality, from inception to consummation, is in a developmental process toward increasing degrees and intensity of form. "Formation," in the sense of a forming process, best captures this notion. "No one," says Hugh, "becomes perfect suddenly."[103]

Second, Hugh is especially drawn to the way in which *forma* gives essential structure, defining pattern, proper arrangement or order, and substantial shape to individual things (as in the phrase "flying in formation"). Here, crucial synonyms are *ordo* and especially *integritas*.[104] For Hugh, formation imparts structure that establishes creaturely wholeness, and facilitates human flourishing.[105] The close link between *forma* and creaturely *integritas* allows Hugh to conceive of the latter in terms of structure and pattern.

Third, for Hugh formation (as both process and pattern) issues forth into aesthetically pleasing result, for instance, the adornment of the creation,[106] the beauty (*pulchritudo*, *venustas*) of the virtuous soul, the *decorum* of good

[103] *Archa Noe*, 4.2 (Sicard 91.47–48; CSMV 127).

[104] See, e.g., the comments in *Didasc.*, 1.5 (Buttimer 12.2–22; Taylor 51–52): The goal of human acts is "the restoring of our nature's integrity." "This is our entire task – the restoration of our nature ..." "The integrity of human nature" is "attained in two things – in knowledge and in virtue."

[105] I borrow the notion of "human flourishing" from Charry, *By the Renewing of Your Minds*, 3ff.

[106] *Sacr.*, 1.1.28 (*PL* 176.216B; Deferrari 26–27).

and well-executed bodily actions, and the harmonious concord (*harmonia*, *concordia*) of community life. In Hugh's words: "Just as our being surpasses nothingness through existence, so does it through its beauty of form surpass the indeterminate. And as existence is pleasing, so ordered existence is even more pleasing."[107] In particular, the soul must become beautiful in order to house the divine presence, since "a fair love demands a pleasant place."[108]

These three aspects of *forma* – dynamic process, integral structure, beautified result – emerge in various contexts (personal, communal, ecclesial), and at many levels (behavioral, intellectual, moral, and mystical) of Hugh's theology. As will be seen below in the chapters on creation, Fall, Christ, Scripture, church, and the soul, he views all levels of reality in these terms. That is, he consistently sees created things progressively receiving essential and ultimately beautifying form, through various processes that impart structure, orchestrate multiplicity, order chaos, and structure confusion. Created reality, at every level, never receives its defining formal nature all at once, but is always gradually, dynamically moving toward increasing degrees of form and thus beauty.

A THEOLOGICAL STYLE

Hugh's own style of thought – the images, metaphors, and conceptual paradigms that he employs throughout his writings – reflects this same tendency. He consistently organizes his thought around structures that facilitate processes of formation and in patterns that result in beauty. In his well-known *Didascalicon*, Hugh notes that "all sciences" were "matters of use" before being "transformed into art," that is, "brought into order by definite rules and precepts,"[109] and then proceeds to offer his own unique overarching arrangement of the liberal disciplines in a pattern most conducive to the formation of students' knowledge and morals.[110] In

[107] *De arrha anime* (*OHSV* 1.252.415–17; Herbert 23). Critical text: *L'Oeuvre de Hugues de Saint-Victor, i: De institutione novitiorum; De virtute orandi; De laude caritatis; De arrha anime*, ed. and trans. H. B. Feiss, P. Sicard, D. Poirel and H. Rochais (Sous la règle de Saint Augustin) (Turnhout: Brepols, 1997). Abbreviated *OHSV* 1, followed by page and line numbers. English translation: *Soliloquy on the Earnest Money of the Soul*, trans. and with an introduction by Kevin Herbert (Milwaukee: Marquette Christianity Press, 1956). Cited hereafter as *Arrha*, followed by page and line number in *OHSV* 1 and by the page number in Herbert's translation.

[108] *Archa Noe*, 4.4 (Sicard 97.54; CSMV 133).

[109] *Didasc.*, 1.11 (Buttimer 21.12f.; Taylor 59). Hugh's penchant for reducing everything to order is summed up in the language/conceptuality of *forma*.

[110] Hugh's interest in *forma* may also be apparent in the fact that, of all the disciplines treated in the *Didascalicon*, he apparently wrote commentaries on only grammar and geometry, the most "formal" arts of the trivium and quadrivium, respectively. See Rorem, *Hugh of St. Victor*, 41–45.

another work, Hugh organizes the historical data of Scripture (persons, places, events) into a pleasing pattern that facilitates a process of memorization, which ultimately "formats" the soul with the historical data of Scripture.[111] His major work of systematic theology, his *De sacramentis*,[112] is, in Hugh's own words, "a brief *summa* ... of all doctrine," to which the mind "may affix and conform its attention." Elsewhere, he organizes five biblical sets of seven (seven vices, seven petitions of the Lord's Prayer, seven gifts of the Spirit, seven virtues, seven beatitudes) into a single conceptual structure that facilitates a process of spiritual formation, resulting in the reformed beauty of the soul. He speaks of a coin maker impressing a form on molten metal to illustrate the soul's capacity to be formed by disciplined thought;[113] similarly, the imitation of virtuous individuals stamps the soft wax of the soul with their exemplary form; and the sustained activity of structured thought is likened to a process whereby the soul is "liquefied" and "poured" into "the mint of divine likeness to be reformed (*reformandum*)."[114] All these examples betray Hugh's interest in the structural dimensions or architectonics of reality and thought.

This is Hugh's penchant: to see everywhere in created reality, but especially in the divine works of restoration, a gradual, beautifying re-formation. And this is his genius: to mirror that perception in his own thought, by reducing intellectual confusion and chaos to orderly and coherent form; by generating thought-paradigms that integrate structure and process,[115] and thus facilitate individual and communal re-formation; and, by espousing practices that facilitate it, that result, namely, in *integritas*, *concordia*, and *pulchrum esse*. In sum, Hugh's thought is oriented toward form and formation. This is a structural feature of his theology. In Mary Carruthers' words, Hugh understood such *formae* "to apply not just to the physical world but also to the cognitive one, to the fabricating of the schemes and patterns for thinking."[116]

PRACTICES OF RE-FORMATION

In a very real sense, Hugh's program of re-formation is a construction project. As noted, the "work of restoration" is the activity of constructing

[111] See Chapter 7 below.
[112] Southern calls it "the first original medieval *Summa theologica*." Richard W. Southern, *Scholastic Humanism and the Unification of Europe*, Vol. II: *The Heroic Age* (Oxford: Blackwell, 2001), 57.
[113] *Didasc.*, I.I (Buttimer 5.23–6.2; Taylor 47).
[114] *Libellus*, 9 (Sicard 150.38–40; Weiss 63).
[115] See Roger Baron's "Introduction" (5) for his observations about Hugh's abilities to structure and order his own thought, his conception of reading, learning, the nature of the soul, the Bible, etc.
[116] Carruthers, *Craft of Thought*, 24.

a dwelling place for God within the soul. Hugh consistently exhorts his listeners in this way: "let us build [a house for God]; for, if we have prepared a place for Him, He will gladly come."[117] "We must build [a divine dwelling] within ourselves" by "an unseen process of construction," an ark "which wisdom builds daily in our hearts" and "grace effects in us."[118] Squarely in the service of this re-forming construction he locates certain theological and communal practices which facilitate it. These practices are the "engine," or in twelfth-century parlance the *machina*[119] driving this overarching theological program of re-formation. A sustained reading of Hugh's corpus turns up three basic practices that are crucial to his re-forming program. An only slightly artificial alliteration labels them thus: *memoria*, *meditatio*, and *mores/moralia*. Hugh nowhere explicitly organizes them into a "program." Yet, careful attention to his theology of re-formation outlined above not only brings these particular practices to the fore, but also suggests a certain arrangement among them.

First, these practices can be correlated with the two aspects of the soul's integrity noted above, knowledge and virtue. Knowledge and virtue, moreover, correspond to the two most basic acts of the soul, cognition and affection. In *De sacramentis*, Hugh describes how these are formable aspects of the soul: the human spirit "is changed by affection and cognition ... and that change in it of knowledge and affection is, as it were, a change of form."[120] *Memoria* and *meditatio* pertain to knowledge;[121] *mores* and *moralia* pertains to virtue.

These practices can also be aligned neatly with the basic structure of Hugh's thought discussed at length above, more precisely, with Hugh's theological "master-structure." *Memoria* is the foundation of the re-formation process; *meditatio* erects a theological superstructure; *mores/moralia* provides a soul-beautifying finish. As Hugh puts it in *De archa Noe*: "knowledge erects the structure of faith (*fidei fabricam*) by its knowing, whereas love like an adorning color embellishes (*pingit*) the building by its virtue."[122] Making a different point regarding Hugh, Mary Carruthers' insightful observation, regarding the formational and practice-oriented nature of Hugh's conception of reading, provides a ready summary of this point: "Medieval reading habits are based upon a model of craft mastery, the 'courses' of stone or brick or other materials which a master mason

[117] *Archa Noe*, 1.2 (Sicard 8.69–71; CSMV 50). [118] *Archa Noe*, 1.3 (Sicard 17.221–39; CSMV 59).

[119] Carruthers, *Craft of Thought*, 22–23. [120] *Sacr.*, 1.3.16 (*PL* 176.222B; Deferrari 47).

[121] *Didasc.*, Pref. (Buttimer 2.9; Taylor 44): "The things by which every man advances in knowledge are principally two – namely, reading and meditation."

[122] *Archa Noe*, 1.3 (Sicard 9.5–7; CSMV 50).

may make in building a wall, with concomitant emphasis upon preparation (the ground), routines of exercise (discipline), and stages in a way toward making a finished artifact, a mastery that affords pleasure."[123]

Finally, these practices can be correlated with Hugh's conception of Scripture and corresponding exegetical theory. "Twofold is the fruit of sacred reading, because it either instructs the mind with knowledge or it adorns it with morals. The first pertains to history and allegory; the second pertains to tropology."[124] *Memoria* corresponds to the literal sense; *meditatio*, to the allegorical sense, *mores/moralia*, to the tropological sense. In another work on exegetical theory, Hugh subsumes this twofold fruit of scriptural reading under the notion of re-form according to the divine likeness: Scripture "reforms the human person to the likeness of God (*ad similitudinem Dei illum reformans*), by instructing him in knowledge and by exhorting him to love of Himself."[125]

Correlated in all these ways, these practices also constitute a dynamic formational process, whose goal is to re-form the soul in the image of God, such that the soul and the church become dwelling places, houses, temples for God.[126] For Hugh, "biblical interpretation is not merely *about* God's restorative work, it is *itself* that work of restoration."[127]

Above all, the task of re-formation is the context in which the profoundly practical orientation of Hugh's theology emerges. As the quotation above suggests, while the divine work of creation was accomplished by God alone, the work of restoration involves human cooperation. Through various activities, exercises, disciplines – in a word, practices – the human person participates in the divine work of reformation. Corrupted and diminished by sin, Hugh says, the goodness of human nature must be "restored by exercise." Accordingly, "God would have us work along with him,"[128] and our "self-reform is patiently awaited by Him."[129] In short, the "restoration of our nature" is "our entire task."[130] Given Hugh's overriding

[123] Carruthers, *Craft of Thought*, 20–21.

[124] *Didasc.*, 5.6 (Buttimer 104.20f.; Taylor 127). Hugh makes the same point, though with a greater emphasis on the aesthetic goal, in *Script.*, 13 (*PL* 175.20C): "Twofold is the fruit of divine reading: for it either instructs the mind in knowledge or decorates (*ornat*) [the mind] with morals. Scripture teaches that which delights to know and that which is expedient to imitate. The first of these, that is, knowledge, looks more to history and allegory; the second, that is, instruction in morals, looks more to tropology. For all divine Scripture refers to this end."

[125] *Script.*, 1 (*PL* 175.10D–11A). Through non-scriptural texts, by contrast, the soul is not "repaired unto true knowledge and love of God."

[126] *Archa Noe*, 1.2 (Sicard 2.69; CSMV 50): "if it has not yet begun to be in us, then let us build it (*aedificemus*)." Again, *Archa Noe*, 1.3 (Sicard 9.10–11; CSMV 51): "Now, therefore, enter your own most inmost heart, and make a dwelling place (*habitaculum*) for God."

[127] Rorem, *Hugh of St. Victor*, 121.

[128] *Archa Noe*, 1.1 (Sicard 4.23; CSMV 46).

[129] *Arrha* (*OHSV* 1.252:415–17; Herbert 35).

[130] *Didasc.*, 1.5 (Buttimer 12.11f.; Taylor 52).

interest in wisdom, the combined executing of these practices may be defined as an intentional participation in the sapiential structures of reality, manifest in creation, salvation, church, Scripture, all founded on Wisdom itself.[131]

REFORMATIO IN MELIUS

In light of the foregoing, Hugh's notion of *reformatio* may be summarized thus: re-formation is that process whereby integral, beautifying form is restored to the rational creature, a process that begins with the post-lapsarian state of lost or corrupted creaturely form but ends in a state that exceeds original created form, and is a *reformatio in melius*, resulting in beautiful existence (*pulchrum esse*). In his treatise on Noah's ark, Hugh offers this lapidary summary. The work of restoration

> is such that it not only reforms (*reformet*) us to our former wholeness, but also gives us greater strength; it not only repairs (*reparet*) that which has been destroyed, but also over and above adds that which formerly we lacked. Wherefore, through it all, God … who freely gives His gift and freely restores (*restaurat*) what has been lost … so refashions (*restituit*) us that we seem to have fallen not to our destruction, but to our further growth. [132]

More precisely, it is a dynamic, gradual, ordered process in salvation history whereby, through the reception of certain structures and patterns, both the human person and the human community are re-formed in the image of God. Re-formation is the reception of, and ever-increasing participation in, salvific, integral form. It should be stressed, moreover, that Hugh's notion of "reform for the better" does not imply a return to a prior pristine state of nature, nor a reinstatement of a sacred cosmos, nor a reification of immutable essences read off the face of original creation, but a Christologically governed, ecclesially enacted transformation into something new. The original *forma* of creation is sin-ravaged; its *reformatio* is not a return to an original creation, but a reaching forward to a new coherence, a new configuration, a new beauty.[133]

Attending to this theme in a comprehensive way sheds light on under-appreciated aspects of Hugh's theology, its Christianized, neoplatonic

[131] Not unlike what, in another context, Pierre Hadot has called "spiritual exercises" and philosophy "as a way of life" (*Philosophy as a Way of Life: Spiritual Exercises from Socrates to Foucault* [Oxford/New York: Blackwell, 1995]).

[132] *Archa Noe*, 3.11 (Sicard 73.75–74.84; CSMV 111).

[133] See Frederick Christian Bauerschmidt, "Order, Freedom, and 'Kindness': Julian of Norwich on the Edge of Modernity," *Theology Today* 60 (2003), 63–81.

exemplarism, for example. It highlights certain structural features of his thought, its tendency to generate conceptual or even actual structures through which to organize and engage a wide array of theological issues. It exposes under-appreciated links between various aspects of this theology, links between his theory of exegesis and his conception of the spiritual life, or between his Christology and his doctrine of creation. Attending to the theme of *reformatio*, moreover, allows his theology to be more fully and precisely contextualized historically in its time and place – an era especially devoted to reform. Above all, it reveals how Hugh combines education, formation, pedagogy, doctrine, spirituality, and art into a single, coherent organic unity.

In short, this study argues that, in crucial, under-appreciated ways, Hugh's is a theology of "re-formation." Analyzing Hugh's theology in this way contextualizes and unifies it afresh. How precisely this is so emerges most clearly by considering the central loci of his theology. In his conception of creation and Fall (Part I), and of salvation, involving Christ, church, Scripture and human person (Part II), the need and the basis for re-formation are made patent, while his account of the practices of *memoria*, *meditatio*, and *moralia* (Part III) describe its implementation.

PART I

Formation in wisdom

CHAPTER I

Creation as formation

INTRODUCTION: THE "WORK OF FOUNDATION"

Hugh of St. Victor conceives of creation – both the divine activity and its non-divine result – from the perspective of form (*forma*). His doctrine of creation,[1] accordingly, is the proper point of departure for an investigation of his theology of re-formation. If, for Hugh, creation as a whole, and in its individual parts, receives being (*esse*) through *forma*, and if being can become beautiful (*pulchrum esse*) through increasing degrees of form, and if this occurs through the very Form of Wisdom, who is none other than the second Person of the Trinity, and if (as will be argued in the next chapter) creation's Fall consists in some sense in the loss of proper and beautifying *forma*, then salvation will fittingly entail the restoration of *forma*, or re-form, and it will fittingly occur through that very same Form of Wisdom which formed it in the first place.

Hugh often emphasizes that the primary focus of his theology – of true, "divine theology" as opposed to "worldly theology" – is the "work of restoration" (*opera restaurationis*) accomplished in the course of the six ages of human history. This, for him, is also the primary subject matter of Scripture. By contrast, creation, the "work of foundation" (*opera conditionis*) is lesser in dignity because created things were made to be of service to pre-lapsarian humankind; "as of little importance," they were

[1] Not surprisingly, Hugh's most extensive discussion of creation occurs in his *De sacramentis* (*PL* 176.173A–618B), his *summa* of Christian doctrine. As early as the first books of the *Didascalicon*, though, as well as in his *De tribus diebus* (see below), his basic view of creation, and the central role of *forma* within it, is evident. Shorter discussions throughout the rest of Hugh's corpus supplement these accounts. The theological ferment of the twelfth century generated a thoroughgoing debate over the doctrine of creation. Chenu notes that a central concern of many twelfth-century thinkers was "the need to affirm the absolute character of creation as against the alleged eternity of matter." M.-D. Chenu, *Nature, Man, and Society in The Twelfth Century: Essays on New Theological Perspectives in the Latin West*, ed. and trans. Jerome Taylor and Lester K. Little (Chicago and London: University of Chicago Press, 1968), 51–52. For a general overview, see Rorem, *Hugh of St. Victor*, 38–47.

accomplished in a mere six days.[2] They are the subject matter of "worldly (*mundana*) theology" and secular philosophy.[3] Not that Hugh has no interest in the created order or in a theology of creation. As he points out, Scripture begins with a brief account of the "works of foundation," treated "briefly and truthfully" at the beginning of its narrative, so that the correspondence between six days and six ages might reveal the identity of Creator and Redeemer.[4] Following this scriptural pattern, Hugh too will begin with works of the six days, but will do so quite explicitly with an eye to the restorative work that follows – "the lower wisdom, rightly ordered, leads to the higher."[5] Concerned neither with a comprehensive nor with a "scientifically" neutral account of creation, he emphasizes certain aspects of the hexameral narrative, "sacramentals" in his terminology – profound symbolic patterns that advertise and anticipate the work of salvation.[6]

At the outset of his account of creation in *De sacramentis*, Hugh observes that the pagan philosophers – he clearly has Plato's *Timaeus* in mind – had posited three co-eternal principles: "an artisan, matter, and form," and that they had argued that all things were "fashioned from matter into form by an artisan."[7] Insisting that God alone is the eternal first principle, Hugh rejects the notion of three co-eternal principles. Yet, he not only retains but revels in the idea of God as an artisan imposing *forma* upon matter: In six days, he says, God "disposed, and ordered, and reduced to form" all that God had made.[8] In this notion of the Creator-Artisan gradually imposing *forma* upon matter are found the crucial features of Hugh's theology of creation.

THE CREATOR-ARTISAN IMPARTING THE FORM OF WISDOM

Hugh's conception of the Creator-Artisan is directly related to his conception of God's Trinitarian nature. The twelfth century saw renewed interest in Trinitarian theology, with such figures as Anselm of Canterbury,

[2] *Sacr.*, 1.Prol.2 (*PL* 176.183C–184A; Deferrari 4).
[3] *Sacr.*, 1.Prol.2 (*PL* 176. 183C; Deferrari 4). [4] *Sacr.*, 1.Prol.3 (*PL* 176.184A–B; Deferrari 4).
[5] *Sacr.*, 1.Prol.6 (*PL* 176.185C; Deferrari 5). [6] *Sacr.*, 1.Prol. 5–6 (*PL* 176.999A; Deferrari 5).
[7] *Sacr.*, 1.1.1 (*PL* 176.187B; Deferrari 7): "ex materia quidem in formam per opificem."
[8] *Sacr.*, 1.1.7 (*PL* 176.193A; Deferrari 13): "Sex diebus disposuit et ordinavit atque in formam redegit Deus …" See also Hugh's *Adnotationes elucidatoriae in Pentateuchon* (*PL* 175.29–86) at *PL* 175.33. Cited hereafter as *In Pent.* Chenu argues that Hugh's account of creation exhibits a tension between Greek and biblical mentalities. The former reflects a dualism between matter and idea; the absence of time; and a view of form organizing primal chaos into a cosmos on the analogy of manual art, viz., Demiurge forming matter. The latter requires the coexistence of time and eternity, and entails no analogy with manual art, no making or fabricating; no notion of cosmos or nature; no notion of form and matter, or of the one moving toward the many (*Nature, Man, and Society*, 59).

Roseclin of Compiègne, Peter Abelard, Gilbert of Poitiers, and Achard and Richard of St.-Victor pursuing speculative, often controversial accounts of the divine nature.[9] The fruit of much of this work will find its way into the Lombard's *Sentences*, and from there pass into the mature scholastic theologies of the following century.[10] In this, Hugh makes his own distinctive contribution.[11]

In his Trinitarian theology, Hugh attends in particular to the ways in which God as Trinity relates to all that is not God (*ad extra*). So, while he speculates concerning God's nature *in se*, his attention moves quickly to a particular triad of divine attributes, which for him not only constitute divine perfection, but also most fundamentally characterize the Creator–creation relationship. Corresponding respectively to the Father, Son, and Holy Spirit are divine "power, knowledge/wisdom, and will/goodness."[12] Through these, God makes all things and brings them to perfection: "nothing could be perfect without these" and they "concur to produce every effect."[13] Significantly, Hugh construes this triad's creative effect in terms of *forma*. Through these three aspects of the divine nature, "the Creator (*artifex*) gave form (*forma*) to His work,"[14] for "the immensity of things received the form (*forma*) of power; the beauty [of things received the form of] wisdom; and utility [of things received the form of] goodness."[15]

9 For a useful overview of these developments, see Peter Gemeinhardt, "Logic, Tradition, and Ecumenics: Developments of Latin Trinitarian Theology between c. 1075 and c. 1160," in *Trinitarian Theology in the Medieval West*, ed. Pekka Kärkkäinen (Vaajakoski: Gummerus Kirjapaino Oy, 2008), 10–68.

10 Ibid., 51–59.

11 Hugh's distinction is in "giving a comprehensive account of the Trinity together with an account of the whole history of salvation" (ibid., 43–44). For Hugh's Trinitarian theology generally, see Poirel, *Livre de la nature*, and Johann Hofmeier, *Die Trinitätslehre des Hugo von St. Viktor dargestellt im Zusammenhang mit den trinitarischen Strömungen seiner Zeit* (Munich: Hueber, 1963).

12 *Sacr.*, 1.3.26–28. See Constant Mews, "The World as Text," in *Scripture and Pluralism: Reading the Bible in the Religiously Plural Worlds of the Middle Ages and Renaissance*, ed. Thomas J. Heffernan and Thomas E. Burman, Studies in the History of Christian Traditions (Leiden: Brill, 2005), 95–122 and A. M. Piazzoni, "Ugo di San Vittore 'auctor' delle 'Sententiae de divinitate'," *Studi medievali* 23.2 (1982), 861–955, at 886–94. Poirel (*Livre de la nature*, 115) reverses that standard scholarly account, which sees Peter Abelard as the originator (in his *Theologia 'Summi boni'*) of this particular triad, power, wisdom, and goodness, divine attributes which are visible in creation. According to Poirel, Hugh first formulated the triad in his *De tribus diebus* some time before 1120 and Abelard subsequently borrowed it from him. For his part, Mews speculates that perhaps both Hugh and Abelard depend on, while also developing in their own distinctive ways, the thought of William of Champeaux, who founded the Abbey of St-Victor in the early twelfth century. Whatever the case, the formulation of this specific triad of divine attributes is a distinctive feature of twelfth-century Trinitarian theology.

13 *Sacr.*, 1.2.6 (*PL* 176.208B; Deferrari 31).

14 *Sacr.*, 1.2.11 (*PL* 176.211A; Deferrari 34).

15 *Sacr.*, 1.2.12 (*PL* 176.211A; Deferrari 34): "Suscepit enim formam potestatis rerum immensitas; sapientiae pulchritudo, bonitatis utilitas." Space does not permit, nor does our argument require, a more detailed discussion of the variation and apparent development in Hugh's writings

Though each member of this triad plays an important and necessary role in divine creative activity, Hugh's interest gravitates toward the role of the Second Person, that is, to the role and effects of Wisdom. Divine power enables God to accomplish His creative purposes; divine goodness or will prompts God to act and benevolently so. Yet it is divine wisdom that determines both *how* God relates to creation and *what* emerges as the result of God's creative act; it is divine wisdom that determines the specific texture, structure, and nature of how and what God creates.[16] As will be evident below, this sapiential relation between God and creation is best described in terms of *forma*. For Hugh, Wisdom is *Forma*; moreover: in, with, and through *Forma*, God engages in a process of creative *formatio*, which results in a creation that is both *formata* and *formosa*, that is, a creation that has both a particular nature or kind of being and a particular beauty. To use one of Hugh's favored expressions, it is Wisdom that "disposes" (*disponit*) all things in form.[17]

At the heart of Hugh's conception of creation is his consistent neoplatonic doctrine of exemplarism. Incorporating various long-standing strands of Christian neoplatonism,[18] Hugh "locates" the substantial forms of all created things eternally within the divine Mind or Word or Reason – the second Person of the Trinity – Who creates all things through these exemplary forms and in Whom as Exemplar all things participate in order to be what they are:[19] "every creature has its cause and likeness in the divine reason (*ratione divina*) ... from which and according to which it is perfected in its subsistence."[20] Again, in the divine Mind "were all things from eternity which were made by Him in time through essence."[21] Hugh puts this in terms of *forma*:

regarding the triad of divine *potentia*, *sapientia*, and *benignitas*. The question of whether and how precisely these should be predicated of the Trinity was intensely debated during this period, and these debates, especially those revolving around Peter Abelard and his followers, seem to have shaped Hugh's treatment of the issue, depending on the time of his writing.

16 Scholars have long noted the important contribution Hugh makes to a view of creation, of *natura*, and even history, as rational, ordered, coherent, having its own integrity that reflects the divine Creator (see Mews, "The World as Text," 116).

17 *Sacr.*, 1.2.6 (*PL* 176.208B; Deferrari 31). See also: *Sacr.* 1.2.10 (*PL* 176.210C; Deferrari 34); *Sacr.* 1.2.11 (*PL* 176.210D; Deferrari 34); *In Pent.* (*PL* 175.33A–B): "In primis Deum Creatorem, et materiam creatam et formationem ejus, et totum hoc ad laudem Dei, et utilitatem hominis: cui utile est Deum admirari et venerari. In eo quod creavit, id est de nihilo fecit mundum, miramur ejus potentiam. In eo quod ornavit, id est pulchrum fecit mundum, ejus sapientiam miramur"; and *In salomonis Ecclesiastes* (*PL* 175.113–256) at *PL* 175.216A: "Opus itaque Dei est creare, formare, disponere universa." Cited hereafter as *In Eccl.*

18 See Chenu, *Nature, Man, and Society*, 47–94, on the confluence of Augustinian, Boethian, and Dionysian neoplatonisms in the early twelfth century.

19 See Sicard, *Diagrammes*, 221–24.

20 *Sacr.*, 1.5.3 (*PL* 176.247D; Deferrari 75).

21 *Sacr.*, 1.3.31 (*PL* 176.232B; Deferrari 59).

This first cause of all things performed its own work according to itself and on account of itself: according to itself, since it did not receive the form (*forma*) of its work from without; on account of itself, since it did not have the cause for operating from any other source. For it made according to its own likeness what it disposed to participation in itself, so that from itself that which was to possess the same good might take the same form (*forma*).[22]

This same neoplatonic, exemplarist tradition, and the central role that *forma* occupies therein, appears immediately in the opening lines of Hugh's *Didascalicon*: "Of all things to be sought, the first is that Wisdom in which the Form of the Perfect Good (*perfecti boni forma*) stands fixed."[23] Divine Wisdom, which is the source of all that exists, is first and foremost the very Form of Goodness. Expanding this definition of Wisdom in relation to creation, Hugh emphasizes the "exemplary" function of Wisdom. Not just the form of the good, Wisdom is also "a living Mind and the sole primordial Idea or Pattern (*ratio*) of things."[24] This is because "to its likeness all things have been formed (*formata*)."[25] Later, Hugh emphasizes this exemplarism as he defines the word "nature":

In the first place, [the men of former times] wished by this word [nature] to signify that archetypal Exemplar of all things which exists in the divine Mind, according to the idea of which all things have been formed; and they said that nature was the primordial cause of each thing, whence each takes not only its being (*esse*) but its "being such or such a thing" (*talis esse*) as well. To the word in this sense they assigned the following definition: "Nature is that which gives to each thing its being."[26]

In short, created things exist as the kinds of things that they are through Wisdom's impartation of substantial form or nature. Created things have been formed according to the Idea or Pattern or Exemplar of Uncreated Wisdom,[27] the second Person of the Trinity.[28]

[22] *Sacr.*, 1.2.3 (*PL* 176.207D; Deferarri 30–31). [23] *Didasc.*, 1.1 (Buttimer 4.4–5; Taylor 46).
[24] *Didasc.*, 1.2 (Buttimer 7.2–4; Taylor 48). [25] *Didasc.*, 2.1 (Buttimer 23.15–16; Taylor 61).
[26] *Didasc.*, 1.10 (Buttimer 18.3–9; Taylor 57): "Primo modo per hoc nomen significare voluerunt illud archetypum exemplar rerum omnium, quod in mente divina est, cuius ratione omnia formata sunt, et dicebant naturam esse unius cuiusque rei primordialem causam suam, a qua non solum esse sed etiam talis esse habeat. Huic significationi talis definitio assignatur: Natura est quae unicuique rei suum esse attribuit."
[27] The difference between the uncreated forms in the divine Mind and those forms as instantiated in time in particular beings is that a timeless, changeless eternity characterizes the former, which (tellingly) has "neither grade nor succession, since they exist in unity and do not pass on in eternity" (*Sacr.*, 1.4.26 [*PL* 176.246A; Deferrari 73–74]). By implication, that which has been created has "grade and succession," and so can decrease or increase.
[28] See Taylor, *The Didascalicon of Hugh of St. Victor*, 186, n. 39: "The primordial causes are the uncreated exemplars of creation subsisting in the divine Wisdom, or Mind." As will be seen in Chapter 4, this formal link between the second Person and created things will allow Hugh to emphasize the Christological dimensions of re-form.

CREATION AS *FORMATIO*

When Hugh turns to the creation account in Genesis, he is forced immediately to take sides in a debate going back to Augustine: Did God create everything all at once or gradually over six days? The bishop of Hippo had argued for the former position. Bolstered by certain biblical texts (e.g., Eccles. 1:18) that seemed to suggest a simultaneous creation of all things, he interpreted Genesis 1–2 as an extended retelling of an instantaneous event. This view hoped to avoid denigrating a divine power that seemed to need an extended period of time (and rest afterwards!) to accomplish the creation. This was a precedent that the "second Augustine" could not easily ignore.[29] Hugh, however, leans toward the latter view, though in the end his interpretation tries to have it both ways. He affirms that the *matter* of the whole creation did in fact come into a certain kind of existence immediately, at the outset of God's creative activity, even before the first day. "Therefore, all things were founded simultaneously."[30] That is, "the works of creation – this sensible world with all its elements – were made indeed in matter before any day, equally in time and with time."[31] But, the creation was not yet in the state of being that God intended. Initially, "the matter of all visible and corporeal things had the form of confusion (*forma confusionis*)"; that is, it was relatively "unformed," though not completely so, otherwise it could not exist at all. But, "it did not yet have the form of disposition (*forma dispositionis*), until it was afterwards formed and yielded order and disposition."[32] Hence, the initial creation of all things had to receive *forma* in order to come fully into being.[33] Put simply, for Hugh, the six days account of creation in Genesis is more precisely an account of formation (*formatio*) – the divine activity of gradually forming

[29] See Dominique Poirel, " 'Alter Augustinus – Der Zweite Augustinus': Hugo von Sankt Viktor und die Väter der Kirche," in *Väter der Kirche: Ekklesiales Denken von den Anfängen bis in die Neuzeit: Festgabe für Hermann Josef Sieben SJ zum 70. Geburtstag*, eds. Johannes Arnold, Rainer Berndt, and Ralf M. W. Stammberger (Munich: Ferdinand Schöningh, 2004), 643–68.

[30] *Sacr.*, 1.5.5 (*PL* 176.249B; Deferrari 77). [31] *Sacr.*, 1.1.29 (*PL* 176.204C; Deferrari 27).

[32] *Sacr.*, 1.5.5 (PL176.249B; Deferrari 77). In the same passage Hugh argues that this procedure in creating is also the case with the invisible realm of spiritual creatures, namely, the angels: "and the nature of the invisible, both unformed (*informem*) according to something and formed (*formatam*) according to something ..."

[33] *Sacr.*, 1.1.4 (*PL* 176.189D; Deferrari 10): "Therefore, before form, matter was in a broken state, yet in form – in a form of confusion (*forma confusionis*), before a form of disposition (*forma dispositionis*). In the first form, that of confusion, all corporeal things were first created as matter simultaneously and once; in the second form, that of disposition, they were afterwards arranged through the interval of the six days." Again (*Sacr.*, 1.1.11 [*PL* 176.195C; Deferrari 16]): "Very possibly the confusion was not worthy of light; yet it received some light, that it might see how to proceed to order and disposition (*ordinem et dispositionem*)."

inchoate being into definite being:[34] in six days all the parts of the sensible world were "disposed into form."[35]

But Hugh says more about creation as formation. The act of gradually disposing into form is twofold: in the first three days, created things were "arranged" (*ordinata*); in the second triad of days, they were "adorned" (*ornata*).[36] Hugh also describes this process as a formation from being (*esse*) to beautiful being (*pulchrum esse*). Hugh subdivided the six days into two halves. In the first three days, formless matter is increasingly disposed (*dispositus*) – ordered, arranged, and reduced to form. In the second three days, the creation formed thus is now decorated and ornamented (*ornatus*). Together these two acts – to dispose and to ornament – constitute Hugh's conception of formation. The result is a visible, corporal creation is that both *formata* and *formosa*, both formed and beautified through a gradual act of divine formation. Hugh sees the Artist's creative act, not as instantaneous, but as a wise, gradual, orderly impartation of form upon chaotic matter.[37] Taking seriously the literal sense of the text and attending to its historical orientation, Hugh is comfortable with a creative process extending over six days, through increasing degrees and successive stages of *formatio*. Like an artist, God creates gradually, through a process that forms matter. For Hugh, this conception of divine activity, which he often emphasizes, is fundamental.

So, does Hugh then see a lack of perfection in the original creation? Was the daily pronouncement of divine approbation – "it was good" – disingenuous? Does an extended creative process impugn divine power? Hugh seems to sense the novelty of his view. His answer is clearly, if awkwardly, stated. Those who suggest such things "do not discern that to make something with a view to perfection ... – in order that it may be

[34] See Chenu, *Nature, Man, and Society*, 53, and n. 4. Regarding "the need to limit the role accorded to beings intermediary between God and man," Chenu observes that Eriugena's own interpretation of the pseudo-Dionysian corpus stressed that "hierarchy" did not involve a hierarchy of beings but a multiplication of "formative" activities. Continuing this approach in the twelfth century, Hugh offered the definitive conclusion: "From the outset, the characteristically Pseudo-Dionysian concept of formation (*formatio*) enters into the commentary (*PL* 175.937; 992) and is invested, moreover, with an Augustinian sense typical of Hugh."

[35] *Sacr.*, 1.1.29 (*PL* 176.204C; Deferrari 27). [36] *Sacr.*, 1.1.29 (*PL* 176.204C; Deferrari 27).

[37] See *Sacr.*, 1.1.3 (*PL* 176.188B–189B; Deferrari 8–9). So, unformed matter, itself created out of nothing, receives form and order so as to receive its essence, to be what it is. Initially, all things are unformed, but not totally unformed, for this is impossible. Thus "in a measure in form (*in forma*)" and "in a measure without form (*sine forma*)"; that is, having "a certain form (*quamdam formam*)," but still "unformed (*informis*)," "not yet disposed and arranged" (*Sacr.*, 1.1.6 [*PL* 176.192C; Deferrari 13]). This begins a process that moves without delay from creation's "unformed form" (*forma informis*) to the "form (*formam*) which it now has" (*Sacr.*, 1.1.5 [*PL* 176.190A; Deferrari 10]).

perfected by Him through whom it was made imperfect that it may be perfected – is not imperfection on the part of the Maker nor a disgrace to what is made." For, "He who made, could have made otherwise, and what was made ought not to have been made otherwise."[38] Though good, the initial creation (*esse*) is yet called to a higher degree of form, namely, "beautiful being (*pulchrum esse*)." Moreover, Hugh sees not divine impotence but sapiential pedagogy in a prolonged process of creation. The actual six days of creation are, as already noted, a "sacrament," a historical occurrence with theological significance, more precisely, a principle that Hugh will also see at work in salvation history and in the life of the individual person. In sum, Hugh's discussion of God's creative activity accents God's constant ordering, disposing, forming of all things in order to provide a pattern for things to come.

This description yields a further dimension of Hugh's theology of creation. Because creation is formation in and through the second Person, who is himself Wisdom and the Form of all forms, and because creation is executed artfully and wisely by the divine Artificer, it is fittingly summarized as formation in wisdom. As might be expected, this notion of the Divine Artisan fosters a profound aesthetic dimension in Hugh's view, not only of how God creates, but of what God creates.

CREATION AS *FORMATA*

An important implication of Hugh's affirmation that the act of creation occurs through the Form of Wisdom, and that the initial act of creation is a process of formation, a gradual imposition of form on matter, is that what comes into being as a result does so precisely as formed (*formata*) by divine wisdom and reflecting it variously. This shifts the focus from the act/process of formation to its result, to that which is formed.

[38] *Sacr.*, 1.5.15 (*PL* 176.253A; Deferrari 81). See also *Sacr.*, 1.5.15 (*PL* 176.253A; Deferrari 81): "But here too it must be said that it is perfect according to something, since it has all that it ought to have, even if it should not have all that it is to have." Again, *Sacr.*, 1.5.16 (*PL* 176.253A–B; Deferrari 82): "For perfection exists in three modes … For there is perfect according to time, and perfect according to nature, and universally perfect. The first perfect is, as it were, the beginning of perfection, making perfect according to time, and there follows what is greater, perfect according to nature, and the third is greatest and superexcellent, universally perfect. That is perfect according to time which has whatever time requires and is suitable to be had according to time. That is perfect according to nature which has all that either was given or was due its nature. That is universally perfect to which nothing is lacking. The first perfection is of a created nature, the second perfection is of a glorified nature, the third and true perfection is of an [un]created nature."

In several works, Hugh emphasizes this sapientially formed aspect of created being. Not only does *forma* give each thing its essential nature,[39] but the creation as a whole is well formed in its overarching order and structure. Throughout the *De sacramentis*, for example, he observes how, both as a whole and in its individual constituent parts, creation is disposed, ordered, arranged, and differentiated by *forma*.[40] The initially "void and empty" earth is "uncomposed (*incomposita*)."[41] From the imposition of *forma* comes "disposition," "order," "arrangement,"[42] and even "harmony."[43] Indeed, Hugh's very definition of created form reflects this: "Form is nothing else at all but the disposition of parts in a whole."[44] In *De tribus diebus*,[45] Hugh marvels at how the manifold propagation of species occurs without altering "the form of the first beginning"[46] and with each creature's own essential *forma* "ruling from within," it "never presumes to exceed its limits."[47] All this leads him to exclaim: "What great wisdom of the creator shines forth in the composition of the human body!"[48] and "… wonderful that in a single body are formed so many members, so many forms of members, so many places, so many tasks … And although all of them are so different, all still cooperate with each other."[49] Again: "We wonder at the shape of certain things, because they are seemly in a certain special way and suitably fit together so that the very disposition of the work seems somehow to suggest the special diligence that its Creator devoted to them."[50] Hugh even wrote a specific treatise on geometry,[51] reflecting his

[39] Form reveals, makes visible, and allows for true perception. See *Sacr.*, 1.1.6 (*PL* 176.190B–192D; Deferrari 10–13); *Sacr.*, 1.1.11 (*PL* 176.195B–C; Deferrari 16): "with increased clarity received a better form (*formam*)"; and *Sacr.*, 1.1.15 (*PL* 176.199A; Deferrari 20).

[40] See especially *Sacr.*, 1.3.14–15; 20; 28; 31.

[41] *Sacr.*, 1.1.6 (*PL* 176.190D; Deferrari 11).

[42] *Sacr.*, 1.1.1–12 (PL176.187A–197B; Deferrari 7–18).

[43] *Sacr.*, 1.1.13 (*PL* 176.197D; Deferrari 19).

[44] *Sacr.*, 1.3.15 (*PL* 176.221D; Deferrari 47): "Non est forma aliquid omnino nisi dispositio partium in toto."

[45] Critical text: *Hugonis de Sancto Victore: De tribus diebus*, ed. Dominique Poirel, *CCCM* 177 (Turnhout: Brepols, 2002). Hereafter abbreviated as *Tribus diebus*, followed by page and line number in Poirel's text. All translations are mine, but I have benefited from an unpublished translation by Hugh Feiss, OFM. See J. Van Zwieten, ed. and trans., *Hugh van St. Victor, De drie dagen* (Kampen: Kok Agora, 1996); Wanda Cizewski, "Reading the World as Scripture: Hugh of St. Victor's *DE TRIBUS DIEBUS*," *Florilegium* 9 (1987): 65–88; Poirel, *Livre de la nature*.

[46] *Tribus diebus*, 11 (Poirel 24.384f.).

[47] *Tribus diebus*, 11 (Poirel 25.399f.).

[48] *Tribus diebus*, 7 (Poirel 17.247–48): "… in compositione humani corporis quanta elucet sapientia creatoris!"

[49] *Tribus diebus*, 11 (Poirel 25.401–2): "Hoc quoque mirabile est quod in uno corpore tot construuntur membra, tot membrorum formae, tot loca, tot officia."

[50] *Tribus diebus*, 11 (Poirel 23.368f.).

[51] See *Practica geometriae*, in *Hugonis de Sancto Victore Opera Propaedeutica*, ed. Roger Baron, University of Notre Dame Publications in Mediaeval Studies 20 (Notre Dame, Ind.: University of Notre Dame Press, 1966). English translation by Frederick A. Homann, *A Practical Geometry*, (Milwaukee, Wis.: Marquette University Press, 1991). Cited as *Practica*.

conviction about and interest in the formal, structural aspects of the created order. For Hugh, all this reflects divine wisdom: each created thing has been "formed by wisdom and discretion."[52]

Hugh also attends to different types of formal change in things.[53] The complete change of form, of course, entails a change in essence: one thing is changed into another thing. But there is also possible a change in form that is not essential but nonetheless intrinsic:[54] "Now the change of form (*mutatio formae*) is alone called intrinsic, since it changes something not about a thing but in the thing itself."[55] "Something changes *formally* when it stays in the same place in regard to its essence, but either receives through augmentation something which it didn't previously have or loses something through the diminishment of what it previously had, or by alteration begins to have something that it previously had otherwise." For Hugh, only God is not susceptible to any of these kinds of changes.[56] So, non-essential but intrinsic formal change involves either augmentation or diminution.[57] The last of these is a change in a thing's intrinsic disposition: "to those which receive alteration, nothing seems to be added which was not, nor is anything shown to depart which was, but what was is only altered and is otherwise disposed."[58]

Similarly, at the macrocosmic level: "Wisdom distributes each thing in a suitable way within the whole, so never, never does the joining of the parts give rise to a conflict of attributes."[59] Again: "from this it is clear how firm are the bonds of things, when each created thing defends its being and nature with such effort, yet at the same time all things cannot be completely loosed from the concord of their association (*concordia societatis*)."[60] "Thus does all nature ... in some wondrous way, by means of a concord of many dissimilar things joined together in unity, fashion (*facit*) one harmonious whole (*armoniam*) in all of them."[61] Accordingly, "in the least of creatures there is lacking nothing of all that nature formed

[52] *Sacr.*, 1.1.6 (*PL* 176.192C; Deferrari 13): "Per sapientiam et discretionem formata est."

[53] *Tribus diebus*, 19 (Poirel 43.735–40). "All mutability occurs in three ways: in place, form and time."

[54] *Sacr.*, 1.3.15 (*PL* 176.221D; Deferrari 47): "When [the disposition] is changed, because the parts change place, the form (*forma*) in the whole is changed, because the disposition of parts is changed, which is the form of the whole (*forma totius*)."

[55] *Sacr.*, 1.3.15 (*PL* 176.222A; Deferrari 47).

[56] *Tribus diebus*, 19 (Poirel 44.750–52): "If, therefore, it is established that God can change neither in form nor in place, there will be no doubt that God is wholly immutable. [Si igitur Deum neque forma neque loco mutari posse constiterit, immutabilem omnino esse dubium non erit.]"

[57] *Tribus diebus*, 20 (Poirel 46.802–4): "Quicquid enim secundum formam mutatur, vel secundum diminutionem, vel secundum alterationem mutatur."

[58] *Sacr.*, 1.3.15 (*PL* 176.221C; Deferrari 46).

[59] *Tribus diebus*, 7 (Poirel 17.244–46).

[60] *Tribus diebus*, 4 (Poirel 14.187–90).

[61] *Tribus diebus*, 4 (Poirel 13.166–68).

(*formavit*) in the greatest"[62] and "in absolutely nothing is the order of things disturbed."[63] This disposition of creatures through *forma* holds true even of times and seasons: "Who can admire sufficiently the wondrous rationale (*ratione*) by which divine providence distinguishes the courses of time?"[64] In all of this, Hugh marvels at the "effectiveness of divine wisdom (*divinae sapientiae efficacia*)."[65] In the end, he settles on a term that best characterizes this formed state of nature: justice. Through sapiential form, all things have been "disposed in the way of justice"[66] and made according "to the order and form of justice (*ad ordinem justitiae formamque*)."[67]

CREATION AS *FORMOSA*

As noted above, for Hugh, the hexameral account in Genesis of the initial formation of creation is not complete with the imposition of mere *forma*. Matter's gradual disposition by form (*dispositus*) is accomplished by the third day; in the remaining three days, the creation receives "adornment,"[68] it is decorated and ornamented (*ornatus*). That which is formed by the end of day three is well formed (*formata*) by the end of day six; that which receives being (*esse*) in the first three days receives beautiful being (*pulchrum esse*) in the last three.[69]

Throughout his corpus, Hugh betrays a consistent sensitivity to the beauty of created things, which for him is the most evident reflection of the Creator within the creation.[70] And beauty, for him, is directly linked to *forma*: "the beauty of creatures deriving from their natural form ..."[71] Hugh elaborates:

> The immensity of creatures pertains more to the being, the beauty of creatures more to the form. The being considered without the form is formlessness. What lacks form, in as much as it exists, is like God, but in as much as it lacks form it is unlike God. What has form is more like God than what does not have form.

[62] *Tribus diebus*, 9 (Poirel 23.352–53). [63] *Tribus diebus*, 5 (Poirel 14.195–15.196).
[64] *Tribus diebus*, 6 (Poirel 16.219–20). [65] *Tribus diebus*, 7 (Poirel 17.244–45).
[66] See *Sacr.*, 1.Prol.3 (*PL* 176.184A–C; Deferrari 4); *Sacr.*, 1.Prol.5 (*PL* 176.185B; Deferrari 5).
[67] *Sacr.*, 1.1.12 (*PL* 176.195C; Deferrari 16). [68] *Sacr.*, 1.1.29 (*PL* 176.204C; Deferrari 27).
[69] *Sacr.*, 1.1.3 (*PL* 176:189A; Deferrari 9).
[70] For Hugh's aesthetic see Edgar de Bruyne, *Études d'esthétique médiévale*, 3 vols. (Bruges: De Tempel, 1946), II:203–50, and Lenka Karfíková, *"De esse ad pulchrum esse." Schönheit in der Theologie Hugos von St. Viktor*, Bibliotheca Victorina: 8 (Turnhout: Brepols, 1998). This is perhaps especially the case in his *De tribus diebus*, with which, according to de Bruyne, Hugh "est le premier auteur [after John Scotus Eriugena] à consacrer un traité complet à beauté" (*Études d'esthétique médiévale*, II:203).
[71] *Tribus diebus*, 16 (Poirel 35.565): "decor creaturarum propter formam naturalem."

Hence, the beauty of creatures, which pertains to form, is a more evident likeness than the immensity of creatures, which concerns only the being.[72]

As before, this perception of *forma* in creation suggests to Hugh the overarching effect of divine wisdom:

If you gaze at the structure of the universe, you will find that the composition of all things is perfect because of wonderful reason and wisdom. How apt, congruent, seemly, how complete in all its parts! In it not only do similar things protect concord, but by the Creator's power diverse and incompatible things that have come into existence by the command of wisdom come together as one in a sort of friendship and federation.[73]

Wisdom's aesthetic impact on the universe as a whole is also evident in relation to the "deeds and deliberations" of rational creatures. For wisdom "so educes all the deeds of human beings, all their volitions, and all the thoughts of their hearts according to the judgment of the will and so tempers and moderates them, that nothing can happen in the universe which wisdom does not wish to happen either by commanding or permitting it for the adornment of Her work."[74] In short, "the supreme beauty (*summa pulchritudo*) of the work shows that the wisdom (*sapientiam*) of the founder is perfect."[75]

Though *forma* is clearly central to Hugh's aesthetic, he does not use the derived term *formosus* ("finely formed, beautiful, handsome") very frequently. Where he does, however, it has special relevance to this study (and serves as a useful *segue* to the next chapter), for he employs the term with respect to the formed beauty of the human person, on analogy with

[72] *Tribus diebus*, 16 (Poirel 34.557–64): "Inmensitas autem creaturarum magis ad essentiam, decor vero creaturarum magis pertinet ad formam. Essentia vero absque forma considerata informitas est. Quod autem informe est, in hoc quidem quod est, Deo simile est, sed in hoc quod forma caret a Deo dissident. Quod ergo formatum est magis Deo simile est quam id quod formam non habet. Unde constat quod plus evidens simulacrum est decor creaturarum, qui pertinet ad formam, quam inmensitas creaturarum, quae ad solam spectat essentiam."

[73] *Tribus diebus*, 4 (Poirel 12.152–13.163): "Si universitatis huius machinam intueris, invenies quam mirabilis ratione et sapientia compositio rerum omnium perfecta sit, quam apta, quam congrua, quam decora, quam cunctis partibus suis absoluta; in qua non solum concordiam servant similia, sed eciam quae creante potentia diversa atque repugnantia ad esse prodierunt, dictante sapientia in unam quodammodo amiciciam et federationem conveniunt."

[74] *Tribus diebus*, 8 (Poirel 21.321–26): "sapientia quae omnia hominum facta, omnes denique uoluntate, omnes cogitationes cordium ita ad suae uoluntatis arbitrium intoquet, ita temperat et moderatur, ut nichil in uniuersitate fieri possit, quod non ipsa ad decorem operum suorum aut precipiendo aut permittendo fieri uelit."

[75] *Sacr.*, 1.3.14 (*PL* 176.221A; Deferrari 46). Ultimately, Hugh's general aesthetic orientation reveals itself in his grappling with issues of theodicy and evil in the world: "with these evils added, good things might be commended and become more beautiful through comparison with evil" and "good things would be adorned from these and commended and would receive greater good to the glory and beauty of the whole" (*Sacr.*, 1.4.6 [*PL* 176.236B–C; Deferrari 63]).

the formed beauty of creation. As noted above, the discussion of creation in *De sacramentis* employed the term *pulchrum esse* to describe the aesthetic culmination of creation. The Victorine sentence collection, the *Miscellania*, which also contains authentic writings of Hugh himself, puts the point thus:

> In the very creation of things, God first made matter; after he added *forma*, in order to show that, similarly, in the rational creature, being (*esse*) was made first, and afterwards beautiful (*pulchrum esse*) or lovely being (*formosum esse*): something better was to be added, so that the rational creature would not glory too much in the good which it had first accepted, but instead would hasten to the better thing he was going to receive afterwards.[76]

The finely formed beauty (*formusus*) of creation, then, is a "sacrament" of the divinely intended state of human beings. Hugh himself makes the same point in his internal dialogue, the *De arrha animae*. Anticipating the re-formative work of salvation, he reminds himself that he is now receiving "beautiful and lovely being (*pulchrum esse, formosum esse*), which far surpasses nothingness in its existence, as it outdoes something merely existent in its beauty."[77] For Hugh, God's gradual imposition of form on matter constitutes a gradual process, not just of formation, but of beautification, and the result is not merely *formata* but also *formosa*.[78]

CONCLUSION

In sum, Hugh's interpretation of the creation account in Genesis reflects a predilection for the language and concept of *forma* to describe the divine source and means of creation, the divine manner of creating, and the

[76] *Miscellanea* I.48 (*PL* 177.497B), "De duabus civitatibus et duobus populis et regibus": "Propter hoc etiam in ipsa rerum conditione, primum materiam fecit; postea formam superaddidit, ut ostenderet quod similiter in rationali creatura primum esse factum erat: postea autem pulchrum esse et *formosum esse*: et melius addendum erat, ut non nimis gloriaretur in eo quod primum bonum acceperat, sed ad illud potius festinaret quod postea melius acceptura erat." To be cited as *Misc.*

[77] *Arrha* (*OHSV* 1.252:413–17; Herbert 23): "Nunc autem amplius dedit, quia dedit non solum esse, sed pulchrum esse, formosum esse, quod quantum superat nihil per existentiam, tantum antecedit aliquid per formam ..." The translator's note here is pertinent: "The form here in question consists in the aspect of things, in the distribution of their parts. Hugh uses the term *informis* to designate a confused distribution and the term *formosus* to indicate an ordered arrangement of the parts of an object. See *De sacramentis* 1.1.13; *PL* 176.188–89." *Soliloquy on the Earnest Money of the Soul*, 23 (n. 8).

[78] *Sacr.*, 1.1.4 (*PL* 176.189C–D; Deferrari 10, trans. altered): "To be sure I might believe that something has being and not any form (*formam*). Thus it is not absurd to call matter unformed (*informem*), because existing in a certain confused and mixed state it had not yet begun [to have] this beautiful and suitable disposition and form (*pulchram aptamque dispositionem et formam*) in which it is now seen."

created result. In his *ex professo* treatment of the topic in *De sacramentis*, and in comments littered throughout his corpus, he interprets the divine creative activity as occurring through the very *Forma* of divine Wisdom, the second Person of the Trinity. Through a gradual process of *formatio*, in the manner of a skilled artisan, Wisdom imparts *forma* upon *materia*, bringing it from the "form of confusion" initially to "a form of disposition," and ultimately to a "form of adornment." For Hugh, creation is a process of *formatio* that results in something both *formata* and *formosa*, formed and well formed, both existing and existing beautifully.[79] In this conception, he privileges divine wisdom and goodness (pedagogy, human benefit) over divine power, though in no way does he understand himself to impugn the latter, only to see it operating always *pro hominibus*, wisely, beneficially, as befitting the well-being and beautiful being of rational creatures.[80]

[79] *Sacr.*, 1.1.6–7 (*PL* 176.190A–193B; Deferrari 10–14).
[80] *Sacr.*, 1.2.1 (*PL* 176.205B–206C; Deferrari 28–29).

CHAPTER 2

Rational creation: Formed by Wisdom for beauty

INTRODUCTION

At the end of the six days of creation God forms the human creature. Hugh's theological anthropology, his conception of human nature, is an important feature in his theology, and figures centrally in his understanding of re-formation. In many respects, his view of human nature is traditional and thoroughly Augustinian. Formed "in the image and likeness of God" (Gen. 1:26), humans are fundamentally "God-oriented," that is, created to know and, especially, to love God above all else, to subsume all else to this overriding goal, and to find ultimate fulfillment and beatitude in that divine–human relationship. Likewise, Hugh insists on the goodness of matter and of humanity's divinely intended, embodied state, including the resurrection of the body, but he privileges the spiritual, immaterial, and interior dimension of the human person. Hugh knows and repeats Augustine's view of the soul as an *imago Trinitatis*, but does not make it central to his own view.

At present, an extended discussion of human nature is premature; only a bare sketch of the human person before the Fall is offered here. The full picture only emerges in the context of restoration, and must be postponed until later in this study. The primary characteristic of Hugh's prelapsarian theological anthropology, to be addressed here in accord with the general account of creation in the previous chapter, is its formability, its openness to a process of formation leading to beautiful being (*pulchrum, formosum esse*), the goal of which is divine indwelling. This feature will continue into his post-lapsarian view as well.

THE RATIONAL CREATURE FORMED BY WISDOM TOWARD BEAUTIFUL BEING

As embodied, the human person is, to be sure, a part of the visible, material creation, but, as an embodied spirit, human nature stands in a middle position between material reality "below" it and the immaterial, spiritual, divine reality "above" it. "Therefore, humankind, as though situated in a kind of middle place, has God above, the world below. By the body humankind is connected to the world below, and by the spirit it is lifted up toward God above."[1] Thus, this middle position creates a particular relationship between human nature and both the invisible Creator and the visible creation. On the one hand, the rational creature was created for participation in God above: "Omnipotent God, whose happiness can be neither increased or decreased in any way, since it is perfect, nor diminished, since it is eternal, by charity alone, not by any necessity on His part, created rational spirit, so that He might make it a sharer in that good which He Himself was, and by which He Himself was happy."[2] On the other hand, what this sharing in God might mean and how it might be accomplished is symbolized by the visible creation below it. That is, ever attentive to the deeper meaning in visible things, Hugh sees in the six days of creation "a great sacrament (*magnum sacramentum*)"[3] regarding the divine intent for rational creatures, especially for human beings, who emerge at the end of the process, but for whom the whole process occurred. "The world was made for the sake of man."[4] So, Hugh observes, "it was necessary that the creation of visible things be so arranged (*ordinaretur*) that humankind recognized in them exteriorly what the invisible good they were to seek within was like; that is, that human beings see beneath them what they desired above them."[5] Or, again, the union of matter and spirit in human nature, just noted, is "a pattern of the future society (*exemplo futurae societatis*) which was to be realized between Himself and rational spirit unto its glorification" and "participation in His own glory."[6]

But Hugh sees a profound symbol of this felicitous divine–human relation, not merely in the creation as accomplished fact, but in the very process and means by which it comes to be over six days. That is, like the visible creation, Hugh conceives of rational creatures themselves receiving from the Creator an initial existence (*esse*), which is capable of – indeed requires – further formation in order that the divine intent for it might be realized. Hugh observes:

For even the rational creature itself was first made unformed (*informis*) in a certain mode of its own, afterwards to be formed (*formanda*) through conversion

[1] *Tribus diebus*, 14 (Poirel 31.488–90). [2] *Sacr.*, 1.6.1 (*PL* 176.263B–C; Deferrari 94).
[3] *Sacr.*, 1.1.12 (*PL* 176.195C; Deferrari 16).
[4] *Sacr.*, 1.Prol.3 (*PL* 176.184B; Deferrari 4). See *Sacr.*, 1.1.19 (*PL* 176.200C–201A; Deferrari 22–23).
[5] *Tribus diebus*, 14 (Poirel 31.491–94). [6] *Sacr.*, 1.6.1 (*PL* 176.263C–D; Deferrari 94).

to its Creator; and therefore matter unformed (*informis*) but afterwards formed (*formata*) was shown to it, that it might discern how great was the difference between being (*esse*) and beautiful being (*pulchrum esse*). And by this it was warned not to be content with having received being from the Creator through creation, until it should obtain both beautiful being and happy being (*pulchrum esse atque beatum esse*), which it was destined to receive from the Creator through a conversion of love.[7]

In this remarkable and crucial passage, Hugh indicates his fundamental conception of divine–human relatedness. The very same pattern visible in the six days of creation – *formatio* across time resulting in a reality both *formata* and *formosa* – is to be replicated in human creatures. So, as an example, Hugh puts forward the dividing of the waters by the firmament:

But why it came to pass that the firmament divided the waters from one another, and that the nature of these waters consisted in part above and in part below, let him not seek outside himself, who believes that these things were made for his sake. For there is in that world which has been constructed (*fabricatus*) interiorly a certain something possessing the form and exemplar (*formam et exemplar*) of this work ... But it sometimes happens that the contrary impulses beget confusion, unless reason (*ratio*), intervening as a mediatrix, divides them from one another ...[8]

In short, Hugh envisions human nature created at the end of the six days' work as existing not in a state of perfection or completion, nor in perfect divine–human relationship, but rather in an imperfect state of partially formed being (*esse*) which is in need of further formation unto beautiful being (*pulchrum*, *formosum esse*). In this sense, Hugh speaks of a "first perfection" of the rational creature. By this he means a state which was as God intended it to be *at that point*. Rational creatures "were good and not evil, and as they were good, so also were they just and happy, but with that goodness and justice and happiness which incipient nature had received." That is, "their goodness, justice, and happiness were not complete."[9]

7 *Sacr.*, 1.1.3 (*PL* 176.189A; Deferrari 9). See *Sacr.*, 1.1.6 (*PL* 176.192C; Deferrari 13): "For just as the matter of bodies to be formed (*formandorum*), when it was first created, had a certain form (*quamdam formam*) in which it began to subsist, and yet was unformed (*informis*), because it was not yet disposed and arranged (*disposita et ordinata*), so likewise that rational creature, when it was first created in the angelic spirits, was soon formed (*formata*) by wisdom and discretion; but because it had not yet fixed itself (*impresserat*) through the conversion of love upon that highest and true good in which it was to be made happy, in a certain measure it still remained unformed (*informis*)."

8 *Sacr.*, 1.1.19 (*PL* 176.200C–D; Deferrari 22).

9 *Sacr.*, 1.5.19 (*PL* 176.254C–D; Deferrari 84): So with the angels: "... angels were not founded perfect, because they were created in the first perfection, and for the second [perfection] under the third [perfection], since, just as they cannot reach the third [perfection], so likewise should they not have begun with the second [perfection]" (*Sacr.*, 1.5.17 [*PL* 176.253B–C; Deferrari 82]).

THE FIRST PERFECTION: "IN THE IMAGE AND LIKENESS OF GOD"

The formation of the rational creature in its "first perfection" was formation in "the image and likeness of God" (Gen. 1:26), a crucial feature of Hugh's theological anthropology:

> For this reason, therefore, not one something, either this or that, could have sufficed in the divine reason as an exemplar for the rational creature, according to whose likeness the latter should be formed (*formaretur*); rather in a manner of speaking it took God entire, that it might be made the image of Himself, and it was represented as completely imitating His perfection ... There shone forth a perfect image imitating its author ...[10]

While all other creatures have, as it were, a particular exemplar in the divine mind, according to which they were created, the rational creature is made according to God Himself, thus establishing the possibility of profound divine–human relatedness, of created participation in the Uncreated.[11] "For [the First Cause] made to its own likeness what it disposed to participation in itself, so that from itself that which was to possess the same good with it might take the same form."[12] For Hugh, divine–human intimacy requires that the rational creature in some sense share the divine *forma*.

For Hugh, this initial image and likeness of God has both a noetic and an affective/moral dimension: "Man was made to the image and likeness of God ... image according to reason, likeness according to love; image according to understanding of the truth, likeness according to love of virtue ..."[13] With respect to the first, the pre-lapsarian human had "perfect knowledge of things in so far as pertained to the beginning of foundation," that is, at the first creation. "At least," Hugh immediately clarifies, "he received a perfect knowledge and understanding of truth (*cognitionem veritatis et scientiam*) *which was appropriate to first perfection* [emphasis added] and he arrived at that not by study or any teaching (*studio aut disciplina*) over periods of time."[14] In the beginning, then, human beings

[10] *Sacr.*, 1.5.3 (*PL* 176.248B; Deferrari 76). Also, *Sacr.*, 1.5.3 (*PL* 176.247C–D; Deferrari 75): "Therefore the rational creature alone is reported as having been made according to the likeness of God, and it is not said that any creature save the rational alone was made to the likeness of God, although every creature had its cause and likeness in the divine reason and in the eternal providence from which and according to which it was perfected in its subsistence."

[11] See Sicard, *Diagrammes*, 220–26. [12] *Sacr.*, 1.2.3 (*PL* 176.207D; Deferrari 31).

[13] *Sacr.*, 1.6.2 (*PL* 176.264C–D; Deferrari 95).

[14] *Sacr.*, 1.6.12 (*PL* 176.270D; Deferrari 102). See *Sacr.*, 1.6.13 (*PL* 176.271A; Deferrari 102): man "received perfect knowledge (*perfectam cognitionem*), in so far as seemed to pertain either to the instruction of his soul or to the needs of his body."

possessed an initially appropriate knowledge of God that was given, not acquired. But this way of putting it clearly implies both something further to be arrived at and a particular way of doing so. Hugh adds, accordingly, that pre-lapsarian man "knew his Creator, yet not so excellently as he would necessarily have known Him thereafter, if he had persisted. For just as the disobedience of man through subsequent ignorance took much from his first knowledge, thus, if the obedience of man had persisted, very much would have had to be added to the same knowledge through subsequent revelation."[15] Hugh here suggests that, even before and apart from any subsequent Fall, God intended that human beings move from an initial, gratuitously granted knowledge of God to a fuller knowledge of God arrived at through obedience, that is, at least in part through human activity, over time in a manner involving study and teaching. Elsewhere, Hugh puts the matter succinctly: "This was, therefore, the one, true good of man, to wit, the full and perfect knowledge of his Maker – full, you must understand, after that fullness which he received at his creation, not after that which he was to receive hereafter, when his obedience was fulfilled."[16]

Hugh seems especially inclined to see things from a developmental perspective. He thus finds it appropriate that, though the first humans were created in a state of maturity, their progeny "would be born small," that is, in an undeveloped or immature state, "and then over intervals of time would receive increase both in sense of mind and in corporeal stature," that is, "to greater and better things." Similarly, "we perceive [this] in all trees and plants and shoots, in all beasts and living things, since they all begin from what is small, and then gradually *by ordered stages*" and "*by increasing over intervals of time*" eventually "arrive at perfection" (emphasis added).[17] So too, the ignorance of immaturity is not a function of sin nor is it culpable, since only that ignorance which is due to human neglect or irresponsibility is culpable. It is, in fact, fitting that humans should be born in this kind of ignorance and then proceed gradually to knowledge and the use of reason.[18] In general, then, Hugh conceives of things from a developmental standpoint, and this is the general context in which his interest in formation emerges.

The Fall, then, will entail a diminishment of that initially appropriate knowledge of God, but it will not negate the overriding goal set in

[15] *Sacr.*, 1.6.14 (*PL* 176.271D; Deferrari 103). [16] *Archa Noe*, 1.1 (Sicard 4.33–37; CSMV 46).
[17] *Sacr.*, 1.6.26 (*PL* 176.279A–B; Deferrari 111).
[18] *Sacr.*, 1.6.26 (*PL* 176.278D–280B; Deferrari 111–13).

place from the beginning: a gradual process of increase and growth in the knowledge of God, finding a culmination and perfection in what Hugh will call contemplation. Thus, the initial knowledge of God, though it "was greater and more certain than the knowledge which now consists in faith alone, so also [it] was less than that which afterwards will be manifestly revealed in the excellence of divine contemplation (*contemplationis divinae*)."[19]

The reference to obedience above introduces the affective or moral dimension of the first perfection. Hugh speaks of a "justice and discipline (*via justitiae et disciplinae*),"[20] which pertain especially to the human will, which for him is the soul's appetitive capacity, its ability to move toward a desired object.[21] Hugh stresses the freedom of the pre-lapsarian will: "free in the voluntary, will in the desire." [22] Before the Fall, "man could incline the desire of his will either to good or evil." He had both "the power to sin (*posse peccare*)" and the "power not to sin (*posse non peccare*)." Yet, even here, "the aid of grace" was necessary.[23] In this state of original justice, the mind assisted by grace moved freely in accordance with "the will of its Creator," which was "its *form and exemplar* and the designed rule which it should follow" (emphasis added). To be conformed to the divine exemplar in this way was, for the creature, to "cling to its rectitude (*rectitudo*)" or to "justice (*justitia*)."[24]

This conformity of the human to the divine will gives rise to Hugh's definition of virtue: "virtue is nothing else than an affection of the mind ordered according to reason."[25] In the first perfection, the rational creature was created with "good affections and ordered according to justice," through which it "was attracted by natural desire to seek out goodness and justice, and in these good affections, indeed, were the natural virtues with which from the beginning the nature of man was formed and instructed (*formata est et instructa*)."[26]

These two basic dimensions of the human mind – cognition and affection, knowledge and love – were to function in tandem in the pre-lapsarian

[19] *Sacr.*, 1.6.14 (*PL* 176.721C–D; Deferrari 103).
[20] *Sacr.*, 1.Prol.3 (*PL* 176.184B–C; Deferrari 4).
[21] *Sacr.*, 1.6.4 (*PL* 176.265C–266B; Deferrari 96).
[22] *Sacr.*, 1.6.4 (*PL* 176.265C; Deferrari 96).
[23] *Sacr.*, 1.6.16 (*PL* 176.272C–D; Deferrari 104). Cf. *Sententiae* (Piazzoni 922.312–14): "He also gave him a free will (*liberum arbitrium*), that is a voluntary desire (*voluntarium appetitum*), so that whichever he willed, either the good or evil, he could desire and by his own will incline his mind to either one."
[24] *Sacr.*, 1.6.4 (*PL* 176.265D; Deferrari 96). For a comparison between Anselm of Canterbury and Hugh on this point, see Roger Baron, "L'Idée de liberté chez S. Anselme et Hugues de Saint-Victor," *RTAM* 32 (1965), 117–21.
[25] *Sacr.*, 1.6.17 (*PL* 176.273B–C; Deferrari 105).
[26] *Sacr.*, 1.6.17 (*PL* 176.274D; Deferrari 107).

state, which collaboration issued forth into praise and contemplation. In its embodied state, the human soul straddled two worlds, the visible, material world without and the invisible, spiritual world within. Both were formed in and by wisdom and both could therefore be the source of sapiential contemplation. Reason's ability to cognize produced admiration, which in turn produced love.

For God would not be praised in all His works by the rational creature, if all the works of God were not known by the rational creature. Therefore, that the praise of God might be perfect, the works of God were shown to the rational creature, so that it might admire Him within and without, and through admiration advance to love.[27]

In this was to be the contemplative fulfillment of human nature: to go inward and contemplate "wisdom," to go outward and contemplate "the works of wisdom," and thus "to find refreshment in both," through cognition and affection, knowledge and love of God.[28] "There are two things by which the whole nature of the rational soul is disposed, namely, cognition and affection, that is, wisdom and love. If the soul perfectly obtains and legitimately disposes these [within itself], it will be blessed."[29] Hugh can put this in terms of *forma*: "cognition and affection" are the *forma* of the human soul. "These two things are the highest and closest to God, and the express image [of God]: the cognition of truth and the love of virtue."[30]

FORMABLE HUMAN NATURE

In this state of first perfection, Hugh conceives of the rational human creature as having been formed to such an extent that it is poised midway between two extremes, expressed in terms of goodness. One extreme, "above" the soul, is God, understood as the *summum bonum*, essential, uncreated Good. The other extreme, "below" the soul, is non-God, non-being, non-good, evil. Arranged between these two extremes is a hierarchy of goods. In this regard, Hugh can appeal to the sapiential triad from

[27] *Sacr.*, 1.6.5 (*PL* 176.266B–C; Deferrari 97). [28] *Sacr.*, 1.6.5 (*PL* 176.266D; Deferrari 97).

[29] *In Eccl.* (*PL* 175.141B): "Duo quippe sunt, quibus animae rationalis natura tota disponitur, videlicet cognitio et affectus, id est sapientia et amor. Quae duo si anima perfecte obtineat et legitime disponat, beata est."

[30] *Misc.*, 1.83 (*PL* 177.518C): "In his duo posuit Deus ad materiam, duo ad formam: vitam et sensum ad materiam, cognitionem et dilectionem ad formam. Ad vitam cognitionem, ad sensum dilectionem. Haec duo suprema et Deo proxima sunt, et expressa imago: cognitio veritatis, et amor virtutis."

Wisdom 11 to describe how all things have been made in "number, weight, and measure," each having "its established boundary and end,"[31] especially rational creatures, who have their proper "measure, mode, and end."[32] Situated thus, the rational creature is capable of movement in either direction, toward the highest Good, which alone is its true good, or toward the lower goods,[33] which when treated as the highest good become in fact evil, not in themselves, but as related to in an unfitting and disorderly way.[34]

This movement is either a "conversion," a turning toward the Creator, or an "aversion," a turning away. Both conversion and aversion, moreover, entail change in the creature, change that occurs through the soul's proper and characteristic acts, namely, knowing and loving, cognition and affection: "We see that spirit can neither increase at all by augmentation of parts, since it is not a body, nor decrease by diminution, since it is a simple nature; and yet spirit is changed by affection and cognition."[35] Again, "change in spirits occurs through knowledge and affect. Spirits change according to affect as at one time they are sad and at another are joyful. They change according to knowledge when they know now less, now more."[36] Hugh conceives of this change, moreover, as a change in *forma*: "the rational creature passes from this to that, it varies and experiences the vicissitudes of joy, grief, repentance and wish; its knowledge increases and forgetfulness befalls it; it varies its thoughts and it knows in succession, and that change in it of knowledge and affection is, as it were, a change in form (*forma*)."[37] Such change is the most profound that a creature can undergo and still remain what it is: "now change of form is alone called intrinsic, since it changes something not about a thing but in the thing itself."[38]

Change "for the better" (*in melius*) is in fact greater goodness; change for the worse is diminution and decreased goodness. Conversion involves

[31] *Super canticum Mariae* (*OHSV* 11.66:597–68:599): "Certum est enim quod omne quod factum est in numero, et pondere et mensura, legitimum terminum et finem suum habet." Critical text: See *OHSV* 11.16–99.

[32] *Sacr.*, 1.5.12 (*PL* 176.251C; Deferrari 80).

[33] See *Sacr.*, 1.2.1 (*PL* 176.206B; Deferrari 29): This middle state is between the "good of necessity," all other created goods created for man's sake, and the "good of happiness," God himself, for whom man was created and in whom man finds his fulfillment. Man receives the goods of necessity that he might make progress and move toward the good of happiness.

[34] *Sacr.*, 1.4.17–19 (*PL* 176.241C–242B; Deferrari 69).

[35] *Sacr.*, 1.3.16 (*PL* 176.222B; Deferrari 47).

[36] *Tribus diebus*, 20 (Poirel 48.825–28): "Alteratio corporum fit in transpositione partium, et uicissitudine qualitatum; alteratio spirituum per cognitionem et affectum. Secundum affectum mutantur spiritus, ut nunc tristes nunc hilares; secundum cognitionem, ut nunc minus nunc amplius sapientes."

[37] *Sacr.*, 1.3.16 (*PL* 176.222B; Deferrari 47).

[38] *Sacr.*, 1.3.15 (*PL* 176.222A; Deferrari 46).

greater and higher degrees of justice, goodness, and beauty (*pulchrum esse*), which is also a state of blessed being – in short, a transformation. Aversion, by contrast, produces loss of justice, goodness, and beauty – in short, a deformation. Thus the movement of conversion or aversion is not merely a change in spiritual "location," either lower or higher. It is a moral, affective conversion, a turning toward the Creator in love,[39] a "conversion of love,"[40] a becoming affectively "fixed (*impresserat*) upon that highest and true good."[41] This is the sure stabilization of form, prior to which there is always a degree of unformedness in the rational creature. When this obtains, the result is "happy being."[42] In short, human nature was created with "original justice," but in this initial state had not yet been "transformed" to the "justice of perfect obedience," which transformation was to be accomplished gradually, over time, through perseverance in obedience. Even had sin not intervened, human nature was "not yet transformed (*transformata*) to true incorruption" or "transformed (*transformata*) to the reward of incorruption" or "transformed from earthly life to a heavenly and spiritual state."[43] In terms of *forma*, the rational creature emerged out of the primal chaos with a certain form, which, though good and beautiful as such, was called to a higher degree of form and beauty.[44] For Hugh, human nature is both formed and formable, dynamic, open to greater and greater degrees of form and beauty.

FORMING PRACTICES

This initial fashioning of human beings had as its final *telos* a glorification[45] and participation in the divine life, for which human nature was to be prepared through a gradual process of formation constituted by certain practices: "Lastly, on the sixth day man was made … and he was placed in paradise, first to abide there and to work, so that, after his work was finished and his obedience fulfilled, he might be transported from there to that place where he was destined to abide forever."[46] The prelapsarian human was "not to be ignorant of his foundation and order

[39] *Sacr.*, 1.1.3 (*PL* 176.188B–189B; Deferrari 8–9).
[40] *Sacr.*, 1.1.6 (*PL* 176.192C; Deferrari 13). [41] *Sacr.*, 1.1.6 (*PL* 176.192C; Deferrari 13).
[42] *Sacr.*, 1.1.6 (*PL* 176.192C; Deferrari 13). [43] *Sacr.*, 1.6.24 (*PL* 176.277D–278A; Deferrari 110).
[44] *Sacr.*, 1.1.6 (*PL* 176.190B–192D; Deferrari 10–13). Hugh consistently locates the status of original creation as suspended between absolute non-being, on the one hand, and a perfected state of created being (typically described as *pulchrum esse*), on the other.
[45] *Sacr.*, 1.6.1 (*PL* 176.263D; Deferrari 94): "Therefore, God confirmed His power and showed His grace, first by fashioning (*fingendo*) man; and this grace He was to show afterwards by glorifying (*glorificando*) man."
[46] *Sacr.*, 1.1.29 (*PL* 176.204D; Deferrari 27).

and obligation, whether above himself or in himself or under himself," but was "to understand of what nature he was made and how he should proceed, what to do, what similarly to avoid."[47] In this "first perfection," the process of either transformation into the good or deformation into evil entailed an external or outer dimension and an internal or inner dimension. Exteriorly, the first humans were given certain activities or practices the doing of which constituted obedience and conduced the transformation unto the good. Interiorly, the rational creature was to be formed by moral and intellectual practices which formed inner virtues or dispositions.

More precisely, Hugh envisions pre-lapsarian humans as receiving two kinds of goods from the Creator – corporeal-temporal goods for the body and spiritual-eternal goods for the soul. Corresponding to these were two kinds of precepts or divine instruction for the "form of right living" (*formam recte vivendi*).[48] The "precept of nature" pertained to the right ordering of "lower," corporeal goods, by which these were "disposed" in the service of the "higher," spiritual goods. This was for protecting what had already been given in creation and involved "ordering, prohibiting, conceding."[49] The latter were in turn governed by "the precept of discipline," obedience to which would eventually culminate in the possession of "perfect justice" and open a way toward "the good that was promised"[50] to man (but not yet possessed). Thus, for Hugh, God enjoined on pre-lapsarian humans a kind of "care" or solicitude over both dimensions of human life. This, then, is the context of the practice-orientation of Hugh's theology. Ideal human life was to be governed by certain disciplines – we might say "practices" – of both body and soul, the execution of which would facilitate and constitute its formation in justice.[51] But Hugh makes a distinction here. The lower goods were given wholly and completely at the first creation, "immediately on his foundation," while the eternal good God "proposed to be given full after merit," such that the "precept of discipline opened a way with divine grace."[52] So, for Hugh, the higher, spiritual goods of the soul were not given fully at first, but were to be arrived at, gradually, over time. Thus, merit entails not only a sense of earning a reward for obedience – in this discussion he does focus narrowly on the particular precept of not eating from the tree of the knowledge of good and evil[53] – but also a grace-enabled formation in justice through

[47] *Sacr.*, 1.6.15 (*PL* 176.272A; Deferrari 104). [48] *Sacr.*, 1.6.15 (*PL* 176.272B; Deferrari 104).
[49] *Sacr.*, 1.6.7 (*PL* 176.268C; Deferrari 99). [50] *Sacr.*, 1.6.7 (*PL* 176.268B; Deferrari 99).
[51] *Sacr.*, 1.6.27 (*PL* 176.280B–281A; Deferrari 113).
[52] *Sacr.*, 1.6.28 (*PL* 176.281B; Deferrari 114). [53] See *Sacr.*, 1.6.29 (*PL* 176.282C–D; Deferrari 115).

the execution of certain practices, that is, a sense of arriving at a point of formation and disposition in justice and capacitation for beatitude: "But since this pertained to the increase of its felicity, that it should recognize the grace of its Creator through whom it was to be glorified, the Creator Himself wished first to show it in its creation what He was afterwards to make in it *according to its worthiness* [emphasis added]."[54]

At one point, Hugh raises the question of what human life would have been like if sin had not intervened, asking "with what zeal human life … would have been cultivated and practiced." His answer continues with the internal/external distinction, but, as is his wont, he sees in the visible and external a pattern of the invisible and interior. Not only would there have been "internal and spiritual zeal of wisdom and contemplation of God," but also an external "cultivating the land, whether in plowing or in sowing or in transplanting and in other works of this kind by which good nature on being cultivated makes progress toward the better," so that "even work was … an example unto instruction." He then pursues the analogy in terms of *forma*:

> For thus the exterior man had to be practiced so that by zeal itself for exterior work *a form* might be taken for interior zeal, and that in what he should do externally he might learn what had to be done by him within. For within also in a similar manner was there a kind of land which had indeed been created good, and yet, if it were well cultivated, could still *be better*; when cultivated it would produce good fruits, but when neglected it would bring forth bad and harmful offshoots [emphasis added].[55]

Had pre-lapsarian humanity continued to cultivate the exterior and interior garden of its good nature, gradually, it would have been formed and prepared for its ultimate destiny.

Here, then, is a crucial feature of Hugh's conception of human being. It is fundamentally orientated toward concrete practices, activities that can be themselves organized and ordered as disciplines, and which also contribute to human formation.

IN MELIUS

As the passage above indicates, Hugh conceives of this formation as change "for the better" (*in melius*). This phrase recurs throughout his corpus and reflects a distinctive feature of his theology. The initial state of creation, the "first perfection," was intended from the beginning for

[54] *Sacr.*, 1.6.1 (*PL* 176.263C; Deferrari 94). [55] *Sacr.*, 1.6.21 (*PL* 176.276D–277A; Deferrari 109).

improvement, for augmentation, for progress, for change beyond and above its first foundation.[56] As Hugh observes:

> [God] imposed ... the law of obedience ... that [human creatures] might ascend from where they were [as initially created] to where they were not ...; thus, when they had so ascended ... they might pass *beyond* that which they had been made to that for which they had been made, and in the end might be with Him by whom they had been made [emphasis added].[57]

Again, looking back from an eschatological vantage point, Hugh states that, "after the resurrection from the dead," the human creature "will be restored not only to that *in which* he was created, but *above* that also even to that *for which* he was created [emphasis added]."[58] Elsewhere, Hugh puts the point thus:

> He Himself cannot be better. But all that He has made can be better, at least if He Himself, who has the power, should so wish. And He Himself can make better what He has made, not, however, by correcting what has been made badly, but by promoting what has been made well to something better.[59]

Again:

> But that God is said to have created something imperfect or unformed is neither injurious nor unfitting; for in comparison to greater perfection or beauty, which He Himself added through Himself when it was necessary, this ought to be affirmed.[60]

In short, Eden was a place of preparatory, formational practices, leading to a better state.

CONCLUSION: *AD PULCHRUM ESSE* AS THE DWELLING PLACE OF GOD

As noted above, in the six days of creation God brought being out of non-being, and beautiful being (*pulchrum*, *formosum esse*) out of being. Both the process and the product of this act are to instruct the rational creature concerning the formative process that should occur in it as well. It too

[56] Similarly, of the angels, Hugh writes: "Otherwise, they could not have found a place for progressing and an avenue for advancing into better, unless there had been left after the first gifts of nature a means whereby they could have increased or failed" (*Sacr.*, 1.5.20 [*PL* 176.253C; Deferrari 82]).

[57] *Sacr.*, 1.6.1 (*PL* 176.264C; Deferrari 94–95).

[58] *Sacr.*, 1.6.10 (*PL* 176.270A; Deferrari 101).

[59] *Sacr.*, 1.2.22 (*PL* 176.216B–C; Deferrari 40–41).

[60] *In Pent.* (*PL* 175.33D): "Quod autem Deus dicitur creasse aliquid imperfectum aut informe, non nocet, nec est inconveniens; quia ad comparationem majoris perfectionis aut pulchritudinis, quas ipsemet per se quando oportuit, addidit, dici debet."

received an initial existence that, though good, was not yet fully formed. In this view, accordingly, God created the human person "leaning forward," so to speak, toward a greater, fuller form of being, which exceeds and fulfills its initial state of being. In this sense, his is an open-ended, dynamic, paradoxically non-essentialist conception of form and essence – an open-ended, dynamic essentialism. It is *forma* "on the move," *forma* with an as yet unrealized *telos* or *Tendenz* toward better, more beautiful existence.

In the end, the goal is divine indwelling – "... that in the end [they] might be with Him ..." This statement indicates the *telos* of creation generally and of the rational creation in particular. Certainly, God is present to the whole creation: "... God is in everything ... without diminution of Himself, and in every place without circumscription, and in every time without mutability ..."[61] For Hugh, though, God intends to dwell in a specific and unique way within the rational creature, especially the human: "how great a pleasure and how great a joy would be that immortal life from the presence of the Godhead in the rational spirit?"[62] More precisely: "by the wisdom of God the heart of man was made, that in it God might dwell as in a temple."[63] As here, Hugh's language for the Creator's indwelling of the creature consistently drifts toward structural and architectural images. Both creation and especially the soul are to be *templum Dei*. As such, moreover, they are in need of construction, of coming into existence and of being made apt for divine indwelling. Accordingly, the practices of formation in Eden were intended to accomplish precisely that: to form human nature so that, both *formata* and *formosa*, both adequately and beautifully formed, it would be a fitting, worthy dwelling place for God.

[61] *Sacr.*, 1.3.17 (*PL* 176.223B; Deferrari 48). God dwells in the creation as a ruler in the kingdom; the house of creation contains the believers, as well as heathen and unbelievers and even the devil, all of whom are present here by virtue of the fact of creation; the House of God is ruled by divine power (*Arca Noe*, 1.1 [Sicard 7.42–8.55; CSMV 49]).

[62] *Sacr.*, 1.6.1 (*PL* 176.263C; Deferrari 94).

[63] *Archa Noe*, 3.7 (Sicard 64.25–28; CSMV 102).

CHAPTER 3

Fall as de-formation

INTRODUCTION

The centrality of *forma* in Hugh's account of creation establishes a useful perspective from which to consider his conception of the primordial Fall of humanity, and a framework within which his view of human sin generally may be appreciated. Deeply Augustinian, Hugh's theology evinces a robust sense of the significance of sin and its effects on human nature. Jerome Taylor's observation regarding the *Didascalicon*, that "a sense of disaster primitively suffered by man pervades Book I," applies to Hugh's theology as a whole.[1]

As described in the previous chapter, Hugh envisions the rational creature in the pre-lapsarian state as situated midway between two extremes, with a nature that could turn and move in either direction. In ontological terms (*esse*), this dilemma can be conceived of in terms of non-being (*non-esse*) and beautiful being (*pulchrum esse*).[2] But, it can also be put psychologically: the creature can turn toward or away from the Creator through intellection and affection, reason and will; the former is justice; the latter is sin. Accordingly, though throughout his corpus Hugh describes this primal turning away and its consequences with diverse concepts and images (e.g., guilt, punishment, infection, illness, ignorance, perverse desire, etc.), these can all be reduced to a single description: a loss or degradation of creaturely integrity or form – in short, a de-formation.

This intuition regarding sin and its effects in Hugh's thought is confirmed by texts emanating from the Abbey of St.-Victor around the mid

[1] Taylor, *The Didascalicon of Hugh of St. Victor*, 11.

[2] See *Arrha* (*OHSV* 1.254:423–25; Herbert 24): "As He took us to himself in love, so He also wished to make us like himself. Therefore, having granted both existence and beautiful existence to us He also granted us to live such that we might both excel by our essence that which does not exist and also excel by our form those things which are disordered or not well-composed. [Dedit ergo nobis esse, et pulchrum esse; dedit et vivere, ut praecellamus et iis quae non sunt per essentiam, et iis quae inordinata aut incomposita sunt, per formam ...]"

twelfth century. Several works, apparently Victorine in their provenance, though now deemed spuriously or doubtfully attributed to Hugh, reflect this notion. The *Explanation of the Rule of St. Augustine*, for example, with a long history of Hugonian association, concludes with this telling observation in regard to sin:

For the sacred writing presents to us our interior image: what is well formed and what is deformed in the soul, how the beauty of justice ought to be observed, how the comeliness of the virtues ought to be composed, and how the stain of the vices ought to be cleansed away ... Holy men never cease daily to look into the sacred writings so as to consider their life and their virtues. If they find something deformed or uncomposed or disordered ... they are zealous to reform and compose themselves.[3]

As if expanding on the theme, the *Summa sententiarum*, which reflects Hugh's writings,[4] explains: "So also, the more the soul is deformed by sin, the more those natural goods which the soul still possesses, such as reason, skill, memory, and the like deteriorate and become darkened."[5] These three texts advertise key features of Hugh's own view: *forma* is an attribute of the soul which can be present or absent in varying degrees; its presence constitutes the soul's justice or righteousness as well as its beauty; its loss, or lessening, by contrast, entails not only forfeiture of justice and beauty, but also the deterioration of the soul's natural or created capacities, as well as the loss of proper arrangement, order, and composition among them.

Similar descriptions are not lacking in Hugh's undisputed works. At one point, he observes that "there are two things in the soul, essence and justice, the latter of which is the soul's form." The soul's essence is immortal and cannot be lost; "but it can be deformed by loss of form."[6] *De sacramentis* asks "whether the reprobate will be resurrected with their vices and deformities (*deformitatibus*)."[7] "The greater you are, the more you are

[3] *Expositio in regulam beati Augustini* (*PL* 176.924A–B): "Scriptura quippe nobis sacra nostram interiorem repraesentat imaginem; ostendit quid formosum, quid deforme sit in anima, et qualiter pulchritudo justitiae debeat observari, qualiter [924B] debeat virtutum decor componi; quomodo vitiorum macula debeat abstergi ... At contra sancti viri in Scripturis sacris quotidie non cessant inspicere vitam suam, moresque suos vigilanter pensare. Et si quid deforme vel incompositum aut inordinatum invenerint, mox quod secundum scriptum vident, reformare et componere se student."

[4] The *Summa sententiarum* (*PL* 176.41–174) is an anonymous theological compilation from the circle of Hugh of St. Victor (*c.* 1138–42), though likely the work of Odo of Lucca. See Marcia Colish, *Peter Lombard*, 2 vols. (Leiden: Brill, 1994), 1.56–65 and *passim*.

[5] *Summa sententiarum* (*PL* 176.112C): "Illa etiam bona naturalia quae adhuc habet anima ut ratio, ingenium, memoria, et caetera; tanto amplius deteriorantur et obtenebrantur, quanto magis anima peccatis deformatur."

[6] *Misc.*, 1.172 (*PL* 177.561A): "Duo sunt in anima, essentia et justitia, quae forma est illius ... Forma enim omnino potest perire; essentia non omnino perit, sed deformatur amissa forma."

[7] *Sacr.*, 2.17.20 (*PL* 176.605C: Deferrari 462).

deformed by your iniquity,"[8] says Hugh in his literal commentary on the book of Kings. In his *Sermons on Ecclesiastes*, he observes how "that vanity, which dominates depraved minds," is "more deforming" than other vices.[9] In one of his richest, best-known spiritual treatises, *De arrha anime*,[10] this theme is prominent. Addressing his own soul, Hugh says: "You do not know how vile you have been in the past, how polluted, how deformed (*deformis*) and squalid, how unkempt and dissipated, plainly a horror and an enormity to all."[11] Shortly thereafter, the soul responds: "How can I please him in my present deformity (*deformitate*), which is even revolting to me? O ancient stains, O stains that are ugly and disfiguring, how long will you remain?[12] By way of consolation, Hugh answers back at length:

> Finally, you began to doubt whether in your deformity (*deformitate*), which you now endure (even though you willingly subjected yourself to it), you could be loved by him. Yet do you not remember that once you were wholly ugly and yet beloved? If then he deigned to love you when you were wholly disfigured and having no comeliness, how much more does he now desire you, now that you are beginning to be adorned and to put off your disfigurement?[13]

Here the corollary of Hugh's positive conception of creation, originally both *formata* and *formosa*, is readily apparent in his negative view of the effects of sin on the human creature in particular, now both deformed and disfigured.

THE ORIGIN AND CONSEQUENCE OF SIN IN *DE SACRAMENTIS*

Hugh's *ex professo* discussion of original sin in his magisterial work of Christian doctrine, *De sacramentis*,[14] provides the fullest account of the

[8] *Adnotationes elucidatoriae in libros regum* (*PL* 175.102A): "Quanto enim major es, tanto iniquitas tua deformior."

[9] *In Eccl.* (*PL* 175.119B): "Porro illa vanitas, quae mentibus pravis dominatur, caeteris tanto deformior existit, quantum a spirituali substantia mutabilitas non solum per gratiam sed etiam per naturam aliena fuit. Propterea sola haec in caeteris omnibus arguitur, et prae caeteris omnibus sola haec iniqua atque perversa demonstratur." Also, *In Eccl.* (*PL* 175.123C): "In ea namque vanitatem posuimus iniquitatis: quae caeteris rebus omnibus eo deformior existit; quod ex ea tantum caeterae habent, vel quod noxiae sunt, vel quod omnino sunt."

[10] See Rorem, *Hugh of St. Victor*, 157–61.

[11] *Arrha* (*OHSV* 1.262:563–65; Herbert 28).

[12] *Arrha* (*OHSV* 1.278:800–3; Herbert 34).

[13] *Arrha* (*OHSV* 1.280:831–37; Herbert 35): "Ad extremum modo dubitare cepisti, an in hac deformitate tua, quam licet invita pateris, ab illo posses diligi. Sed quando hoc dubitasti, olim te totam fedam et tamen dilectam fuisse non meministi. Si ergo te nunc diligere dignatus est quando tota turpis, et nichil adhuc decoris habens fuisti, quanto magis nunc diliget te quando decorari et priscam turpitudinem deponere ian cepisti?"

[14] *Sacr.*, 1.7 (Deferrari 121–41).

deforming nature of sin in his theology. After its initial creation, the human person stands poised before the challenge of progress in formation: "for the preservation of the goods which he possessed he was fortified by divine providence added to human reason"; at the same time, "for seeking and obtaining those goods which he was to acquire" he was equipped with "the precept of obedience along with the assistance of grace."[15] Endowed with some goods, but destined for greater ones, the task of the pre-lapsarian rational creature was not simply to maintain an ideal state given by God at the outset, but rather actively to engage with divine assistance in a progression to something further. Precisely here sin will emerge, sin which "vitiates good nature and takes away its beauty and integrity (*pulchritudinem et integritatem*)."[16]

Hugh's analysis here is crucial and telling as he probes to the interior dynamics of the soul from which this first sin emerged. Externally, of course, the one act of original sin was the eating of the forbidden fruit from the tree of the knowledge of good and evil (Genesis 1). In and behind this one act, though, Hugh espies two dimensions of disobedience, and, deeper still, three basic vices. In eating, the primal parents succumbed to pride, greed, and gluttony. By pride and greed, they disobeyed the precepts of nature; by gluttony, they disobeyed the precept of discipline.[17] Eden's edible fruit stood for divine likeness and divine knowledge. Reaching for it, the human creature consciously desired these excellent things. Yet, the root problem was not *that* the human creature desired these: "Nowhere," insists Hugh, "is it read that God prohibited man from desiring likeness to God or knowledge of good and evil." Rather, the crucial factor was *how* the rational creature desired it, its manner or mode, and the subsequent action that this prompted. For Hugh, the characteristic feature of these three vices is excess or immoderation: pride is "the inordinate desire to excel." Greed is "the excessive passion for holding and possessing." Gluttony is "the immoderate desire to eat."[18] God-likeness and divine knowledge were goods rightly desired. Yet, the creature desired these inordinately (through pride) and excessively (through greed), thus violating the precepts of nature by being contrary to reason; it then desired them immoderately (through gluttony) in eating the forbidden fruit, thus violating the precept of discipline by being contrary to divine command.

Shortly thereafter, he extends his analyis to consider more fully the interior dynamics of the will, from which these vices emerged. He

[15] *Sacr.*, 1.7.1 (*PL* 176.287B; Deferrari 121). [16] *Sacr.*, 1.7.10 (*PL* 176.291B; Deferrari 125).
[17] *Sacr.*, 1.7.7 (*PL* 176.289B–C; Deferrari 123). [18] *Sacr.*, 1.7.6 (*PL* 176.289A–B; Deferrari 123).

observes that "from the beginning God had placed two things in man, by which his whole nature might be ruled and led to the fulfillment of its end," namely, "a desire for justice (*appetitus justi*) and a desire for benefit (*appetitus commodi*)."[19] These two desires are possessed by the soul in different ways. The desire for benefit is necessarily and inextricably present in human nature. It cannot be lost. Yet it can go unfulfilled. The soul does not automatically or necessarily possess the benefit it desires. By contrast, the desire for justice is contingently and voluntarily present in human nature; it can be lost. Yet, when present, this desire is *ipso facto* fulfilled, at least to some extent, since "the desire for justice can not exist without justice."[20]

With this background, Hugh can now turn to the question at hand. The deep cause of the primal lapse was the loss of this desire for justice. But how to explain this? For "it seems marvelously strange, if man first had a desire for justice, how afterwards he lost it."[21] He either lost this desire willingly or unwillingly. If unwillingly, then it was somehow imposed externally, and so culpability would be absent. But if willingly, how did man cease to will what he willingly willed? Hugh's answer is perhaps surprising, even if not fully satisfying. For our Victorine, the primal parents did not cease to will justice *per se*, that is, by beginning to will something else; rather they continued to will justice, but *in the wrong way*! And here he introduces a crucial term: What else can be said, he asks, "except that man willed something outside the measure (*extra mensuram*) in which alone was justice? For whatever exceeds proper measure cannot be just."[22] Strikingly, for Hugh, the root problem of human sin entailed at the outset, not a radical turning away from God or the goods that God willed to bestow, but rather the exceeding of a pre-established measure. The root problem was not *what* they desired, but *how*. What does this mean?

Adapting Augustine's distinction between enjoyment and use to his own purpose, Hugh asserts that God had prepared two goods for rational creatures, a temporal one, to be used, and an eternal one, to be enjoyed. To be sure, justice entailed not transposing these, by enjoying what was to be used and using what was to be enjoyed. But Hugh goes further: "to use or to enjoy goods is not praiseworthy, unless you use and enjoy them *well*" (emphasis added). So, in Eden "a measure was defined for man according to which he should use temporal goods and enjoy eternal goods

[19] *Sacr.*, 1.7.11 (*PL* 176.291B; Deferrari 125). [20] *Sacr.*, 1.7.11 (*PL* 176.291B; Deferrari 125).
[21] *Sacr.*, 1.7.12 (*PL* 176.292B; Deferrari 126). [22] *Sacr.*, 1.7.12 (*PL* 176.292D–293A; Deferrari 127).

well (*bene*)."[23] The measure of using well differed from that of enjoying well. Right use was fourfold: the proper object, along with the proper time, manner, and extent.[24] Right enjoyment, for its part, needed only to determine the proper time and manner, since it is self-evident both that God is the proper object of delight and that God should be enjoyed as much as possible.[25] Proper manner was the desire to be like God "according to imitation" as befits a creature," not "according to equality, which exceeds creaturely capacity." Proper time was only after the human being had completed its obedience.[26] In Eden, Hugh avers, the first humans exceeded measure on both counts:

But from the time that he began to will something outside measure (*extra mensuram*), he ceased to will measure (*velle mensuram*). Moreover, after he had ceased to will measure, he failed to love justice (*amare justitiam*). And he lost justice in this, wherein he lost the very love of justice. For as justice can not be lacking to its lover, so it can not by any means by present to him by whom it is not loved. In this therefore was the injustice of man: that he extended his desire beyond measure, both according to manner (*secundum qualitatem*), when he wished to be made like his Creator, and according to time (*secundum tempus*), when he hastened to forseize reward before merit. When, therefore, he desired the highest good, he desired good but he did not desire *well* (*bene*), because he sought to seize this both immoderately and unseasonably (*immoderate et intempestive*) [emphasis added].[27]

Original sin, then, was a violation of proper measure: It was excessive desire and immoderate haste. In short, the rational creature was rapacious and impatient.[28] Hugh puts all this more explicitly in terms of *forma* elsewhere:

For the one who does the good, works in good matter, but if he does not do the good well the good matter is deformed through a bad form. The good is a form, where it is neither more nor less it is just. If it is more than just, it is sin; if it is less than just it is a transgression. Thus, he who does the good well imprints as it were a good form upon good matter.[29]

[23] *Sacr.*, 1.7.13 (*PL* 176.293A; Deferrari 127). [24] *Sacr.*, 1.7.14 (*PL* 176.293A–B; Deferrari 127).

[25] The fall of angels (*Sacr.*, 1.5.29 [*PL* 176.259C–260C; Deferrari 87–88]) occurs similarly. They too sinned by exceeding measure (*extra mensuram*) and thus not acting "according to justice (*secundum justitiam*)."

[26] *Sacr.*, 1.7.15 (*PL* 176.293B–C; Deferrari 127–28). A similar discussion is found in Hugh's *De sacramentis legis naturalis* (*PL* 176.25) and in the *Summa sententiarum* (*PL* 176.97A–C).

[27] *Sacr.*, 1.7.15 (*PL* 176.293D–294A; Deferrari 128). [28] See also *Sacr.*, 1.5.29–32 (Deferrari 87–90).

[29] *Misc.*, 1.107 (*PL* 177.536C): "Qui enim bonum facit in bona materia operatur, sed si bonum bene non facit, per malam formam bona materia deformatur. Bona est forma, ubi nec plus nec minus justo est. Si plus justo sit, peccatum est; si minus justo sit, delictum. Igitur qui bonum bene facit, quasi bonae materiae bonam formam imprimit."

Here, then, is the deeper explanation for the initial description of the three internal vices that converged to produce the external act of illicit eating. The extension of good desire beyond measure manifested itself in pride, greed, and gluttony, all of which are vicious precisely because they are inordinate, immoderate, and excessive. They are distorted desires, not because they have abandoned that which ought to be desired by substituting non-goods for genuine goods, nor even because they have inverted the hierarchy of goods by placing inferior over higher goods; but rather because they have pursued the highest good *poorly*. This was the primal evil: "For the good that was sought was not evil, nor the will likewise by which it was sought, in so far as it was will; and in so far as it was for good, there was not evil, but what was sought beyond measure this alone was evil." For "that which is sought beyond measure is evil."[30] The Victorine *Miscellania* agrees: vice emerges when valid needs exceed "mode and measure," and "expand into superfluity"; "vice is nothing else than the natural affection outside of order and above measure."[31] Elsewhere, Hugh himself states that "the fecundity of the virtues must be encircled, guarded, and constrained, lest in their multiplication, they are relaxed beyond the measure of justice."[32] This, then, is the loss of the "form of justice," described in the previous chapter.[33] It is a loss of composure, an excess, a failure of discipline. The whole matter turns on the notion of measure, which for Hugh does not so much describe an external, fence-like boundary set up by God, but rather traces the border of the rational nature itself, and thereby establishes the bounds of its integrity, the proper mode of its activity.[34]

In all of this, a subtle yet persistent aesthetic dimension, already intimated above in Hugh's *Soliloquy*, is present in the sense of lost poise and balance, of flawed execution. One is tempted to call it "bad form." Indeed, Hugh himself says as much: "This is its sin and injustice and

[30] *Sacr.*, 1.7.16 (*PL* 176.294B; Deferrari 128).

[31] *Misc.*, 1.54 (*PL* 177.501C): "Omne vitium ex natura originem trahit; quia non est aliud vitium, quam affectus naturalis praeter ordinem et supra mensuram."

[32] *In hierarchiam* (*PL* 175.1145D): "quae custodia ipsas virtutes ambit, et custodit, vel constringit, ne in sua multiplicatione extra metas justitiae relaxentur, aut diffluant."

[33] See *Sacr.*, 1.7.10–15 (Deferrari 124–27).

[34] See the Victorine *Misc.*, 2.69 (*PL* 177.628B–C): "The way of man is mutable and is inflected toward diverse things; that is, either toward the way of God or the way of the devil. For if necessity is twisted toward cupidity and cupidity toward iniquity, the way of man is inflected toward the way of the devil. But if the way of man is arranged according to measure, and measure according to justice, the way of man is directed toward the way of God. [Via hominis mutabilis est, et ad diversa inflectitur; hoc est, vel ad viam Dei vel ad viam diaboli. Si enim necessitas intorquetur ad cupiditatem, et cupiditas ad iniquitatem, via hominis flectitur ad viam diaboli. Si autem diriguntur ad mensuram, et mensura ad justitiam, via hominis directa est ad viam Dei.]"

blame, from which it appears base and reprehensible and worthy of reprobation, for it no longer has its form (*formam*) or comeliness (*decorem*) or beauty (*pulchritudinem*)."[35] Elsewhere, Hugh sums up the results of this primal injustice as a forfeiture of beauty: By "transgressing measure," the rational creature became "shameful," "depraved," and "disordered"; "issuing forth," it no longer "held fast to the measure and law of its beauty."[36]

The loss of measured form in Eden had several crucial consequences for the rational creature. First, as a punishment for loss of measure in the rational will, a similar loss of measure was inflicted upon the body. Initially created "sound," that is, not liable to corruption, and "whole," that is, not lacking anything, its needs were "tempered by a certain measure" so that "a few things could have sufficed for nourishment, and moderate amounts for satiety." In all of this, the spirit, which ruled and presided over the body, was given the care and duty of providing for these things. Like a rider for his horse, the soul was to provide fodder for the body, not as an onerous task, but as a "pleasure and exercise," if man had "maintained justice." But when the rational will forfeited justice, God, by inflicting mortality as a punishment, "destroyed the integrity of the human body," such that it now needs more nourishment than before to restore and preserve its soundness, and its desire exceeds the proper measure initially set for it. "Because the spirit exalted above itself did not wish to restrain desire within measure, on this account was it brought about to its toil and misery that now in the desire of its flesh it could not keep measure." Thus, the spirit-rider must now not only provide fodder, but also use "bridle and spurs; a bridle, indeed, that he may check the body when fiery and violent from evil; spurs, however, that he may excite body when slothful to do good." In short, the primal "distension" in the rational will, in losing the form of justice, resulted in a correspondingly dis-integrated body.[37] Hugh sums up:

Since the flesh was struck with mortality, dissipated by the very infirmity of its languor, it extended its desire beyond the measure of the first disposition. For this is what is called concupiscence of the flesh itself, namely, the natural desire or affection transgressing order and exceeding measure – transgressing order

[35] *Sacr.*, 1.7.16 (*PL* 176.294C; Deferrari 129). Later in the same discussion (*Sacr.*, 1.7.21 [*PL* 176.296D; Deferrari 131]), Hugh notes that "the beauty (*pulchritudo*) and dignity of reason (*dignitas rationis*) appear in this, that it checks its affection from inordinate things."

[36] *Sacr.*, 1.5.29 (*PL* 176.258A–B; Deferrari 88): "Hoc itaque malum factum est voluntati avertenti se et transgrediendi mensuram, quod turpis facta est et prava et inordinata, effluens et non tenens modum et legem pulchritudinis suae."

[37] *Sacr.*, 1.7.19–20 (*PL* 176.295B–296A; Deferrari 129–30).

when it moves toward those things to which it ought not; exceeding measure, when it moves otherwise than it ought.[38]

As a punishment for willingly departing from just measure in the mind, a similar loss of measure was imposed unwillingly upon the body. The first of these Hugh calls "the concupiscence of the spirit"; the second is the "concupiscence of the flesh."[39]

Within the rational spirit, Hugh identifies a further consequence of original sin: ignorance.[40] *De sacramentis* ties this directly to the penal mortality imposed upon the body. The corruption that attends to the body also affected the bodily senses. If they had retained their integrity, through growth and exercise, they would have easily facilitated the mind's perception of divine truth from the visible, external creation.[41] But now, because "the instrument for conceiving truth is lacking in the vigor of integrity,"[42] "the light of the truth is taken away from the mind,"[43] such that, "deprived of its integrity, it can not drink in pure truth without the confusion of error."[44] Paul's statement in Rom. 1:20, accordingly, that "the invisible things of God are clearly seen from the creation of the world, being understood by the things that are made," no longer holds true for the fallen rational creature.[45]

In sum, Hugh's account of original sin in his *summa* of Christian doctrine describes a primal forfeiture of original justice in the rational will through loss of measure. This is most basically a distending concupiscence of the will that deforms the soul and mars its beauty. In consequence, a similar loss of measure is imposed upon the body through penal mortality, and a concupiscence of the flesh, which exceeds the original bounds of physical need and desire.[46] This in turn, because of its deleterious effects on the bodily senses, "rebounds" upon the mind, resulting in ignorance. This original "vitiation of nature" through ignorance and concupiscence is transferred to posterity.[47]

[38] *Sacr.*, 1.7.31 (*PL* 176.301C–D; Deferrari 136). [39] *Sacr.*, 1.7.23 (*PL* 176.297C; Deferrari 132).

[40] *Sacr.*, 1.7.26 (*PL* 176.298C–299A; Deferrari 133).

[41] *Sacr.*, 1.7.32 (*PL* 176.302B–C; Deferrari 137).

[42] *Sacr.*, 1.7.34 (*PL* 176.302D–303A; Deferrari 138).

[43] *Sacr.*, 1.7.27 (*PL* 176.297C; Deferrari 133). [44] *Sacr.*, 1.7.32 (*PL* 176.302B–C; Deferrari 137).

[45] *Sacr.*, 1.7.33 (*PL* 176.302C–D; Deferrari 138).

[46] The *Didascalicon* describes the proper soul–body relationship in musical-aesthetic terms: "Next, the soul, from its being virtually threefold, steps down by a second progression to controling the music of the human body, which music is constituted in the number nine, since nine are the openings in the human body by which, according to natural adjustment (*contemperantiam*), everything by which the body is nourished and kept in balance flows in or out" (*Didasc.*, 2.4 [Buttimer 28.9ff.; Taylor 65]).

[47] *Sacr.*, 1.7.27 (*PL* 176.297C; Deferrari 133).

"DIS-INTEGRATION": THE NATURE AND CONSEQUENCE OF SIN IN *DE QUINQUE SEPTENIS*

Scattered throughout Hugh's corpus are additional descriptions and images of sin and its effects that confirm and expand on the description found in *De sacramentis*. In his brief *On the Five Sevens* (*De quinque septenis*),[48] for example, he gives an account of sin as developing organically from one vice to the next, and eventually blooming in full, yet devastating, flower.[49] Though this discussion differs somewhat from that in *De sacramentis*, the overall thrust is consistent: The traditional seven "capital" or "deadly"[50] vices, the "seeds of all evil"[51] from which "all evils originate,"[52] disintegrate and deform the soul. "We will speak," he says, "concerning these seven vices, devastators which corrupt the whole integrity of nature."[53] At the outset, he previews the soul's progressive disintegration thus: "There are seven [vices]," he says, and the first three "despoil (*expoliant*) humanity." For "pride carries man away from God; envy carries him away from his neighbor; anger carries him away from himself." Then, having been despoiled, "sadness lashes him." Finally, "greed expels the beaten one, gluttony seduces the outcast, and lust enslaves the one seduced."[54] In effect, Hugh divides the vices into two groups of three, the fourth vice acting as a "hinge" between them. Throughout, he accentuates the psychological aspect: sin affects both reason and will, intellect and affect.

Hugh begins with pride, the root vice, defined as "the love of one's own excellence when the mind loves only the good which it possesses, that is, without Him from whom it receives the good."[55] In *De quinque*, pride loves

[48] See Chapter 1, n. 74.

[49] Standing in a venerable patristic and medieval tradition that sees spiritual growth as proceeding through identifiable stages, Hugh finds five distinct series of such steps in Scripture. Given the symbolic significance medieval thinkers attributed to certain numerical values, Hugh identifies seven such steps in each of these five series. Hence, the "five sevens." They are as follows: the seven vices, followed by the seven petitions in the Lord's Prayer, the seven gifts of the Holy Spirit as traditionally found in the Septuagint and Latin versions of Isaiah, the seven virtues found in the Beatitudes and the seven beatitudes also found in the Beatitudes.

[50] *Quinque sept.* (Baron 100.6–8). On the history of the "seven deadly sins," covering such authors as Evagrius of Pontus, John Cassian, Gregory the Great, and Aquinas, see David L. Jeffery, ed., *A Dictionary of Biblical Tradition in English Literature* (Grand Rapids: W. B. Eerdmans, 1992), 698–701. Though Hugh claims to have found the seven vices there, "the Bible is not the direct source of the traditional list of vices. The individual sins that compose the catalog of seven all occur in the Bible, however, and medieval exegetes found it relatively easy to provide scriptural warrant for the list" (698).

[51] *Quinque sept.* (Baron 104.47). [52] *Quinque sept.* (Baron 102.38–39).

[53] *Quinque sept.* (Baron 102–4.45–49). [54] *Quinque sept.* (Baron 104.50–56).

[55] *Quinque sept.* (Baron 104.58–62).

the good which it has received from God *as if* it had not received it from God, *as if* it were *its own*. The prideful one loves "the gift apart from the giver," and thus "perversely claims for himself the part of the good which is given to him from [God]."[56] The problem of pride is not that it loves its own excellence, but rather, the way it does so – *as if* it were its own, reflecting the concern with proper measure or mode discussed above. The Augustinian Hugh sees pride as born in a refusal to acknowledge creaturely dependency and the resulting willful divorce of gift from Giver, of creaturely possession from gratuitous reception. This mis-construal of the gift-nature of creaturely existence yields a perverse love for one's own excellence, as if it were one's own. Piling up illustrations, Hugh says that pride urges man "to the rivulet, so that he separates himself from the fountain," and to the sun's ray as if it were separable from the sun itself.[57] The effect of pride's perverse affection is the loss of that very good which the creature had already received. When man "ceases to be filled," says Hugh, he "dries up," and when the sinner "turns away from the one who illuminates," he "becomes darkness."[58] When the proud thus "cease to receive that which they do not yet possess, immediately they lose what they already possess," forfeiting "all the good" which is in them.[59] Hugh explains:

> He is not able to possess *usefully* that which he has, as long as he does not love it in Him from Whom he has [received] it. For just as every good is truly from God, so no good can be possessed *usefully* apart from God. But rather that very thing which man has is lost through this: that what he has is not loved in God, and with God, and from God.[60]

The essential character of this loss of creaturely good is that it ceases to be a cause of the soul's delight in God. This loss of useful possession of creaturely excellence refers to the lost capacity for delighting in God on the basis of what one has received from God and what one truly possesses only in and with God. The immediate fruit of pride, therefore, is the loss of God: "pride carries man away from God."[61]

Such pride naturally gives birth to envy. Once one's own excellence is loved in the wrong way, as one's own, and not as wholly from God and therefore necessarily in and with God, then all the goods of others become rival excellences.[62] Hugh's underlying intuition here is that when human

[56] *Quinque sept.* (Baron 104.66–69).
[57] *Quinque sept.* (Baron 104.61–63).
[58] *Quinque sept.* (Baron 104.63–65).
[59] *Quinque sept.* (Baron 104.65–66).
[60] *Quinque sept.* (Baron 104.70–75).
[61] *Quinque sept.* (Baron 104.58).
[62] *Quinque sept.* (Baron 106.80–83): "Hence, envy always follows pride. For whenever someone does not attach his love where all good is, then, the more perversely he extols himself, the more gravely he is tormented by the good of another."

goods are loved as from God, and thus in and with God, then such delight is possible regardless of who possesses such goods. Loved in this way, another's excellence is no less a source of delight in God than one's own. By contrast, the one who "does not wish to love the good common to all, is now rightly consumed with envy regarding another's good."[63] The success of another "burns" the envious one, says Hugh, because he does not possess through love "Him in Whom is every good." The envious one considers "another's good to be foreign from himself," when he does not through love "possess his own good and another's good together" in God.[64] Thus, the lost affectivity of pride with respect to God gives birth to a lost affectivity with respect to the neighbor, "since [the soul] is not delighted at the good of another through charity."[65] Rather than loving the neighbor as co-recipient of gratuitous goods, envy burns and pines for the goods of the neighbor as a rival competitor. And, just as the perverse affection of pride resulted in loss of God, so envy's perverse affection loses the neighbor as well.[66]

Envy, however, is not the only offspring of pride. Together with pride, envy engenders anger. Anger (which captures Hugh's meaning better than "wrath") is but the corollary of envy. To desire another's excellence for oneself implies, of course, that one lacks such goods. And for the person both proud and envious, the awareness of such deficiency produces anger at himself or self-hatred "in light of his own imperfection."[67] So, even that which he already possesses now "begins to displease," "since he recognizes in another that which he is not able to possess."[68] A perverse anger directed at the self for lacking another's excellences results now in self-alienation.

The cumulative effect of this vicious triad is the "despoiling" of human nature. Pride's failure to recognize God as the supremely good source of all creaturely goods inhibits proper delight in either the good God or his good gifts, yielding other-envy and self-hatred. The end result is the forfeiture of all goods, created and uncreated:

> He who could have everything in God through charity loses through envy and anger what he attempted to have through pride. After he loses God through pride, he loses his neighbor through envy and himself through anger.[69]

[63] *Quinque sept.* (Baron 106.84–86). [64] *Quinque sept.* (Baron 106.86–90).

[65] *Quinque sept.* (Baron 106.97–98).

[66] *Quinque sept.* (Baron 106.90–93): "Now, therefore, the more he extols himself through pride against the Creator, the more he falls under his neighbor through envy; the more he falsely rises up in one place, the more he is truly brought low in another."

[67] *Quinque sept.* (Baron 106.94–97): "This corruption, once begun, cannot stop here: for as soon as envy has been born of pride, anger is born from envy, since the wretched soul is now angered at itself because of its own imperfection."

[68] *Quinque sept.* (Baron 106.98–100). [69] *Quinque sept.* (Baron 106.100–4).

Perverse affectivity results in the loss of basic creaturely integrity – loss of God through love of one's own excellence apart from God; loss of neighbor through love of one's own excellence in opposition to the neighbor; loss of self through hatred of one's own lack of excellence.

De quinque's sad tale now reaches a transition point: "Since, therefore, everything has been lost ... the soul is cast down within itself by sadness."[70] "Confined within itself," having lost God, neighbor and self, "nothing remains in which the unhappy conscience can delight." This fourth vice, moreover, is a punishing sadness, illustrated graphically: "After pride, envy, and anger ... sadness follows immediately, which lashes the one now stripped."[71] Yet this punishment is not inflicted from without, but rather is the natural outcome of the preceding vices. "He who would not rejoice lovingly over another's good," he says, is "justly tortured (*cruciatur*)."[72]

Now comes the final triad of vices: greed, gluttony, and lust, treated with surprising brevity. "Once interior joy has been lost," avarice or greed compels the soul "to seek consolation in external things,"[73] projecting the soul outside of itself. Next, gluttony seduces the one thus "externalized."[74] And, finally, "lust arrives, which violently subjects to servitude the one thus seduced." As Hugh explains: gluttony's inebriating excess has inflamed the flesh such that "its resolution has been softened and weakened" and it can no longer resist "the supervening ardor of lust." The mind, now "unseemly subjugated, serves this domination most cruelly."[75]

This is *De quinque*'s overall conception of vice. This progressive despoliation, dissipation, and bondage is a movement from interiority to exteriority, as Hugh indulges an Augustinian priority on the integrity of the former and a corresponding horror at the dissipation of the latter. Vice here is centrifugal: It flees the centeredness of the soul.

After completing his analysis, Hugh pauses to emphasize its destructive effects by offering another "similitude," which adopts an equally graphic metaphor:

> Through pride, then, the heart is puffed up, through envy it is dried out, through anger it is shattered, through sadness it is pounded and as it were reduced to dust, through avarice it is scattered, through gluttony it is infected and as it were moistened, through lust it is trampled under foot and reduced to mud.[76]

[70] *Quinque sept.* (Baron 106.105–6). Following Gregory the Great, Hugh prefers *tristitia* "sadness" over the more traditional *acedia* or "sloth."

[71] *Quinque sept.* (Baron 108.108–10).

[72] *Quinque sept.* (Baron 108.107–8).

[73] *Quinque sept.* (Baron 108.111–13).

[74] *Quinque sept.* (Baron 108.114).

[75] *Quinque sept.* (Baron 108.118–21).

[76] *Quinque sept.* (Baron 108–10.135–39).

Here, Hugh graphically depicts the overall effect of vice as the loss of integral creaturely form, whereby the person is reduced to a state of inchoate, unformed matter reminiscent of the state in Genesis prior to God's imposition of creaturely form upon the slime of the earth. Ultimately, in *De quinque* sin and vice "dis-integrate" the human person.

IMAGES OF SIN AND VICE IN HUGH'S THEOLOGY

Hugh's overall conception of sin and vice is consistent, even as the details vary. In addition to these sustained discussions, Hugh's writings are littered with other images that round out the overall account of sin.

In the ark treatises, Hugh likens the soul to the diluvian ark – a pregnant and crucial association for this study – afloat upon and threatened by the watery chaos of this world. Before the Fall, the soul "remained one in the love of the One." But then it was "divided into as many channels as there were objects that it craved, once it had begun to flow in different directions through earthly longings."[77] Again, from the integrated unity of its initial formation, with full and perfect knowledge of its Maker and cleaving to Him in love, the fallen person is divided into multiplicity.[78] This loss of integrated unity pertains especially to the soul's love. The affection, now bent downward and dissipated outward into exteriority and love of the world, is restless, unstable, and mutable.[79] The dominant image here is that of liquid excess, of superfluity, "issuing forth (*effluens*)" like overflowing water, dispersing rivulets, and raging floods: "The desire for the world is likened, therefore, to waters because it is liquid and slippery ... because it makes those who pursue it unstable and disintegrated."[80] But neither is the intellect spared in this loss of unity. In the intellect, the "eye of contemplation" is now blinded; the "eye of reason" is deeply impaired – "the light of reason (*lumen rationis*) in man was obscured by sin, but was not taken away."[81] Only the eye of the body still functions, though not as a perfect vehicle of sense knowledge. Accordingly, the soul is now beset by confusion, ignorance, blindness, and forgetfulness.[82]

[77] *Archa Noe*, 1.1 (Sicard 5.46–50; CSMV 47). [78] *Archa Noe*, 1.1 (Sicard 5.52–53; CSMV 47).

[79] *Archa Noe*, 1.1 (Sicard 3.17–5.64; CSMV 45–47).

[80] *Archa Noe*, 4.12 (Sicard 103.14–17; CSMV 139); see also the similar image in *Sacr.*, 1.1.12 (*PL* 176.196C–D; Deferrari 17).

[81] *Lament.* (*PL* 175.270B–C). [82] *Archa Noe*, 1.1 (Sicard 4.37–41; CSMV 46).

In his *Sermons on Ecclesiastes*, Hugh shifts the image of the sin-ravaged soul from storm-tossed bark to desperate exile,[83] but to similar effect. "The soul is rightly here called a wanderer and a fugitive. The soul is a wanderer due to disordered concupiscence, and a fugitive through a sinful conscience. As long as concupiscence divides it in thought, and it turns away in its conscience through desperation, the sinner himself is not able to return, [and] hides himself from the light of truth."[84] Recalling the discussion above, Hugh here also describes how in the vice of curiosity, whereby the mind reaches forth to illicit things and excessive investigations, the mind dissipates (*dissipat*) and pours itself out (*illaqueat*); it is distended (*distendantur*) and dilates beyond measure (*dilatat ultra mensuram*).[85]

In his commentary on the book of Lamentations, Hugh develops an extended allegory between the ruined city of Jerusalem and the ruined state of the fallen human person. With various points of comparison, the overall image is of the soul constructed originally as a royal *civitas* in which God dwelt as sovereign lord. In that pre-fallen state, the divine presence was known and loved through interior contemplation: "The first man, before he sinned, was Israel – Israel means *a man seeing God* – since he saw God through the presence of internal contemplation."[86] Divine rule presided over order and integrity: "The kingdom of the soul was the flesh, as long as it possessed God within itself through the regency of love; the princes of the kingdom were the virtues of the soul, through which the soul ruled the movements and appetites of the flesh."[87] In this there was beauty: "In his first creation, this Jacob was beautiful (*speciosus*) within and without: his conscience flowered through innocence, his flesh through chastity."[88] Sin, however, has dismantled the city-soul: "Rightly was it first said: 'he has overthrown all its walls,' and then was added: 'he has dissipated his strongholds,' since when the sinful soul was given up [to destruction], first those goods which had been given in order to be visible were dismantled, and then the foundations (*fundamenta*) of faith, hope, and love were overturned."[89] This dismantling of the rational creature begins in

[83] In the ark treatises, the sinner is a "fugitive in guilty conscience" and a "wanderer" in disordered desires: in the former, devoid of satisfying truth; in the latter, ever insatiable in his cravings (*Archa Noe*, 1.1 [Sicard 4.37–41; CSMV 46]).

[84] *In Eccl.* (*PL* 175.156D–157A): "Unde bene illic dicitur, vagus et profugus. Vagus enim per inordinatam concupiscentiam, et profugus per peccatricem conscientiam, dum se in concupiscentia per cogitationem dividit, et in conscientia per desperationem [157A] avertit, ipse sibi peccator ne redire valeat, ad se lumen veritatis abscondit."

[85] *In Eccl.*, 5 (*PL* 175.157B–C). See also *In Eccl.*, 7 (*PL* 175.160A–B).

[86] *Lament.* (*PL* 175.270C).

[87] *Lament.* (*PL* 175.271D).

[88] *Lament.* (*PL* 175.271B).

[89] *Lament.* (*PL* 175.274A–B).

"the confusion of the mind" and then proceeds to "the corruption of the flesh," since "the flesh would not have descended into corruption, unless first the mind had descended into blindness."[90] This darkening of the mind is moral as well as intellectual, as "concupiscence polluted the beauty of chastity and the guilt of sin rendered his conscience equally dark and disfigured."[91] The result is that the rational creature has lost the "knowledge of invisible good from his mind," and the "sight of visible things" has changed from "spiritual delight to the concupiscence of the flesh."[92] In short, lost integrity renders the soul incapable of divine contemplation.[93]

This particular image in the commentary on Lamentations has an overarching fittingness for this present study. Hugh's construal of the soul as edifice – constructed to house the divine presence, de-constructed by sin and vice – reflects his basic tendency to think in terms of dynamic, organizing structures, *formae*. Through these, he conceives of and expresses his view of creation and salvation.

CONCLUSION

The upshot of these vignettes describing the nature of sin and its effects in Hugh's theology is that in the most basic sense the primal human sin issued forth from an inner disruption within the soul. The original integrity of the essential powers (*intellectus* and *affectus*/reason and desire) of the rational creature was fundamentally vitiated by an ultimately mysterious loss of balance, poise, and measure – in a word, the loss of justice. This, in turn, dishabilitated and distorted the proper activity of these powers (reason was blinded; desire was distended); in turn, the rightly ordered relationship *between* the person and other realities (God and other creatures) made possible by knowing and loving was perverted, and the harmonious relation *among* its various parts (soul and body) was lost. For, having perverted true knowledge and right love "against nature," "it suffers either defect or confusion of those things ..."[94]

90 *Lament.* (*PL* 175.270C–D).

91 *Lament.* (*PL* 175.271B): "quia et castitatis decorem concupiscentia polluit, et conscientiam reatus sui sceleris foedam pariter et tenebrosam fecit."

92 *Lament.* (*PL* 175.271B–C): "quia Deus in ultionem primi reatus a mente ejus invisibilium bonorum cognitionem abscondit, et visibilium rerum aspectum ab illa spiritali jucunditate in concupiscentiam carnis commutavit."

93 Shifting the metaphor, Hugh also sees the soul as a sterile piece of soil, which when watered by the Holy Spirit begins to become fertile and grow with the virtues, etc. (*Lament.* [*PL* 175.257B–259B]).

94 *In Eccl.* (*PL* 175.141B–C): "... cognitio et affectus ... Si vero vel in his quantum natura expetit obtinendis [141C] deficiat, vel obtenta, contra naturam pervertat, in ea procul dubio parte qua vel defectum vel confusionem horum patitur, misera, necesse est, efficiatur."

Consistently, Hugh describes all this in aesthetic terms. Measure is the mode and law of the creature's beauty. Sin is a failure to maintain a certain moral-intellectual composure (*non tenens*). In the Fall, "the confusion of ugliness contorted"[95] the beauty of the soul; "through incontinence" a once stable and secure mind is "relaxed to the point of ugliness."[96] The impression emerges that for Hugh the creature was to live before the Creator, if the expression be permitted, in the manner of a dancer executing a move or a singer a note, with a sense of proper modulation and moderation, balance, equilibrium, timing, method, and procedure. It is this that seems to prompt Hugh to define the soul's beauty by measure, for measure is beautiful because it is the essence of proportion, integrity, and comely form.[97]

The frequent recourse to terms like issuing forth (*effluens*), decomposition, dissipation, distension, disintegration, and dilation suggest a distortion of the creature's proper dimensions; that is, its *forma*: The sinful creature "does not have its form or comeliness or beauty, for which it should have been loved and brought to glory."[98] The notion of deformity as an overarching term seems apt. The result of sin is a kind of grotesque enormity and ugly malformation of the soul. It is the loss of the proper being of the soul: for the rational will, evil was "not to be what it ought to have been."[99]

For Hugh, though, the proper *forma* and integrity of the rational creature is not an end in itself. Rather, it enables proper, indeed creature-fulfilling, activity – which reaches its zenith in *contemplatio* (loving-knowing) of God, which activity also makes the human person a *templum*

95 *Arrha* (*OHSV* 1.256:460–61; Herbert 24): "… ne te cum damno amissae pulchritudinis simul torqueret confusio foeditatis."

96 *In Eccl.* (*PL* 175.200B): "Vena sollicitudo reprehenditur, ut male secura mens per torporem, et otium, et incontinentiam ad turpitudinem relaxetur."

97 *Arrha* (*OHSV* 1.256:456–58; Herbert 24): [961C] "lest you destroy such a gift, lest you defile such an ornament, lest you corrupt such a beauty … [*ne tale donum perderes, ne tale ornamentum foedares, ne tantum decorem corrumperes*]." Again, *Arrha* (*OHSV* 1.256:465–66; Herbert 25): "You have corrupted your integrity, you have defiled your beauty, you have dispersed your ornament. [*Corrupisti integritatem tuam, foedasti pulchritudinem tuam, dispersisti ornatum tuum*]." And, *Arrha* (*OHSV* 1.254:445–256.451; Herbert 24): "Externally He adorned you with the senses, within He enlightened you with wisdom, giving the one as an outer garment, the other as inner garb. His gifts of the senses are, as it were, precious and resplendent jewels for display, and the faculty of wisdom within is like the natural beauty of your countenance. Indeed your attire far surpasses the beauty of any gems and your countenance is the most beautiful of all. [Sensibus foris decoravit, intus sapientia illustravit. Sensus dans quasi exteriorem, sapientiam quasi interiorem habitum. Sensus quasi quasdam gemmas fulgentes appendens exterius, sapientiam quasi naturali pulchritudine faciem vultus tui decorans intus. Ecce ornatus tuus, omnium gemmarum vincit pulchritudinem, ecce facies tua omnium formarum superat decorem.]"

98 *Sacr.*, 1.7.16 (*PL* 176.294C; Deferrari 129).

99 *Sacr.*, 1.7.16 (*PL* 176.294B; Deferrari 128).

Dei, a living structure in which God can dwell, being made present to the soul through its knowledge and love of God.[100] Hugh's conception of the "image and likeness of God" is dynamic and structural: it pertains to the soul's proper activity. Put simply, the loss of integral structure within the soul renders it incapable of proper activity and function *vis à vis* God and other creatures. For Hugh the soul is a structure that facilitates the contemplative act and enables divine indwelling. Loss of integral form – deformity – renders contemplation (loving-knowledge) impossible and divine presence "un-housable." Hugh sums it up thus: "by the wisdom of God the heart of man was made, that in it God might dwell as in a temple." But now, this temple "is filled with a cloud. For man, once created and by his sin falling away from the vision of inward contemplation, has sunk down into the wretched darkness of this present life . . ."[101]

PROSPECT

The Creator, of course, has no intention of leaving the sinful creature in its deformed state. Yet, the remedy will be neither instantaneous nor unfitting. Hugh is sensitive to the pedagogical and re-formative import of the divine response to human sin. In salvation, "not the punishment but the guilt is taken away." For "guilt is taken away, that humans may be justified, but punishment remains, that they may be exercised."[102] Ultimately, human restoration will involve a re-formation of the soul achieved through gradual exercise. "For, without any doubt this will come to pass – if we do not fall away from our hope and from good patience – namely, that full and integral peace will be re-established after the laborious struggle is completed."[103] Again: "during this present time the human will [submits] itself to the divine will, either by willingly conforming to those things that ought to be done or by enduring those things that have to be suffered."[104] Returning to the discussion of sin in *De sacramentis* clarifies Hugh's meaning. Noting how, in the first three days of creation,

[100] Hugh's categories for sin stress more the way it alters human nature for the worse (disordered desire, ignorance, blindness, loss of contemplation) than moral guilt or personal estrangement in relation to God, though the former is not absent and the latter is the result of the lost integrity – deformed nature is rendered unfit for housing the divine presence.

[101] *Archa Noe*, 3.7 (Sicard 64.27–33), CSMV 102–3.

[102] *Sacr.*, 1.7.24 (*PL* 176.297D; Deferrari 132).

[103] *In Eccl.* (*PL* 175.236A): "Nam, et hoc sine dubitatione proveniet, si non defecerimus a spe nostra et patientia bona, ut tandem pax plena et integra restituatur post consummatum laborem concertationis."

[104] *In Eccl.* (*PL* 175.213D): "Et omnia haec tempus habent, cum voluntas hominis se per justitiam pro tempore divinae voluntati, vel ad haec agenda sponte conformat, vel ad patienda supponit."

Genesis narrates a movement from confusion to formation, from darkness to light, Hugh allegorizes thus:

> I think that here a great sacrament is commended, because every soul, as long as it is in sin, is in a kind of darkness and confusion. But it cannot emerge from its confusion and be disposed to the order and form of justice (*ad ordinem justitiae formamque disponi*), unless it be first illumined to see its evils, and to distinguish light from darkness, that is, virtues from vices, so that it may dispose itself to order and conform to truth (*conformet veritati*).[105]

What this means, Hugh then explains: the sinful soul must "recognize the horror and shameful ugliness of its confusion." Such a one, accordingly, must "extricate itself, and harmonize itself to that rational disposition and order of truth." That is, the soul must be "disposed according to the exemplar of reason and the form of wisdom." For Hugh, as will be seen in the following chapter, "truth," the "exemplar of reason," and the "form of wisdom" all refer to the divine Word and Wisdom, the second Person of the Trinity, who is not only the source of creaturely form in the "work of creation," but as Incarnate Wisdom is also the source of creaturely re-form in the "work of restoration."

[105] *Sacr.*, 1.1.12 (*PL* 176.195C–D; Deferrari 16).

PART II

Re-formation in wisdom

Preface to Part II

Restoration as re-formation

As argued thus far, for Hugh of St. Victor, the primal events that set the stage for salvation history – original creation and subsequent Fall – are best described as formation and de-formation. For the rational creature, the event of creation was an initial forming, which began a further process of formation that was to result in beautiful (*pulchrum esse*) and blessed (*beatum esse*) being, constituted and consummated by divine indwelling. The result of sin, however, was not merely an interruption of this formation, but also a forfeiture of even what had been initially granted in creation, a dis-figuring dis-integration in the very structure of its being. Hugh's conception of salvation, accordingly, will entail a process of re-formation, a process that will not merely resume the formation interrupted in Eden, but will also re-store, re-integrate, re-establish – in short, re-form – what had been deformed by sin and its effects. As Hugh apparently put it in one of his lectures: "The work of creation is to make what did not exist or to form what was formless (*formare quod informe erat*). The work of restoration is to reform what had been ruined (*restituere quod perierat*)."[1]

A twelfth-century collection of theological opinions (*sententia*), known as the *Miscellania*, which includes material by Hugh himself, as well as other brief texts, some of which come from his teaching and influence, describes this salvation history thus:

> You were created, cleansed, and saved ... The first is formation, the second is reformation, the third is consummation. In the first, we were formed by God in Christ; in the second, we were reformed through Christ; yet, we will be consummated both through Christ and with Christ. Since that which did not exist had to be created in [Christ], that which did exist and was deformed had to be reformed through form, and the members [of the body] could only be perfected by the head; that will be *when we all arrive at the perfect man, at the measure of the age of the fullness of Christ* (Eph. 4:13).[2]

[1] *Sententiae* (Piazzoni 920.233–35).

[2] *Misc.*, 6.9 (*PL* 177.815B–D): Crearis, sanaris, salvaris. Qui recte sapiunt, hanc triplicem divinae gratiae confitentur operationem. Prima est formatio, secunda reformatio, tertia consummatio. Primo

Whether directly from Hugh or not, this text aptly summarizes his theology of re-formation and clearly articulates the dimensions of this re-forming process that are the focus of the remainder of this study. After noting the three phases of salvation history – *formatio*, *reformatio*, *consummatio* – largely in terms of *forma*, the text grounds each in the person of Christ. Christ is the *Forma* by which the rational creature was initially formed; now deformed, it must be reformed by Him as well. At the same time, this Christological re-formation happens through union between Christ, the Head, and His body, the church composed of individual members of the believing community. This reflects the necessarily ecclesial aspect of reformation. The Christic shape and the ecclesial locus of re-form are the focus of the following two chapters.

in Deo Christo formamur, secundo per ipsum reformamur, tandem per ipsum et cum ipso consummabimur. Siquidem quod non erat in illo creari oportuit; quod erat et deformatum erat, per formam reformari, et membra non nisi a capite perfici; quod erit *cum occurremus in virum perfectum et mensuram aetatis plenitudinis Christi* (Eph. 4)."

CHAPTER 4

Christ

The Form of Wisdom

INTRODUCTION

Taking the hexameral narrative in Genesis as a polyvalent "sacrament" (having depths of meaning beyond the surface), Hugh finds there not only an account of God's mode of creating – occurring in time, gradually, through successive stages, unto increasing degrees of form and beauty – but also an indication of the way in which God will proceed in salvation. Both instances of divine action reflect, not a deficiency of power, but the fittingness of wisdom. God the Creator, who is "wise because He is Wisdom,"[1] creates and restores through Wisdom, and so creation and redemption have a sapiential quality that reflects their Source. For Hugh, this sapiential character is manifest in structure, order, harmonious diversity, fittingness, stability, integrity, and, ultimately, in beauty. "In Wisdom is all beauty and truth, and the whole of it is desire, invisible light and immortal life. ... It is simple and perfect, full but not excessive, alone but not solitary, one and containing all."[2] Hugh's Christology,[3] accordingly, has a consistently sapiential orientation.

This sapiential Christology is behind Hugh's clear conviction that the humble, compassionate, suffering, human nature of Jesus has, in the Incarnation, been united to the divine nature that is hypostatic Wisdom itself, the eternal Exemplar and Pattern of all things and eternal Form of the Good. Hugh consistently affirms this juxtaposition of humble humanity and majestic divinity in Christ. "Wisdom reaches forth

[1] *De sapientia Christi* (*PL* 176.848B): "Creator vero sapiens est, quia ipse sapientia est." To be cited as *Sapientia*.

[2] *Tribus diebus*, 22 (Poirel 55.978–56.982).

[3] On Hugh's Christology generally see Rorem, *Hugh of St. Victor*, 89–91; Baron, *Science et sagesse*, 125–28; Hofmeier, *Die Trinitatslehre*; Lasic, *Theologica perfectiva*, 328–38; Eberhard Poppenberg, *Die Christologie des Hugo von St. Viktor* (Hiltrup/Münster: Herz Jesu-missionshaus, 1937); H. R. Schlette, "Die Eucharistielehre Hugos von St. Viktor," *Zeitschrift für katholische Theologie* 81 (1959), 67–100, 163–210, at 83–100.

from end to end, above and below. Above in majesty, below in humility. If you look to the heights, no one is more sublime than Christ. If you reach to the depths, no one is more humble. Humbled even to the lowest, exalted even to the highest."[4] Christ is Wisdom in both dimensions. Restoration, accordingly, is the process of being re-formed according to Christ, of being con-formed to His likeness. In His humanity Christ is, for Hugh, the exemplary Form of all humanity, the measure – described in Chapter 3 – of ideal humanity, whose fullness or perfection is the goal of this re-forming process. At the same time, in His divinity Christ is the uncreated *Forma* of all created *formae*, the originary patterning, structuring, ordering, beautifying – in a word, forming – Wisdom within all created reality. Ultimately, then, to be conformed to the humanity of Christ is to participate in the Wisdom that formed and is re-forming all creation. Re-formation is "Christification."

CHRIST THE WISDOM OF GOD

Hugh conceives of the personal identity of the second Trinitarian Person in terms of wisdom. Commenting on the opening lines of John's Gospel, Hugh ponders the significance of calling the second Person "Word." "The word of a man is not a man," but Scripture asserts that "the Word of God is God." Hugh offers a sapiential rationale: "Just as the word of the heart is the heart, and a word comes from (*de*) the heart, and the word of the heart is not other than the heart itself, so the Word of God cannot be other than God." But, he continues:

> Wisdom is the word of the heart; which is born from (*de*) the heart, and is not separated from the heart. The heart itself is wisdom, and from the heart itself is wisdom, the heart and its wisdom is one wisdom. So God is wisdom, and from God himself is wisdom, and God and his wisdom is one wisdom. The wisdom of God is the Word of God.[5]

Within the Trinity itself, the Word is the hypostatic expression of divine wisdom. "The Word is Wisdom and Wisdom is the Word."[6]

4 *Misc.*, I.71 (*PL* 177.507C): "Sursum et deorsum pergit sapientia, a fine usque ad finem. Sursum majestate, deorsum humilitate. Si altitudinem respicis, nemo Christo sublimior. Si dejectionem intendis, nemo Christo humilior … Usque ad infimum humiliatus, usque ad summum exaltatus."

5 *De Verbo incarnato*, II (*PL* 177.318D): "Sapientia est verbum cordis; quae de corde nascitur, et a corde non separatur. Ipsum cor sapientia est, et de corde ipso sapientia est, et una sapientia cor et sapientia sua. Sic Deus sapientia est, et de ipso Deo sapientia est, et est una sapientia Deus et sapientia sua. Sapientia Dei verbum Dei est."

6 *Sapientia* (*PL* 176.848C): "Verbum sapientia, et sapientia Verbum."

Hugh's identification of the second divine Person and Wisdom is the centerpiece of a distinctive, and likely original, contribution that Hugh makes to Western Trinitarian theology.[7] The specific Trinitarian triad – power, wisdom, goodness[8] – seems to have emerged in the early twelfth-century school discussions in Paris and has long been attributed to Abelard.[9] Recently, scholars have mounted an argument for a Hugonian origin. Whether the first to formulate this view or not, Hugh allots it a central place in his theology.

CHRIST THE CREATING FORM OF WISDOM

This sapiential conception of the divine nature also finds expression for Hugh in his account of God's activity *ad extra*. In creating, God acted through Wisdom. This is apparent first in Hugh's basic exemplarism. As Wisdom and Word (*Verbum/Logos*), the Son "contains" within himself all the "ideas" of created things to which God grants actual being (*esse*). "Wisdom," says the *Didascalicon*, "is a living Mind (*vivax mens*) and the sole primordial Idea or Pattern (*ratio*) of things ..."[10] In the same breath, drawing from Boethius' *De consolatione*, Hugh refers to this Wisdom as the "Form of the Good," which the medieval commentary tradition prior to and including Hugh "identifies ... with the Second Person of the Trinity, to whom is assigned the role of formal cause or exemplar of Creation."[11] From this perspective Hugh interprets the biblical "book of life" as the hypostatic Wisdom "by which God made all His works ... in which from eternity He had written beforehand all the things that He was going to make according to the purpose of His providence and His predestination."[12] Elsewhere, he says that "in Him I have eternally arranged whatever I have made in time."[13] As the uncreated formal and exemplary cause of all created things, the Son is also fittingly the efficient cause as well; the Word is the Agent of creation, "because through His wisdom the Father is manifested ... when He created the world through His wisdom."[14] "He is the Wisdom through whom I made all things."[15]

[7] See Gemeinhardt, "Logic, Tradition, and Ecumenics," 51–59.
[8] *Tribus diebus*, 1 (Poirel 3–4.6–9). [9] See the discussion above in Chapter 1.
[10] *Didasc.*, 1.2 (Buttimer 7.7f.; Taylor 48).
[11] Taylor, *The Didascalicon of Hugh of St. Victor*, 175, n. 1.
[12] *Archa Noe*, 2.10 (Sicard 48.7–10; CSMV 88).
[13] *Tribus diebus*, 24 (Poirel 58.1032–33): "In ipso aeternaliter disposui, quicquid temporaliter feci."
[14] *Tribus diebus*, 16 (Poirel 35.577–80): "quia per sapientiam suam Pater manifestatur ... sed tunc quoque quando per sapientiam suam mundum creauit."
[15] *Tribus diebus*, 24 (Poirel 58.1031–32): "Ipse est enim sapientia, per quam feci omnia."

This same sapiential perspective also lies behind the profound aesthetic dimension in Hugh's theology, clearly apparent in his view of the ordered harmony and beauty of creation.[16] The original creation was a highly differentiated world, wherein all things were arranged in hierarchical gradations of power, subtlety, wisdom, and freedom, such that each had its proper "measure, mode, and end."[17] Hugh employs the triad from Wisdom 11 to describe how all things have been made in "number, weight, and measure (*in numero, et pondere et mensura*)," each having "its established boundary and end (*terminum et finem*)."[18] This arrangement – establishing creatures as certain kinds of things, with distinct boundaries and unique modes of being – is aesthetically pleasing, since "in the composition and order of the universe that diversity is beautiful in which less good is not evil and different good is greater good."[19] In an important though understudied work, *De tribus diebus*, Hugh declares that the "beauty of created things is the likeness of invisible wisdom" and that in "the beauty of visible things," in various and myriad ways, "the invisible wisdom of God shines forth (*elucet*)." In an oft-cited passage, Hugh compares the beauty of the whole universe, and the beauty of its individual parts, to a beautifully illuminated manuscript: "For this whole sensible world is a kind of book written by the finger of God, that is, created by divine power, and each creature is a kind of figure, not invented by human convention, but established by the divine will to manifest and in some way signify the invisible wisdom of God." When someone rightly "considers the external beauty of one of God's artifacts, he perceives inwardly how wondrous is the wisdom of the Creator."[20] Describing this sapiential beauty, Hugh is often prolix, frequently lyrical, and sometimes personal, as here:

> Would that I could examine these as subtly, and tell of their beauty as ably as I can ardently love them! I find delightful that it is so very pleasant and agreeable to treat frequently these matters where simultaneously sensation is instructed by reason and the mind delighted with sweetness, and feeling aroused to exultation,

[16] See *Tribus diebus*, 1 (Poirel 4.18–29): "The beauty of creatures is found in their location and movement, in their appearance and their quality. [Decor creaturarum est in situ et motu, in specie et qualitate.]"

[17] *Sacr.*, 1.5.12 (*PL* 176.251C; Deferrari 80).

[18] *Super canticum Mariae* (*OHSV* 11.66:597–68:599).

[19] *Sacr.*, 1.5.9 (*PL* 176.250D; Deferrari 79).

[20] *Tribus diebus*, 24 (Poirel 58.1031–32): "Vniuersus enim mundus iste sensibilis quasi quidam liber est scriptus digito Dei … et singulae creaturae quasi figurae quaedam sunt, non humano placito inventae, sed divino arbitrio institutae ad manifestandam et quodammodo significandum invisibilem Dei sapientiam … Qui autem spiritualis est et omnia diiudicare potest, in eo quidem quod foris considerat pulcritudinem operis, intus concipit quam miranda sit sapientia creatoris."

so that stunned and admiring we shout with the psalmist: "How magnificent are your works, O Lord! You have done everything wisely …"[21]

In short, the beauties of creation are "witnesses to the wisdom of God (*testes sapientiae Dei*)" and a "true and clear proof of divine wisdom (*verum et evidens divinae sapientiae argumentum*)."[22] Or, as in another work:

For this work, this lovely work, this work worthy of the Divine Worker, this work that befits the Wise, this work that the Omnipotent alone could do, at one and the same time in its beauty proclaims as with voice the might of its Creator, and speaks His wisdom. This wisdom has made all things so fertile that the whole of it dwells in each of the things that He has made …[23]

As will be evident, Hugh's conviction regarding the beauty of Wisdom's acts in creation will carry over into his view of Wisdom's salvific activity as well.[24]

It should be noted that Hugh associates beauty in particular with *forma*. "The immensity of creatures," he says, "pertains more to the essence," while "the beauty of creatures [pertains] more to the form." He explains: The essence considered without the form is formlessness. What lacks form, in as much as it exists, is like God, but in as much as it lacks form, it is unlike God. What has form is more like God than what does not have form. Accordingly, "the beauty of creatures, which pertains to form, is a more evident likeness [of God] than the immensity of creatures, which concerns only the essence."[25]

Hugh never divorces the beauty of creation from its Christological source. In fact, he directly links the intensity or degree of beauty in created things to their proximity and participation in the Son:

Therefore, He said: "This is my beloved Son in whom I am well pleased." He did not say He was pleased with earth or heaven, nor in the sun and moon and stars, not even in the angels and what things are the most excellent in creatures, because even these things, though in their way they are pleasing, yet cannot please except in Him and through Him. They are the more worthy of my love,

[21] *Tribus diebus*, 4 (Poirel 8–9.83–89): "Et haec utinam ego tam possem subtiliter perspicere, tam competenter enarrare, quam possum ardenter diligere! Delectat enim me, quia ualde dulce et iocundum est de his rebus frequenter agere ubi simul et ratione eruditur sensus, et suauitate delectatur animus, et emulatione excitatur affectus, ita ut com psalmista stupentes et admirantes clamemus: 'Quam magnificata sunt opera tua, Domine! Omnia in sapienta fecisti …' "

[22] *Tribus diebus*, 11 (Poirel 24.382–84).

[23] *Archa Noe*, 2.14 (Sicard 52.10–15; CSMV 91).

[24] For Hugh's aesthetic see Bruyne, *Études d'esthétique médiévale*, II:203–50, and Karfíková, *"De esse ad pulchrum esse."*

[25] *Tribus diebus*, 16 (Poirel 34.563–64): "decor creaturarum, qui pertinet ad formam, quam inmensitas creaturarum, quae ad solam spectat essentiam."

the more closely they approach His likeness. Thus, God does not love Wisdom on account of His works, but His works on account of Wisdom.[26]

Hugh envisions a variegated universe of creatures in one degree or another participating in, and thus reflecting through their beauty, the Wisdom that is the second Person of the Trinity:[27] So strong is this link that even the aesthetic delight of the Father in the beauty of creation is mediated by the Son. The Father delights principally in this Wisdom, and then, secondarily and by extension, takes delight in all that reflects this sapiential beauty in creation. Wisdom's "appearance is so desirable that it can delight the eyes of God." So, "whatever pleases me does so in Him and through Him … And the more perfectly I see each work of mine to be in harmony with that first arrangement, the more fully I love it." Again, "through Him also the creation of all creatures becomes praiseworthy and pleasing in my sight. In Him I consider all the works I do, and I cannot not love what I see is similar to Him Whom I love."[28]

While all created things were made by Wisdom and through Wisdom, and all variously reflect Wisdom, Hugh adds a further dimension to his sapiential theology of creation – especially relevant to this study – when he argues that rational creatures were also made for or toward Wisdom. "All things were made through (*per*) the wisdom of God; but for (*ad*) [i.e., oriented toward], that wisdom, nothing was made, except those things alone which are able to enjoy (*frui*) wisdom." What he means by this sapiential teleology, Hugh explains in terms of modes of existence. The rational creature was made "through (*per*) the wisdom of God, so that he might exist (*esset*)." But mere existence was not the goal. Rather, "man was also made for (*ad*) the wisdom of God, so that he might exist blessedly (*beate esset*)."[29] That is, only those creatures that can enjoy wisdom were made with an orientation toward it.

[26] *Tribus diebus*, 22 (Poirel 55.971–78): "Propterea enim dixit: 'Hic est Filius meus dilectus in quo michi complacui'; non in terra aut in caelo, non in sole et luna et stellis, non eciam in angelis et quae excellentissima sunt in creaturis, quia et ista, si suo modo placita sunt, tamen nisi in ipso et per ipsum placere non possunt. Tanto enim amplius amore meo digna sunt, quanto uicinius ad eius similitudinem accedunt. Non ergo propter opera sapientiam, sed propter sapientiam opera sua diligit Deus."

[27] *Sapientia* (*PL* 176.850D–851A): "et tamen secundum participationis differentiam minus et magis de illo percipiunt omnes, qui secundum [851A] conditionem suam aut donum gratiae largitoris minus ac magis hujus ejusdem communicationis ac participationis capaces sunt."

[28] *Tribus diebus*, 24 (Poirel 58.1037–39): "In ipso examino cuncta opera mea quae facio, et non amare nequeo quod intueor simile illi quem amo."

[29] *De Verbo incarnato*, III (*PL* 177.320B–C): "Omnia per sapientiam Dei facta sunt; ad ipsam autem sapientiam facta non sunt, nisi illa solum quae sapientia frui possunt … Igitur homo non solum per sapientiam Dei factus erat ut esset, sed etiam ad sapientiam Dei factus erat ut beate esset, ut illa videlicet frueretur eo sensu quo sapientia percipi potest."

THE NEED TO RECOVER THE FORM OF WISDOM

If participation in divine wisdom is the *telos* or vocation of rational creatures, the source of their blessedness, and if the exercise of created wisdom is the highest likeness to divine wisdom, then, as noted in the previous chapter, the Fall entailed a deforming interruption of their progress toward this end. Accordingly, Hugh's theology of restoration will require a restoration of human wisdom by an assimilation to divine wisdom. In the *Didascalicon*, Hugh expresses this need in philosophical language. As Jerome Taylor notes, "a sense of disaster primitively suffered by man pervades Book I [of the *Didascalicon*], though never set forth in familiar religious or doctrinal terms."[30] With a faint echo of the *exitus–reditus* dynamic at the heart of neoplatonic metaphysical schemes like those found in Augustine, the Pseudo-Dionysian corpus,[31] and later in Thomas Aquinas, Hugh suggests that not only do rational creatures receive their form and existence from Wisdom, but that, through an illumination of their mind, Wisdom draws them back to Itself, to a kind of friendship with Itself: "Of all things to be sought, the first is that Wisdom in which the Form of the Good (*boni forma*) stands fixed."[32]

This love of wisdom is an illumination of the apprehending mind by that pure Wisdom and, in a certain way, a drawing and a calling back to Itself of man's mind, so that the pursuit of Wisdom appears like a friendship with that Divinity and pure Mind. This Wisdom stamps (*imponit*) upon every manner of souls the benefit of its own divinity and brings them back to their proper force and purity of their nature.[33]

This "retraction" back toward God leads the (fallen) rational creature back to the fullness of its creaturely form, the "force and purity" of its nature. At one point in this discussion, Hugh depicts this reception of the Form of Wisdom on the human mind in terms of a coiner stamping a form on molten metal to make a coin:

We see how a wall receives a likeness when the form of some image (*forma imaginis*) or other is put upon it from the outside. But when a coiner imprints a figure (*figuram imprimit*) on metal, the metal, which itself is one thing, begins to

[30] Taylor, *The Didascalicon of Hugh of St. Victor*, 11.

[31] Chenu notes (*Nature, Man and Society*, 50) how Hugh combined Augustinian and Dionysian neoplatonisms; but see Rorem's reservations regarding the influence of the Dionysian corpus (*Hugh of St. Victor*, 167–76).

[32] *Didasc.*, 1.1 (Buttimer 4.4–5; Taylor 46).

[33] *Didasc.*, 1.2 (Buttimer 7.4ff.; Taylor 48, slightly altered).

represent a different thing, not merely extrinsically, but from its own power and its natural aptitude to do so.[34]

So, for Hugh, the mind is formed by or "imprinted (*insignita*) with the likeness" of all that it knows.[35] In his *Commentary* on *The Celestial Hierarchy*, Hugh expresses the same idea in terms of the Dionysian light metaphysic. The notion of re-form emerges at the central pivot of the Dionysian dynamic of procession and return. "Gazing upon the beauty of the Father we are refashioned, that is, reformed again, that is, converted to it by being led back … into the simplicity of its ray."[36] "For this reason," he says, "the one light pours itself out to many lights, in order that, having been illuminated, the many lights might be reformed according to that one light, so that the many … might all appear as one in its form."[37]

Hence, "the need of fallen man for reunion with the divine Wisdom lies at the basis of Hugh's thinking on education,"[38] which is itself part of Hugh's overall program of restoration (to be examined in Part III). This program entails a "progressive assimilation to wisdom."[39] In Hugh's own words:

> This, then, is what the [liberal] arts are concerned with, this what they intend, namely, to restore (*reparetur*) within us the divine likeness, a likeness which to us is a form (*forma*) but to God is his nature. The more we are conformed (*conformamur*) to the divine nature, the more do we possess Wisdom, for then there begins to shine forth again in us what has forever existed in the divine Idea or Pattern (*ratione*).[40]

Hugh thus depicts created reality as receiving, losing, and recovering the *Forma Sapientiae*, the Form of divine Wisdom.

THE SAVING FORM OF WISDOM IN HISTORY

Ever attentive to the narrative texture of Scripture, and perhaps reflecting an emergent, twelfth-century sensitivity to history and the historical

[34] *Didasc.*, 1.1 (Buttimer 5.23–6.2; Taylor 47).
[35] *Didasc.*, 1.1 (Buttimer 5.26; Taylor 47).
[36] *In hierarchiam* (*PL* 175.942B): "Respicientes enim claritatem Patris restituimur, id est reformamur iterum, hoc est reductive conversi ad illud, unde venimus, in simplum ejus radium."
[37] *In hierarchiam* (*PL* 175.937B): "Propter hoc ergo unum lumen in multa se lumina participatione profudit, ut multos illuminatos ad unum lumen reformaret, ut dum illud participando multi acciperent, in illius forma omnes unum apparerent."
[38] Taylor, *The Didascalicon of Hugh of St. Victor*, 175, n. 1.
[39] On definitions of wisdom, see ibid., 181, n. 19.
[40] *Didasc.*, 2.1 (Buttimer 23.17–20; Taylor 61).

nature of both reality and revelation,[41] Hugh's conception of salvation is especially sensitive to the dimension of time. He took history and temporality seriously. Salvation occurs in time, through a historical process, both corporately and individually. After treating creation and Fall in *De sacramentis*, accordingly, he notes that his ensuing discussion of restoration will be organized around three heads: "time, place, remedy." The time is "this present life from the beginning of the world even to the end of the world." Elsewhere he divides this time of salvation into two states (*status*), three times (*tempora*), and six ages (*aetates*).[42] The place is "this world." The remedy consists in three things: "in faith, in the sacraments, in good works." Though "the time is long" and "the place is rough," the remedy is "efficacious that the weak may be healed."[43] This too has a sapiential rationale. Divine wisdom ordained that "judgment be deferred" for fallen humanity, so that it might not be found wanting. That is, "since divine mercy foreordained man to salvation, in this time of expectation and delay it assigned him a place for repentance and correction, in order that meanwhile through its grace it might make him such that it could judge him finally not only with mercy but also with justice unto salvation."[44] God's wise and merciful intent in salvation history is to provide a time, place, and means for the recovery of lost justice. And though divine power could have accomplished this instantaneously, divine wisdom ordained that the "renewal (*innovatio*) of human life which is accomplished through the grace of Christ until the end of the world"[45] occur gradually, in time, through the course of history. In this way, "the divine economy of our restoration" is "supremely well-ordered."[46]

The same sapiential aesthetic, noted above in regard to creation, appears in Hugh's view of God's saving activity in history. In one of his *Sermons*

[41] See R. W. Southern, "Presidential Address: Aspects of the European Tradition of Historical Writing: 2. Hugh of St. Victor and the Idea of Historical Development," *Transactions of the Royal Historical Society*, 5th series, 21 (1971), 149–79.

[42] See *Script.*, 17 (*PL* 175.24B). The six ages (Adam to Noah, Noah to Abraham, Abraham to David, David to the Babylonian deportation, Babylonian deportation to the coming of Christ, Christ to the end) correspond to the ages of a human life span; the three times are the time of natural law (from Adam to Moses), of written law (from Moses to Christ), and of grace (from Christ to the end of history); the two states are the old and the new, divided by the Incarnation.

[43] *Sacr.*, 1.8.1 (*PL* 176.305D–306C; Deferrari 142).

[44] *Sacr.*, 1.8.1 (*PL* 176.305C–D; Deferrari 142).

[45] *Script.*, 17 (*PL* 175.24C): "Status dicuntur, quia adesse hominis pertinent ... Novus autem dicitur propter innovationem vitae humanae, quae per gratiam Christi facta est usque ad finem saeculi."

[46] *Archa Noe*, 4.3 (Sicard 93.38; CSMV 129).

on Ecclesiastes,[47] he observes the omnipresent activity of divine wisdom ordering all of history to its end:

[Wisdom] reaches forth from end to end mightily, in order that by its power it might contain evil within measure (*ad mensuram*), and that evil might be restrained to order (*ad ordinem*) by reason (*ratio*), lest corruption extend itself to the end, destroying everything, or confusion pour itself out to the extreme, deforming (*deformans*) everything. For this reason, therefore, wisdom reaches forth everywhere mightily, subjecting evil to its domination: and whatever that [wickedness] of corruption brought to confusion, this wisdom converts to the beauty (*ad decorem*) of its works by a marvelous law (*lege mirabili*) and by a secret disposition (*secretaque dispositione*), bringing this about from something not beautiful (*ex non pulchro*), so that what is beautiful (*pulchrum*) becomes most beautiful (*pulcherrimum*), and that which is constituted good arises from that which is not good, in the consummation of the good.[48]

Hugh repeats this sapiential, aesthetic theodicy – an explanation for the presence of evil in the world by an appeal to its wisely implemented contribution to the overall and ultimate beauty and goodness of the world – in other places as well.[49] God does not directly intend or will that evil exist, yet Hugh allows that God permitted evil, so that good might come from it, through divine providence.[50] This was a greater good than if only good had existed and not evil: "It was a greater good that there be good from good and from evil, than from good alone."[51]

Evident throughout these discussions is the power of wisdom to form the beauty of the whole, not only by secretly ordering and marvelously disposing "all things pleasingly (*suaviter*)," "without violence," "without tumult," and "without coercion" into a "most peaceful (*pacatissimo*) kingdom," characterized "by justice";[52] but to do so by raising all things to a mode of existence that is a consummation exceeding what was originally granted in creation. Not only does the ugly become beautiful, but the beautiful becomes most beautiful, not merely a return, but an advance. God does this with sapiential art, wisely disposing all things, gradually, within and over time, and through created beings and processes, in particular, through the activity of rational creatures themselves. The goal is in fact a greater good, a greater beauty than that which was present at the beginning of creation, even pre-lapsarian creation. Hugh is profoundly

[47] *In Eccl.* (*PL* 177.113–256).
[48] *In Eccl.* (*PL* 175.188D–189A). Thanks to Hugh Feiss for improving my translation.
[49] *In Eccl.* (*PL* 175.188C–D). [50] *Sacr.*, 1.4.5–6 (*PL* 176.236A; Deferrari 62–63).
[51] *Sacr.*, 1.4.6 (*PL* 176.236B; Deferrari 63): "Fuitque majus bonum esse bonum ex bono et malo quam ex solo bono."
[52] *In Eccl.* (*PL* 175.189A–B).

attuned to the ways in which God brings about at the end of creation and history a result that far exceeds its good beginning. In a word, apparently banal, but full of profound implications, it is "better (*melius*)."[53] This concern with the greater good is indicative of a crucial aspect of Hugh's theology. He is attentive to the way in which the divine will is providentially accomplished with the creation in history.

CHRIST THE FORMAL/STRUCTURAL CENTER OF SALVATION HISTORY

Hugh consistently stresses the identity of the Creator and the Redeemer[54] and finds a parallel between the "works of restoration" (*opus restaurationis* – "the Incarnation of the Word and all its sacraments") and the "works of creation" (*opus conditionis* – "the creation of the world and all its elements").[55] The works of foundation are "those which were made at the beginning of the world in the six days," while the works of restoration are "those which from the beginning of the world are made in six ages for the renewal of man."[56] Initial formation required the presence of and participation in Wisdom. Re-formation will too. But, for Hugh, salvation through the *Forma sapientiae* requires its incarnate presence in history. In the Trinitarian text cited above, after identifying God's Word as the hypostatic expression of divine Wisdom, Hugh immediately declares in Johannine language that "this Word was made flesh."[57] In a similar discussion elsewhere, he expands this point: "But that very wisdom of God did not wish to lose man who had been made in his image. And since divine wisdom was above and man below, divine wisdom came to where man was, and called man back from whence he had fallen."[58] Hugh thus extends his sapiential Christology to the Incarnation and its effects.

It is appropriate here to note that Hugh's understanding of the hypostatic union itself fits nicely within this larger soteriological scheme. For him, the Incarnation involves the second Person of the Trinity assuming

[53] See *Sacr.*, 1.4.26 (*PL* 176.244C–D; Deferrari 73–74).

[54] In *De sacramentis* (*Sacr.*, 1.10.4), Hugh argues that Christian faith differs from both Jewish and pagan views of God in affirming that God is both Creator and Savior.

[55] *Sacr.*, 1.Prol.2 (*PL* 176:183A–B; Deferrari 3). Nearly the same description is in *Script.*, 2 (*PL* 175:11B). See also *De vanitate mundi*, 2 (*PL* 176:716B–C).

[56] *Sacr.*, 1.1.28 (*PL* 176.204A; Deferrari 26).

[57] *De Verbo incarnato*, II (*PL* 177.318D): "Ipsum Verbum caro factum est."

[58] *De Verbo incarnato*, III (*PL* 177.320C–D): "Ipsa autem Dei sapientia [320D] noluit amittere hominem qui propter ipsam factus fuerat. Et cum ipsa sursum esset, ille, deorsum, venit ubi ille erat, ut eum revocaret ad se unde ciciderat."

a complete human nature (rational soul and body), such that the divine Person is the sole subject of that nature and such that that human nature has no personal existence prior to or posterior to its assumption as the personal human existence of the divine Word.[59] The salvific activity of the God-Man, accordingly, is directly and unequivocally that of divine Wisdom, who is thus not only the forming agent of creation, but also the re-forming subject of the Incarnation. Hugh stresses this sapiential dimension in his discussion of the Incarnation, noting that, in that ineffable union, the fullness of divine Wisdom was communicated to the human soul of Christ, such that "fully and perfectly from Wisdom itself and through Wisdom was it wise."[60] So constituted, Christ was able to "complete the dispensation of human salvation according to His ineffable ordination."[61] At the heart of the divine work of restoration, then, is the incarnate, reforming presence of the *Forma sapientiae*, the foundation, source, means, and pattern or exemplar of human re-form, the *telos* of Christ's advent: "[it was] necessary that first [man] be justified from fault in order to be reconciled, afterwards that he be liberated from wretchedness in order to be reformed (*reformaretur*)."[62]

Here too, in the Incarnation of Wisdom itself – "when He put on beauty, that is to say, when He took flesh, unspotted, stainless, fair flesh from a virgin body"[63] – Hugh perceives God's wisdom in its accommodation to human modes of experience:

> The true bread [came] as milk, so that He might be received by little ones. Wisdom was bread above and that same wisdom was milk here below. In divinity, bread; in humanity, milk. For the little ones were thus nourished in their minds (*sensu*) through the milk of humanity, and were made strong for the bread of divinity, so that the same one might refresh by both, and by refreshing those languishing He repaired them to incorruption.[64]

59 See *Sacr.*, 2.1.9 (*PL* 176.394A–B; Deferrari 230–31). Much twentieth-century scholarship on medieval Christology has tended to associate Hugh's view with what came later to be called the *homo assumptus* theory of the hypostatic union. This view, the first of the three Christological opinions listed by Peter Lombard in his *Sentences*, was interpreted by later readers as a subtle form of Nestorianism, which posited the presence of two distinct subjects in Christ, divine and human, both before and after the union. Recently, however, Franklin Harkins has argued that this is a misreading of Hugh's Christology ("Victorine Christology," *The Thomist* 72 (2008): 595–624, at 600–8).

60 *Sacr.*, 2.1.6 (*PL* 176.383C; Deferrari 219). 61 *Sacr.*, 2.1.6 (*PL* 176.384A; Deferrari 219).

62 *Sacr.*, 2.1.12 (*PL* 176.412A; Deferrari 249).

63 *Archa Noe*, 1.5 (Sicard 26.60–62; CSMV 66).

64 *De Verbo incarnato*, III (*PL* 177.320D): "Et versus est panis ille in lac, ut a parvulis sumi possit. Sapientia sursum panis erat, et eadem ipsa sapientia deorsum lac erat. In divinitate panis, in humanitate lac. Sic enim parvuli sensu per lac humanitatis nutriti sunt, et roborati sunt ad panem divinitatis."

When John's Gospel claims that "grace and truth have come through Jesus Christ" (John 1:17), and when Paul calls Jesus "the power of God and the wisdom of God" (1 Cor. 1:24), Hugh produces a synthesis:

> If the wisdom of God is Jesus Christ, and truth came to be through Jesus Christ, it follows that truth came to be through the wisdom of God. The day of wisdom is the truth. The truth of God is the redemption of the human race. He had first promised it. When later He showed it, surely what else did He show than His own truthful self? Rightly this truth was fulfilled through Wisdom, from whom all truth is. What was sent to fulfill the truth was nothing else than Him in whom all the fullness of truth resided.[65]

Jesus of Nazareth, for Hugh, is eternal truth and wisdom manifest in time for human salvation. "Therefore the fullness of wisdom dwells in the humanity of Christ."[66] The Incarnation is the "day of wisdom."

Hugh then situates this Christological "day of wisdom" as the center between two other "days" in salvation history appropriated respectively to the Father and the Spirit. In the first "day," after the Fall, but before Christ, "human beings ... were rebuked by the law and began to fear God, the judge, because they knew their wickedness." After this "day of fear" came the "day of truth," the day of Christ and salvation, "which destroyed sin [and] illumined the brightness of the previous day." This "day" did not "take away fear, but turned it *into something better*" (emphasis added). But "there was not yet full brightness, until charity was added to truth." This charity of the third "day" comes from the Holy Spirit, the "Spirit of truth," sent to "teach you all truth" (John 16:12–13). Brought to completion by the Spirit, the historical work of Christ is thus effective "both to remove evils and to *reform* good things" (emphasis added).[67] Hugh sees the work of restoration implemented gradually in time to re-form what was already good into something better. "For that is how 'Jesus' is translated, that is, 'salvation' ... because through him humanity is *reformed* for salvation" (emphasis added).[68] Here, then, the language of re-form emerges as an apt description of the macro-historical process of gradually and wisely restoring humanity to its Christological *forma*.

Within this sapiential, salvation-history framework, Hugh incorporates much that is traditional regarding the work of Christ. Christ

[65] *Tribus diebus*, 27 (Poirel 66–68:1172–1208).
[66] *Sapientia* (*PL* 176.851C): "Ergo plenitudo sapientiae Dei habitat in humanitate Christi."
[67] All citations in this paragraph from *Tribus Diebus*, 27 (Poirel 68.1208–36).
[68] *Tribus diebus*, 27 (Poirel 66–68:1172–1208).

conquers the devil and despoils Hades,[69] makes satisfaction for sin,[70] reconciles humanity to God, mediates as a high priest between God and man,[71] restores health to ailing humanity as a physician.[72] Christ assumed genuine human nature, even that damaged by sin and its penalty (though not the guilt),[73] and in so doing cleansed human nature.[74] Yet, the overall emphasis in Hugh's soteriology is the wise restoration of humanity: "Wisdom came that it might conquer malice, that the enemy, who had conquered by astuteness, might be conquered by prudence."[75] And, "wisdom came that the enemy might be overcome by reason."[76] And, "all these things were done according to the judgment and dispensation of the Physician, who … knew what kind of remedies should be applied to it on every occasion."[77] For "although in His omnipotence God could have employed many methods to restore mankind, this, the most fitted to our weakness, was the one that He preferred; so that the works of His mercy might be fulfilled not only mightily and righteously, but wisely too."[78]

This overarching concern with a sapiential soteriology is perhaps most apparent in Hugh's unique deployment of the biblical imagery of the "book of life," noted above. If the original creation could be compared to a book, the book of wisdom, written by the finger of God, the divine response to the Fall can be seen as the writing of another sapiential book!

> God willed afterwards [i.e., after the Fall] that [a book of wisdom] be written still outwardly, yet in a different way, that wisdom might be seen more manifestly and be recognized more perfectly, that the eye of man might be illumined to the second writing, since it had been darkened to the first. Therefore he made a second work after the first …[79]

This second "writing" is the Incarnation. "He assumed flesh not losing divinity, and was placed as a book written internally and externally; externally in humanity, internally in divinity … Internally, 'in the beginning was the Word' (John 1), externally, 'the Word became flesh.'"[80] Hugh sums up: "Therefore, there was one book written once

[69] *Sacr.*, 1.8.11 (*PL* 176.312A–313C; Deferrari 148–50).
[70] *Sacr.*, 1.8.10 (*PL* 176.311D–312A; Deferrari 148), where Hugh takes up the soteriological notions of Anselm of Canterbury.
[71] See *De Verbo Dei*, 5.4. Critical edition in Hugues de Saint-Victor, *Six opuscules spirituels*, SC 155, ed. Roger Baron (Paris: Cerf, 1969), 60–80, at 78.259–63. To be cited as *Verbo*.
[72] *Sacr.*, 1.8.12 (*PL* 176.313C–314C; Deferrari 150–51).
[73] *Sacr.*, 2.1.6–7 (*PL* 176.C; Deferrari 218–28).
[74] *Sacr.*, 2.1.5 (*PL* 176.382B; Deferrari 217).
[75] *Sacr.*, 1.8.6 (*PL* 176.310C; Deferrari 146).
[76] *Sacr.*, 2.1.2 (*PL* 176.372C; Deferrari 206).
[77] *Sacr.*, 1.8.12 (*PL* 176.3134A; Deferrari 150).
[78] *Archa Noe*, 4.3 (Sicard 93.29–33; CSMV 129).
[79] *Sacr.*, 1.6.5 (*PL* 176.266D–267A; Deferrari 97–98).
[80] *Sacr.*, 1.6.5 (*PL* 176.267A; Deferrari 98).

internally and twice externally; first externally through the creation of visible things; second externally through the assumption of flesh …"[81] The internal writing is none other than hypostatic Wisdom itself: "the Wisdom by which God made all His works … in which from all eternity He had written beforehand all the things that He was going to make" in time, namely, "the Book of Life" (Revelation 5).[82] This parallel between the visible book of creation and the visible book of salvation, both reflecting the invisible book of divine Wisdom, not only reflects Hugh's consistent emphasis on the "two works of God," accomplished by the one Worker, but buttresses his impulse to espy parallel attributes of wisdom in both works.

Lastly, these sapiential dimensions of Christ's saving presence in history are also apparent in Hugh's symbolic interpretation of Noah's ark. There, he situates the entire cosmos, and within it the world and its history from Adam to the Final Judgment, within a Christological frame by depicting these as held and contained by Christ himself enthroned in majesty. Christ is depicted "so that He seems to embrace all things" for "the supreme, true Unity holds the central and highest place." Out of Christ's mouth at the top of the image proceed the six days of creation, reflecting Christological agency in creation. At the center of time, as it proceeds "downward" through the states (*status*) and times (*tempora*) of salvation history toward consummation and judgment, stands Christ crucified, depicted as a spotless lamb. Furthermore, "the column that is raised up in the middle of the Ark signifies the Tree of Life, which was planted in the middle of paradise, that is, it signifies Our Lord Jesus Christ, who is both God and man, planted in the middle of the church in the form of the humanity which He assumed."[83] Both cosmos and history are thus Christologically structured and governed – embraced by, proceeding from, flowing through, and ordered toward the Incarnate Christ. In a sense, He is the formal structure of world and history, the life-giving "tree" in the center of a new paradise.[84]

[81] Ibid.

[82] *Archa Noe*, 2.10 (Sicard 48.10–12; CSMV 88).

[83] *Libellus*, 1 (Sicard 125.108–11; Weiss 47–48): "Columna ista, quae in medio arcae erigitur, significat lignum vitae, quod plantatum est in medio paradisi, id est Dominum Jesum Christum secundum formam humanitatis susceptae in medio Ecclesiae plantatum, qui Christus Deus et homo est." See also *Archa Noe*, 2.12 (Sicard 49.5–9; CSMV 89): "the Lord Jesus Christ who, according to the form of His manhood that He has assumed, is planted in the midst of His Church, like the tree of life in the midst of paradise."

[84] *Libellus*, 11 (Sicard 160.72–75; Weiss 68–69).

CHRIST THE FORMAL/STRUCTURAL CENTER OF THE SOUL

This macro-history is mirrored by a micro-narrative within persons.[85] The six ages of history have an analogue for Hugh in the six ages of a single life.[86] Indeed, his primary focus lies there.[87] Here too, he locates Christ at the center, both of the restorative activity and of the product of that restoration. That is, Christ is the agent of the soul's restoration by a process that reconstitutes the soul around a Christological center.

This formal role that Christ plays in the re-formation of the human person is clearly symbolized in the ark treatises. The ark is not only a symbol of cosmos and history; it also represents the re-structured and re-integrated soul. Here, Hugh's "structural intuition" comes to the fore. Depicting world and history, the ark-symbol is read two-dimensionally; representing the soul, it is seen three-dimensionally, as a structure rising "upward" (viewed longitudinally). From this perspective, the two-dimensional square at the center of the flat surface, with a lamb depicted upon it representing Christ, becomes a pillar rising to the apex of the three-dimensional structure: "The pillar set up in the middle of the ark to the height of thirty cubits, to which the entire structure (*universa fabrica*) leans, and the top whereof measures a single cubit from corner to corner, this is … our Lord Jesus Christ."[88] Hugh interprets this vertical dimension of the ark-symbol, where it rises as an edifice, tropologically or morally, which for him embraces the whole spiritual life of the individual, the various "stories" of the ark representing the different dimensions of the person or phases of the spiritual life. As argued in the Introduction, for him the spiritual life is a process whereby the de-formed soul is re-constructed, re-structured, and so re-formed, and this tropological process is described more fully in later chapters. What merits attention here is that this "re-construction" is deeply and formally Christological. Christ is not only the center of cosmos and time, but also the structural center and architectural apex of the soul, since the ark narrows as it ascends, so that its very top corresponds completely to the dimensions of the Christological pillar

[85] Hugh consistently plays with salvation history schemes, overlaid onto individual history schemes. See *Sacr.*, 1.8.11.

[86] *Script.*, 17 (*PL* 175.24D). See also *Sacr.*, 1.1.11, where in each of the three "times" there were individuals of all types: "men of the natural law," "men of the written law," and "men of grace."

[87] See *Sacr.*, 1.1.12 (*PL* 176.195C–197B; Deferrari 17); the soul is a microcosm of the world and its re-formation follows that of the world; moreover, reason presides over this as mediatrix and as the firmament, overcoming confusion, dividing and judging within the soul.

[88] *Archa Noe*, 2.6 (Sicard 42.1–6; CSMV 82).

in the center.[89] Moreover, Christ himself is in some sense the master-architect and builder, the "Noah," who precisely as Wisdom accomplishes this work wisely: "He is Himself the wisdom whereof it is said, 'Wisdom hath builded her house,' ... it is clear, therefore, that wisdom builds herself a house in the heart of man ..."[90] The ark-symbol thus images the salvific process of receiving the *Forma sapientiae*.[91]

How this happens, Hugh consistently describes as a process of imitation leading to con-formation. This is evident in his use of the "book" and "tree" imagery noted above: "yet He becomes especially for us the Book of Life according to His humanity that He has assumed, since as man He gives us an example. He is for us the Tree of Life in respect of His divinity, since in virtue of his Godhead He supplies us with a remedy."[92] Or again: "because Jesus Christ is true God and true Man, He gives us a model in His manhood and a medicine in His divinity."[93] For our Victorine, as for Augustine, the humanity of Christ is the starting place, which becomes the door and path to the divinity: "do not wish to despise the humility in the Word of God, for it is through the humility that you will be illumined to divinity."[94]

So, Hugh begins by commending the imitation of the humanity of Christ. Pursuing the book image, he likens human hearts to books. "Our books have been written according to the book of God, because our hearts are created in the likeness of the wisdom of God, as it is said: 'Your light is imprinted upon us, O Lord' (Ps. 4:7)." But sin has in a sense effaced and erased the text of wisdom! So, "our books must be inscribed according to the pattern of the book of life, as the Apostle says: 'Be imitators of Christ, like most dear children' (1 Cor. 4:16)." Imitation of Christ begins to restore the lost "text-image" as Hugh sharpens the admonition: "Let us compare our books with this book so that if they have any differences they can be corrected, so that they will not be thrown away in that ultimate 'collation'[95] because they are found to have something different."[96] The humanity of Christ is thus a "book" to "be read externally through imitation."[97]

89 *Archa Noe*, 1.3 (Sicard 9.1–95; CSMV 51–54).

90 *Archa Noe*, 4.1 (Sicard 88.56–64; CSMV 124).

91 Châtillon, *Le Movement canonial au moyen âge*, 302: "Christ is the first and unique in himself artisan of the work of restoration; he is primarily efficacious in the order of redemption."

92 *Archa Noe*, 2.11 (Sicard 46.11–14; CSMV 87).

93 *Archa Noe*, 2.7 (Sicard 43.22–24; CSMV 84).

94 *Script.*, 5 (*PL* 175.14D).

95 Hugh Feiss notes that Hugh's example comes from the world of manuscript copying with which he was intimately familiar. Scribes would be given a manuscript (or one would be read to them) and they would copy it. Then they or a corrector would compare (collate) the copy with the original (exemplar) and any errors of transcription would be fixed. Hugh envisages the possibility that a copy would be so bad that it would have to be thrown away.

96 *Verbo*, 5.2 (Baron 76.221–36).

97 *Sacr.*, 1.6.5 (*PL* 176.267A; Deferrari 98).

But Hugh's notion of visible example descends rapidly into the metaphysical depths of formal exemplarity, as Christological imitation becomes ontological participation.[98] This is clear in a homiletical imperation, where Hugh adopts rhetorically the posture of the Father speaking to fallen humanity:

"Listen to Him" (Matt. 17:5). And, if by chance you have departed from His likeness by acting badly, return by imitating Him … "Listen to Him." He is the creator and He is also the redeemer … "Listen to Him." For He is the *forma*; He is the medicine; He is the example; he is the remedy. "Listen to Him."[99]

The use of *forma* here is crucial, as it is in similar exhortations elsewhere: "Put on the Lord Jesus Christ (Romans 13), namely, the *forma* of Christ, the likeness of Christ; put that on! Assume that! Conform (*conformare*)! Take on that measure!"[100] Again, comparing the *forma* of Christ to the heavenly city of Jerusalem, which is built on earth, Hugh says:

The [city] descended from heaven and was built on earth. The *forma* from heaven, the matter from earth. Thus man is the *forma* of man and Christ is the *forma* of Christ. Hence that verse: "Put on the Lord Jesus Christ" (Romans 13); the *forma*, therefore, that is, the image of Christ. He is the image and he is the imitation. This then occurred as an example for you, so that you might "put on Christ" by imitating Him. He acted bodily, you should imitate spiritually.[101]

In all this, Hugh identifies *imitatio Christi* with *conformatio Christi*. "Go with him, so that you may grow in him!"[102] But the language of *forma* does not lose its connection to the wider, sapiential framework of Hugh's Christology, outlined above, in which the Second Person of the Trinity is the eternal Form of the Good, the Exemplar of all creation, the formal, structuring principle of cosmos and history.[103] Indeed, in that light it is fitting for Hugh to see the *Forma sapientiae* as the formal pattern of

98 See Sicard, *Diagrammes*, 220–26.

99 *Tribus diebus*, 24 (Poirel 59.1050–51): "Ipse est forma, ipse est medicina; ipse est exemplum, ipse est remedium."

100 *Misc.*, 1.71 (*PL* 177.507B): "*Induimini Dominum Jesum Christum* (Romans 13), formam scilicet Christi, similitudinem Christi; hanc indue, hanc assume. Conformare, commetire."

101 *Misc.*, 1.81 (*PL* 177.516B–C): "*Vidi civitatem sanctam Jerusalem novam, descendentem de coelo* (Revelation 21). De coelo descendit, et fabricata est in terra. De coelo forma, de terra materia. Sic forma hominis homo, et forma Christi Christus. Unde illud: *Induimini Dominum Jesum Christum* (Romans 13); formam igitur, id est imaginem Christi. Ipsa imago et ipsa est imitatio. Idcirco factus est tibi exemplum, ut tu illum imitando indueres. Fecit corporaliter, tu spiritualiter imitare."

102 *Misc.*, 1.71 (*PL* 177.507C): "Perge cum ipso, ut crescas in ipso."

103 Commenting on this very passage, Ivan Illich (*In the Vineyard of the Text: A Commentary to Hugh's* Didascalicon [Chicago: University of Chicago Press, 1993]), observes: "The need of fallen man for reunion with wisdom is central to Hugh's thought. This makes the concept of 'remedy' or 'medicine' crucial for an understanding of Hugh … The ultimate remedy is God as wisdom" (10).

redeemed human nature. Always finding parallels between creation and salvation, Hugh sees the sin-ravaged soul "in a kind of darkness and confusion," which is remedied when the soul is "disposed to the order and form of justice," when it "conforms to truth," "fits itself to that rational disposition," is "put in order" and "disposed according to the exemplar of reason and the form of wisdom."[104] Christ is example because he is Exemplar: "I have now another Exemplar (*exemplar*) to whom I desire to be conformed (*conformari*) and to whom I unceasingly look, and in so far as I am able, I desire to become more and more like Him."[105] Hugh's conception of medicine and remedy, moreover, will now be seen to entail a different meaning than a modern sense of an ingested substance that provides nearly instant healing, passively received. Christ is, rather, the medicinal remedy as the formal pattern or structural *forma* to which one needs actively to conform: "Since what was done in Him was not only a remedy, but also an example and a sacrament" – that is, something both to imitate and to participate in – "it was necessary that it happen visibly and outwardly, so that it might signify what needed to happen in us invisibly."[106] The creature thus recovers "the likeness of that first exemplar within itself."[107]

Here, finally, emerges in the microcosm the same aesthetic dimension in Hugh's Christology that was noted above in the macrocosm. As *forma* is the source of beauty in the visible creation, so does the *Forma sapientiae* bestow beauty on the fallen rational creature. Sapientially disposed, ordered, and conformed – in a word, re-formed – the soul too acquires beauty and becomes, as it were, aesthetically pleasing to God: "Whatever pleases Me does so in Him and through Him. The only one that offends Me is the one who departs from His likeness … Therefore, if you wish to please Me, be like Him."[108] Moreover, this work of "re-beautification," like the work of creation, is a function of divine wisdom, appropriated to the second Person, working in tandem with divine power and benevolence (appropriated to the Father and the Spirit respectively): "Have no doubts about His power; see how great are His works. Do not doubt His wisdom; see how beautiful are His works. Do not doubt His good will; see how His works serve you by their utility."[109]

[104] *Sacr.*, 1.1.12 (*PL* 176.195D; Deferrari 17).
[105] *Arrha* (*OHSV* 1.278:814f.; Herbert 34f.).
[106] *Tribus diebus*, 27 (Poirel 68–69.1220–23).
[107] *Tribus diebus*, 25 (Poirel 61.1093).
[108] *Tribus diebus*, 24 (Poirel 58.1031–63).
[109] *Tribus Diebus*, 24 (Poirel 60.1059–63): "Noli dubitare de potentia eius, uide opera illius quanta sunt! noli dubitare de sapientia, uide opera eius quam pulcra sunt! noli dubitare de beneuolentia, uide opera eius quomodo ad utilitatem tibi seruiunt!"

CONCLUSION: SALVATION AS RE-FORMATION ACCORDING TO THE PATTERN OF FORMATION

Wisdom, which Hugh consistently appropriates to the incarnate second Person, is common to all the phases and facets of divine activity. Wisdom, moreover, is for him inherently formational, structural, pedagogical, aesthetic, and symbolic-sacramental. That is, Wisdom delights in bringing into being myriad creaturely natures with diverse structural forms, as so many marvelous reflections of Itself. Wisdom works gradually, delicately, subtly – in a word, sweetly or winsomely (*suaviter*) – to order, to configure, to pattern, and to shape. It pursues processes that work with the structured nature of creatures, even cooperatively within free, rational creatures, to realize simultaneously both their own individual flourishing and the divine intent for all of reality. It acts in ways that are fitting and appropriate to creatures, in time and in history, accommodated to their creaturely status. The results of Its actions are aesthetically pleasing, beautiful. Created reality's sapiential character, accordingly, is itself perceivable, not only to God, Who delights in His own works, but also to rational creatures themselves for whom all reality should be a *simulacrum*, a symbolic representation of its Source – "a drawing together [*coaptatio* or *collatio*] of visible forms to demonstrate an invisible thing,"[110] sacramentally revelatory of the very Wisdom that is God. Hugh finds this sapiential character in both the "works of creation" and the "works of restoration," in both formation and re-formation.

In creation, in salvation history, and in the human soul, therefore, Christ as Wisdom is central to Hugh's theology.[111] More precisely, he consistently presents the second Person of the Trinity as the forming, ordering, structuring, and ultimately beautifying *Forma sapientiae* for all of reality. In his humanity, Christ is the exemplar, the ideal pattern or structure, the *forma* to which the fallen human being must be conformed in order to be restored. But through Christ's humanity comes remedial access to his divinity, the very Wisdom of God. Salvation is a process of being increasingly conformed to the whole Christ, "Christo-formation," which ultimately restores the beautifying "image and likeness of God" (Gen. 1:26) in human beings.

While Hugh sees Christ as the foundation of reform, he posits two further realities deriving from Him, namely Church and Scripture, which are deeply implicated in the re-formation of individual and community.

[110] *In hierarchiam* (*PL* 175.941B): "Symbolum est collatio formarum visibilium ad invisibilium demonstrationem." Ibid. (*PL* 175.960D): "Supra iam diximus quid sit symbolum, collatio videlicet, id est coaptatio visibilium formarum ad demonstrationem rei invisibilis propositarum."

[111] Zinn, "Mandala Symbolism," 318.

CHAPTER 5

Church and sacraments

Edifice and agents of re-formation

INTRODUCTION

Hugh's concluding remarks on the topic of the Incarnation in *De sacramentis* describe the ultimate goal for which Christ assumed human nature. Reform of the creature according to the *Forma sapientiae* facilitates divine indwelling. "God is everywhere through the presence of divinity but not everywhere through the grace of divinity and of habitation." So, we do not pray "Our Father who art everywhere," though this is true, but "Our Father who is in heaven," that "in prayer we may rather recall His temple which even we ourselves ought to be." In this, though, are varying degrees: "He Himself ... can be present wholly to all things and wholly to each, although those in whom He dwells have Him according to the diversity of their capacity, some more, others less." To whatever extent God indwells human beings, this is possible only because each has been constructed by Christ Himself as a kind of temple: "those more whom He himself builds (*aedificat*) as a most loving temple (*dilectissimum templum*) for Himself." This temple is "the unity and the congregation of the saints, especially in heaven ... where He dwells, building (*aedificans*) His home to be dedicated at the end of time."[1] Christ came, then, to form human persons, both individually and communally, into a place of divine habitation.[2] In heaven, this has been fully realized; in this present life, it is in process, and the community of those moving toward this eschatological goal is the church (*ecclesia*).

Hugh's view of the church must be seen within the historical context of the late eleventh-century Investiture Controversy and the Gregorian reform of the church,[3] which brought the question of the church in all its aspects to the fore of theological debate and ecclesiastical practice in Europe generally,

[1] *Sacr.*, 2.1.13 (*PL* 176.414A–416A; Deferarri 251–53).

[2] Rorem, *Hugh of St. Victor*, 92: "the incarnational union of divine and human leads directly to the broader union of humanity with the incarnate Christ in the church, specifically in its sacramental life."

[3] See Fassler, *Gothic Song*, 211–40.

certainly among the Victorines. "Beginning with Hugh, the body of writings emanating from the Abbey of St. Victor in the twelfth century was, therefore, dominated by the subject of the church and its ministers, its structures and organization, its purpose in contemporary life, and its significance throughout history."[4] In all of this, Hugh is an important early theorist.[5]

Within this context, "Hugh's all-encompassing vision of the church is a reformer's church."[6] That is, his conception of the church reflects the emerging Gregorian ideals about how the church is to be reformed and what a reformed church should look like. He envisions a church unified both temporally and institutionally or hierarchically, purified from secular influence, and led by virtuous, well-educated, and faithful clerics.[7] Less commonly noted is the fact that for Hugh the church is also a *re-forming* entity.[8] Its fundamental purpose is to re-form all the faithful through its clergy, liturgy, and sacraments. The institutional church must be reformed because it is the locus and means of the re-form of history, accomplished through the re-form of the individual members of the body of Christ. In this way, the church occupies a crucial place in the execution of the "works of restoration," the gradual working out of salvation in history. But because, as will be seen, Hugh images the church structurally-architecturally, it can be seen as a re-forming structure or *forma*, derived from the Christ-*Forma*, extending and mediating that *forma* to its members. The process of re-form, then, is one of ecclesial formation, or "churchification," of both the individual and the community.

A VICTORINE ECCLESIOLOGY IN SYMBOLS

Hugh is a profoundly ecclesial theologian. The church plays a crucial role in his theology, and his ecclesiology, though not extensively studied, has been noted for its distinctive contribution to the development of medieval ecclesiology.[9] Hugh does address ecclesiological issues explicitly in his theological treatises, but, as Châtillon noted, the very nature of the church, which is above all a mystery, cannot be fully expressed in logical

4 Ibid., 212–13.

5 See Châtillon, *Le Movement canonial*, 293–323, and Fassler, *Gothic Song*, 211–42.

6 Fassler, *Gothic Song*, 214. 7 Ibid.

8 Fassler gestures at, but does not pursue in detail, this dimension of Hugh's ecclesiology: "The reformer makes his ultimate statement: the church must be ordered and presented in its ideal form because only in this way can its purposes be known, and only if its purposes are known can human beings begin to become part of it" (ibid., 219).

9 F. Vernet praised, without exploring, Hugh's ecclesiology and noted its importance for the development of ecclesiology in the tradition between Augustine and Aquinas (Châtillon, *Le Movement canonial*, 298). Châtillon argued that Victorine ecclesiology, Hugh's in particular, avoided the

or dialectical modes. "It does not fit into a genus or category that contains it. It is best approached symbolically; concepts applied to ecclesiology must be transposed and used analogously."[10] Accordingly, Hugh expresses his deepest understanding of the church symbolically and allegorically, and an adequate appreciation of it requires careful attention to these descriptions.

Hugh's ecclesiology deploys various biblical and traditional images. The church is an army,[11] boat,[12] city,[13] vineyard,[14] paradise,[15] and spouse of Christ.[16] Increasingly to the fore in his time is the organic image of the church as the mystical body of Christ (*corpus mysticum*),[17] united to Christ as its head[18] and spiritually vivified thereby.[19] Indeed, in *De sacramentis* he

pitfalls of later medieval and modern views of the church that tended to focus either on church–state issues or on apologetic defense of the institutional church against Protestant criticisms. For Châtillon, Hugh's ecclesiology possessed a mystical and symbolic orientation, more often associated with the Eastern churches (emphasizing life in Christ through the Spirit, in the unity of faith and charity), while not neglecting the juridical, institutional, and hierarchical conception typically associated with the Western approach (stressing the discipline of obedience and submission to authority). Reflecting the distinctive Victorine integration of exegesis, theology, and spirituality, Hugh's was a patristic conception of the church, though more systematically conceived, but in a particular way – more symbolic than dialectic, meant to nourish the soul and promote contemplation, seeing in the realities of the visible church the symbolic means to penetrate to the invisible realities (*Le Movement canonial*, 293–96).

10 Ibid., 306. 11 *Sacr.*, 1.Prol.2 (*PL* 176.183B–C; Deferrari 3).

12 "The Church is herself the ark, which her Noah, our Lord Jesus Christ, the Helmsman and the Haven, is guiding through the tempests of this present life, and leading through Himself unto Himself" (*Archa Noe*, 1.5 [Sicard 23.1–5; CSMV 64]). "He it is who makes a track across the sea; for, guiding His body the Church through the storms of this life, as it were the ark in the flood, He brings her at last to the haven of eternal rest" (*Archa Noe*, 1.3 [Sicard 16.217–20; CSMV 59]).

13 *Lament.* (*PL* 175.300C): "Urbs namque in hoc loco, Ecclesia catholica intelligenda est."

14 *Lament.* (*PL* 175.314B): "Ecclesiam sanctam vineam appellari plurimis Scripturarum testimoniis comprobatur."

15 *Archa Noe,* 2.15 (Sicard 53.13; CSMV 89).

16 *De beatae Mariae virginitate* (*OHSV* II.208:356–62): The union of man and woman "is a sacrament of the invisible society/union, which is to be accomplished in the spirit between God and the soul, in which indeed the fact that two become one flesh is a sacrament of the invisible participation which was accomplished in the flesh between Christ and the Church (*Christum et Ecclesiam*). It is a great sacrament, therefore, that two become one flesh in Christ and the Church (*Christo et Ecclesia*); but it is a greater sacrament that two are one in heart, in one love, in God and the soul." See also *Pro assumptione Virginis*, (*OHSV* II.116:51–55). Cited hereafter as *BM Virg.* and *Assumpt.*, respectively.

17 *Sacr.*, 2.2.1–2 (Deferrari 253–55). See Henri de Lubac, *Corpus Mysticum: The Eucharist and the Church in the Middle Ages* (Notre Dame: University of Notre Dame Press, 2007), for an extended argument that this phrase originally designated the Eucharist and gradually over the centuries, but especially in the course of the twelfth century, came to refer to the church.

18 *Sacr.*, 2.2.1–2 (Deferrari 253–55). See also *Sacr.*, 2.1.5 (PL176.382C; Deferrari 218): "through the Word the Christian is freed from sin, that he may be associated with the same nature in Christ his Head and that ... grace may so appear to us in our Head, whence according to the measure of each one it diffuses itself through all his members." *In Eccles.*, Homily 12: "Christ was constituted by God as head of the whole church, and that church ... the body of Christ ..." [194D] "Et caput omnis Ecclesiae Christus constitutus est a Deo. Et ipsa Ecclesia sponsa Christi, et corpus Christi ..."

19 *Script.*, 1 (*PL* 175:10A). Only "made sensate by their Head" (*sensificentur a capite*) can members of the *ecclesia* perceive the divine nature.

uses this image in the definition of the church: "Holy Church is the body of Christ vivified by one Spirit, united by one faith and sanctified."[20] He stresses two things about the church as body of Christ. First, it is a living body because it has received the Holy Spirit: "called the body of Christ on account of the Spirit of Christ which it received."[21] Second, this animating, vivifying Spirit is always the Spirit of Christ, and so the members of the body share in Christ's own anointing and ministry. The very name "Christian" "designates the members of Christ sharing in the Spirit of Christ, so that each is anointed by the Anointed."[22] As Châtillon argued, Hugh's church is above all a mystery of life in Christ.[23] Participating in Christ through the Spirit, members of the body receive from "the best dispenser" and "most wise distributor" diverse graces and gifts for the good of the whole body (reflecting the sapiential accent of Hugh's Christology).

More central than all of these images, though, and often integrating them, is the architectural or structural image of the church as an edifice, mansion, or temple, as is clearest in the ark-symbol, where "the ark denotes the Church."[24] But, more generally, "God's house is the Catholic Church," in which God dwells "as head of the family in His own house."[25] This image is apparently derived from the New Testament Letter to the Ephesians, which speaks of believers as an edifice "built upon the foundation of the apostles and prophets, Jesus Christ himself being the chief cornerstone: In whom all the building, being framed together, grows up into an holy temple in the Lord. In whom you also are built together into an habitation of God in the Spirit" (Eph. 2:19–22). Like the First Epistle of Peter, Hugh will assimilate the organic within the architectural by speaking of "living stones built up, a spiritual house" (1 Pet. 2:5).

TWO ARCHITECTURAL IMAGES OF THE CHURCH

As noted, Hugh's ecclesiology is best grasped from his symbolism. One of his original contributions to ecclesiology (and to theology generally) was

[20] *Sacr.*, 2.2.2 (PL176.416B–C; Deferrari 254). [21] *Sacr.*, 2.2.2 (PL176.416D; Deferrari 254).

[22] Ibid.

[23] Châtillon argues that for Hugh Christ is the primary and deepest "subject" of the church; only secondarily is the community the subject. "When the church protects, enlightens, comforts, or sanctifies, it is Christ himself" who does these things. Before all else, the church is a mystery of life, where the activities of exchange and growth hold first place. The church in effect is born of Christ, lives from Christ, grows in Christ, leads to Christ, and it is this that first of all defines it and gives it its *raison d'être* (*Le Movement canonial*, 306–7).

[24] *Archa Noe*, 1.3 (Sicard 10.40–41; CSMV 52). [25] *Archa Noe*, 1.2 (Sicard 8.47–48; CSMV 49).

to employ what Fassler has aptly called a "visual model of the church."[26] In this regard, two textual loci in Hugh's corpus are crucial for an appreciation of his view of the church. The first is the ark treatises, *De archa Noe* (and the *Libellus*); the second is the *De sacramentis*.

As with his Christology, Hugh put his essential ecclesiology on display in the ark-symbol, since in it "is represented the state of the universal Church."[27] The ark-symbol[28] depicts the church both spatially and temporally. Spatially, the church is seen as a rectangular-shaped edifice, the dimensions of which (300-cubit length, 50-cubit width, 30-cubit height) are taken from the literal account of Noah's ark in Genesis 6. This structure rises up from a foundation through five stories, the final two of which slope gradually inward, narrowing finally at the top to the dimensions of a single, square cubit. This cubit is in fact the top of a pillar, representing Christ, that itself stands in the center of the edifice as the central architectural support of the entire structure: "[t]he pillar set up in the middle of the ark to the height of thirty cubits, to which the entire structure leans, and the top whereof measures a single cubit from corner to corner."[29]

Here, the church is an ark-edifice with Christ as its structural center.[30] With respect to his humanity, Christ has been placed "in the middle of the Church (*in medio Ecclesiae*),"[31] and just as "the ark leans on the central pillar," so "the Church leans on Christ, since it surely would be unable to remain standing without His support."[32] At the same time, Hugh depicts the whole ark-edifice, from top to bottom, as embraced by Christ. At the top is His head; at the bottom His feet. Graphically, the church is thus also represented as the body of Christ: "This ark denotes the Church, and the Church is the body of Christ." "To make the illustration clearer for you I have depicted Christ's whole person, the Head with the members, in a form that you can see."[33] Hugh thus fuses the organic and architectural images of the church.

The five interior stories of the ark represent the different states of ecclesial life. "Just as the column extends through the height of the individual

[26] Fassler, *Gothic Song*, 214. [27] *Archa Noe*, 4.9 (Sicard 116.136; CSMV 152).

[28] Despite Hugh's apparent reliance on prior authors, such as Ivo of Chartres, William of Champeaux, Anselm of Laon, and Rupert of Deutz, "the visual model of the church" was apparently Hugh's own (Fassler, *Gothic Song*, 214).

[29] *Archa Noe*, 2.6 (Sicard 42.1–4; CSMV 82).

[30] In this central position, Hugh can also see Christ as the Tree of Life planted in the center of the Church, as a new Garden of Eden. Christ, "according to the form (*formam*) of manhood that He has assumed, is planted in the midst of His Church, like the tree of life in the midst of paradise" (*Archa Noe*, 2.12 [Sicard 49.5–9; CSMV 89]).

[31] *Libellus*, 1 (Sicard 125.11; Weiss 47–48). [32] *Libellus*, 1 (Sicard 126.138–39; Weiss 48).

[33] *Archa Noe*, 1.3 (Sicard 10.43; CSMV 52).

rooms (*mansionum*), so Christ apportions the virtue and progress of each individual."[34] The first three levels pertain to the church in this present life, correlated to carnal, sensual, and spiritual believers respectively. The last two levels pertain to the life to come: the dead as yet separated from their bodies in purgatory and the resurrected in soul and body.[35] At the same time, polyvalently, they represent different hierarchical offices within the institutional church, as "some are given positions of authority in the Church."[36] For "just as the column sets apart the stations [of the Ark], so Christ in accordance with His own judgment distributes the gifts of grace in the Holy Church, making some prophets, others apostles, others evangelists, and letting others share in other sorts of spiritual gifts."[37]

Viewed from above, the rectangular shape of the ark contains the whole of the church conceived of temporally, both diachronically and synchronically, in its historical existence. "The length of the Church is its temporal duration, just as its width is the multitude of its peoples. For we say that the Church is increased when the number of those believing is augmented and many are gathered to the faith."[38] Hugh depicts historical figures, from Adam through the patriarchs to Christ and Peter's successors up to Pope Honorius II (1124–30), representing Hugh's view that the church has existed from the beginning of post-lapsarian human history up until the present day.[39] "This body is the Church, which began when the world began, and will last till the end of the age. This is the ark, of which we have set out to speak; and it reaches from the head to the feet, because through successive generations Holy Church reaches from the beginning to the end."[40] Again, "we believe that there has been no time … in which there were no people who had faith in Christ."[41] Christ's Incarnation stands at the center of this procession through time, around which stand the twelve apostles, who in turn are surrounded by the preceding prophets and subsequent popes, as well as other participants in the faith of Christ.[42] In this way, the 300-cubit length of the ark represents all believers from the beginning to the end,[43] while the 50-cubit breadth denotes all believers everywhere. All "are established under one Head, that is, Christ."[44] Fassler remarks that, "in Hugh's hands, all history worth knowing becomes church history and its agents and explicators, churchmen."[45]

[34] *Libellus*, 1 (126.141–43; Weiss 48). [35] *Archa Noe*, 1.15 (Sicard 27.96–99; CSMV 67).
[36] *Archa Noe*, 2.4 (Sicard 36.33; CSMV 76). [37] *Libellus*, 1 (Sicard 126.143–47; Weiss 48).
[38] *Libellus*, 2 (Sicard 127.5–8; Weiss 49). [39] See *Libellus*, 2 (Sicard 128.53–131.125).
[40] *Archa Noe*, 1.3 (Sicard 16.197; CSMV 58). [41] *Libellus*, 2 (Sicard 127.13–14; Weiss 49).
[42] See *Libellus*, 2 (Sicard 128.53–131.125). [43] *Archa Noe*, 1.5 (Sicard 23.6–10; CSMV 64).
[44] *Archa Noe*, 1.5 (Sicard 23.11; CSMV 64). [45] Fassler, *Gothic Song*, 220.

The ark-symbol allows Hugh to navigate the relationship between time and eternity, between history and metaphysics in complex ways. This is especially so with respect to the church, which spans the whole of salvation history, but is also directly and intimately linked to the historical event of the Incarnation. In one sense, the church "began with the beginning of the world." In another sense, equally true, the church "was fashioned when the Church's sacraments flowed forth in blood and water from the side of Christ, while He was hanging on the cross." (Hugh uses various symbols for this: "When the Lamb was sacrificed, then was the Lamb's Bride born. When Adam slept, then Eve received her form.")[46]

The crucial ecclesial import of the ark treatises, both symbolically depicted and explicitly affirmed by Hugh's own commentary, is the notion of the church as edifice or structure, composed of individuals united by a common faith,[47] into a single dwelling place for God. "God's house is the Catholic Church," wherein God dwells "as head of the family in His own home," and wherein humans dwell "through the faith whereby He called" them.[48] This house is built in time, over the course of history, through the active presence of Christ, mediated and facilitated by members of the church, especially the clergy. The "ark of the Church" is that "which Christ made through His preachers, by gathering the nations into a single confession of faith."[49] God dwells there, Christologically, so to speak: "the Church of the saints, which … Christ founded and indwells (*fundavit et inhabitat*)."[50] At the same time, the ark-symbol represents this "churchification" process within individuals too: "If you review the Church in thought and, having contemplated the believer's way of life, adopt it as your pattern (*exemplum*), you stretch your heart (*cor extendis*) to fifty cubits wide … This is the ark you ought to build (*aedificare*) [within yourself]."[51]

This same conception of the church, as an architectural structure that forms believers individually and corporately, appears clearly in Hugh's theological *summa*, *De sacramentis*.[52] Here too, the organic and architectural images of the church are both present. We will focus on the latter.

[46] *Archa Noe*, 1.5 (Sicard 25.35–39; CSMV 65). [47] *Libellus*, 2 (Sicard 127.13–14; Weiss 49).
[48] *Archa Noe*, 1.2 (Sicard 8.56; CSMV 49). [49] *Archa Noe*, 1.3 (Sicard 17.235–36; CSMV 59).
[50] *Archa Noe*, 2.15 (Sicard 53.4; CSMV 92). [51] *Archa Noe*, 2.1 (Sicard 34.38–43; CSMV 74).
[52] This work also contains an extended discussion of the church in which Hugh focuses on the church's offices and hierarchy, clergy and laity, and the relation between ecclesial and secular authority, between spiritual and temporal power. Châtillon (*Le Movement canonial*, 318–21) observes the narrower, limited nature of this discussion in relation to the other discussions in Hugh's corpus.

In a short but crucial chapter dealing with the dedication of a church building, Hugh draws extensive parallels between the ecclesial edifice and the individual psyche as well as the corporate ecclesial body.[53]

Hugh calls the ritual and liturgical dedication of a church building a sacrament, because, in a sense, it is the baptism of the building in which the baptism of individual souls will subsequently occur.[54] He begins by introducing the parallel between edifice and individual: "Regeneration is first symbolized in the dedication of a church; then it is exhibited in the sanctification of a faithful soul. For what is expressed visibly in a figure in this house is exhibited entirely through invisible truth in the faithful soul."[55] Two aspects of the dedication liturgy are noteworthy. First, the pavement of the foundation. The bishop, who represents Christ, processes across the floor from the left corner of the east to the right corner of the west, inscribing the Latin alphabet on the floor, and then from the right corner of the east to the left of the west, inscribing the Greek alphabet. In so doing, he traces intersecting lines that express "the form of the cross which is impressed upon the minds of the people by the faith of the evangelical preaching."[56] The second is the altar. The ark treatises had represented Christ symbolically as the center of the ark-symbol, and thus at the center of cosmos, history, church, and soul; similarly, here, "the altar is Christ upon whom we offer to the Father the gift of our devotion." From this architectural, sacramental, liturgical center flow, in Fassler's words, "the meaning and power from Christ to his apostles and then to the people,"[57] as the evangelical preaching "of the faith of the Trinity" spread throughout the world.

These features of the dedication in view, Hugh can pursue their allegorical significance. "A house to be dedicated is a soul to be sanctified." The pavement stands for "the human heart"; the inscribing of the alphabet

53 Rorem, *Hugh of St. Victor*, 96: "Here [Hugh] makes heavy use of Ivo of Chartres' fourth sermon, 'On the Sacrament of the Dedication' of a church," but "Hugh emphasizes more than Ivo did how the biblical parallels of a building with the faithful pertain to particular features of a church's dedication."

54 On baptism in Hugh, see Hugh Feiss, "*Bernardus Scholasticus*: The Correspondence of Bernard of Clairvaux and Hugh of Saint Victor on Baptism," in *Bernardus Magister: Papers presented at the nonacentenary celebration of the birth of Saint Bernard of Clairvaux, Kalamazoo, Michigan, sponsored by the Institute of Cistercian Studies, Western Michigan University, 10–13 May 1990*, ed. John Sommerfeldt, Cistercian Studies 135 (Spencer, Mass.: Cistercian Publications, 1992), 349–78; and Emero Stiegman, "Three Theologians in Debate: Saint Bernard's Tract on Baptism," in *Bernard of Clairvaux: On Baptism and the Office of Bishops, on the Conduct and Office of Bishops, on Baptism and Other Questions: Two Letter-treatises*, trans. Pauline Matarasso, Cistercian Fathers Series 67 (Kalamazoo, Mich.: Cistercian Publications, 2004), 85–147.

55 *Sacr.*, 2.5.1 (*PL* 176.439B–C; Deferrari 279). 56 *Sacr.*, 2.5.3 (*PL* 176.441B;, Deferrari 281).

57 Fassler, *Gothic Song*, 235.

represents the instruction of the uninitiated "by first and simple teachings of the faith."[58] Hugh continues:

For the faithful soul is the true temple of God by the covenant of virtues which is built (*aedificata*), as it were, by a kind of structure (*structura*) of spiritual stones, where faith makes the foundation, hope constructs the building, charity imposes the finish.[59]

In the very next breath, though, Hugh stresses the corporate nature of the parallel:

But the Church herself also, brought together as one from the multitude of the faithful, is the house of God constructed of living stones (*vivis lapidibus constructa*), where Christ has been placed as the cornerstone, joining the two walls of the Jews and the gentiles in one faith.[60]

Fassler has argued, following Gerhard Ladner, that Hugh understood the biblical cornerstone as a coping stone, "the final stone of an arch or wall,"[61] rather than the first stone laid at the foundation of an edifice. However understood, in the ecclesiology of *De sacramentis*, the structural-architectural orientation of the ark treatises is thus also evident. Both individually and corporately, the church is imaged as an edifice that must be constructed. "The church building made of many stones is like both the faithful soul made of many virtues and the Body of Christ made of many saints."[62]

Significantly, these texts construe all this in terms of *forma*. In the ark treatises, Hugh speaks of the "form of our ark,"[63] a "single form,"[64] "a visible form."[65] God's mysterious activity is "producing in our hearts the form of an invisible ark."[66] But this is a work in which humans too take an active part:

And now, then, as we promised, we must put before you the pattern of our ark. Thus you may learn from an external form, which we have visibly depicted, what you ought to do interiorly, and when you have impressed the form of this

[58] *Sacr.*, 2.5.3 (*PL* 176.441B; Deferrari 281). [59] *Sacr.*, 2.5.1 (*PL* 176.439C; Deferrari 279).
[60] Ibid.
[61] Fassler, *Gothic Song*, 269. Such an interpretation of the cornerstone, found in the *Historia scholastica* of Peter Comestor (a student at St.-Victor in the second half of the twelfth century), is, according to Ladner, "rare and represents a special trend."
[62] Fassler, *Gothic Song*, 234.
[63] *Archa Noe*, 4.2 (Sicard 90.37–91.38; CSMV 126): "tunc spiritaliter videre poterimus formam arcae nostrae."
[64] *Archa Noe*, 1.3 (Sicard 17.245; CSMV 60): "una est forma."
[65] *Archa Noe*, 1.3 (Sicard 10.43; CSMV 52): "forma visibili depinxi."
[66] *Archa Noe*, 4.5 (Sicard, 100.60–64; CSMV 137).

pattern on your heart, you may rejoice that the house of God has been built within you.[67]

Similarly, in *De sacramentis*: "thus we set forth first what is shown in the dedication of the church as the form (*forma*) of this sacrament, that we may seek next the mystical understanding of the faith which is formed (*formatur*) in it."[68] In a profound way, for Hugh, the visible, physical edifice of the church (and, as will be seen below, its visible liturgy and sacraments) is the *forma* which forms the ecclesial faith of the invisible, spiritual church, both individually and communally.

These symbolic descriptions of the church reveal the essential features of Hugh's ecclesiology. While Hugh can also employ the language of the church as Christ's body and bride,[69] the architectural image affords him certain key emphases. First, the church's connection to Christ is imaged, not nuptually or organically, but structurally. A twelfth-century Victorine liturgical text sings of Christ as the "*architectus*," who "stands resplendent at the apex of his church."[70] Both the Pauline cornerstone image (whether a coping stone at the top or foundation stone at the bottom) and the ark-symbol's 30-cubit central column indicate clearly enough the church's dependence on Christ. Both images, though, graphically portray how the Christological center informs the rest of the structure. The size and shape of a cornerstone determine the structure depending on it. Even more do the ark-symbol's nested, geometric rectangles depict the formal shape of the Christological column extended ecclesially in time and space. This allows Hugh to encompass, in one symbolic representation, the temporal (diachronic) dimension of the church through successive periods of salvation history, its corporate (synchronic) dimensions in time and space, and its individual dimension in the human soul (psychological). That is, its re-forming power is mediated macro-historically and micro-psychologically in the world and in the soul, respectively. The *ecclesia-forma* mediates the Christ-*Forma*. In short, for Hugh, the *ecclesia* is a re-forming *forma*, derived from and participating in the *Forma Christi*, which extends and

[67] *Archa Noe* 4.9 (Sicard, 117.166–72; CSMV 153: "arche nostre exemplar ... quod exterius depingimus" (Latin text not found in *PL* edition).

[68] *Sacr.*, 2.5.1 (*PL* 176.439C; Deferrari 279).

[69] Châtillon, *Le Movement canonial*, 302–3: "But the Church is in a sense identified with Christ, of whom she is the spouse and body. It is moreover in her bosom that Christ carries out this work of reconciliation and restoration that the God-Man came to accomplish. Accordingly, all that is said of Christ in Scripture will thus be linked to the Church, with certain transpositions. The Church is therefore at the same time and like Christ, the object of Scripture ... Hugh here clearly affirming the first rule of Tychonius: ... Scripture speaks now of Christ, now of the Church."

[70] "Stola regni," strophe 11.2, in Fassler, *Gothic Song*, 305.

mediates the reforming power of Christ.[71] "The form is one, though the matter differs ..."

LITURGICAL RE-FORMATION

At one point in the treatises on Noah's ark, Hugh describes the collective "ascent" of human beings to heaven as an apparently liturgical procession of all humanity into the "house of the Lord."[72] Liturgy was a central part of the common life at St.-Victor.[73] Margot Fassler's massive and important work on Victorine liturgy, in particular on Victorine liturgical sequences (texts set to music and sung just before the reading of the Gospel at Mass),[74] has shed helpful light on the place of liturgy within the Abbey of St.-Victor. She has also uncovered the extensive influence of Hugh's ecclesiology on the sequences[75] and gestured at the importance of liturgy within Hugh's own thought. "With Hugh, the works of restoration always take place inside the church, through the sacramental action of the liturgy. Thus the church and its liturgy become a kind of second world, and are both model and effective agent."[76] The re-forming agency of Christ, mediated by the church, is carried out, accordingly, liturgically and sacramentally.[77] That is, at St.-Victor, there was a vital culture of liturgical formation, or re-formation. In a sense, borne out throughout the ark treatises, the liturgical procession "into the house of the Lord" reaches its goal in as much as both individually and collectively believers are formed into that very house of divine indwelling. In as much as formation is liturgically enacted at St.-Victor, the liturgical procession itself contributes to the realization of that toward which it moves: divine inhabitation of the human.

An assumption to be noted here concerns the hierarchical nature of this formation. The "[liturgical] motion" was from the top down, through the

[71] Châtillon, *Le Movement canonial*, 321: "This ecclesiology is therefore an extension or prolongation of Christology. It is not accurate to say, as is sometimes said, that the church is at the center of Victorine thought; in reality it is Christ who is the center; the church on the contrary puts forward and diffuses the influence of Christ, creating the spiritual ambiance or the divine milieu in which humans and creation find their salvation and sanctification."

[72] *Archa Noe*, 2.7 (Sicard 44.39; CSMV 84–85).

[73] Rorem, *Hugh of St. Victor*, 8: "The church year provided the familiar annual rhythm, but the Victorines had a distinctive weekly highlight; every Saturday evening featured the foot-washing service (*mandatum*) otherwise associated with Maundy Thursday, thus dramatically reinforcing the lesson that all this prayer and study is for serving the neighbor."

[74] Fassler, *Gothic Song*, 9–10.

[75] Fassler argues that, "in the [liturgical] sequences, the pictograms [of the church] described in Hugh's treatises on Noah's ark have been turned into another medium" (ibid., 292).

[76] Ibid., 212–15. [77] See Châtillon, *Le Movement canonial*, 313–15.

ordained priesthood, whereby spiritual influence and power flowed down through clerical ranks all the way to the laity. Conversely, as Fassler notes, all participants were "gathered up into the hierarchical structure and ordered, in hope that divine power could thereby flow smoothly through them all, unite them, restore them, cleanse and heal them."[78] This was not simply a "local" hierarchical mediation, but rather linked the clergy at St.-Victor historically back to those who first received Christ's power, namely the apostles: "the understanding that this power [of Christ] was transmitted first through the apostles, then to the clergy, and finally, through them, to the people was a part of the ritual life at St. Victor."[79] A twelfth-century Victorine liturgical sequence thus speaks of canons regular, successors to the Levites of the Old Testament and the apostles of the New Testament, as "the foundation of the temple, the living stone and mortar binding the edifice together."[80] In *De sacramentis*, Hugh is careful to link every clerical order and function, from porter to pope, to the words and deeds of Christ Himself, suggesting thereby that all these in different ways perpetuate and mediate His saving power and ministry.[81]

Central to the formation mediated liturgically through the clergy at St.-Victor was preaching and teaching the faith. In every sense, this was foundational. "Great emphasis is given in Hugh's writings to the clerical responsibility for teaching and preaching."[82] As already noted, the "ark of the Church" is that "which Christ made through His preachers, by gathering the nations into a single confession of faith."[83] The possession of faith is the *sine qua non* condition of ecclesial membership: "in that they have faith," persons "are in the Church."[84] A distinctive feature of

[78] Fassler, *Gothic Song*, 264. [79] Ibid., 267.

[80] "Stola regni," strophe VII.1, in ibid., 306.

[81] Rorem, *Hugh of St. Victor*, 94: "For each order … Hugh's composite text summarizes the office biblically, mentions what objects are given at ordination and what is expected of the recipient, and links the office to Christ's earthly activity. The porters or doorkeepers, to take the first example, receive the keys and guard the doors, as Christ 'the door' cleansed the temple. Readers receive a book of scripture readings, and the charge to read effectively, as Christ read the lesson from Isaiah (vi). Exorcists supervise catechumens and upon receiving a book of exorcisms from the bishop are ready to cast out unclean spirits just as Christ did (vii). Acolytes or candlebearers receive a candelabrum at ordination, as Christ is the light of the world (viii). The subdeacons who prepare the altar receive the towel and basin used in ritual cleansing, as Christ washed and dried his disciples' feet (ix). The deacons, initially the spiritual number of seven, instruct the congregation, proclaim the gospel, and dispense the sacraments that have been consecrated by priests (x). The diaconal office is full of assisting duties, as symbolized by the stole/yoke they receive, especially in reading the gospels they receive from the hand of the bishop. Their model too is Christ who spoke and dispensed."

[82] Fassler, *Gothic Song*, 236.

[83] *Archa Noe*, 1.3 (Sicard 17.235–36; CSMV 59). Fassler, *Gothic Song*, 235: "The walls of the ark and the walls of the church represent the teaching of the faith."

[84] *Libellus*, 3 (Sicard 137.125; Weiss 56).

Hugh's theology emerges here in his conception of the unified and unifying nature of faith throughout salvation history. In a debate with Abelard, Hugh (famously) argued for a common faith uniting both Jews and Gentiles in belief in Christ, even before the Incarnation! Even though the cognition or understanding of that faith varied, dependent upon the historical era, the *forma* of the faith remained the same. Hugh's comment merits extended quotation:

[Abraham] was called, therefore, that he might go out of his land and withdraw from those with whom he had been united, not that he might be joined with those to whom he was going. And *form* was given him which he might transmit to all who were to be born from him and to all who were to be one *in the one form* itself so that, although the number of the faithful might be increased, yet the unity of the faith might not be multiplied, so that first they might be one *in his form* who were born from him, afterwards also that they might be made one who were associated with him in the same faith [emphasis added].[85]

For Hugh, this common *forma* of (Abrahamic) faith has existed since the beginning of salvation history in the faithful people of Israel, but finds a greater intensification after the Incarnation and the birth of the church, which forms a unified people, Jew and Gentile, into a single house of God. The ark-symbol depicts Jews and Gentiles as "crowding into the faith and making one City of God: the Church, that is, made out of both," these who "had been divided among themselves, but afterward were united in their faith in Christ."[86] "The first man" was created and fell and was dispersed throughout the earth and across time; from there, "when he is gathered and called together, first from the four parts of the world he approaches the Ark, which is the Church, and ascending upward from there he gathers himself into a whole little by little, until he reaches the highest point."[87] This theme of Jews and Gentiles united in faith through the church emerges consistently in Victorine liturgy, "especially through the symbols of the cornerstone joining two sides of a building and the cross representing the joining of two peoples."[88] In one sequence, Jews and Gentiles are "adopted under one faith" as "the headstone of the angle/corner" is "interposed between the two."[89] In another, Christ "as the headstone of the corner … creates a new creature, holding in Himself the joining of both people."[90] Here, the structural image of the church facilitates Hugh's description of his basic ecclesiology.

[85] *Sacr.*, I.12.1 (*PL* 176.348C–349A; Deferrari 188). [86] *Libellus*, 4 (Sicard 139.20–24; Weiss 56).
[87] *Libellus*, 4 (Sicard 147.206–10; Weiss 61). [88] Fassler, *Gothic Song*, 285.
[89] "Lux iocunda, lux insignis," strophe V.1–2, in ibid., 275.
[90] "Ecce dies celebris," strophe VIII.1–2, in ibid., 281.

This macro-historical formation of unifying faith in and through the church, over time and across salvation history, is accomplished by a corresponding micro-formation of faith within time and space (see Chapter 8 below). True to the Victorine charism of *docere verbo et exemplo*, this is accomplished not only through the taught word, but also through lived example. In their liturgies, "the Victorines emphasized their ideals of instruction through deeds and words, attempting to teach through symbolic, ritualized action."[91] Indulging the venerable allegory of the city of Jerusalem as the church, Hugh writes: "city in this text is understood to be the Catholic Church, in which the gates and the walls are those who both inform (*informant*) others with the doctrine of truth and who walk circumspectly."[92] Again, the lives of the faithful are to be "informed with virtue (*ad virtutem informatur*)" by the exemplary zeal and labor of the clergy, so that those "who are cultivated through the teaching of the faith (*per fidei doctrinam excoluntur*)" might also bring forth "the fruit of good works."[93] This reflects a basic pattern in Hugh's theology: doctrinal formation leads to moral formation. "To have faith" is to be "in the Church"; to be "good" through virtue is to be "of the Church."[94] As seen above, he often depicts this structurally. Upon a foundation of faith, an edifice of doctrine is constructed, which is then adorned and decorated with virtue: "This church will have perfect beauty when virtue adorns wisdom in its prelates and the obedience of good works [adorns] discipline in its subjects."[95] This formation in faith leading to virtue, in "faith that works through love,"[96] facilitates the overriding goal of Hugh's theology: divine indwelling. As long as someone is in the Ark, they are "in the unity of the Church," and if "we hold to right and unviolated faith, Christ himself will come to us, so that He might stand in our midst, co-rejoicing in our good beginning, prepared to assist and lift us higher, so that He might be one in all …"[97]

Again, Victorine liturgical sequences, many of which speak of the church as the formation of a unified community of believers, reflect this theme. This unity is founded historically by Christ, and is perpetuated in time through the on-going activity of the church, so that the members of Christ have "conformity (*conformitatem*) with their head."[98] The liturgical

91 Fassler, *Gothic Song*, 266. 92 *Lament.* (*PL* 175.300C).
93 *Lament.* (*PL* 175.314B–C). 94 *Libellus*, 3 (Sicard 137.125–27; Weiss 55).
95 *Lament.* (*PL* 175.300C–D): "quae videlicet Ecclesia tunc perfectum decorem habet quando, et in praelatis virtus ornat sapientiam, et in subjectis obedientia bonorum operum disciplinam. Hujus ergo [300D] civitatis decor, recte gaudium universae terrae dicitur; quia ejus disciplina jam per omnes mundi partes dilatatur."
96 *Libellus*, 3 (Sicard 137.160; Weiss 56). 97 *Libellus*, 1 (Sicard 126.153–57; Weiss 48–49).
98 "Lux illuxit dominica," strophe III, in Fassler, *Gothic Song*, 281.

singing of these themes, though, is clearly meant not only to teach this unity, but also, both in the teaching and in the very singing, to effect it among those participating in the liturgy, especially the clergy, but also the laity. In a Pentecostal sequence, for example, the same fire that descended upon the first disciples, by which "the church is founded,"[99] invites those singing "to concordant modes of heart and tongue."[100] Another mentions that a "harmony of diverse things reduced into one is a sweet union,"[101] brought about, in the words of still another, as "the finger of God harmonizes (*aptet*) the strings with sweet instruction."[102] Fassler concludes: "the singing itself has become a sacrament of communal unity, creating a place in the liturgy for the worshipping clerics to emit the light of well-lived lives, the sound of tongues that harmonize with pure hearts."[103] By modeling the unity of the church in the very act of liturgical singing, the harmony of voices forges the harmony of hearts and minds.

RE-FORMATION THROUGH CHURCH AND SACRAMENTS

With Hugh's overall conception of the church and its liturgy now in view, it is possible to consider the re-forming force of the sacraments celebrated therein. Hugh was an important and influential twelfth-century theorist regarding the sacraments, and, as Fassler notes, the *De sacramentis* is often seen as "one of the first attempts to identify and standardize the major sacraments – here baptism, confirmation, communion, marriage, penance, and extreme unction – and give these special prominence."[104] At the same time, as Rorem notes, Hugh's title for his *summa* of Christian theology is often misunderstood to refer to the sacraments in this narrower sense of a specific set of rites, leading to the erroneous assumption that it is a work on sacramental theology. Rather, Hugh's "own usage of the term 'sacraments' is broad and varied,"[105] and plays a role in his theology far beyond and, indeed, apart from the narrower sense of the term.

Though a full discussion of sacraments in Hugh's theology is neither possible nor necessary here, the central and distinctive features of his sacramentology can be duly noted. Most generally, a sacrament is a "sign of a sacred reality," something visible and material containing and communicating an invisible, spiritual power or grace.[106] More precisely, Hugh gives

[99] "Lux iocunda, lux insignis," strophe IV.1, in ibid., 275.
[100] "Lux iocunda, lux insignis," strophe I.2, in ibid., 275.
[101] "In natale salvatoris," strophe I, in ibid., 301.
[102] "Ex radice caritatis," strophe VI.1, in ibid., 318.
[103] Fassler, *Gothic Song*, 288. [104] Ibid., 229.
[105] Rorem, *Hugh of St. Victor*, 66. [106] *Sacr.*, I.9.2 (*PL* 176.317B–C; Deferrari 154).

the following definition of a sacrament: "a corporeal or material element set before the senses without, representing by similitude and signifying by institution and containing by sanctification some invisible and spiritual grace."[107] The sacraments can be divided into distinct classes. The "sacraments of salvation," principally baptism and Eucharist, are necessary for salvation. Others, like "the water of aspersion and the reception of ashes," while not salvific, yet transmit a "fuller grace." Still others, sacraments of "preparation" or "administration," such as ordination, clerical orders, even liturgical vestments and sacramental vessels, support and facilitate the principal sacraments.[108] He views the sacraments, like the church itself, as existing from the beginning of salvation history.[109] At the same time, the Incarnation is the deep source of sacramental grace and power, which are "retroactively" communicated to the sacraments prior to Christ's first advent in history.[110]

Reflecting the sapiential orientation of his theology generally, Hugh stresses that God in his omnipotence could have saved human beings in any manner whatsoever.[111] That he should "reform (*reformet*)" human beings through the Incarnation and its sacraments was, however, a more fitting strategy.[112] Here, Hugh espies a wise pedagogy at work. Gradually, over time, the salvific effects of the sacraments would intensify; their meaning and significance be clarified: "all sacraments were certain signs of the spiritual grace which is granted through them, that with the progress of time the signs of the spiritual graces would be made ever more and more evident and declarative so that with the effect of salvation would grow the knowledge of truth."[113] Specifically, Hugh identifies a threefold rationale in the institution of the sacraments. First, because humans fell by a perverse attachment to material things, their salvific restoration will begin with material things as well. In this there is a salutary humiliation. Second, because in every sacrament the material element reflects in some way the spiritual grace communicated therein (e.g., baptism cleanses the soul, as water cleanses the body), the sacraments provide instruction. Third, God instituted the sacraments "for the sake of exercise (*exercitatio*),"[114] so that various external liturgical and sacramental practices might produce an interior fertility (*fructum interius*), an interior

[107] *Sacr.*, 1.9.2 (*PL* 176.318A–B; Deferrari 155).

[108] *Sacr.*, 1.9.7 (*PL* 176.327A–B; Deferrari 164); see also 2.3.1–23 (Deferrari 259–73) and 2.4.1–17 (Deferrari 273–78).

[109] *Sacr.*, 1.8.12 (*PL* 176.313C–314C; Deferrari 150–51).

[110] *Sacr.*, 1.8.11 (*PL* 176.312A–313C; Deferrari 148–50).

[111] *Sacr.*, 1.9.5 (*PL* 176.323C–326B; Deferrari 160–63).

[112] *Sacr.*, 1.8.10–11 (*PL* 176.311D–313C; Deferrari 148–50).

[113] *Sacr.*, 2.6.3 (*PL* 176.448D; Deferrari 289).

[114] *Sacr.*, 1.9.3 (*PL* 176.320C; Deferrari 157).

medicine (*medicinam interioris hominis*), and an interior edifice (*ad aedificationem interiorem*).[115] For this reason, "certain places were consecrated, churches (*aedificatae basilicae*) built, and certain times appointed at which the faithful should assemble together" for corporate worship.[116] Herein, through the manifold liturgical actions of prayer and praise, silent reflection and audible reading, standing, kneeling, bowing, the faithful receive within themselves the "formation of character (*formam morum*)" and "instruction for a good life (*vitae bonae instructionem*)." The ultimate effect in them is recreation (*causam recreationis perfectam*) and renewal unto holiness (*ad sanctitatem innovatur*).[117]

Again, like his discussion of the church itself, Hugh's treatment of the sacraments, individually and generally, in *De sacramentis* invokes numerous metaphors. Baptism and Eucharist, not surprisingly, cleanse and nourish, respectively. Linked to the idea of the church as *corpus mysticum*, baptism also unites the believer to Christ's mystical body, while the Eucharist vivifies the one so united.[118] They can also be seen as military weapons in Christ's battle against the devil,[119] a means of intellectual and moral exercise, a source of interior fertility and life. The most prominent image, though, is medicinal. Christ is the physician,[120] who, in instituting the sacraments, provides invisible antidotes for restoration within (*intus reparetur*)[121] and spiritual medicines (*medicinae spiritales*) in material containers,[122] to make whole the infirm (*ut infirmus :anetur*).[123] Throughout, accordingly, diversity and fluidity characterize Hugh's discussion.

SANCTIFYING SACRAMENTS IN THE CHURCH

Perhaps the most unifying notion is also the most prosaic and obvious. Holy things themselves through Christ's institution and the church's consecration, the sacraments have a sanctifying effect.[124] Most literally, they "make holy," or more precisely, in light of the Fall and sin to which they are the remedy, they "re-make" or "re-fashion" human nature unto

[115] *Sacr.*, 1.9.3 (*PL* 176.321A–B; Deferrari 158). See Fassler, *Gothic Song*, 231ff. Fassler argues that this threefold rationale for the sacraments is intimately linked to Hugh's reforming program (*Gothic Song*, 232).

[116] *Sacr.*, 1.9.3 (*PL* 176.321C; Deferrari 158). [117] *Sacr.*, 1.9.3 (*PL* 176.321D; Deferrari 158).

[118] On the former, see *Sacr.*, 2.6.1–15; the latter, *Sacr.*, 2.8.1–14.

[119] *Sacr.*, 1.9.8 (*PL* 176.328B; Deferrari 165). [120] *Sacr.*, 1.8.12 (*PL* 176.314A; Deferrari 150).

[121] *Sacr.*, 1.9.3 (*PL* 176.320B; Deferrari 157). [122] *Sacr.*, 1.9.5 (*PL* 176.325B; Deferrari 162).

[123] *Sacr.*, 1.8.1 (*PL* 176.306C; Deferrari 142).

[124] *Sacr.*, 1.9.6 (*PL* 176.326B–327A; Deferrari 163–64).

holiness. It is this notion that embraces and unites the re-forming and re-structuring notion of the church and its sacraments with the other images Hugh invokes, especially the medicinal. For him, to restore spiritual health (*sanet*) with sacramental medicine entails a more robust conception than fighting infection by ingesting a substance in the modern sense; rather, it is a return to wholeness, to restore integrity. This connection between health and structure, between remediation and re-formation is explicit elsewhere in his corpus. Exhorting his readers to ask for the gift of the Spirit, Hugh likens the Spirit to medicine: "he will give his own Spirit, in order to make your spirit whole (*sanet*): he will give the Holy Spirit, and the Holy Spirit will make whole (*sanabit*) the spirit of sinners. Here is illness, he is medicine." In the next breath, though, Hugh indicates the *telos* of this wholistic sanitation:

> He will come to you in order to make a mansion (*mansionem faciat*) in you. For he will not find [a mansion] when he comes, but he will come in order to construct [a mansion]. First he will construct (*aedificabit*) it, then he will indwell (*habitabit*) it. First he will make whole (*sanabit*), afterward he will illuminate. First, for wholeness (*sanitatem*), then for delight.[125]

Here, to make well is to make whole in the sense of re-building or re-constructing. The metaphor of health is construed as or subsumed within that of structural integrity. Restored to wholeness, the soul can be a structure of divine indwelling. In this sense, the sacraments can be seen as agents of re-formation in Hugh's thought.

This conception is filled out elsewhere. In the *De sacramentis* discussion of the above-mentioned threefold rationale for the institution of the sacraments (for humility, instruction, and exercise) in the wider sense of the term, Hugh notes that "the present life is a time of sickness and a time of remedy,"[126] in which the sacraments were instituted as so many "invisible antidotes."[127] Yet, this sacramental medicine is presented as a structured, "pedagogical progression"[128] that moves from the inculcation of humility, to theological knowledge, to moral virtue. Obeying the divine command to seek salvation through material elements produces humility; perceiving a deeper, theological significance in "that which is seen" instructs the mind; engaging in various kinds of works and exercises produces "multiple fruits of virtue within."[129] The goal of this progression is an "interior edification"

[125] *Quinque sept.* (Baron 100.5). [126] *Sacr.*, 1.8.12 (*PL* 176.313D; Deferrari 150).
[127] *Sacr.*, 1.9.3 (*PL* 176.320B; Deferrari 157).
[128] On this phrase, see Rorem, *Hugh of St. Victor*, 121 and Poirel, *OHSV* 1.123.
[129] *Sacr.*, 1.9.3 (*PL* 176.320C; Deferrari 157).

(*aedificationem interiorem*),[130] which in light of the foregoing clearly accents its literal denotation of "building up," of constructing. The sacraments are medicinal in this way: as a structured and indeed re-structuring regimen.

Something similar emerges in Hugh's account of the dedication of a church, noted above. As he launches his discussion of the sacraments in the narrower sense, the "sacraments of salvation," which then opens out to a broader discussion of the sacraments of exercise, he begins not with baptism or Eucharist but with "the sacrament of the dedication of a church in which all other sacraments are celebrated."[131] Hugh is quite explicit about the rationale. The subsequent sacraments will be celebrated in this ecclesial structure and by their liturgical enactment will both erect a structure of faith, hope, and love within individual believers, and form them all into a temple of living stones. The meaning and function of the sacraments is thus directly tied to the overall re-forming purpose of the church itself.[132]

CONCLUSION

Perhaps the richest symbolic expression of Hugh's ecclesiology is found in a spiritual meditation on the love of God, *The Soliloquy on the Earnest Money of the Soul*, couched as a dialogue between Hugh and his own soul. Toward the end, Hugh rehearses a version of salvation history in terms of royal nuptials. God is a king who comes seeking a worthy consort. The ministers of this king, accordingly, were sent forth "as apostles to bring together souls throughout the world and lead them to the city of the King, which is his holy Church, in which is a house and mansion (*domus est et mansio*) of royal women, that is, of holy souls."[133] By faith (*per fidem*), those invited enter the church, which is cast as a preparatory antechamber, "a sanctum of preparation," where believers receive the "sacraments of Christ." These "are like certain unguents and antidotes prepared for the reparation and beautification of souls (*ad ornatum animarum*)";[134] they are like cosmetics and delicacies "brought to the soul for its wholeness (*ad sanitatem*) and nourishment (*ad refectionem*), for restoring its beauty (*ad reparandam speciem*) and augmenting its comeliness (*ad augendum decorem*)."[135] Prepared thus, the soul will be able to enter the bridal chamber itself and consummate the bridal bond.

[130] *Sacr.*, 1.9.3 (*PL* 176.321B; Deferrari 158). [131] *Sacr.*, 2.5.1 (*PL* 176.439A; Deferrari 279).

[132] Fassler, *Gothic Song*, 233–34: "The *De sacramentis* joins the idea of renovation and re-creation as found in salvation history with the sacraments of the church ..."

[133] *Arrha* (*OHSV* 1.266:605–9; Herbert 29). [134] *Arrha* (*OHSV* 1.266:612–15; Herbert 29).

[135] *Arrha* (*OHSV* 1.266:621–5; Herbert 30).

Presented with this image, the student-soul responds to Hugh the teacher: "I beg you not to be unwilling to teach me those particular remedies by which I must reform (*reformare*) my features to that comeliness."[136] Hugh's response is to direct the soul to the church and to "decode" the allegory as follows:

In this room of preparation [i.e., the church] you will first find the font of baptism and the basin of regeneration in which you wash away the stains of past sins. Next the chrism and the oil, in the unction of which you are bathed by the Holy Spirit. Then, anointed and imbued with the unction of gladness you come to the table and take there the nourishment of the body and blood of Christ. Filled and refreshed within by this you dispel the harmful emancipation of previous hungers and in a wondrous manner are rejuvenated with the recovery of your former plentitude and fortitude. Next you put on the garments of good works and by the fruit of almsgiving, with fasts and prayers, with holy vigils and other deeds of piety you become arrayed as though with finery of the most varied kinds. Finally the fragrance of the virtues comes forth and their sweet odors welling up dispel all the stench of past filth, so that somehow you seem to be wholly changed (*mutari*) and to be transformed (*in aliam transformari*) into someone else.[137]

Here is Hugh's church "in action," with its liturgy and sacraments, as a reforming structure, a transforming agent, through which the soul receives wholeness, integrity, beauty – in a word, sanctity – and is thus rendered fit and worthy of divine indwelling, for union with the divine. Subsumed within this overarching image are the others – cleansing, nourishment, adornment, and healing – which he associates with individual sacraments. The entire process is aptly characterized as "ecclesial re-formation."

Hugh's penchant for thinking "symbo-structurally" emerges clearly in his ecclesiology, as Fassler rightly notes: "Several of Hugh's treatises when studied together outline a plan for applying theological principles to the structures of actual buildings," which gives his writings "an immediately practical dimension."[138] But this movement from theology to architecture goes the other way too, and so reflects an even deeper and more basic feature of his theology, namely, his consistent use of architectural/structural models.[139] One could argue then that the structures of actual buildings

[136] *Arrha* (*OHSV* 1.268:646–48; Herbert 30).

[137] *Arrha* (*OHSV* 1.270:672–85; Herbert 31). [138] Fassler, *Gothic Song*, 215.

[139] Fassler has even argued that the Victorine sequences themselves can be organized according to an architectural model, in which two key sequences, "Laudes crucis" and "Zima vetus," form the architectural center or foundation (like the column in the center of the ark or the cornerstone/coping stone of the building), the remaining sequences, derived from these two, are built up upon this foundation, and then still others decorate this structure. Fassler sees this happening over several generations in the twelfth century (ibid., 295).

offered a means for organizing and presenting theological principles. Not only that, but the parallel between actual buildings and the structure of Hugh's theology extends widely, to the structure of systematic theology, the nature of Scripture and its exegesis (as will be seen in the next chapter), to the ark-symbol, and to the soul itself. It too was meant to be structured, or, better, re-formed so as to become the *templum Dei*. In this sense, one could speak of a profoundly ecclesio-structural dimension pervading all of Hugh's theology.

CHAPTER 6

Scripture

A re-forming *forma sapientiae*

INTRODUCTION

Much of Hugh of St. Victor's renown, especially in the modern era, derives from his view of Scripture and its interpretation. In very different ways, Beryl Smalley's *The Study of the Bible in the Middle Ages*[1] and Henri de Lubac's *Exégèse médiévale*[2] – both of which devote considerable attention to our Victorine – show his importance in this regard. Both his innovative insistence on the foundational and controlling role of the literal sense of Scripture (Smalley's concern) and his systematic theorizing regarding the spiritual senses of the text (de Lubac's interest) are central to his contribution to medieval exegesis.

This chapter will not offer a detailed account of Hugh's conception of scriptural exegesis – that will figure centrally in Part III. Its aim, rather, is to sketch his view of the essential nature and structure of Scripture as a whole, and to appreciate its overall function within his theology of re-formation. Hugh views Scripture as an entity whose multiple senses taken together constitute a structure or *forma* (like the church), the exegetical engagement with which "re-forms" the reader.

SCRIPTURE AND CHURCH

At the outset, the relation in Hugh's thought between Scripture and church (see Chapter 5) needs clarification. Years ago, Châtillon noted the "essential rapport" that exists for Hugh between church and Scripture.[3] Certain texts

[1] On Hugh's exegesis, the standard introduction remains Beryl Smalley, *The Study of the Bible in the Middle Ages* (Oxford: Blackwell, 1952), 83–195. See also Jean Châtillon, "La Bible dans les écoles du XIIe siècle," in *Le Moyen âge et la Bible*, eds. Pierre Riché and Guy Lobrichon (Paris: Beauchesne, 1984), 163–97, at 178–83.

[2] See Henri de Lubac, *Exégèse médiévale: les quatre sens de l'écriture*, 4 vols. (Paris: Aubier, 1959–64), esp. III:287–359.

[3] Châtillon, *Le Movement canonial*, 301: "There exists between Scripture and Church an essential rapport that the allegorical method alone is able to detect and which the liturgy for its part expresses."

in Hugh's corpus suggest a priority of Scripture over church, as do some features of the ark-symbol. *De sacramentis*, for example, refers to "Sacred Scripture" as that "whence Holy Church takes her form of living (*vivendi formam*)."[4] The central column of thirty cubits rising up in the center of the structure, for example, represents Christ, derived from and conformed to whom is the ark of the church, as noted in the previous chapter. Yet, Hugh explicitly affirms that the central column also represents the thirty books of Scripture (twenty-two of the Old Testament and eight of the New by his reckoning), not only suggesting a near identification between Christ and Scripture, but perhaps also intimating that the church is derived from and conformed to Scripture too. From an eschatological viewpoint, moreover, the church is coming into existence through the agency of Scripture, which (as will be argued below) figures centrally in the re-forming process of restoration.

At the same time, the reverse relationship is apparent. The church is chronologically prior to Scripture, as the church has existed since Abel, and Scripture was produced by and for the church, established and defined by its authority.[5] The symbolism of the ark-symbol can also be interpreted this way. As a symbol of the church, the ark contains all of salvation history, the "works of restoration," which are the true subject matter of Scripture. Scripture is thus circumscribed within the church.[6]

This ecclesial view of Scripture is evident in Hugh's very definition of it. "Sacred Scripture" consists of those writings "which were produced by men who cultivated the catholic faith and which the authority of the universal church has taken over to be included among the Sacred Books."[7] These, the "catholic faith traditionally calls Sacred Scriptures."[8] Perhaps suggestive in this regard is the symbolism of the church dedication, described in *De sacramentis* and discussed in Chapter 5. Here, the bishop carries a "cambria or pastoral branch," which represents Scripture and signifies the ministry of teachers and preachers in the church.[9] Here too, Scripture finds its proper place within an ecclesial and liturgical context.

The view adopted here is that for Hugh Scripture is best seen as existing and functioning within the ecclesial context, its re-forming effects part of the overall re-forming effects of the church. Yet the more fundamental

4 *Sacr.*, 2.Prol. (*PL* 176.363; Deferrari 205). 5 *Didasc.*, 4.1 (Buttimer 70.21–71.5; Taylor 102–3).

6 *Archa Noe*, 1.5 (Sicard 24.16–19; CSMV 64): "The height of thirty cubits denotes the thirty volumes of the Holy Writ ... wherein is contained the sum all the things that God has either done, or else is going to do, for his Church."

7 *Didasc.*, 4.1 (Buttimer 70.21–24; Taylor 102).

8 *Didasc.*, 4.1 (Buttimer 70.12–13; Taylor 102). 9 *Sacr.*, 2.5.3 (*PL* 176.441B; Deferrari 281).

claim, which need not in the end delineate the precise church–Scripture relationship in Hugh,[10] is that Scripture is, in some sense, analogous to church, which analogy is most apparent in the architectural symbolism that he employs to discuss both. Along with and in conjunction with church, Scripture mediates the re-forming power and presence of Christ.

SACRED AND SECULAR WRITINGS

Writing during the "twelfth-century Renaissance," which witnessed an immense interest in ancient writings of all kinds, Hugh is keen to distinguish Scripture from other texts, not merely from secular poetry or philosophy or ethics,[11] but even those that might be termed "theological," i.e., that may speak of God, invisible goods, the immortality of the soul, and eternal judgment. In contrast to these "writings of the philosophers," whose speculative eloquence has merely the whitewashed appearance of truth, Scripture is like a honeycomb, with its simple, dry language concealing the sweetness of sacred truth.[12] In particular, he observes the practical, this-worldly orientation of Scripture, in contrast to philosophical speculations. Scripture "is devoted almost entirely to the state of this present life," and it "is read for the strengthening of the [catholic] faith."[13]

More precisely, Scripture for Hugh plays a unique and crucial role in the "works of restoration." In his short *accessus* to Scripture, his *De scripturis et scriptoribus*,[14] Hugh rehearses this fundamental distinction between the "two works" of God in order to distinguish two corresponding kinds of writings.

[10] Châtillon notes the complexity of this relationship: "Scripture is to be sure the good of the church to which it has been entrusted by Christ. In a certain sense Scripture forms part of the church, as Hugh indicates in the ark treatises by comparing Scripture to the central column. Equally so, though, Scripture in a sense contains the church, for Scripture was made for the church and for the sake of the church. It is not absolutely prior to the church, since the church has in a sense existed from Adam. It is for him, however, anterior to the church, for Scripture assists in the understanding of the church which will not be fully manifest until the end of time" (*Le Movement canonial*, 301).

[11] *Script.*, 1 (*PL* 175:9A–10A): "For indeed through the spirit of this present world the loquacious have written many things. We read the songs of the poets, in which with the delectation there is also some utility; as someone has said: 'poets intend to benefit and to delight' (Horace, *Art. Poet.* 333). Logic, mathematics, and physics teach a certain kind of truth, but they do not extend to that truth in which there is salvation of the soul, without which, whatever is, is empty. The philosophers of the Gentiles also wrote ethics in which they depicted certain virtues like a member severed from the body of goodness; but the members of the virtues are not able to be alive without the body of the charity of God."

[12] *Didasc.*, 4.1 (Buttimer 70.13–18; Taylor 102). [13] *Didasc.*, 4.1 (Buttimer 70.22–23; Taylor 102).

[14] See Zinn, "Hugh of St. Victor's *De scripturis et scriptoribus sacris.*"

There are two works of God, by which everything that has been made is accomplished. The first is the work of creation, by which were made those things which were not. The second is the work of restoration, by which are repaired (*reparatur*) those things which had come to nothing (*perierant*). The work of creation is the creation of the world with all its elements. The work of restoration is the Incarnation of the Word with all the Word's sacraments – either those which came before the Incarnation, from the beginning of the world, or those which followed afterwards until the end of the world.[15]

These two works, for Hugh, are the distinguishing subject matter of two distinct kinds of writings: The subject matter "of all other writings is in the works of creation (*operibus conditionis*)"; but the subject matter "of divine Scriptures consists in the works of restoration (*operibus restaurationis*)."[16]

Not only the subject matter, but also the manner or mode of treating their subjects differs between these two literary genera: "if the other writings teach something true, it is not without the contagion of error; if they seem to commend something good, it is either mixed with malice, so that it is not pure, or it is lacking knowledge and love of God, so that it is not complete."[17] The *Didascalicon* chimes in: The "writings of the philosophers" speculate only plausibly regarding states of affairs in the next life and, though often superficially attractive, are in fact mixed with falsehood and error. Scripture, by contrast, though simple and rude on the surface, contains within the honey-sweet truth of how this present life ought to be lived.[18] In Scripture "whatever is taught, is true; whatever is prescribed, is good, whatever is promised, is happiness. For God is truth without fallacy, goodness without malice, happiness without misery."[19] How does Scripture come to be thus? Divine inspiration. "Only those writings are rightly called divine, which were inspired by the Spirit of God, and through which the Spirit of God speaks ..." Because of their inspired character, the Scriptures are truly to be called "divine," and through them, the truth is "perceived without the contagion of error," and the soul is "repaired (*reparatur*) unto true knowledge and love of God."[20] Precisely in this are they distinguished from all other writings.

[15] *Script.*, 2 (*PL* 175:9A–11A–B): "Duo sunt opera Dei, quibus consummantur omnia quae facta sunt. Primum est opus conditionis, [11B] quo facta sunt quae non erant: secundum est opus restaurationis, quo reparata sunt quae perierant. Opus conditionis est creatio mundi cum omnibus elementis suis. Opus restaurationis est incarnatio Verbi cum omnibus sacramentis suis; sive quae ante incarnationem praecesserunt ab initio saeculi, sive quae post subsequentur usque ad finem mundi."

[16] *Script.*, 2 (*PL* 175:11C).

[17] Ibid.

[18] *Didasc.*, 4.1 (Buttimer 70.13–18; Taylor 102).

[19] *Script.*, 1 (*PL* 175.11A).

[20] Ibid.

THE SENSES OF SCRIPTURE

Its inspired character gives Scripture a special nature in that, not only do its words (*voces*) signify (as is the case with all other writings), but also, and more importantly, the things (*res*) to which Scripture refers also have divinely intended meaning.[21] In the Augustinian terminology shaping Hugh's thinking, in Scripture the things (*res*) to which the words refer are themselves also signs (*signa*);[22] these things are "the voice of God speaking to men," having been dictated by "Nature." A word is a mere sign of human perception; a thing is the *simulacrum* of the divine idea.[23] Scripture provides the occasion for moving from a sign (*voca*) to a concept (*intellectum*), to a thing (*res*), to an idea (*ratio*), in order to arrive at Truth.[24]

This additional depth or dimension that distinguishes Scripture from other texts is behind Hugh's affirmation (along with the tradition before him) that Scripture has not only a literal sense or meaning, the first meaning of the words (*voces*) on the page, but also deeper, spiritual meanings that are found through an interpretation of the things (*res*) to which the words refer. For Hugh, there are two spiritual senses in addition to the literal, namely, the allegorical and the tropological. In his *Chronicon*,[25] he gives a helpful description of the multi-sense nature of Scripture:

> All exposition of Scripture is treated according to a threefold sense: history, allegory, and tropology or morality. History is the narrative of things done, expressed through the first meaning of the letter. There is allegory when through the facts of history, which is found in the literal sense, some other fact, either of past, present or future time, is indicated. There is tropology when, in that which we hear was done, we recognize what it is that should be done by us. Whence, it rightly receives the name of tropology, that is, speech that has changed direction or discourse folded back on itself, for without a doubt we turn the word of another narrative to our own instruction when, having read of the deeds of others, we conform (*conformamus*) ourselves to their example of how to live.[26]

21 *Sacr.*, 1.Prol.5 (*PL* 176.185A; Deferrari 5). See also *Script.*, 5 (*PL* 175.13B–D).

22 *Didasc.*, 5.3 (Buttimer 96.24–25; Taylor 120): "Sciendum est etiam, quod in divino eloquio non tantum verba, sed etiam res significare habent."

23 *Script.*, 14 (*PL* 175.20D–21A): "quia hanc usus instituit, illam natura dictavit. Haec hominum vox est, illa vox Dei ad homines. Haec prolata perit, illa creata subsistit. Vox tenuis est nota sensuum, res divinae rationis est simulacrum."

24 *Didasc.*, 5.3 (Buttimer 97.7–9; Taylor 122).

25 William Green, "Hugo of St. Victor: *De tribus maximis circumstantiis gestorum*," *Speculum* 18 (1943), 484–93.

26 *Chronicon, vel de tribus maximis circumstantiis gestorum* (Green 491.3–11; trans. altered from Mary Carruthers, "The Three Best Memory Aids," *The Medieval Craft of Memory: An Anthology of Texts and Pictures*, eds. Mary Carruthers and Jan M. Ziolkowski [Philadelphia: University of Pennsylvania Press, 2002]). See also *Sacr.*, Prol. 4 (Deferrari 5).

Speaking generally, the literal sense of the text is the first meaning of the words and also the meaning of the historical narrative of Scripture. Allegory is the doctrinal sense, which indicates that which is to be believed; tropology is the moral sense, which indicates that which ought to be done. In the ark treatises, Hugh compares these three senses to the dimensions of Noah's ark:

In these three measurements the whole divine Scripture is contained. For history measures the length of the ark, because the order of time consists in the succession of events. Allegory measures the breadth of the ark, because the fellowship of faithful people consists in their sharing in the mysteries. Tropology measures the height of the ark, because the worth of merits increases with advance in virtue.[27]

With this description, Hugh adumbrates his inclination to think of Scripture in structural, indeed architectural, terms, which will become more evident below.

THE SUBJECT MATTER OF SCRIPTURE: "CHRIST AND HIS SACRAMENTS"

Before exploring Scripture's agency in re-formation, its link to Christ merits comment. As noted above, Scripture's subject matter is the "works of restoration," at the center of which stands "the Incarnate Word." Later in that same work, Hugh says quite pointedly: "the material of divine Scripture (*materia divinae Scripturae*) is the Incarnate Word."[28] In the treatise on Noah's ark, Hugh develops this link between Christ and Scripture to the point of near identity:

When we said that the height of thirty cubits signified Divine Scripture, and then asserted that the fact of the pillar being thirty cubits high meant Christ, we were not making any contradiction. For the whole Divine Scripture is one Book, and that one Book is Christ, for the whole divine Scripture speaks of Christ and is fulfilled in Christ.[29]

Thus, for Hugh, "Christ is the first object of Scripture, which has been made for him and speaks only of Christ."[30] In his short treatise, *De verbo Dei*, Hugh makes this point even more forcefully. The Word, of course, is the second divine Person, the single, eternal, divine utterance,[31] "through which He made all things." That single divine Word is mediated to human

[27] *Archa Noe*, 4.9 (Sicard 113.67–73; CSMV 149). [28] *Script.*, 17 (*PL* 175.24A).
[29] *Archa Noe*, 2.7 (Sicard 45–46.84–89; CSMV 86). [30] Châtillon, *Le Movement canonical*, 302.
[31] *Verbo Dei*, 1 (Baron 60.1–5): "The Word is his utterance. The utterance of God is one, because the Word of God is one. And therefore it is truly one, because it is one from one, who does not contain multiple statements, but is perfected by one, simple word."

beings through the multiple human words of the Scriptures, both Old and New Testaments. Yet, persisting behind the many human words of Scripture is the one divine Word: "whatever things He has brought forth through the mouths of men, He was one in all of them, and all of them were one in this one, without whom they cannot have been brought forth in any place or time."[32] Hugh calls this a "great sacrament" and compares it to the Incarnation:

> The Word of God clothed in human flesh appeared once visibly, and now the same Word comes to us daily fashioned with a human voice [i.e., Scripture]. And although He becomes known to men in one way through the flesh and in another through the human voice, in a sense, what here is to be understood to be the voice of the Word is there the flesh of God.[33]

The many words of Scripture mediate the one Word of God, as did human flesh in the Incarnation. It is for this reason that Scripture has life-giving power, "because Life is in it," such that "what is heard externally stirs up, vivifying the heart within" and "what falls upon the ears outside inspires the heart."[34] In short, "Christ confers on Scripture the power to protect and illuminate the faith."[35]

In this light, the claim that Scripture mediates the re-forming power of Christ to its readers will not surprise. Through Scripture, the community of exegetes is both drawn together and conformed to Christ:

> Our purpose in reading Scripture is that, by gaining knowledge of what He did and said and commended, we may be enabled to do what He told us and receive what He has promised. Growing in this way both in the knowledge of the truth and in the merit of virtue, spiritually we strive towards conformity (*conformitatem*) with Him and the "measure of the age of His fullness" (Eph. 4:13).[36]

By thus linking the ecclesial community to Christ, the source of spiritual life, Scripture is the "Book of Life": "the whole Divine Scripture is that one Book, which is the Book of Life."[37] This is Scripture's *raison d'être* – to unite God and humanity, to enable the divine indwelling of the human. Waxing rhapsodic, Hugh extols the close association between the Incarnation and Scripture in the economy of salvation: "And to sum it all up, it was for this, with a view to this, on account of this, that the whole of Scripture was made. For this, the Word was made flesh, God was made humble, man was made sublime."[38]

[32] *Verbo Dei*, 1.1 (Baron 60.14–17). [33] *Verbo Dei*, 1.2 (Baron 60.19–62.24).
[34] *Verbo Dei*, 1.3 (Baron 62.31–33). [35] Châtillon, *Le Movement canonial*, 302.
[36] *Archa Noe*, 2.7 (Sicard 46.90–95; CSMV 86). [37] *Archa Noe*, 2.7 (Sicard 45.87–88; CSMV 86).
[38] *Archa Noe*, 1.3 (Sicard 10.30–31; CSMV 51).

Reflecting his consistent conviction about the historically enacted, materially mediated nature of salvation, about the profoundly sacramental character of the "works of restoration," Hugh takes care to insist that the subject matter of Scripture is not Christ alone, but Christ "and His sacraments," more precisely, "all His sacraments, as much those of the past since the beginning of the world as those of the future up until the end of the world."[39] Hugh has in mind here not just the narrow sense of sacraments (which were in the process of being codified and defined in his time), but the broader sense of the term, meaning any visible, material reality that has become "significant" with respect to divine revelation and has thereby become part of the works of restoration. For Hugh, Christ (as seen in Chapter 4) stands at the center of history, and, "flowing" out from him backward toward Eden and forward to the *eschaton*, are his sacraments, deeds done in time, which are revelatory and salvifically effective. These are inextricably linked to Christ and together with him constitute the subject matter of Scripture, "the collection of spiritual realities that restore fallen man."[40]

THE SAPIENTIAL COMPOSITION OF SCRIPTURE

Above, Hugh associated Scripture with Christ by linking both to the biblical symbol of the "book of life." This raises the issue of the other "book" often associated with medieval thinkers, including Hugh, namely the "book of creation." An adequate appreciation of Hugh's view of Scripture requires that the relation between these two "books" be specified. The short answer is that, for our Victorine, the "book of Scripture" intervenes between fallen humanity and the "book of nature." Scripture replaces the inner voice of revelation that sin silenced and facilitates a correct reading of creation. Whereas, prior to the Fall, the rational creature could "read" the "book of nature" rightly, i.e., for spiritual profit, post-lapsarian man is now blind and can no longer read creation well. Accordingly, God has provided a new set of material objects in place of, or at least overlaid upon, the "works of creation," namely the "works of restoration," that is, Christ and his sacraments – deeds done in history, centered on the Incarnation, and recorded in Scripture. These are analogous to the creative acts of wisdom in creation. They are the *simulacrum* of grace, which are now the proper visible forms or patterns (*species*, *exemplaria*) declaring and revealing the divine nature. Only these have the power to heal

[39] *Script.*, 17 (*PL* 175.24B). [40] Châtillon, *Le Movement canonial*, 302.

spiritual blindness and thus reveal the divine nature.[41] The works of creation merely declare. The works of restoration heal and reveal, illuminate and demonstrate.[42] Only Scripture, for Hugh, provides access to these salvific, sacramental realities.[43]

As long as man was able to hear God speaking within himself, he did not have [exterior teaching]; but after the interior eye was no longer strong enough to look into the book of life, Scripture was set down outside, so that at least by the inspection of it, man might be renewed unto the understanding of truth.[44]

So, in the treatise on Noah's ark, Hugh warns his reader "not to pry into such mysteries of God as He has not intended to open to us through his Scripture."[45]

The claim that Hugh thinks of the "book of Scripture" as now intervening between fallen humanity and creation finds a confirmation in the fact that, just as the "book of creation" was well formed and beautiful, so too is the book of Scripture. In his *Didascalicon*, Hugh compares the structure and composition of Scripture with a musical instrument. Here, the various scriptural senses – the historical, allegorical, and tropological – have been divinely brought together like the strings of a musical instrument strung across a wooden frame. He notes that not every part of the instrument produces the musical sound: only the strings. Yet the wooden frame, to which the strings are attached, is crucial.[46] After introducing the simile, he pursues an extended comparison, asserting that whatever

[41] *In hierarchiam* (*PL* 175.926C): "In both [simulacra] God was shown, but God was not understood in both; for to be sure by its appearance nature showed its Creator, but it could not illumine the eyes that contemplated it. But the humanity of the Savior was both medicine, so that the blind might receive sight, and at the same time instruction, so that the ones who saw might recognize the truth." (My translation.)

[42] *In hierarchiam* (*PL* 175:925D–926B): "For nature, created for servitude, pointed to its Creator, but it was a likeness distant from his excellence and lordly majesty. Nor could the nature that was to be taught find an evident declaration in all those things, since it too was not sound enough to gain much clarity in contemplation. For it did not have the patterns formed by grace for soundness of internal vision; nor did it know the ark of wisdom, and of created treasures, namely, the flesh of the eternal Word in the humanity of Jesus." (My translation.)

[43] See Zinn, "*Historia fundamentum est*," 155.

[44] *Misc.*, 1.13 (*PL* 177.484C): "Quandiu homo intus Deum audire loquentem potuit, doctrina exteriori opus non habuit; sed postquam librum vitae oculo interiori inspicere jam non valet, Scriptura foris apponitur, ut ejus saltem inspectione ad cognitionem veritatis renovetur."

[45] *Archa Noe*, 2.1 (Sicard 34.50–51; CSMV 75).

[46] *Didasc.*, 5.2 (Buttimer 95.21ff.; Taylor 120, slightly adapted): "Sicut enim in citharis et hujusmodi organis musicis non quidem omnia quae tanguntur canorum aliquid resonant, sed tantum chordae; cetera tamen in toto citharae corpore ideo facta sunt, ut esset ubi connecterentur, et quo tenderentur illa quae ad cantilenae suavitatem modulaturus est artifex." Hugh is quoting verbatim from Isidore, *Quaestiones in Vetus Testamentum*, praef., 4 (*PL* 82.208), but independently making the comparison with Scripture (Taylor, *The Didascalicon of Hugh of St. Victor*, 219 n. 2). See similar passage in *Script.*, 4 (*PL* 175.12D–13A).

is contained in Scripture either "resounds with the sweetness of spiritual understanding in the manner of strings" or as a historical or literal narrative "binds [the spiritual meanings] together all at once as the wood does which curves under the taut strings." The result is "a sound which the string alone has not yielded, but which the wood too has formed by the shape of its body."[47] Here, the literal sense is associated with the instrument's wooden frame, while the spiritual senses are the strings stretched across it. Both Scripture and the lyre are composed of diverse parts, each of which functions in a manner proper to it, so as to produce a pleasing effect.

Crucial to note here is that Hugh credits this marvelous construction of the sacred text to the Wisdom of God: "thus it is that, in a wonderful manner, all of sacred Scripture is so suitably adjusted and arranged in all its parts through the Wisdom of God."[48] The sapiential form of Scripture mirrors the sapiential form of the cosmos, since both receive their essential structure by participation in the *Sapientia Dei*. The very same Wisdom of God that figured so prominently in the first half of the *Didascalicon* reappears in the second half as the structuring form of Scripture, as Hugh's depiction of the composition of Scripture parallels his description of nature. Like nature, Scripture exhibits "a wonderful ordering of the divine dispensation."[49] Similarly, *De sacramentis* speaks of Scripture as "interwoven in its diction with beautiful variety"; and such "variety itself is apt, that it may not generate schism and diversity, concordant that it may not produce adversity."[50] In short, for Hugh, the book of Scripture is for fallen humanity the wisely composed mediator of divine revelation and means of access to God.

SCRIPTURE AS FORMATIVE STRUCTURE

But what precisely is the role or function of Scripture for post-lapsarian humanity in the economy of salvation? Or, since its subject matter is the

[47] *Didasc.*, 5.2 (Buttimer 96.7f.; Taylor 121, slightly adapted): "quidquid in ea continetur aut vice chordarum spiritualis intelligentiae suavitatem personet, aut per historiae seriem, et litterae soliditatem mysteriorum dicta sparsim posita continens, et quasi in unum connectens, ad modum ligni concavi super extensas chordas simul copulet, earumque sonum recipiens in se, dulciorem auribus referat, quem non solum chorda edidit, sed et lignum modulo corporis sui formavit."

[48] *Didasc.*, 5.2 (Buttimer 96.5; Taylor 121): "unde modo mirabili omnis divina scriptura ita per Dei sapientiam convenienter suis partibus aptata est atque disposita ..."

[49] *Didasc.*, 4.2 (Buttimer 72.22; Taylor 104): "et mira quadam divinae dispensationis ratione actum est, ut cum in singulis plena et perfecta veritas consistat, nulla tamen superflua sit."

[50] *Sacr.*, 2.Prol (*PL* 176.363; Deferrari 205).

"works of restoration," how does it contribute to restoration? The answer is that Scripture addresses the two primary deficiencies of fallen humanity with an eye toward a single result: re-form of the creature in the divine likeness. Scripture "makes man divine, *reforming* (*reformans*) him to the likeness of God, by instructing him in knowledge and by exhorting him to love of Himself" (emphasis added).[51] This is the "work of restoration" that Scripture brings about. Scripture facilitates this re-forming of human nature by instructing it in the knowledge of God and by exhorting it to the love of God.[52] Knowledge and love are the two basic dimensions of the human soul for Hugh. Change in them constitutes "formal" change in the soul.[53] Later in the same work, Hugh elaborates, by aligning these two objectives with the different spiritual senses of the text:

> Twofold is the fruit of divine reading: for it either instructs (*erudit*) the mind in knowledge or decorates (*ornat*) [the mind] with morals. Scripture teaches that which is delightful to know and that which is expedient to imitate. The first of these, that is, knowledge, looks more to history and allegory; the second, that is, instruction in morals, looks more to tropology. For all divine Scripture refers to this end.[54]

That morals are rightly associated with love is confirmed by Hugh's statement in the treatise on Noah's ark. There, he interprets the word "seraphim" (following Gregory the Great) to mean "burning," beautifully signifying "Holy Scripture, which causes those whom it has first enlightened by knowledge afterwards to burn mightily with love. For when it shows our heart what it should desire, it first enlightens it, and then makes it burn."[55] Shortly thereafter, he says again: allegory "is an illumination of our minds to the knowledge of His Godhead,"[56] while through tropology "we are prepared for doing good works"[57] Thus, "in all Scripture there is to be sought either the cognition of truth or the form of virtue."[58]

[51] *Script.*, 1 (*PL* 175.10D–11A): "Sola autem illa Scriptura … hominem divinum facit, ad similitudinem Dei illum reformans, instruendo ad cognitionem, et exhortando ad dilectionem ipsius."

[52] *Script.*, 1 (*PL* 175.11A).

[53] See Chapter 2: "change in [the soul] of knowledge and affection is, as it were, a change in form (*forma*)" (*Sacr.*, 1.3.16).

[54] *Script.*, 13 (*PL* 175.20C): "Geminus est divinae lectionis fructus: quia mentem vel scientia erudit, vel moribus ornat. Docet quod scire delectat, et quod imitari expediat. Quorum alterum, id est scientia magis ad historiam et allegoriam, alterum, id est instructio morum, ad tropologiam magis respicit. Omnis divina Scriptura refertur ad hunc finem." Nearly the verbatim description found in *Didasc.*, 5.6; see also *Misc.*, 1.13 (*PL* 177.484C–485A).

[55] *Archa Noe*, 1.3 (Sicard 12.98–100; CSMV 54).

[56] *Archa Noe*, 1.3 (Sicard 14.145–48; CSMV 56).

[57] *Archa Noe*, 1.3 (Sicard 15.179–81; CSMV 57).

[58] *Misc.*, 1.13 (*PL* 177.484D–485A): "In omni autem Scriptura aut cognitio veritatis quaerenda est, aut forma virtutis."

At first glance, these descriptions might suggest a certain exegetical distance between text and reader. Hugh's extended descriptions of Scripture and its interpretation, however, indicate a more intimate encounter with the sacred text in which instruction and exhortation occur as the exegete is in some sense formed by and conformed to Scripture. An adequate appreciation of this requires a fuller analysis of Hugh's view of Scripture. In addition to the analogy with the lyre, the *Didascalicon* also compares Scripture to an architectural edifice. Addressing the question of the relation between the different scriptural senses, Hugh advises his students "to call to mind what we see happen in the construction of buildings, where first the foundation is laid, then the structure is raised upon it, and finally ... the house is decorated by the laying on of color."[59] He then links these three parts of a structure to the three senses of Scripture. The foundation is the literal sense; the structure the allegorical sense; the decoration is the moral or tropological sense. He then brings the analogy to bear on the act of exegesis:

> As you are about to build, therefore, lay first the foundation of history; next, by pursuing the "typical" meaning, *build up a structure in your mind* to be a fortress of faith. Last of all, however, through the loveliness of morality, paint the structure over as with the most beautiful of colors [emphasis added].[60]

The significance of this passage is manifold. First, it illustrates Hugh's tendency to think in structural/architectural terms.[61] Here is his "master-symbol," noted earlier in this study. Hugh can deploy various images for Scripture. In addition to the lyre, noted above, he can also call it a dense wood to be explored[62] or a honeycomb whose hard, dry surface conceals sweet honey within.[63] But this simple, structural form dominates. More importantly, this text indicates that scriptural exegesis is not merely the detached study of the multi-sense structure of Scripture, but an interior act of self-construction, so to speak. The scriptural edifice is a structure that the exegete replicates within himself. "As *you* are about to build ..."

59 *Didasc.*, 6.2 (Buttimer 113.17–21; Taylor 135).

60 *Didasc.*, 6.3 (Buttimer 116.20ff.; Taylor 138): "Fundamentum autem et principium doctrinae sacrae historia est, de qua quasi mel de favo, veritas allegoriae exprimitur. Aedificaturus ergo 'primum fundamentum historiae pone; deinde per significationem typicam in arcem fidei fabricam mentis erige; ad extremum vero, per mortalitatis gratiam quasi pulcherrimo superducto colore aedificium pinge.'" Hugh is quoting with slight adapations from Gregory the Great, *Moralium Libri* Epistula missoria iii (*PL* 75.513C) (Taylor, *The Didascalicon of Hugh of St. Victor*, 223, n. 9).

61 See also, for example, *Misc.*, 1.75 (*PL* 177.510C–511A), where Hugh pursues an extended comparison of Scripture with the structure of a bishop's chair: "Cathedra doctoris sacra Scriptura est, in qua jugiter populo praesidere debet, et per auctoritatem praeceptionis, et per exemplum conversationis ..."

62 *Didasc.*, 5.5 (Buttimer 103.25f.; Taylor 126–27). 63 *Didasc.*, 6.3 (Buttimer 116.21; Taylor 138).

(emphasis added), says Hugh in the second person (betraying the communal origin and setting of this teaching). As you pursue the spiritual interpretation, he exhorts, "build up a structure *in your mind*." In *Archa Noe*, Hugh tells his charges: "if you have acquired the science of holy writ, which is comprised in thirty books, you build your heart up to the height of thirty cubits."[64] In short, the aim of scriptural exegesis is the noetic and moral re-formation of the human person, which is accomplished as the reader is in-formed by and con-formed to Scripture itself. For Hugh, "the effect [Scripture] produces in the hearts of its hearers is wont to be attributed to Scripture itself."[65] In some sense, Scripture and soul coalesce, as the sapiential *forma* of Scripture comes to in-form the soul.

CONCLUSION

As seen in preceding chapters, for Hugh, created being was formed *in* and *by* Wisdom and the well-being of creatures was continued participation in Wisdom. This was especially so for the rational creature, which was created especially *for* such participation, a participation conceived of as a personal indwelling of the creature by the Creator. The Fall and sin brought de-formation, by which the rational creature forfeited not only its created integrity, but also divine indwelling – indeed, the latter precisely because of the former. Salvation, accordingly, entails restored participation in wisdom, which requires re-formation of the creature by and according to the *Forma sapientiae*.

For this it is necessary – and fitting – that Wisdom become present in history, which occurs, of course, first and foremost in the Incarnation (see Chapter 4). But the salvific presence of Christ at a particular time and place in salvation history must, for Hugh, be further mediated throughout history (both before and after the Incarnation) through various created means, "sacraments" in the broad sense. Recall that the "works of restoration" are "Christ *and* his sacraments." Before the Fall, life-giving access to Wisdom occurred through the visible creation and through interior inspiration; now, in the post-lapsarian context, a new work of Wisdom, "the works of restoration," have been wisely wrought. These now mediate access to Wisdom. This mediation occurs in one sense in the church (see Chapter 5), again, in a broad sense, beginning with Abel and extending to the end of history, wherein these "sacraments" find their proper place; but access to Christ and his sacraments is also mediated

64 *Archa Noe*, 2.1 (Sicard 34.40–42; CSMV 74). 65 *Archa Noe*, 1.3 (Sicard 13.107–9; CSMV 55).

through Scripture, which records and bears the historical account of the salvific deeds of Wisdom and makes them available to subsequent readers. Now, Scripture has been interposed, which has the power, not only to reveal the Creator, but also and first to heal the defects that prevent the creature from receiving revelation. For Hugh, Scripture can do this because the creating *Forma sapientiae*, which bestowed form in creation, and from which creation departed when it lapsed, is made available now in and through it. In short, Scripture, itself wisely wrought like the first creation, mediates re-forming access to the *Forma sapientiae* and thus makes it available to fallen readers.

Herein lies the significance of the fact that Hugh visualizes Scripture itself, in its totality, as a sapiential *forma*, and specifically as an architectural structure. To engage it exegetically is to be formed by it architecturally, so to speak, as one constructs a building, or, as will be seen, an ark. This occurs gradually, through a specific, ordered, and inter-related sequence of steps. First, a foundation is laid with the literal sense; then, upon it a structure is built up through allegory; finally, the structure is adorned and decorated through tropology. Such is the threefold structure of Scripture; such is the structure replicated in the soul. When Hugh's exegetes engage Scripture thus, "their salvation grows by steps (*gradibus suis crescit salus*)."[66]

[66] *Misc.*, 1.13 (*PL* 177.485A).

PART III

Practices of re-formation

Preface to Part III

The twelfth-century, Victorine *Miscellania*, quoted at the outset of the Preface to Part II, continues thus:

Therefore, creation occurred *without* us; consummation [will occur] *of* us: but neither one *by* us. Only reformation occurs in a certain way *with* us, on account of the consent of the will. Hence, it is reckoned among merits, which are our fastings, vigils, works of mercy, and the exercise of other virtues, by which our inner man is "being renewed from day to day (2 Cor. 4:16) [emphasis added].[1]

This text reflects a crucial feature of the re-forming dimension in Hugh's theology, which he himself expresses elsewhere in terms of creating and saving grace:

By creating grace were made those things which were not; by saving grace are restored those which had perished. Creating grace first implanted certain goods in created nature, saving grace both restores the goods which nature lost when first corrupted and inspires those goods which nature being imperfect has not yet received. Through the first goods [of saving grace] free will is restored, through the second goods [of saving grace] free will operates. In the first goods [of saving grace] God operates in man, in the second goods [of saving grace] God cooperates with man.[2]

In contrast to initial formation, re-formation involves active, cooperative participation by the rational creature. While in creation God acts alone, in salvation, as Hugh puts it elsewhere: there are "two employed upon the work, God, and the man himself; and these two work together."[3] More precisely, "He who works along with us when we do good, and He who grants us the desire and the power to do good when we are not doing it, are One and the

[1] *Misc.*, 6.9 (*PL* 177.815B–D): "Creatio ergo fit sine nobis; consummatio de nobis: neutra a nobis. Sola reformatio quodammodo fit nobiscum, propter consensum voluntarium. Unde reputatur inter merita, quae sunt jejunia nostra, vigiliae, opera misericordiae, et caetera virtutum exercitia, quibus constat nostrum interiorem hominem renovari de die in diem."

[2] *Sacr.*, 1.6.17 (*PL* 176.273C–D; Deferrari 105).

[3] *Archa Noe*, 4.1 (Sicard 88.66–67; CSMV 124).

Same."[4] Evident here is his concern to make room for human involvement in the divine work of re-formation. "The good [of human nature], because it is [humanity's] nature, because it has suffered corruption, because it has been lessened, requires to be restored by exercise (*exercitio*)."[5] This active participation entails concrete practices, specific activities that renew the *imago Dei* in the "inner man."[6] "The intention of all human actions is resolved in a common objective: either to restore in us the likeness of the divine image or to take care of the necessity of this life."[7]

This reflects the distinctively practical, that is, the practice-oriented nature of Hugh's theology. There is, for example, his consistent interest in the practical implications of theology in history, church, and individual lives.[8] In *De sacramentis*, for instance, he often refrains from pursuing certain questions or topics that he deems not useful or profitably knowable. Certainly, the very choice to take up the notion of "divine works" – of foundation and restoration – as the fundamental framework and organizing principle of his theology reflects this practical orientation. Yet human works and activities also figure centrally in his thought. As noted in the chapter on the creation of the human person, this practical orientation is evident in Hugh's vision of pre-lapsarian life:

> Now if the question is raised regarding what zeal human life would have had to be cultivated and practiced, if man had not sinned, it is not unfittingly said that beyond the internal and spiritual zeal of wisdom and contemplation of God, externally also in cultivating the land, whether in plowing or in sowing or in transplanting and in other works of this kind – by which good nature on being cultivated makes progress toward the better – men at first were not [made] for practicing labor but pleasure, so that even work was for pleasure and example for the purpose of instruction. For thus the exterior man had to be practiced so that by zeal itself for exterior work a form (*forma*) might be taken for interior zeal, and so that in what he should do externally he might learn what had to be done by him within. For within also in a similar manner was there a kind of land which had indeed been created good, and yet, if it were well cultivated, could be still better.[9]

Before the Fall, human beings not only enjoyed divine contemplation, but also engaged in the cultivation and gradual betterment of nature,

[4] *Archa Noe*, 4.1 (Sicard 88.73–75; CSMV 124).
[5] *Didasc.*, 1.5 (Buttimer 12.7–9; Taylor 52).
[6] For an extended discussion of the importance of "exercises" in the spiritual life, see Sicard, *Diagrammes*, 229–54.
[7] *Didasc.*, 1.7 (Buttimer 14.5f.; Taylor 54).
[8] *Tribus diebus*, 26 (Poirel 62.1110–12): "For what good is it to us if we know in God the sight of his majesty, but glean from it nothing useful (*utilitatem*) to us."
[9] *Sacr.*, 1.6.21 (*PL* 176.276D–277A; Deferrari 109).

including, perhaps especially, human nature. Again, Hugh's predilection for the notion of form and his preoccupation with formation appear. The external cultivation of literal land was not only good and proper in itself, but was also the form (pattern, example, external expression) of a kind of internal cultivation of the soil of the soul. And, both internally and externally, Hugh's emphasis is on cultivation, not simply on labor or activity, but on structured processes that result in change for the better (*in melius*).

While the post-lapsarian situation changes many things – a shift from pleasurable to laborious work, for example – it does not remove the necessity of practices in the service of formation for the better. But what would have been gradual formation now, in light of the Fall, becomes gradual re-formation, both recovery of lost goods, and the acquisition of goods not yet possessed. In both contexts, however, practices are necessary and integral. "Times were divided and places distinguished ... pursuits and works to be practiced [were] enjoined."[10] In the activities of imitation and contemplation, humans find their "health," "happiness," "merit," "joy."[11] Not only that, but Hugh retains the inner/outer, the interior/exterior distinction. The two basic parts of human nature, body and soul, each have their respective spheres and corresponding practices in the service of either the renewal of the soul or the relief of bodily necessities. They are both part of a single re-formation of the human person and they mirror each other as much after the Fall as before:[12] "in every one of us, the disposition of the exterior man, and the ordering of his living and acting, show the form and habit of the interior man."[13]

Hugh's interest in practices in the post-lapsarian context of re-formation is variously visible. In describing God's saving response to the Fall in *De sacramentis*, Hugh notes that "guilt is taken away, that [human beings] may be justified, but punishment remains, that they may be exercised."[14] He conceives of vice and virtue similarly: "for struggles with the vices are exercises in the virtues."[15] So too, he identifies certain sacraments as sacraments "of exercise," which were instituted "for practice"[16] or "for the sake of exercise, that, while the human mind is exercised and cultivated by various species of works without, it may be made fertile for the multiple

[10] *Sacr.*, 1.9.3 (*PL* 176.321A–B; Deferrari 158). [11] *Sacr.*, 1.6.5 (*PL* 176.276A; Deferrari 97).
[12] *Sacr.*, 1.8.11 (*PL* 176.312A–313C; Deferrari 148–50).
[13] *In hierarchiam* (*PL* 175.951A–B): "Sed et in unoquoque nostrum exterioris hominis dispositio, et ordo vivendi, atque agendi modus interioris hominis formam habitumque demonstrat."
[14] *Sacr.*, 1.7.24 (*PL* 176.297D; Deferrari 133). [15] *Archa Noe*, 3.11 (Sicard 76.154–55; CSMV 113).
[16] *Sacr.*, 2.5.1 (*PL* 176.439B–C, Deferrari 279).

fruits of virtue within."[17] God instituted marriage, for example, "so that those joined in matrimony might be exercised through obedience unto virtue."[18] The divine rationale for the delay in the consummation of salvation history is the need for gradual re-form accomplished through various practices, so that "by some care and zeal [the soul] might first regain [its] former comeliness."[19] And "good performance is the road by which one travels toward life."[20] Ultimately, "in all these things … God's servant is practiced to his profit,"[21] so that perforce "right faith and good operation make perfect."[22]

While numerous references to practices and exercises may be culled from his works, in the post-lapsarian context there is a central task that Hugh identifies, which dominates his entire theology and elicits a specific set of practices in its service. In the *Didascalicon*, he puts it thus: "this is our entire task – the restoration of our nature …"[23] This restoration, which is a recovery of the divine likeness, is identical to the restoration of the integrity of human nature: "of all human acts or pursuits, then, governed as these are by Wisdom, the end and intention ought to regard … the restoring of our nature's integrity (*naturae nostrae reparetur integritas*)."[24] More precisely, this consists principally in two things: knowledge and virtue. "The integrity (*integritas*) of human nature, however, is attained in two things – in knowledge and in virtue (*scientia et virtute*)."[25] In short, the primary task for human beings is now the recovery of integrity through the acquisition of knowledge and virtue. "Now there are two things which restore the divine likeness in man, namely the contemplation of truth and the practice of virtue."[26] This restoration of *integritas* is, more precisely, a re-formation. The discussion in the *Didascalicon* as a whole, moreover, is in fact framed as a renewed participation in the divine mind or *Forma*. As Taylor notes: "For Hugh, the ultimate concern of the arts is with the changeless archetypal patterns in the divine Wisdom, to whose likeness the arts restore man."[27]

17 *Sacr.*, 1.9.3 (*PL* 176.320C; Deferrari 157).
18 *Sacr.*, 1.8.13 (*PL* 176.315C; Deferrari 152).
19 *Arrha* (*OHSV* 1.262:566–68; Herbert 28).
20 *Didasc.*, 5.9 (Buttimer 110.12; Taylor 132–33).
21 *Archa Noe*, 3.11 (Sicard 75.138–39; CSMV 113).
22 *Sacr.*, 1.12.5 (*PL* 176.352B; Deferrari 192).
23 *Didasc.*, 1.5 (Buttimer 12.12; Taylor 52).
24 *Didasc.*, 1.5 (Buttimer 12.3–5; Taylor 51–52). Hugh also mentions another aspect of restoration, which, though not the focus of this present study, is yet an important part of twelfth-century theological reflection, namely, attention to the bodily needs of fallen human life (e.g., weakness, illness, mortality, etc.). He speaks of the task as also pertaining to "the removal of our deficiency" and "the relieving of those weaknesses to which our present life lies subject."
25 *Didasc.*, 1.5 (Buttimer 12.13–14; Taylor 52).
26 *Didasc.*, 1.8 (Buttimer 15.11–12; Taylor 54–55).
27 Taylor, *The Didascalicon of Hugh of St. Victor*, 196, nn. 2–3.

At the outset of *Archa Noe*, Hugh tantalizingly describes what must have been the typical communal aspect of theological practices at St.-Victor: "Sitting with the assembled brethren" and "replying to the questions they asked," Hugh says that "with one accord" they collectively marveled over the restlessness of the human heart and together sought both the reason and the remedy. Might such an evil as this, they asked, "be countered by any skill or by the practice of some discipline"?[28] The ensuing treatise is Hugh's response to this inquiry, offering a practical program by which the members of the Victorine community together might pursue their re-formation. Yet there is one crucial difference between the pre- and post-lapsarian contexts of human activity – the dominant organizing principle or image. When Hugh looks back to Eden he sees an agricultural enterprise, both spiritually and physically, the latter symbolizing the former; when he looks forward he sees a construction project, the architectural form of which both organizes the practices by which the soul is re-formed and symbolizes the soul thus re-formed. This is the tripartite, architectural structure or form, in which a foundation is laid, upon which is built an edifice, which is then beautifully adorned.[29] As noted in Part II, this structural form is at once Christological, ecclesial, and scriptural.

In Hugh's program of re-formation, the "work of restoration" is thus the activity of constructing a dwelling place for God within the soul. In *Archa Noe*, he exhorts: "We must build [a divine dwelling] within ourselves" by "an unseen process of construction," an ark "which wisdom builds daily in our hearts" and "grace effects in us."[30] This, in some sense actual, re-forming process restores the soul's lost integrity and measure (see Chapter 3). In short, the *instabilitas* of the soul, offered as the presenting symptom of human fallenness at the beginning of *Archa Noe*, is remedied when the soul becomes again a *templum Dei*, a house for the divine presence. Fittingly, at the conclusion, when perhaps the actual ark-symbol was unveiled before his hearers, Hugh expresses himself in terms of *forma*:

And now, then, as we promised, we must put before you the pattern of our ark (*archa*). Thus you may learn from an external form, which we have visibly depicted, what you ought to do interiorly, and when you have impressed the

[28] *Archa Noe*, 1.1 (Sicard 3.1–9; CSMV 45).

[29] Sicard (*Diagrammes*, 210–20) makes similar observations and provides helpful background to this architectural orientation in Hugh's thought. Before Hugh, both Gregory the Great and Isidore of Seville had employed the image, though not in the same way.

[30] *Archa Noe*, 1.3 (Sicard 17.221–39; CSMV 59).

form (*forma*) of this pattern on your heart, you may rejoice that the house of God has been built within you.[31]

Ultimately, three basic practices are crucial to his re-forming program: *memoria*, *meditatio*, and *moralia*. These practices correlate with the two aspects of the soul's integrity noted above, knowledge and virtue. *Memoria* and *meditatio* pertain to knowledge;[32] *moralia* pertains to virtue. Knowledge and virtue, moreover, correspond to the two most basic acts of the soul, cognition and affection, by which the soul undergoes "formal" change: the human spirit "is changed by affection and cognition ... and that change in it of knowledge and affection is, as it were, a change of form."[33] These practices also fit with Hugh's theological "master-structure." *Memoria* is the foundation of the re-formation process; *meditatio* erects a theological superstructure; *moralia* provides a soul-beautifying finish. "Knowledge erects the structure of faith by its knowing, whereas love like an adorning color embellishes the building by its virtue."[34] Finally, these practices can be correlated with Hugh's conception of Scripture and corresponding exegetical theory, described in the chapter above. "Twofold is the fruit of sacred reading, because it either instructs the mind with knowledge or adorns it with morals. The first pertains to history and allegory; the second pertains to tropology."[35] Or again, adapting Gregory the Great's construction metaphor to Scripture, as already noted in Chapter 6, Hugh says:

As you are about to build, therefore, "lay first the foundation of history; next, by pursuing the 'typical' meaning, build up a structure in your mind to be a fortress of faith. Last of all, however, through the loveliness of morality, paint the structure over as with the most beautiful of colors."[36]

Memoria corresponds to the literal sense; *meditatio*, to the allegorical sense; *moralia*, to the tropological sense. Correlated in all these ways, these practices also constitute a dynamic, formational process, whose goal is to re-form the soul in the image of God. Given Hugh's overriding interest in wisdom, the combined execution of these practices may be defined

[31] *Archa Noe*, 4.9 (117.166–72; CSMV 153): "Nunc igitur ipsius arche nostre exemplar proponamus, sicut promisimus, quod exterius depingimus, ut foris discas quid intus agere debeas, ut cum huius exemplaris formam in corde tuo expresseris domum Dei in te edificatam esse leteris." (Latin is not in the *PL* edition.)

[32] *Didasc.*, pref. (Buttimer 2.9–10; Taylor 44): "The things by which every man advances in knowledge are principally two – namely, reading and meditation."

[33] *Sacr.*, 1.3.16 (*PL* 176.222B; Deferrari 47).

[34] *Archa Noe*, 1.3 (Sicard 9.5–7; CSMV 50).

[35] *Didasc.*, 5.6 (Buttimer 104.20–24; Taylor 127).

[36] *Didasc.*, 6.3 (Buttimer 116.22–25; Taylor 138).

as a participation in the sapiential structures of reality, manifest in creation, salvation, incarnation, church, Scripture, all founded on Wisdom itself; it is acting in accord with and inscribing them in one's person, body and soul.

Finally, grace-enabled, human cooperation with divine activity is the source of human merit, "grace for grace," which lifts man "above nature" – another way of saying "for the better." "For the virtues, which are formed by restoring grace superadded to nature, … are worthy of being requited in reward also above nature, so that for those to whom love of God is the cause in work, the presence of God is a reward in requital."[37] The content of this reward is thus, as noted in previous chapters, the indwelling of the divine presence.[38] "For the faithful soul is the true temple of God (*templum Dei*) … built (*aedificata*), as it were, by a kind of structure (*structura*) of spiritual stones."[39]

[37] *Sacr.*, 1.6.17 (*PL* 176.274B; Deferrari 106). [38] *Archa Noe*, 1.2 (Sicard 8.71; CSMV 50).
[39] *Sacr.*, 2.5.1 (*PL* 176.439C; Deferrari 279).

CHAPTER 7

Memory practices

INTRODUCTION

The subtitle of Hugh's *Didascalicon* is "On the Study of Reading" (*de studio legendi*), reflecting the importance he placed on this activity. As he notes in the Preface, human progress in knowledge occurs through reading and meditation, and it is the first of these that he will treat,[1] considering in turn the reading of both secular and divine texts. In the remainder of the work, he sets out a program and a method of reading.[2] Hugh's theorizing on reading reflects both his priorities and those of his era. The late eleventh and early twelfth centuries generated a resurgence of zeal for education, which was based on reading (*lectio*), and so on grammar, on which Hugh wrote a separate treatise.[3] His careful and extensive theoretical reflection on *lectio* accords with his overarching commitment to pedagogy (as Rorem's study emphasizes) and to formation. Reading is the first and foundational practice in his program of re-formation. It is not that his program lacks loftier intellectual goals; only that the ambitious must also be patient: "once grounded in things small," he will quip, "you may safely strive for all."[4] He "who proceeds by stages moves along best. Certain fellows, wishing to make a great leap of progress, sprawl headlong."[5]

For Hugh, reading is much more than a means for acquiring information or a technique for amassing knowledge. Rather, *lectio* is a profoundly

[1] *Didasc.*, pref. (Buttimer 2.11; Taylor 44).

[2] It must be noted that Hugh is here creating a model, bringing together in a coherent form and unified order things that in his time and place were often separated and scattered. This is Hugh's penchant and genius – reducing confusion and chaos to form, setting up structures that result in *integritas* and *concordia*. At the outset of his *Practica geometriae* he says that he is "gathering together old things that had been scattered about" (*vetera colligens dissipata*) (Baron, *Hugonis de Sancto Victore Opera Propaedeutica*, Prologue, 15.2).

[3] *De grammatica* (Baron, *Opera Propaedeutica*, 75–156).

[4] *Didasc.*, 6.3 (Buttimer 114.11; Taylor 136). Hugh is quoting Mardobus, *De ornamentis verborum* (*PL* 171.1687), cited in Taylor, *The Didascalicon of Hugh of St. Victor*, 222, n. 5.

[5] *Didasc.*, 3.13 (Buttimer 63.1–2; Taylor 95).

soul-forming activity, but not simply (*pace* much modern theorizing) by the sheer act of reading itself. Rather, for him (like many medievals), to read is to be formed by the content of one's reading, to have it impressed upon oneself. His very definition of reading itself reflects this: "Reading consists of forming our minds (*informamur*) by rules and precepts taken from books."[6] *Lectio* is thus a subsidiary activity, located within a larger practice, whose goal is the formation of the human person by the text itself. That practice is interiorization by memorization, not highly esteemed in contemporary Western society, but central to the intellectual and moral culture of the Middle Ages, as Mary Carruthers has shown.[7] Hugh was concerned with reading, not merely for reading's or even for understanding's sake, but for memory's sake.[8] "Indeed the whole usefulness of education consists only in the memory of it, for just as having heard something does not profit one who cannot understand, likewise having understood is not valuable to one who either will not or cannot remember."[9] Of Hugh, Carruthers observes: "What Hugh describes here is a process of completely internalizing what one has read … and the agency by which this is accomplished is … the process of memory-training, storage, and retrieval."[10] To be precise, then, the first and foundational re-forming practice is memorization or reading-for-memory (*lectio-ad-memoriam*). "I charge you, then, my student, not to rejoice a great deal because you may have read many things, but because you have been able to retain them."[11]

READING THE LIBERAL ARTS FOR MEMORY

While Scripture is the central and most important object of *lectio-memoria*, it is not the only or even the first to be read and retained. Rather, like Augustine's *De doctrina Christiana*, Hugh's *Didascalicon* assumes that fruitful exegetical engagement with the Bible requires a prior formation in the liberal arts and philosophy. The *Didascalicon*'s program of reading, accordingly, contains two parts. The first is the reading of secular texts,

6 *Didasc.*, 3.7 (Buttimer 57.25–26; Taylor 91): "lectio est, cum ex his quae scripta sunt, regulis et praeceptis informamur."

7 *The Book of Memory: A Study of Memory in Medieval Culture* (Cambridge: Cambridge University Press, 1990).

8 This chapter is much indebted to Carruthers' fine study, in which Hugh figures centrally. We attempt here to situate Hugh's theorizing on memory within the larger framework of his theology, especially his program of re-form.

9 *Chronicon* (Green 490.39–41).

10 Carruthers, *Book of Memory*, 163.

11 *Didasc.*, 3.11 (Buttimer 61.3–5; Taylor 94).

which are propaedeutic to the second, the reading of sacred Scripture. "For this reason it appears to me that our effort should first be given to the arts, in which are the foundation stones of all things,"[12] says Hugh, indulging his "architectural intuition." Much has been written on this aspect of Hugh's thought and his unique contribution to the *didascalos* tradition. Standing in a venerable genre of works that lay out a program of learning via the liberal arts,[13] this work takes up traditional material in a distinctively Hugonian fashion.[14] It has long been studied for Hugh's theory of the liberal arts, his view of the nature of theology, and the implications such study has for reading and interpreting Scripture. It need only be reprised here.

In the *Didascalicon*, Hugh lays out an educational program, in the sense of a disciplined, orderly arrangement, prescribing what ought to be read, in what order, and in what manner. "Philosophy is the discipline which investigates comprehensively the ideas of all things, human and divine."[15] He lays out a comprehensive overview of all learning, comprised not only of the theoretical (including the quadrivium – arithmetic, music, geometry, and astronomy), practical (including ethics, economics, and politics), and logical arts (including the trivium – grammar, dialectic, and rhetoric), but also famously the so-called "adulterate" or mechanical arts (including textile fabrication, armament and construction, commerce, agriculture, culinary arts, medicine, and theatre). All these, he observes, "were matters of use before they became matters of art. But when man subsequently considered that use can be transformed into art, and what was previously vague and subject to caprice can be brought into order by definite rules and precepts, they began, we are told, to reduce to art the habits which had arisen partly by chance, partly by nature."[16] Similarly, Hugh is thus creating a model – a *forma* for learning – bringing together in a structured process and unified order things that in his time were often separated and scattered.[17]

While Hugh gives a comprehensive discussion of the origin and nature of all the arts – twenty-eight in all, if the mechanical arts are also included – he commends especially the classical seven liberal arts, divided into the trivium and quadrivium, for careful study. These "comprise the tools of

[12] *Didasc.*, 3.4 (Buttimer 55.8–9; Taylor 88–89).
[13] See Taylor, *The Didascalicon of Hugh of St. Victor*, 30–36.
[14] See ibid., 28–30. [15] *Didasc.*, 1.4 (Buttimer 11.13–16; Taylor 51).
[16] *Didasc.*, 1.11 (Buttimer 11.21.12f.; Taylor 59).
[17] What Rorem called "pedagogical patterns" (*Hugh of St. Victor*, 45; 121); see Taylor, *The Didascalicon of Hugh of St. Victor*, 201, n. 37.

all philosophy"[18] and "constitute the best instruments, the best rudiments, by which the way is prepared for the mind's complete knowledge of philosophic truth."[19] "The trivium pertains to the meaning of words. The quadrivium pertains to the meaning of things. Grammar teaches correct speech and the competent pronunciation of words. Dialectic is useful for distinguishing meanings in words and for inquiring into the truth through disputation. Rhetoric looks to both. Physics teaches the interior natures of things, mathematics the exterior figures and numbers."[20]

The crucial point here is that reading-for-memory in the arts or philosophy plays an indispensable part in Hugh's re-forming program. The fact that Hugh conceives of all the arts as arising after the Fall, and in response to it, nicely situates the arts in the project of restoration and reformation.[21] That this program is formational in a very real – we might say ontological – sense is apparent from his comparison of reading the liberal arts with the process of minting coins (which reflects his context of an emerging, money-based, urban economy). When an image is painted on a wall, only the surface receives the "form of some image." By contrast, "when a coiner imprints a figure on metal, the metal, which itself is one thing, begins to represent a different thing, not just on the outside, but from its own power and its natural aptitude to do so." Similarly, by reading-for-memory "the mind, imprinted with the likeness of all things, is said to be all things and to receive its composition from all things and to contain them ..."[22] Whatever is read and retained forms the mind in this way.

But such educational formation has a spiritual *telos*. By it, the soul begins to be formed again according to the very Wisdom in whose image it was originally created.[23] Hugh explicitly situates the arts thus:

> This, then, is what the arts ... intend, namely, to restore (*reparetur*) within us the divine likeness, a likeness which to us is a form (*forma*), but to God is His nature. The more we are conformed (*conformamur*) to the divine nature, the more do we possess Wisdom, for then there begins to shine forth again in us what has forever existed in the divine Idea or Pattern (*ratione*).[24]

[18] *Didasc.*, 3.4 (Buttimer 55.11; Taylor 88). [19] *Didasc.*, 3.3 (Buttimer 53.5–7; Taylor 87).

[20] *Script.*, 13 (*PL* 175.20C): "Trivium ad significationem vocum. Quadrivium ad rerum significationem respicit. Grammatica recte loqui et competenter pronuntiare voces docet. Dialectica ad distinguendas in eis significationes et ad veritatem per disputationem inquirendam valet. Rhetorica ad utrumque spectat. Physica interiores rerum naturas, mathematica exteriores figuras et numeros docet."

[21] *Didasc.*, 1.5 (Buttimer 12.1–22; Taylor 51–52). [22] *Didasc.*, 1.1 (Buttimer 5.23–6.2; Taylor 47).

[23] "Hugh offered encouragement to the study of everything for reasons that are entirely religious: the Fall of man has to be repaired by the recovery of the wisdom which man has lost." David Luscombe, "Thought and Learning," in *The New Cambridge Medieval History, vol. iv c.1024–c.1198*, 478–79.

[24] *Didasc.*, 2.1 (Buttimer 23.17–20; Taylor 61).

Reading the liberal arts begins the pursuit of wisdom, *philosophia*, or, more precisely, a process of participation in divine Wisdom. This participation is in truth a re-formation. Initiated by reading and study, the soul's noetic encounter with all other things, which variously reflect divine Wisdom, gradually impresses the contours of Wisdom upon it, re-forming it by con-forming it to the primordial pattern of Wisdom, identified with the second Person of the Trinity.

READING SCRIPTURE FOR MEMORY: THE FOUNDATION OF *HISTORIA*

While the study of the liberal arts holds a genuinely important place, such "philosophy" is not the primary or central object of study; it is only preparatory for the study of Scripture. This must be stressed: Hugh does not view the *artes* as an independent means of access to wisdom; rather, they are taken up into the service of scriptural reading. So, Hugh's discussion of the liberal arts in the first half (Books 1–3) of the *Didascalicon* leads to the discussion of reading Scripture in the second half (Books 4–6).[25] The formation process which the arts course initiates is consummated by the reading of Scripture. Just as he prescribed an order of study in the disciplines of the liberal arts, so he posits an order of study in the scriptural "disciplines," namely, of literal, allegorical, and tropological interpretation. As noted, Hugh schematizes this order according to the architectural model of a building: first, a foundation of the literal or historical sense; then, an allegorical or doctrinal superstructure built upon it; finally, an adornment through the tropological or moral sense applied to the whole. So, prepared by the study of the liberal arts, reading-for-memory turns to the study of the literal sense of Scripture.

Hugh is justly recognized for his stress on the importance of Scripture's literal sense, an issue of some debate in the early twelfth century.[26] Several works (*Disdascalicon*, *On the Scriptures*, *Chronicon*) offer theoretical reflection on literal reading. In *On the Scriptures*,[27] he defines the literal sense as the "historical interpretation (*expositio historica*)." "Historical" here harbors two meanings. Strictly speaking, history refers to events, persons,

[25] Taylor, *The Didascalicon of Hugh of St. Victor*, 222, n. 2: "these are separate studies, to be pursued successively."

[26] See Smalley, *The Study of the Bible*, 83–195; Zinn, "*Historia fundamentum est*," 135–58; and H. J. Pollitt, "Some Considerations on the Structure and Sources of Hugh of St. Victor's Notes on the Octateuch," *Recherches de théologie ancienne et médiévale* 33 (1966), 5–38.

[27] See Zinn, "Hugh of St. Victor's *De scripturis et scriptoribus sacris*," 111–34.

and objects existing in time past; more broadly, history also "denotes the sense in which the meaning of the words refers to states of affairs described by the words."[28] That is, the literal or historical sense treats the "primary meaning of the words" with respect to the "things to which they refer."[29] The *Didascalicon* clarifies: "history" is "not only the recounting of actual deeds but also the first meaning of any narrative which uses words according to their proper nature."[30] Both aspects of this definition are important, and they afford Hugh a certain flexibility in approaching the Scriptures literally. Because the literal-historical sense includes the first or primary meaning of the words on the page, he can speak meaningfully of the literal-historical sense of a passage even when the historical state of affairs to which it refers is ambiguous or even unknown, or when the first meaning is already figurative, as in poetry, or metaphor and other figures of speech. Thus, provided that a text is not defective and the reader understands the language and the words written in it, there is always a literal meaning to a text, even if that meaning is first of all metaphorical:

> Something is said and signified literally, and this is so even when the words uttered are not to be understood at their face values, but signify something else through what they say. Therefore, taken all together, something is both said and signified literally and that is to be taken as the interpretation which is primarily signified by the letter; then, what is thus signified by the letter can be further interpreted.[31]

Most precisely, then, the literal sense is the first signification of the words.

Strictly speaking, then, it is not the scriptural words that have deeper, inspired meaning, but the realities (*res*) to which the words (*signa*) refer. "These literally recorded facts" represent "spiritual realities," and are thus called "sacraments"[32] in the broad sense that Hugh affords the term. These "are things which the Holy Spirit has shaped (*depinxit*) for the grasp of fleshly minds, which lack the power to grasp invisible realities except by means of visible, as, so to speak, simulacra of mystical meanings; and the Spirit constructs (*figuravit*) a clear revelation, by means of the likeness he sets forth, of the things which are to be interpreted spiritually."[33] In order for these *res* to become themselves effective *signa* of deeper things, they must be known and understood. This is the rationale for the propaedeutic

[28] *Script.*, 3 (*PL* 175.12A): "Secundum hoc proprie et districte dicitur historia; sed solet largius accipi, ut dicatur historia sensus qui primo loco ex significatione verborum habetur ad res."

[29] *Script.*, 3 (*PL* 175.11D). [30] *Didasc.*, 6.3 (Buttimer 115.28–116.5; Taylor 137).

[31] *Script.*, 5 (*PL* 175.14B–C). [32] *Script.*, 3 (*PL* 175.11D).

[33] *Script.*, 5 (*PL* 175.14C).

study of the liberal arts. Through the trivium, facility with words and their interpretation is gained; a proper understanding of the realities to which the words refer is acquired via the quadrivium. Both are essential for exegetical success. To use his own example in *On the Scriptures*, the scriptural word "lion" does not refer directly to Christ, as some of his contemporaries held, but rather to the animal itself. On the basis of the properties of lions – that they (as was supposed) slept with their eyes open, for example – a deeper, spiritual interpretation might be offered, namely that, while Christ died with respect to his human nature, he remained "wide awake with his eyes open in divinity."[34] In this way, the literal sense is both the source and norm for all subsequent, spiritual interpretation. Through the first meaning of the words, the reader has access to the divinely intended historical realities, which are susceptible, according to their actual properties and characteristics, to further interpretation.

Behind this emphasis on the revelatory significance of the created realities (*res*), to which Scripture refers and so privileges, is Hugh's exemplarism (see Chapter 4). In Scripture, "not only words but even things have a meaning," and while the meaning of words is merely a function of human usage, the meaning of things was established by Nature, that is, by God. Accordingly, "the thing is a resemblance of the divine Idea" or form, and thereby reflects in some way the very Wisdom of God which created it: "divine Wisdom, which the Father has uttered out of His heart, invisible in Itself, is recognized through creatures and in them." Hugh links this to Scripture:

> From this is most surely gathered how profound is the understanding to be sought in the Sacred Writings, in which we come through the word to a concept, through the concept to a thing, through the thing to its idea, and through the idea arrive at Truth.[35]

Scripture, then, is the means of access to the Wisdom of God embedded in created things.

In this light, it might be supposed that Hugh would have advocated the kind of quest for scientific knowledge of creation generally that other contemporaries, such as Adelard of Bath, pursued. He does advise: "Learn everything; you will see afterwards that nothing is superfluous."[36] In fact, however, it is the *res* of salvation history, the deeds and events of the scriptural narrative, that are of greater interest.[37] The historical realities (*res*)

[34] *Script.*, 5 (*PL* 175.13D). [35] *Didasc.*, 5.3 (Buttimer 97.6–9; Taylor 122).
[36] *Didasc.*, 6.3 (Buttimer 115.19; Taylor 137).
[37] See Southern, "Presidential Address," 149–79.

to which the literal sense of Scripture (in its non-figural mode) refers, the events, time, places, and persons of the past, are of immense significance. As recorded in Scripture – this must be emphasized: his concern is not history generally, but sacred history – these hold deeper meaning. They will be the proper object of further, spiritual interpretation. He exhorts his students, accordingly, to an assiduous investigation of salvation history. For "you have in history the means through which to admire God's deeds"[38] and "you will [not] be able to become perfectly sensitive to allegory unless you have first been grounded in history."[39] For "the foundation and principle of sacred learning ... is history, from which like a honeycomb, the truth of allegory is extracted."[40] Though the whole of Scripture has a litero-historical meaning, Hugh directs his students to the more historically oriented books of both Testaments (Genesis, Exodus, Joshua, Judges, Kings, and Chronicles, as well as the four Gospels and the Acts of the Apostles). "These eleven seem to me to have more to do with history than do the others."[41]

Just as Scripture mediates access to created things (*res*), which in turn mediate access to divine Wisdom itself, structurally present in created natures themselves, so do the historical deeds and events (*res*) recorded in Scripture mediate access to divine Wisdom, which is in some sense structurally present in salvation history too. As described in Chapter 4, these historical realities are the "works of restoration," namely, the Incarnation and its sacraments. For Hugh, then, history has a Christological center and shape, and its "sacraments" are the foundational aspect of Scripture, upon which its spiritual senses will be built up. In short, for him, *historia fundamentum est* and *historia* is essentially Christo-form, Christically structured from beginning to end. As Grover Zinn has aptly noted: theology "is grounded in the Biblical text by more than the fact that it draws upon Scripture for insights. The very 'economy' or dispensation of sacred history becomes the integrating structural principle of order in the exposition of the truth of the Christian religion."[42]

FORMING MEMORY

To proceed to spiritual interpretation, the reader of Scripture must not merely know the proper techniques of literal interpretation (through skills derived from the liberal arts, namely, facility with language and

[38] *Didasc.*, 6.3 (Buttimer 116.26; Taylor 138). [39] *Didasc.*, 6.3 (Buttimer 114.4–5; Taylor 136).
[40] *Didasc.*, 6.3 (Buttimer 116.20–22; Taylor 138).
[41] *Didasc.*, 6.3 (Buttimer 115.25; Taylor 137). [42] Zinn, "*Historia fundamentum est*," 141.

knowledge of things); he must also assimilate within himself the historical data of Scripture. This is done through memorization. While "aptitude," the ability to read well, gathers wisdom, "memory preserves it."[43] Hugh's conception of memory, though, differs widely from the modern view, which tends to see memorization simply as data storage and memory itself as a data repository, both of which can be "out-sourced" to external substitutes (i.e., reference books or electronic media). Put simply and with obvious relevance to this study, for Hugh (and for many medievals, as Carruthers' study has amply shown), by contrast, memorization is an activity that forms the soul, and a well-formed memory is an indispensable foundation for all subsequent intellectual and moral activities. Thus, even regarding the names, number, and order of the biblical books, Hugh advises: "let the student prepare himself once and for all by fixing these matters in the forefront of his mind, in certain little formulae, so to say, so that thereafter he will be able to run the course before him …"[44] Again:

> Therefore, read Scripture and learn diligently what it speaks of first in a bodily fashion [i.e., the literal sense]. For if you zealously impress (*impresseris*) upon your mind (*anima*) the form (*forma*) of those events in the narrative sequence in which they are set down, you will shortly take with you by meditation (*meditando*), as from a kind of honeycomb, the sweetness of spiritual understanding.[45]

To impress upon the mind the form of the data of Scripture is thus the essential task of reading Scripture for memory.

The Preface to a unique work of Hugh's, entitled *De tribus maximis circumstantiis gestorum, id est personis locis temporibus*, but dubbed (mercifully) *Chronicon*, evinces his conception of the soul-forming activity of reading Scripture for memory.[46] The short title captures the work's purpose; it is a massive, multi-column time-line, chronicling the scriptural persons, places, and occasions – thirty-seven folios in all! – to be memorized by Hugh's students.[47] The *Chronicon* is thus clearly an adjunct to the litero-historical reading of Scripture, confirmed by Hugh's comment in the *Didascalicon*: "First you learn history and diligently commit to memory the truth of the deeds that have been performed, reviewing from beginning to end what has been done, when it has been done, where it has been done, and by whom it has been done." These, he continues, "are

[43] *Didasc.*, 3.7 (Buttimer 57.19; Taylor 91). [44] *Didasc.*, 5.1 (Buttimer 95.7f.; Taylor 120).
[45] *Script.*, 5 (*PL* 175.15A). [46] See Chapter 6, n. 25 above.
[47] Green, "Hugo of St. Victor: *De tribus maximis*," 484. Carruthers claims "seventy folio pages worth in the fullest versions" (*Book of Memory*, 81).

the four things which are especially to be sought for in history – the person, the business done, the time, and the place."[48]

The preface begins pedagogically (as Rorem stresses[49]) with Hugh, echoing the Gospel admonishment about storing up treasure in heaven (Matt. 6:19), exhorting his students to consider wisdom a treasure and their hearts an *archa* in which to store it. "Son, wisdom is a treasury and your heart is its strongbox (*archa*). As you study all of wisdom, you store up for yourselves good treasures, immortal treasures, incorruptible treasures, which never decay nor lose the beauty of their brightness."[50] Carruthers and Rorem both render *archa* here as "strongbox," a place to store and secure money. As Hugh develops a comparison between memory and a money-changer, such a translation is apt. But an additional, more significant connotation is present, which recalls Noah's ark (*archa*), Hugh's symbol for the soul constructed as a *templum Dei*. Both senses are mutually compatible and indeed the meaning shifts from the first to the second through the course of the Preface.

At first, Hugh depicts memory as a box with numerous compartments, "filing places in the storehouse of your heart." As one reads, one separates and distinguishes the various pieces of data, like so many precious stones; this is to distinguish and to dispose (*disponere*). Then, these can be assembled in an orderly fashion; this is to gather (*collocare*). Memorization begins then with *disponere* and *collocare*: "Memory retains through gathering" those things "which we have analyzed in the course of learning."[51] The result is an "orderly arrangement" of knowledge, and the "pay-off" of such a well-organized memory is that, like a money-changer who can easily and accurately produce the required amount of currency in the appropriate denominations, the mind can retrieve such knowledge as needed.[52] Hugh sums up: "return, then, to your heart … and consider how you should dispose and collect (*disponere et collocare*) in it the precious treasures of wisdom," so that, "when your reason asks for it, you are easily able to find it by means of your memory …"[53]

But how exactly is this to be done? Hugh now proposes three different strategies for memorization – by number (*numerus*), by location (*locus*), and by occasion (*tempus*) – and discusses each in turn. (While these seem

[48] *Didasc.*, 6.3 (Buttimer 114.2–4; Taylor 136). [49] Rorem, *Hugh of St. Victor*, 15.

[50] *Chronicon* (Green 488.5).

[51] *Didasc.*, 3.11 (Buttimer 60.15–16; Taylor 93): "memoria colligendo custodit … quae discendo divisimus …"

[52] *Chronicon* (Green 488.13–489.6; Carruthers 261).

[53] *Chronicon* (Green 489.8–12; trans. adapted from Carruthers 262).

at first to correspond to the three kinds of things to be remembered, adumbrated in the work's title – *persona*, *locus*, *tempus* – they are in fact not.) By visualizing a number grid, the titles of all 150 Psalms, for example, may be committed to memory and by the same strategy the contents of each psalm can be retained. By associating what is read with the visual or sensory characteristics of its placement on the page, that is, "the color, shape, position, and placement of the letters," or with where and when it was read, the mind more easily retains the contents. Behind this memorial strategy is the telling assumption that the *forma* of an external object enters the soul through sight.[54] In Rorem's paraphrase of Hugh: "Yes, it sounds childish," but "it helps children learn";[55] and Carruthers treats the tradition of memory and rhetorical training on which Hugh draws here.[56]

What merits emphasis here is that Hugh clearly conceives of these memorial strategies as mentally visual or imaginable schematizations of data, organized according to some ordering principle or rationale which captures the essential nature of the material to be memorized. A parallel discussion in the *Didascalicon* defines "gathering (*colligere*)" as "reducing to a brief and compendious outline (*summam*) things which have been written or discussed at some length," or a "short restatement, by headings, of things already said,"[57] produced by identifying the "organizing principle (*principium*)" of the entire work and reducing the work to this essential form.[58] Again:

> We ought, therefore, in all that we learn, to gather (*colligere*) brief and dependable abstracts to be stored in the little chest (*arcula memoriae*) of the memory, so that later on, when need arises, we can derive everything else from them. These one must often turn over in the mind and regurgitate from the stomach of one's memory to taste them, lest by long inattention to them, they disappear.[59]

In the *Chronicon*, each of these strategies is a "form of disposition (*ratio dispositionis*)"[60] for organizing the data. In effect, these are, like Hugh's ark-symbol, symbolic, mental representations of data.[61] Carruthers notes that such medieval memory devices were often called "forms (*formae*),"

[54] *In Eccl.* (*PL* 177.141B): "Per visum namque ad animi cognitionem ex rebus pervenit substantia et forma"; *In Eccl.* (*PL* 177.141C–D): "Forma vero rerum per visum intrans."

[55] Rorem paraphrasing Hugh at *Chronicon* (Green 490.30f.) and noting "pueris puerilia" at *Chronicon* (Green 490.38) (*Hugh of St. Victor*, 16).

[56] See the extensive discussion of these strategies in Carruthers, *Book of Memory*, 80–85.

[57] *Didasc.*, 3.11 (Buttimer 60.16–18; Taylor 93).

[58] *Didasc.*, 3.11 (Buttimer 60.20; Taylor 93).

[59] *Didasc.*, 3.11 (Buttimer 60.26–61.3; Taylor 94).

[60] *Chronicon* (Green 489.12). Carruthers renders it "a method for such classification" (*Book of Memory*, 262).

[61] Carruthers (*Book of Memory*, 30) and Fassler (*Gothic Song*, 217) note that the ark-image/symbol is a visual aid to memory.

which in this context can mean "geometric shape" or "outline" or "the sort of thing that a diagram is." She suggests that this massive chart of columns of persons, places, and dates, which Hugh constructed in the *Chronicon*, should be understood as one such *forma*.[62] Hugh himself calls it a "form of learning (*formam discendi*)."[63]

Equally significant is Hugh's consistent description of memorization as the stamping or impressing (*imprimere*) of such *forma* onto the matter of the soul. After laying out his numbering stratagem, he says: "then I stamp this mental visualization upon my heart with vigilant concentration."[64] Similarly, failure to use such a stratagem can cause difficulty in "stamping upon his memory what the student has read."[65] He explains why in terms of *forma*: "For when a memory image is assembled from all [the copies of books] indiscriminately – one superimposed upon another, and always the earlier being wiped away by later ones – to be formed (*informari*) [upon the heart], nothing personal or familiar remains which by use and practice can be clearly possessed."[66] So one ought "to stamp upon the memory through the use of the imagination" all the sensory characteristics of the reading experience.[67] Gesturing then toward the tables of historical data to follow, he says: "these are as it were the basics of knowledge, which, if they are firmly stamped upon your memory, open up all the rest readily."[68] So he exhorts: "now indeed you have enough to do to stamp upon your memory the matters which are written out below, according to the mode and form of learning demonstrated for you above."[69] To thus impress or stamp upon the mind the visualized diagram or *forma* – Carruthers frequently emphasizes Hugh's metaphor of a coiner impressing a form upon molten metal or stamping a seal upon wax[70] – entails a process of soul formation.

[62] Carruthers, *Book of Memory*, 251. [63] *Chronicon* (Green 491.30; Carruthers 265).

[64] *Chronicon* (Green 489.35; trans. adapted from Carruthers, *Book of Memory*, 262).

[65] *Chronicon* (Green 490.14; trans. adapted from Carruthers, *Book of Memory*, 263): "difficilius id quod legitur memoriae imprimere possit."

[66] *Chronicon* (Green 490.17f.; trans. adapted from Carruthers, *Book of Memory* 263): "Nam cum omnibus indiscrete informari cogitur, alia alii superveniente, semperque posteriore priorem detergente, nulla domestica remanet aut familiaris quae usu et assiduitate certa habeatur."

[67] *Chronicon* (Green 490.22; trans. adapted from Carruthers, *Book of Memory*, 264): "situm positionemque litterarum per imaginationem memoriae imprimere."

[68] *Chronicon* (Green 490.44–45; trans. adapted from Carruthers, *Book of Memory*, 264): "Sed sunt quaedam fundamenta scientiae, quae si memoriae firmiter impressa fuerint, facile cetera omnia patescunt."

[69] *Chronicon* (Green 491.29–31; trans. adapted from Carruthers, *Book of Memory*, 265): "Nunc ergo satage ut ea quae subter describentur ita memoriae tuae imprimas, secundum modum et formam discendi superius tibi demonstratem ..."

[70] *Book of Memory*, 180.

MEMORY AS FOUNDATION

As noted above, the Preface to the *Chronicon* begins by comparing the heart or soul, well disposed by an orderly memory, to a strongbox (*archa*) for organizing, accessing, and dispensing the diverse monies of memorized knowledge drawn from Scripture. By the end of the Preface, though, the metaphor for memory has subtly but surely shifted to that of an architectural foundation for an ark-like structure that is to be built upon it in the soul. "These [the historical data]," says Hugh toward the end, "are like the foundations of knowledge (*fundamenta scientiae*)," laid down in the soul, "so that whatever afterwards we construct (*superedificaverimus*) it may be solid."[71] Then, after recalling the three senses of Scripture – history, allegory, and tropology – Hugh reminds the reader that the present work pertains to the first: "we have now in hand history, as it were, the foundation (*fundamentum*) of all teaching/doctrine (*doctrinae*), the first to be laid out (*collocandum*) in memory." "But," he continues, "because, as we have said, memory rejoices in brevity, though the events of history are nearly infinite, it is necessary for us, from among all of that material, to gather together (*colligere*) a kind of brief *summa* – as it were the foundation of a foundation (*quasi fundamentum fundamenti*), that is, a first foundation (*primum fundamentum*), which the soul can most easily comprehend and the memory retain."[72] That is, in order to lay down the foundation of history, one must begin by memorizing its most rudimentary aspects: persons, places, and times. For, "whoever possesses these three by memory in his soul, will find that he has for himself a good foundation (*fundamentum bonum*), upon which afterward he may without difficulty construct (*superedificaverit*) anything through reading and rapidly take it in and retain it for a long time."[73] Cinching the point, Hugh describes how this occurs in the "ark of the heart" (*archa cordis*), not now a strongbox for money, but an architectural structure in the manner described in the treatise on Noah's ark: "time and number measure off the long side in the ark of the heart, place extends the area transversely."[74] The final result is the formed memory as the foundation of the *archa sapientiae* or *archa cordis*.

In this way, the specific purpose of the *Chronicon* finds its place within Hugh's overall project of re-formation, in which the soul is to be built

[71] *Chronicon* (Green 490.43–44; 491.1–2; trans. adapted from Carruthers, *Book of Memory*, 264).
[72] *Chronicon* (Green 491.11–16; trans. adapted from Carruthers, *Book of Memory*, 265).
[73] *Chronicon* (Green 491.18–21; trans. adapted from Carruthers, *Book of Memory*, 265).
[74] *Chronicon* (Green 491.24f.; trans. adapted from Carruthers, *Book of Memory*, 265).

up as an *archa*, an ark-like structure. This structure, of course, requires a foundation and the burden of Hugh's *Chronicon* is to describe how that foundation is laid in the soul's memory, a foundation for the structure to be raised upon it – the structure of allegory and the decoration of tropology. The memorization facilitated by reading lays the foundation for the remaining practices, both intellectual and moral: "... afterwards by meditation (*meditando*) you gather together that which you draw out through likeness either for the construction of faith (*fidei aedificationem*) or the instruction of good morals (*instructionem bonorum morum*)."[75]

Toward the end of the *Chronicon*'s Preface, significantly, Hugh turns to the Genesis account of the six days of creation, the point of departure, of course, for the salvation history that his charts will chronicle. He recalls that the world was formed (*formata*) in six days: in the first three, the world was *dispositus* – disposed, arranged, put in order; in the second three, it was *ornatus* – adorned, decorated, beautified (see Chapter 2). It is intriguing that the same word, *disponere*, is used here in the Preface for the practice of memorization, for arranging things properly and in an orderly fashion in memory. The *res* of history are themselves disposed in the tables that follow, which he explicitly refers to as establishing a *forma*. In both creation and memorization, the disposition of order (*dispositio ordinis*) is opposed to chaos and confusion, "the mother of ignorance and oblivion (*confusio ignorantiae et oblivionis mater est*)." The apparent implication is that the initial disposition of creation, forfeited in the Fall, is restored in subsequent salvation history, the form and pattern of which (with all the Christological, ecclesial, and scriptural links noted in previous chapters) is also reproduced in the soul through reading-for-memory. The soul is disposed and formed by receiving *historia* within itself, through memorization, in a manner that recalls and perhaps recapitulates the original act of creation. Thus does memorization find a fundamental place in Hugh's re-forming program. He advocates reading in the service of memorization (*lectio-ad-memoriam*), because memory forms the soul.

CONCLUSION: A FOUNDATION FOR THE EDIFICE OF DOCTRINE

For our Victorine, memory so formed is not an end in itself, but rather the beginning of a process of re-formation that will engage the whole person, not only intellectually, but also morally. In a comment worthy of

[75] *Script.*, 5 (*PL* 175.14A).

extended citation, Carruthers notes that for medievals generally, and for Hugh in particular, "memory was considered to be the prerequisite for character itself." She continues:

> The link is suggested in the fact that Greek *charakter* means literally "the mark engraved or stamped" on a coin or seal ... [I]n *Orator*, Cicero translates it with the Latin word *forma*, which had a similar range of meanings. One basic conception of a memory phantasm, as we have seen, employs exactly the same model, that of "seal" or "stamp," in wax most commonly, but also on a coin (as in Hugh's *Didascalicon*). The Greek concept of *hexis*, crucial to an understanding of moral behavior, is a predisposition that "stamps" or "forms" the embodied soul towards behaving in certain ways rather than others. Perhaps here as clearly as anywhere else in ancient and medieval culture, the fundamental symbiosis of memorized reading and ethics can be grasped, for each is a matter of stamping the body-soul, of *charakter*.[76]

In light of the foregoing, this moral *telos* of reading-for-memory can be appreciated within the larger framework of Hugh's theology of re-formation. More precisely, in terms of Hugh's architectural intuition, the well-formed memory is a foundation for the remaining soul-construction process, which will involve theological reflection and moral action. Let not the reader "despise this primary foundation of doctrine," he admonishes, nor "think worthy of contempt the knowledge of those things which Scripture lays down through the primary significance of the letter."[77] "Lest we," he adds elsewhere, "disdaining the least rudiments of doctrine (*minima haec rudimenta doctrinae*), start little by little to dissipate (*diffluere*)."[78] In the end, reading-for-memory, the study of the liberal arts leading to the study of Scripture, begins to dispose (*disponere*) and so re-establish the intellectual and moral integrity of fallen human nature, overcoming the dissipating and dis-integrating effects of sin. Ultimately, as was the case for the original creation, the result will be the beautiful adornment (*ornatio*, *pulchrum esse*) of the soul.

[76] Carruthers, *Book of Memory*, 180. [77] *Script.*, 5 (*PL* 175.14C).
[78] *Chronicon* (Green 490.37–39; trans. adapted from Carruthers, *Book of Memory*, 264).

CHAPTER 8

Meditative practices

INTRODUCTION

In Hugh's theory of scriptural interpretation, as noted, the literal-historical discipline of reading-for-memory comes first, and lays a foundation in the soul. But Hugh knew that, as McGinn puts it, "a foundation was not a building."[1] The restoration of fallen humanity, best understood as a re-formation of the divine image and likeness, requires that it be re-structured, built up again, and this new structure in the soul is produced by, and indeed consists in, well-ordered, rightly structured theological thought. This activity, moreover, corresponds to the second "discipline" of scriptural exposition, namely, allegorical reading. For Hugh, allegorical interpretation of Scripture is akin to "theological interpretation" as well as to systematic or constructive theology in the modern sense. Indeed, he wrote his massive, pioneering *summa* of theology, *De sacramentis*, quite explicitly as an aid to this particular dimension of scriptural exposition: "Since, therefore, I previously composed a compendium on the initial instruction in Holy Scripture, which consists in their historical reading (*historica lectione*), I have prepared the present work for those who are to be introduced to the second stage of instruction, which is in allegory (*allegoria*)."[2] Thus, reading-for-memory has established a foundation and fund of scriptural or historical knowledge, but as yet there is no edifice in the soul. The memorial strategies noted in the prior chapter certainly form the soul in ways that allow ease of retention and retrieval, but

[1] Bernard McGinn, *The Growth of Mysticism: Gregory the Great through the 12th Century* (New York: Crossroad, 1996), 374.

[2] *Sacr.*, 1.Prol. (*PL* 176.184; Deferrari 3, trans. altered). See the discussion in Rorem, *Hugh of St. Victor*, 52, who notes that Jan W. M. van Zwieten ("The Preparation to Allegory: Hugh of St. Victor's *De Sacramentis* and His Notes on the Octateuch," *Nederlands archief voor kerkgeschiedenis* 68 [1988], 17–22) has argued that, when Hugh refers to a previous "compendium" of historical reading of Holy Scripture, he cannot mean the *Chronicon* (*De tribus maximis*) as some have argued (cf., Baron, *Science et sagesse*, 70), but rather intends his *Adnotatiunculae* on certain books of the Old Testament. See also Poirel, *Livre de la nature*, 99ff.

they have not effected a *theological* structure, that is, a structure organized around theological principles.

How is this to occur? We recall that re-formation pertains to knowledge and virtue, and that knowledge is acquired through two distinct practices: "The things by which every man advances in knowledge are principally two – namely, reading and meditation."[3] If reading pertains to the literal-historical sense, as argued in the previous chapter, does meditation then correspond to the allegorical sense, as apparently implied? In *On Writings*, Hugh answers affirmatively:

> Therefore, read Scripture and learn diligently what it narrates first in a bodily way [i.e., the literal sense]. For if you zealously impress (*impresseris*) upon your mind (*anima*) the form (*forma*) of those events in the narrative sequence in which they are set down, you will shortly take with you *by meditation* (*meditando*), as from a kind of honeycomb, the sweetness of spiritual understanding [emphasis added].[4]

Here, the relationship between the foundation formed in memory and the subsequent practice of theological meditation emerges, as Hugh associates meditation with the spiritual, that is, the non-literal, senses of the biblical text. After careful, historical reading, he specifies, "you may *by meditation* gather together (*colligas*), through similitudes that you adduce, whatever is either constructive of faith (*ad fidei aedificationem*) or instructive of good morals" (emphasis added).[5] *Meditatio* pertains then to *allegoria*, the construction of faith, and *tropologia*, instruction in morals. Yet, Hugh links meditation especially to the former, the construction of faith through allegory, even though the reflection on morals that also pertains to meditation will facilitate the transition to the third re-forming practice, namely, *moralia*, the practices of virtue (addressed in the next chapter). *Meditatio* is thus the second step, after *lectio*, in the restoration of knowledge, and it is the re-forming practice that both follows *memoria* and prepares for *moralia*. "Reading provides the matter for exercising virtue and for understanding truth; then meditation imposes the form."[6]

As will be seen, *meditatio* is a term of wide application for Hugh. The claim advanced below, though, is that its primary place in Hugh's program is as a practice of theological thinking, employing allegorical exegesis, that is both constructive and personally appropriated. In terms of Hugh's master-symbol, meditation erects a structure of Christian doctrine

[3] *Didasc.*, pref. (Buttimer 2.9–10; Taylor 44).
[4] *Script.*, 5 (*PL* 175.15A). [5] *Script.*, 5 (*PL* 175.14A).
[6] *Misc.*, 1.93 (*PL* 177.524B): "lectio cognoscendae veritatis et exercendae virtutis materiam tribuit; deinde meditatio formam apponit."

within the soul. "Next [after the literal-historical reading] by pursuing the 'typical' meaning, build up a structure in your mind to be a fortress of faith."[7] In the *Libellus*, Hugh graphically illustrates this effect of meditation in terms of re-form. Two human figures are described: one shatters a vase against a rock, indicating how ignorance "through various errors destroys the integrity of the soul (*animae integritatem*)";[8] the other, symbolizing the act of theological mediation, is depicted as a craftsman, who gathers the fragments together in a process that, after smelting the fragments in the fire of divine love (*per ignem divini amoris liquefaciendo*), "reforms (*reformandam*) the soul in the mould of the divine likeness."[9]

A TAXONOMY OF MEDITATIVE PRACTICES

Bespeaking the intellectual climate of the twelfth-century renaissance is Hugh's preoccupation with the nature of *thinking* itself; reflecting the emergent scholastic impulses animating early twelfth-century Paris is his interest in the nature of *theological* thought; and indicating the Victorine ethos and his own priorities is his interest in theological *meditation*. He was intensely interested in and valued highly what might be called "meditative practices," on which he often heaps praise. In meditation "is to be found the greatest delight (*maximum oblectamentum*),"[10] for "if anyone will learn to love it very intimately and will desire to be engaged very frequently upon it, meditation renders his life joyful indeed, and provides the greatest consolation to him in his trials. This especially takes the soul away from the noise of earthly business and allows it to enjoy even in this life a kind of foretaste of the sweetness of the eternal quiet."[11] This high estimation is perhaps most evident in his conclusion to the *Didascalicon*. Having "explained as lucidly and briefly" as possible "those things that pertain to reading," he gestures at the "remaining part of learning, namely, meditation," which he has not treated. "So great a matter requires a special treatise," for it is "a thing truly subtle and also delightful," one that "both educates beginners and exercises the mature." Better to be silent than treat it poorly. Then this: Meditation "has not yet been treated

[7] *Didasc.*, 6.3 (Buttimer 116.20ff.; Taylor 138). [8] *Libellus*, 5 (Sicard 150.24–37; Weiss 62).

[9] *Libellus*, 5 (Sicard 150.38–40; Weiss 63). See Zinn, "*De gradibus ascensionum*," 74–75.

[10] *Didasc.*, 3.10 (Buttimer 60.2; Taylor 93).

[11] *Didasc.*, 3.10 (Buttimer 59.20ff.; Taylor 93, trans. altered): "... in meditatione, quam si quis familiarius amare didicerit eique saepius vacare voluerit, iucundam valde reddit vitam, et maximam in tribulatione praestat consolationem. Ea enim maxime est, quae animam a terrenorum actuum strepitu segregat, et in hac vita etiam aeternae quietis dulcedinem quodammodo praegustare facit."

in writing" and therefore "deserves all the more to be followed up" with the aid of divine Wisdom illuminating us within.[12] The implication seems to be that, while Hugh relies on his predecessors for much, he espies a lacuna in that patrimony regarding meditation, which he intends to fill up. However that may be, theological meditation holds a crucial place in his theology of re-formation.

The term *meditatio* recurs often in Hugh's corpus. He even devoted a short treatise, *De meditando*, to the topic. Briefly surveying and analyzing the notion of meditation in his corpus will help clarify the ensuing discussion. In several places, he situates *meditatio* as a second intellectual activity within a threefold framework. In his first sermon *On Ecclesiastes*, for example, he distinguishes three kinds of spiritual speculation or rational vision in the soul: "thought (*cogitatio*), meditation (*meditatio*) and contemplation (*contemplatio*)."[13] The first is simply the mind's awareness of the mental image of something "passing through it," arising either from sense experience or memory. The third is a more intuitively direct and encompassing insight into something, either created or Uncreated.[14] Between these, meditation is "the concentrated and sagacious reconsideration of thought (*cogitatio*) that tries to unravel something complicated or scrutinizes something obscure to get at the truth of it."[15] Hugh emphasizes meditation's intense labor on particular matters that are obscure or poorly understood. At times, his imagery is agonistic, almost violent. Meditation is "a sort of wrestling-match" in which knowledge gradually gets the upper hand and eventually victory over ignorance. It "consumes and penetrates" its object, not resting until "reaching the very center" of the matter, when it has "absorbed into itself everything that it had found outside itself."[16] Elsewhere, his imagery is more irenic: meditation "delights to range along open ground, where it fixes its free gaze upon the contemplation of truth, drawing together now these, now those causes of things, or now penetrating into profundities, leaving nothing doubtful, nothing obscure."[17]

Hugh provides expanded definitions elsewhere. The *Didascalicon*[18] defines meditation as "frequent, purposeful cogitation (*cogitatio*) which prudently investigates the cause and the source, the manner and the utility

[12] *Didasc.*, 6.13 (Buttimer 130.5–14; Taylor 151).
[13] *In Eccl.* (*PL* 177.116D): "Tres sunt animae rationalis visiones, cogitatio, meditatio, contemplatio."
[14] *In Eccl.* (*PL* 177.116D–117A).
[15] Ibid.: "Meditatio est assidua et sagax retractatio cogitationis, aliquid, vel involutum explicare nitens, vel scrutans penetrare occultum."
[16] *In Eccl.* (*PL* 177.117C). [17] *Didasc.*, 3.10 (Buttimer 59.16ff.; Taylor 92–93).
[18] Essentially the same discussion is found in *De contemplatione*, "Contemplation and Its Forms," ed. Roger Baron in *Hugues de Saint-Victor. La Contemplation et ses espèces* (Desclée: Tournai,

of each thing."[19] It then distinguishes three kinds: (1) on morals (virtues and vices); (2) on commandments (injunctions, promises, prohibitions); and (3) on divine works (that which divine power creates, wisdom disposes, and grace co-effects).[20] *On Meditation*[21] offers this: "meditation is frequent cogitation, investigating the manner (what it is), cause (why it is), and reason (how it is) of anything whatsoever."[22] It also distinguishes three major kinds: (1) on creatures (*in creaturis*), arising from admiration; (2) on Scripture (*in scripturis*), arising from reading; (3) on morals (*in moribus*), arising from circumspection,[23] but then further distinguishes twelve sub-species within these three. Both the definitions and the divisions of types of meditation in these two works are similar, though not identical. The commandments are scriptural commands, the divine works encompass creation as well as salvation history; in both, there is reflection on morals.

Most generally, then, *meditatio* is described, as Hugh himself puts it, as the practice of sustained, intense, thoughtful scrutiny into matters,[24] pertaining either to creation, to Scripture, or to the moral life. In the same breath, he helpfully situates meditation in relation to the practice of reading (*lectio*), considered in the previous chapter: "*Meditatio* takes its beginning from *lectio*, but it is not constrained by the rules and precepts of reading. ... The beginning of doctrine, therefore, is in reading, but its consummation is in meditation ..."[25] Clearly, *meditatio* holds both a crucial and a carefully specified place among the intellectual practices that Hugh prized. Yet its full import and centrality only emerge when placed in the context of his theology as a whole.

PRE-LAPSARIAN KNOWLEDGE

Before doing so, though, and in order to appreciate the significance of theological meditation as a means of salvific re-formation, Hugh's conception of pre-lapsarian knowledge must first be sketched.

1955). There is a partial translation by Bernard McGinn in *The Essential Writings of Christian Mysticism* (New York: Random House, 2006), 336–340.

19 *Didasc.*, 3.10 (Buttimer 59.13–15; Taylor 92). 20 *Didasc.*, 3.10 (Buttimer 60.3ff.; Taylor 93).

21 Hugh of St. Victor, *De meditatione*, in *Six opuscules spirituels*. Introduction, critical text, translation (into French), and notes by Roger Baron. SC 155 (Paris: Editions du Cerf, 1969), 44–59. Hereafter abbreviated as *Meditatione*, followed by line numbers in Baron's edition. All translations are mine.

22 *Meditatione* (Baron 44.1–3). 23 *Meditatione* (Baron 44.4–7).

24 *Didasc.*, 3.17 (Buttimer 67.22–68.2; Taylor 99–100).

25 *Didasc.*, 3.10 (Buttimer 59.15–21; Taylor 92).

Humans were created with a threefold knowledge: of creation, of self, and of God, all of which they received "simultaneously and immediately" upon their creation, "not by study or any teaching over periods of time."[26] With respect to the first kind, the human creature had perfect knowledge of the rest of creation, knowing of creatures "the nature and the use and the offices of each from the reason implanted in him"[27] – what might be called scientific knowledge. With respect to the third kind, Hugh describes a kind of interior, contemplative knowledge of the divine presence, "through inspiration (*per inspirationem*)."[28] This was not, however, full contemplative knowledge of the kind that it would have come to enjoy if it had not disobeyed (nor of the kind to which it will eventually be restored).[29] Hugh does not elaborate, except to say that, "taught visibly through internal inspiration," the creature "in no way could have doubted about his Creator Himself."[30] With respect to self-knowledge, the rational creature knew what sort of relationship it ought to have both with the rest of creation "below" it and with its Creator "above" it.[31] Elsewhere, Hugh correlates this threefold knowledge with three "eyes": with the "eye of the body," it could see "the world outside itself and those things which were in the world"; with the "eye of reason," it could see "itself and those things which were within itself"; and with the "eye of contemplation," it could see "God within itself and those things which were in God."[32]

As an embodied, rational creature, moreover, the human person was created straddling a line between rational, disembodied angels, on the one hand, and embodied, irrational animals, on the other. Like the angels, humans had an interior "rational sense," through which they could know invisible, spiritual realities, and like the animals they had an exterior "bodily sense," through which they could know visible, physical realities. Thus equipped, the human person could both go within himself to contemplate Wisdom and also turn to external things to contemplate "the works of wisdom." Hugh can put this in terms of a book: "Wisdom was a book written internally; the work of wisdom a book written externally."[33] The former, though, had priority: the first human creature was always "directed inwardly towards its Maker," having "its attention

[26] *Sacr.*, 1.6.12 (*PL* 176.270C–D; Deferrari 102).
[27] *Sacr.*, 1.6.13 (*PL* 176.271A; Deferrari 102).
[28] *Sacr.*, 1.6.14 (*PL* 176.271C; Deferrari 103).
[29] *Sacr.*, 1.6.14 (*PL* 176.271D; Deferrari 103).
[30] Ibid.
[31] *Sacr.*, 1.6.15 (*PL* 176.272A–C; Deferrari 103–4).
[32] *Sacr.*, 1.10.2 (*PL* 176.329C–D; Deferrari 167).
[33] *Sacr.*, 1.6.5 (*PL* 176.266D–267A; Deferrari 97).

and desire within to its Maker alone"[34] in the "high point (*acies mentis*)" of his mind.[35]

Hugh seems to imply that there was for pre-lapsarian humanity a perfect harmony between the internal and external knowing. What was known internally, through direct, inspired knowledge of God, was also easily and delightfully corroborated through the knowledge of external realities. The human person could "contemplate both and be refreshed by both" – contemplation through cognition, refreshment with affection. Both internally and externally, contemplation provoked delight and love, which issued forth in doxology.[36]

POST-LAPSARIAN KNOWLEDGE: *PER VISIBILIA AD INVISIBILIA*

The Fall, however, radically altered human knowing, afflicting "the mind with ignorance,"[37] "because the light of truth is taken from the mind."[38] In terms of the three "eyes," the "eye of contemplation" was "extinguished so that it saw nothing"; the "eye of reason" was "made bleary so that it saw doubtfully"; the "eye of the body" alone "remained in its clarity."[39] The Fall entailed a forfeiture of immediate, contemplative knowledge of God *interiorly* or *within* the soul through the "eye of contemplation." Beforehand, direct intuition of invisible things was corroborated through knowledge of visible things; now, a kind of expulsion and extroversion has occurred. The soul is turned outward and must find knowledge of God in *visibilia*. Having lost direct and immediate contemplation, the human person must now "advance to knowledge of truth through intervals of time," and be "stimulated and instructed to knowledge of truth through the forms of temporal and visible things externally."[40] But even this process is faulty. After the Fall, though it retains in some way an ability to make judgments regarding the natures of visible things, the soul is impaired in its ability to derive deeper truths from those things, that is, to arrive at "the judgment of truth instructed by those things which were seen externally."[41] Now, "it can not drink in pure truth without confusion of error."[42] As Grover Zinn has put it, "fallen man is now deaf

[34] *Archa Noe*, 4.5 (Sicard 98.6–7; CSMV 135).
[35] *Archa Noe*, 4.5 (Sicard 99.15; CSMV 135). [36] *Sacr.*, 1.6.5 (*PL* 176.266D; Deferrari 97).
[37] *Sacr.*, 1.7.26 (*PL* 176.298B; Deferrari 133).
[38] *Sacr.*, 1.7.27 (*PL* 176.298D; Deferrari 133). See Chapter 3 above.
[39] *Sacr.*, 1.10.2 (*PL* 176.329C–D; Deferrari 167). [40] *Sacr.*, 1.7.33 (*PL* 176.302C–D; Deferrari 138).
[41] *Sacr.*, 1.7.32 (*PL* 176.302C; Deferrari 137). [42] Ibid.

and blind ... and no longer perceives the world as a symbol revealing the Creator ... [and is] unable to read the book of creation."[43] Thus, St. Paul's claim in Rom. 1:20 – that "the invisible things of God are understood through the things that are made" – does not perfectly obtain for post-lapsarian humanity.[44] The post-lapsarian plight of human ignorance emerges here: having completely lost immediate knowledge of God internally, it must now turn outward to seek a mediated knowledge from created things. It can indeed still know these; scientific knowledge of the created world is not impaired. Yet, it cannot profit from these in deriving knowledge of God. "The disobedience of man through subsequent ignorance took much from his first [contemplative] knowledge."[45]

How, then, is this to be remedied? For Hugh, the divine response is to write another sapiential book!

> God willed afterwards [i.e., after the Fall] that [a book of wisdom] be written still outwardly, yet in a different way, that wisdom might be seen more manifestly and be recognized more perfectly, that the eye of man might be illumined to the second writing, since it had been darkened to the first. Therefore he made a second work after the first ...[46]

This second book is the Incarnation itself. "He assumed flesh not losing divinity, and was placed as a book written internally and externally; externally in humanity, internally in divinity, so that he might be read externally through imitation, [and be read] internally through contemplation."[47] Hugh sums up: "Therefore, there was one book written once internally and twice externally; first externally through the creation of visible things; second externally through the assumption of flesh ..."[48] In short, the visible God-Man affords a means by which to recover both interior, contemplative knowledge of God and proper exterior contemplation of creatures.[49]

This distinction between these two "books" corresponds to Hugh's distinction between two kinds of *visibilia*, the two kinds of divine works, noted in Chapter 7. The "works of foundation (*opera conditionis*)" are the creation of the world and all its elements; the "works of restoration (*opera restaurationis*)" are the Incarnation of the Word and all its sacraments.[50] Corresponding to these, moreover, are also two kinds of

[43] Zinn, "*De gradibus ascensionum*," 69. [44] *Sacr.*, 1.7.33 (*PL* 176.302D; Deferrari 138).
[45] *Sacr.*, 1.6.14 (*PL* 176.271D; Deferrari 103). [46] *Sacr.*, 1.6.5 (*PL* 176.267A; Deferrari 97–98).
[47] *Sacr.*, 1.6.5 (*PL* 176.267A; Deferrari 98). [48] Ibid.
[49] *Archa Noe*, 4.5 (Sicard 99.30–32; CSMV 136): "God, therefore, wishing to collect our hearts from this distracted state, and to recall them to the contemplation of interior joys, speaks outwardly, in order that He may exhort us to return into ourselves."
[50] *Sacr.*, 1.Prol.2 (*PL* 176.183A–B; Deferrari 3).

texts: non-sacred texts, which treat the works of creation, and sacred Scripture, which primarily treats the works of restoration (after initially and briefly treating the works of creation).[51] The works of restoration are the material, the subject matter of Scripture.[52] The book of Scripture, then, in some sense coincides with the "book" of incarnate Wisdom.

In the post-lapsarian context, human knowledge must advance to invisible things through visible things (rather than simply having the latter confirm the former, as in Eden). *But*, this cannot occur by simply turning again to the "book of nature." Rather, now a second "book," the Incarnation and all its *sacramenta*, has been written and made available in Scripture, as the new and privileged set of *visibilia* through which to access the *invisibilia*. In his *Commentary* on *The Celestial Hierarchy* of (Pseudo-)Dionysius, accordingly, Hugh derives two kinds of theology from these two kinds of divine works. Secular theology (*mundana theologia*) considers the book of creation directly; divine theology (*divina theologia*) reads it in light of the book of restoration. Both theologies use visible things to understand invisible realities, yet they are critically different. Worldly theology considers the "work of creation and the elements of this world (*opera conditionis assumpsit et elementa hujus mundi*)."[53] Divine theology, by contrast, treats the work of restoration, that is, the humanity of Jesus and his sacraments (*humanitatem Iesu et sacramenta ejus*).[54] The former is the *simulacrum* (symbolic representation) of nature (*simulacrum naturae*); the latter, the *simulacrum* of grace (*simulacrum gratiae*).[55] Hugh sharply criticizes the practitioners of worldly theology, who look directly at the beautiful appearance of creation, rather than at the humanity of the incarnate Word and his sacraments.[56] For him, only the *simulacrum* of grace offers the proper visible forms or patterns (*species*, *exemplaria*) declaring and revealing the divine nature. Only the *simulacrum* of grace can both heal spiritual blindness and demonstrate divine Beauty.[57] The

[51] *Sacr.*, 1.Prol.3 (*PL* 176.184B; Deferrari 4).

[52] *Sacr.*, 1.Prol.2 (*PL* 176.183A; Deferrari 3); *Sacr.*, Prol.2 (*PL* 176.183C; Deferrari 4); see also *Script.*, 2 (*PL* 175.11C).

[53] *In hierarchiam* (*PL* 175.926D). [54] *In hierarchiam* (*PL* 175.927A).

[55] *In hierarchiam* (*PL* 175.926B).

[56] *In hierarchiam* (*PL* 175.928B): "Here, thus, God made 'the wisdom of this world' to be foolish; for it could not recognize the truth, since in its erudition it disdained to hold to the form of humility."

[57] *In hierarchiam* (*PL* 175.926C): "In both [kinds of *simulacra*] God was shown, but God was not understood in both; for to be sure by its appearance nature showed its Creator, but it could not illumine the eyes that contemplated it. But the humanity of the Savior was both medicine, so that the blind might receive sight, and at the same time instruction, so that the ones who saw might recognize the truth."

works of creation merely declare. The works of restoration heal and reveal, illuminate and demonstrate.[58] Christ incarnate and his visible sacraments thus provide the "text" of divine theology, which alone offers true knowledge of God.[59] In short, God has "written" another "book," which provides another set of *visibilia*, the Incarnation and its *sacramenta*, which have the requisite power, not only to reveal but also, first, to heal the human knowing apparatus.

Under the heading "works of restoration," then, Christ, church, and Scripture coalesce (as described in Part II). The central divine work is the Incarnation, but linked to it inextricably are the *sacramenta*, both in the narrow, ecclesial sense and in the wider, symbolic sense, extending throughout the course of salvation history, constituting the time of the church, before and after the Incarnation (see Chapter 5). These sacramental *visibilia* are made known through Scripture in the church. The "sacred eloquence" points to and thus mediates the divinely instituted subset of *res* (persons, objects, places, and events) that have revelatory significance.[60] Scripture is the lens through which God is perceived in created things.[61] In some sense, the second "book" has been superimposed upon the first "book," as the interpretive lens through which the first must be read. In the present situation, "we must observe in doctrine those things which authority approves, because human reason unless it has been illumined by the word of God can not see the way of truth."[62] In short, this constellation of Christ, church, and Scripture has become a new sacramental, theophanic universe.[63] So, Zinn: "because of the effects of sin upon man's noetic and volitional capabilities the efficacy of the cosmos as a set of representations (*simulacra*) of the Triune God and of spiritual realities

[58] *In hierarchiam* (*PL* 175.925D–926B): "For it did not have the patterns formed by grace for soundness of internal vision; nor did it know the ark of wisdom, and of created treasures, [namely,] the flesh of the eternal Word in the humanity of Jesus; but employing only the evidence of nature with the vision of bleary eyesight, applying only a cloudy and uncertain light, it contemplated the appearance of created things."

[59] See Zinn, "*Historia fundamentum est*," 155.

[60] Hugh's comment in *Sacr.*, 1.6.13 (*PL* 176.271B; Deferrari 103) clearly implies this post-lapsarian need for Scripture with respect to certain things, though not all: "Now since man by sinning did not lose this knowledge [scientific knowledge], just as he did not lose that by which also he had to provide the comforts and the necessities of his flesh, God on this account did not afterwards care to instruct him on such matters through the Scriptures …"

[61] See Hugh's remarks in *Misc.*, 1.83 (*PL* 177.518B): "Si quis omnem creaturam theophaniam dixerit, non errabit." Yet, in *Misc.*, 1.63 (*PL* 177.505A), he says: "Scriptura explicat quae creatura probat." This seems to correspond to Hugh's comments in his *Commentary* on *The Celestial Hierarchy*, noted above, which argue that the works of creation merely declare the divine beauty, but only the works of restoration can heal the soul and enable it to perceive creation aright. Thus, Scripture explains what creation shows forth.

[62] *Sacr.*, 1.3.31 (*PL* 176.234C; Deferrari 61).

[63] See Smalley, *Study of the Bible*, 90–91.

depends squarely upon the work of restoration in healing the disorders of man's inner self so that he may again 'see' the deeper sense of the visible cosmos as a symbol of the invisible world of the spirit."[64] Hugh's is thus not a "generally symbolic cosmos, but a specifically Christo-centric one."[65] Accordingly, as suggested in Part II, the hermeneutical key to this cosmos is Christ, mediated through church and Scripture.

At the same time, the post-lapsarian state entails a different kind of divine "availability" to human knowing and a different "posture" on the part of the human knower. God and the things of God are now in a sense absent, and, accordingly, human knowing occurs now by faith rather than by sight. The pre-lapsarian "eye of contemplation" saw divine things that were directly present to it; now there is only that "knowledge whereby God absent is now sought in faith."[66] "Man now seeks through faith the Maker whose face he does not see."[67] Thus, "if the highest good is rightly believed to be man's contemplation of his Creator, not unfittingly is faith, through which he begins in some manner to see [God] absent, said to be the beginning of good and the first step in his restoration."[68] Faith itself, then, "is the sacrament," the efficacious sign, "of future contemplation."[69]

All this is a backdrop for Hugh's conception of post-lapsarian, theological meditation. To meditate *theologically* "is to search out the hidden things of the sacraments of God."[70] "From the beginning at no time were the sacraments of God lacking by which the faithful people might be nourished unto the perception of the invisible and excited unto cognition."[71] So, still speaking of the sacraments in the most general sense – pertaining to things, deeds, and words[72] – Hugh observes:

> The sacraments were also instituted on account of instruction (*eruditionem*), so that, through what is seen externally in the visible species of the sacrament, the human mind may be instructed to recognize the invisible power which is within in the reality of the sacrament. For man, who knew visible things but did not know invisible things, could by no means have recognized divine things unless stimulated by human things. And on this account, while the invisible

[64] Zinn, "Book and Word," 149.

[65] Zinn, "Suger, Theology, and the Pseudo-Dionysian Tradition," 35.

[66] *Sacr.*, 1.6.14 (*PL* 176.271C; Deferrari 103). [67] *Archa Noe*, 4.3 (Sicard 93.34–35; CSMV 129).

[68] *Sacr.*, 1.10.4 (*PL* 176.342D; Deferrari 181).

[69] *Sacr.*, 1.10.4 (*PL* 176.342D; Deferrari 181). Not surprisingly, Hugh analyzes faith in terms of matter and form: the "matter" of faith is the understanding of things that are absent, "received from hearing" and "made manifest from the significance of words"; faith's "form" is the posture or intentionality of belief that such things are true. So, when the "form" (*substantia*) of belief is added to the "matter" (*materiam*) of cognition, there is faith (*Sacr.*, 1.10.3 [*PL* 176.331D; Deferrari 169]).

[70] *Sacr.*, 1.10.3 (*PL* 176.332A; Deferrari 169). [71] *Sacr.*, 2.6.8 (*PL* 176.455C; Deferrari 296).

[72] *Sacr.*, 1.9.6 (*PL* 176.326B–327A; Deferrari 163–64).

good which he lost is returned to him, the significance of the same is offered to him externally through visible species, that he may be stimulated externally and restored internally.[73]

Yet, as has just been shown, what is needed is not simply the recovery of accurate, notional knowledge of God, derived from created *visibilia*, but the restoration of the interior, contemplative knowledge of God *within* the soul.

THEOLOGICAL MEDITATION AND ALLEGORICAL EXPOSITION OF SCRIPTURE

In light of the foregoing, the claim that the "book of Scripture" is the primary object of meditative practices does not surprise. "We shall give ourselves up gladly to meditation, and to the teaching of Divine Scriptures, so that by applying ourselves to reading and meditation the eye of our mind may once more be enlightened."[74] Again: "But what shall I call Scripture if not an orchard? Its thoughts, like so many sweetest fruits, we pick as we read and chew as we consider them."[75] *On Meditation* notes that "meditation in reading [Scripture]" occurs in three ways: "according to history, allegory, and tropology."[76] The first "exercises" the reader in reflecting on and especially admiring God's works, as recorded in Scripture.[77] The third (to be considered in the next chapter), explores the moral meaning. The second attends to the deeper meaning of the historical events "as is required for understanding and for constructing the form of the faith (*ad intelligentiam et fidei formam fabricandam*)."[78] Meditation through allegorical exposition, *allegoresis*, is in fact the quintessential intellectual practice, by which believers pursue an understanding of the mysteries of the faith, conceived of as an act of intellectual construction.[79] This, for Hugh, is what the work of theology entails.

Book 6 of the *Didascalicon* considers the practice of allegorical exposition at length. As he had done for literal-historical reading, Hugh indicates which biblical books are most appropriate for *allegoresis*:

The beginning of Genesis on the works of the six days; the three last books of Moses on the mysteries of the Law; Isaias; the beginning and end of Ezekiel; Job, the Psalter, the Canticle of Canticles; two Gospels in particular, namely those of Matthew and John; the Epistles of Paul; the canonical Epistles, and the

[73] *Sacr.*, 1.9.3 (*PL* 176.320A–B; Deferrari 157). [74] *Archa Noe*, 2.7 (Sicard 45.72–74; CSMV 86).
[75] *Didasc.*, 5.5 (Buttimer 103.25–27; Taylor 126–27).
[76] *Meditatione* (Baron 48.46–47). [77] *Meditatione* (Baron 48.49–50).
[78] *Meditatione* (Baron 48.56–57). [79] *Didasc.*, 6.3 (Buttimer 116.13ff.; Taylor 138).

Apocalypse; but especially the Epistles of Paul, which even by their very number show that they contain the perfection of the two Testaments.[80]

This list follows the canonical, largely historical, sequence of the biblical books, but Hugh cautions that the proper order for allegorical reading is not the "order of time," as in literal-historical exposition, but the "order of knowledge." So, the New Testament, "in which the evident truth is preached," should be read before the Old, "in which the same truth is announced in a hidden manner."[81] Order is crucial, for "whoever does not keep to an order and a method in the reading of so great a collection of books wanders as it were into the very thick of the forest and loses the path of the direct route."[82]

Indulging the Gregorian, architectural image of Scripture as an edifice, Hugh locates allegory as the constructive activity of building up a theological structure upon the foundation laid by *memoria*: "by pursuing the 'typical' meaning, build up a structure in your mind to be a fortress of faith."[83] The construction image is especially apt here because the transition from history to allegory (we might say from historical-critical to constructive theology) is not necessarily straightforward. It requires well-honed theological sensibilities, "matured mental abilities,"[84] which Hugh compares to the skills of medieval stone-masons. The foundation of the literal-historical meaning is rough and uneven: "It contains many things which seem both to be opposed to each other and, sometimes, to impart something which smacks of the absurd or the impossible." It lacks "smoothly fitted stones."[85] On the other hand, the theological structure to be built upon it "demands a smoothly proportioned construction (*aequalem structuram*)."[86] At the literal level, "many things are found to disagree," yet "the divine deeper meaning can never be absurd, never false"; it "admits no contradiction, is always fitting, always true (*semper congrua, semper vera*)."[87] In it "many things can be different from one another, but none can be opposed."[88] What Hugh suggests here is that the theological structure cannot be constructed *directly* upon the rough, uneven foundation of history. Rather, an apt placement of smooth, well-shaped stones to form a flush surface is required. He elaborates:

The first course of stones to be laid upon the foundation [of history] is placed flush with a taut cord – and these are the stones upon which the entire weight of

80 *Didasc.*, 6.4 (Buttimer 122.18ff.; Taylor 144).
81 *Didasc.*, 6.6 (Buttimer 123.13–16; Taylor 145).
82 *Didasc.*, 5.5 (Buttimer 103.27–29; Taylor 127).
83 *Didasc.*, 6.3 (Buttimer 116.24; Taylor 138).
84 *Didasc.*, 6.4 (Buttimer 117.28; Taylor 139).
85 *Didasc.*, 6.4 (Buttimer 118.20–21; Taylor 140).
86 *Didasc.*, 6.4 (Buttimer 118.21; Taylor 140).
87 *Didasc.*, 6.11 (Buttimer 128.20–23; Taylor 149–50).
88 *Didasc.*, 6.4 (Buttimer 118.25–26; Taylor 140).

the others rests and to which they are fitted [*coaptatur*] … This is like a sort of second foundation … This foundation both carries what is placed upon it and is itself carried by the first foundation. All things rest upon the first foundation but are not fitted [*coaptantur*] to it in every way. As to the second foundation everything else both rests upon it and is fitted [*coaptantur*] to it.[89]

Allegoresis, then, begins by laying an initial, *theological* foundation – a "second foundation" – which mediates between the first foundation of history, rough and uneven, and the theological structure to be constructed subsequently upon it. What is this "second foundation"? It is the core principle of the Christian faith, the "principles of the mysteries"[90] and "certain principles of the faith,"[91] and "sound faith";[92] in short, it is the rule of faith.

Upon this second foundation, the "superstructure rises in many courses of stones." Hugh now lists eight levels: (1) Trinity; (2) Creation; (3) Fall/Sin; (4) Natural Law; (5) Mosaic Law; (6) Incarnation; (7) New Testament and Church; and (8) Last Things.[93] These comprise the "whole of divinity," and together are a "spiritual structure raised on high."[94] Hugh does not indicate where this particular arrangement of theological "stone courses" originated. It appears to be his own ordering of theological *loci*, derived in large part from the theo-logic of salvation history. Whatever the case, early in the twentieth century, scholars noticed that this eight-course theological structure in the *Didascalicon* corresponds (in large part) to the outline of Hugh's great *summa* of theology, his *De sacramentis*,[95] and this correspondence forges a crucial link between these two works. The *De sacramentis* emerges as an adjunct text for the practice of allegorical reading of Scripture, outlined in the *Didascalicon*, as is patent in the Prologue to the *summa*: "By this work, if they firmly establish their souls on that foundation (*fundamentum*) of the knowledge of faith, so that other things acquired by reading or hearing may be constructed upon (*superaedificare*) it, they may remain unshaken."[96] In effect, Hugh presents the *De sacramentis* as a means by which a doctrinal structure may be constructed upon a foundation of faith (itself in turn resting on the first foundation laid down through literal-historical exposition). The sheer size and scope

89 *Didasc.*, 6.4 (Buttimer 118.26–119.2; Taylor 140–41).
90 *Didasc.*, 6.4 (Buttimer 119.26–27; Taylor 141).
91 *Didasc.*, 6.4 (Buttimer 120.2; Taylor 142). 92 *Didasc.*, 6.4 (Buttimer 121.10; Taylor 143).
93 *Didasc.*, 6.4 (Buttimer 119.9ff.; Taylor 141). 94 *Didasc.*, 6.4 (Buttimer 119.25–26; Taylor 141).
95 See Taylor, *The Didascalicon of Hugh of St. Victor*, 223, n. 15, crediting G. Robert, *Les Ecoles et l'enseignement de la théologie pendant la première moitié du XIIe siècle* (Paris, 1909), 140–48, with noticing in *Didasc.*, 6.4 "a sketch later filled out in the *De sacramentis*."
96 *Sacr.*, 1.Prol. (*PL* 176.183; Deferrari 3; trans. modified).

of the *De sacramentis* easily distracts from the fact that the overarching structure is of greatest importance. Acquaintance with this structure and familiarity with the essential principles associated with each doctrinal heading allow the allegorical exegete to interpret with theological competence any scriptural passage whatsoever. That is, to this doctrinal structure, further theological affirmations may be added without compromising its architectural integrity. Returning to the *Didascalicon*, Hugh indicates how this occurs by comparing *allegoresis* to the guild-craft of stone-masons. "Take a look at what a mason does," says Hugh:

> When the foundation has been laid, he stretches out his string in a straight line, he drops his plumb line, and then, one by one he lays the diligently polished stones in a row. Then he asks for other stones, and still others, and if by chance he finds some that do not fit with the fixed course he has laid, he takes his file, smoothes off the protruding parts, files down the rough spots, and the places that do not fit, reduces to form (*forma*), and so at last joins them to the rest of the stones set into the row. But if he finds some to be such that they cannot either be made smaller or be fitly shaped (*congrue coaptari*), he does not use these lest perhaps while he labors to grind down the stone he should break his file.[97]

Again: equipped with the principles of faith, the exegete should "take those things which [he finds] clear and, if it should be that they conform, add them to the proper base. The doubtful things interpret in such a way that they may not be discordant (*discordent*)."[98] Hugh does not hesitate here. His exegete knows how to "bend all Scriptural passages whatever into fitting interpretations and to judge both what is out of keeping with sound faith and what is consonant with it."[99] He offers the Trinity as an example. "First learn briefly and clearly what is to be believed about the Trinity, what you ought unquestionably to profess and believe."[100] Thus doctrinally formed, one can read widely, though also critically and judiciously, on matters Trinitarian, determining what is consonant with right faith. In sum, *allegoresis* is an act of theological construction that builds up a doctrinal structure of faith.

It must be recalled and stressed at this point that for Hugh *allegoresis* is a species of *meditatio*; or, better, *allegoresis* is a tool and strategy for a central meditative practice. Just as he conceived of reading-for-memory (see previous chapter), so he posits allegory-for-meditation, or what might be called "meditative *allegoresis*." This link between allegory and meditation is clear in the common act that he ascribes to each. Both penetrate

97 *Didasc.*, 6.4 (Buttimer 118.10–18; Taylor 140).
98 *Didasc.*, 6.4 (Buttimer 120.24; Taylor 142).
99 *Didasc.*, 6.4 (Buttimer 121.7–11; Taylor 143).
100 *Didasc.*, 6.4 (Buttimer 120.18–20; Taylor 142).

the surface of things in order to apprehend deeper realities "under" what appears; in Hugh's terms, both penetrate the sacramental *visibilia* of created reality, more precisely, the visible realities (*res*) of salvation history mediated through Scripture, in order to arrive at the *invisibilia* of divine things. This is, however, only the preliminary task, which yields the material for the next. Subsequently, as noted in the Introduction above, meditation "gathers together" the theological "similitudes" drawn from allegorical interpretation that are "constructive of faith (*ad fidei aedificationem*),"[101] and "imposes form"[102] on the matter derived from historical reading, just as allegory erects a theological structure of faith. In short, meditative *allegoresis* is an act of constructive, theological thinking that produces a coherent synthesis of doctrine.

Linking *allegoresis* and *meditatio* thus allows the density and sophistication of Hugh's conception of theological thought to begin to emerge. It requires the mental energy and effort required in any act of meditation, described above. It is intellectually demanding, even agonistic. To give theological scrutiny to the deeper meaning of Scripture summons forth all the cognitive resources that can be mustered in its effort, all the training in the liberal arts, both the trivium and especially the quadrivium, as well as the requisite time, diligence, and commitment. At the same time, the constructive dimension entails a degree of creative freedom and individual, theo-aesthetic judgment, not only in uncovering fitting, doctrinal meanings in the *sacramenta*, but even more so in the construction of the larger theological structure or synthesis of doctrine. Although the individual theological insights or affirmations (excavated by *allegoresis* from the quarry of history laid out in memory) must be made to conform to ecclesially determined orthodoxy (e.g., to Christological or Trinitarian dogma, i.e., the "second foundation") like so many well-hewn stones, the ultimate arrangement of the "stone courses" in the theological superstructure is, to some degree, a function of the theo-aesthetic judgment of the architect. Orthodoxy is not "pre-fabricated" *in its overarching structure*; that is, the arrangement of the "stone courses" is not pre-determined. Ultimately, fittingness, proportion, and coherence, in relation to the rule of faith and the overarching "logic" of salvation history, determine the probity of theo-exegetical judgments. Accordingly, for Hugh at least, *allegoresis* is much more than finding a deeper, theological meaning in a particular scriptural pericope (which can indeed seem fanciful and forced to moderns); that is only the preliminary task. The ultimate goal is a well-built, doctrinal

[101] See page 164, n. 5 above. [102] See page 164, n. 6 above.

synthesis, both sound and pleasing "architecturally," into which further theological insights may be inserted without compromising the structural integrity of the whole.

But more must be said. Hugh's second-person directives in the *Didascalicon* regarding *allegoresis* are not merely rhetorical flourishes. When he says, "as *you* are about to build," lay the foundation and build up the structure "in *your* mind";[103] or "*you* are about to construct the spiritual building," the litero-historical foundations of which "have been laid *in you*"[104] (emphases added), these are more than figures of speech. At the very least, this language gestures at the profound way in which meditative *allegoresis* entails an interiorization of theological thought, a personal appropriation of doctrine, imaged here as an act of interior construction, in which layer upon layer of doctrinal "stone courses" are built up into a theological structure within. Similarly, of the entire *De sacramentis* he says: "I have compressed this brief *summa*, as it were, of all doctrine into one continuous work, that the soul may have something definite to which it may affix and conform (*conformare*) its attention,"[105] and we recall from above that meditation "re-forms the soul" fragmented by ignorance.[106] The theologian-exegete must do the construction within. The doctrinal construct is neither "ready-made," nor an external system of doctrinal propositions disconnected from the believing exegete, remote from his lived existence.

For Hugh, then, contrary to modern conceptions of both exegesis and theology, neither exegetical facility with the biblical text, nor the text of his *De sacramentis* were the ultimate concern or the final product of theological endeavor; rather, the theologically formed soul of the exegete was. Accordingly, it seems likely that his *summa* is not meant to be an expression of theological originality in its content, which may explain why he so liberally incorporates large tracts of material from earlier authors; nor is it meant to be a final statement of all Christian doctrine, in the manner in which such *summae* were later conceived. His goal is not "Hugonian theology," but a useful, theologically structured compendium of doctrine, drawing deeply from the tradition, to equip his students to be theologically deft readers of Scripture and to be themselves changed and formed – rather, re-formed – in the process.

In fine, *allegoresis* is meditative; *meditatio* is allegoro-theological. Meditation gives *allegoresis* an internalized, personally appropriated

[103] *Didasc.*, 6.3 (Buttimer 116.22–24; Taylor 138; emphasis added).
[104] *Didasc.*, 6.4 (Buttimer 119.27–28; Taylor 141; emphasis added).
[105] *Sacr.*, 1.Prol. (*PL* 176.183; Deferrari 3; trans. modified). [106] See page 165, n. 8 above.

quality and a soul-forming *telos*; allegory gives *meditatio* theological content. Meditative *allegoresis* for Hugh, as Carruthers emphasized, is a constructive theological practice of thought that generates a theological structure in the soul on the basis of the salvation-historical realities – the "works of restoration" – which have already been assimilated through reading-for-memory as a foundation.

THEOLOGICAL MEDITATION AND THE *ARCHA NOE*

This conception of meditative *allegoresis* is nowhere more evident in Hugh's corpus than in his oft-noted treatise, *On Noah's Ark*. That treatise begins with the literal ark of Noah, as described in Genesis 6, but this biblical boat soon becomes a symbol of Christ, the church, Scripture, the whole of salvation history (and indeed the cosmos), as well as the individual human person.

As noted in the Preface to Part III, the treatise is the product of a *collatio*, a discussion of student-brothers gathered around Master Hugh, which finds its point of departure in their collective wonder at the restlessness of the human heart. Significantly, restlessness is cast in terms of *instabilitas*. The question is whether it can be remedied "by any skill or practice of some discipline."[107] Hugh's affirmative answer emphasizes that, though the remedy is a work of grace, God yet desires that we "work along with him."[108] Both God and man are "employed upon the work," and "these two work together."[109]

The root of *instabilitas* is disordered love. Before the Fall, the human soul was unified and stable in its interior, contemplative love of the One God. The Fall, however, produced the blindness of ignorance and the extroversion to the external multiplicity of created things, noted above. These became the illicit objects of human affection and the result was disordered love, which dissipates and disintegrates the soul (see Chapter 3). This is "love of the world." The remedy is to recover the "love of God,"[110] which will "integrate and stabilize our hearts."[111] But how? Hugh's starkly simple answer is this: recovery of the knowledge of God. "Nobody can love that which he does not know; and so, if we desire to love God, we must first make it our business to know him."[112] Once rightly known, God will be loved "automatically," for "so great is the beauty of his loveliness

[107] *Archa Noe*, 1.1 (Sicard 3.1–9; CSMV 45). [108] *Archa Noe*, 1.1 (Sicard 4.23; CSMV 46).
[109] *Archa Noe*, 4.1 (Sicard 88.66–67; CSMV 124). [110] *Archa Noe*, 1.1 (Sicard 5.59–60; CSMV 47).
[111] *Archa Noe*, 1.2 (Sicard 7.22–25; CSMV 48). [112] *Archa Noe*, 1.2 (Sicard 7.26–27; CSMV 48).

(*species pulchritudinis*)" that "he cannot be known without being loved."[113] Such knowledge, though, can only come from familiarity with God and so one must inhabit the place that God does. "Let us inquire where God dwells."[114] Where is the house of God?

To be sure, God inhabits the whole creation as a king in a kingdom; he abides in the church as a *paterfamilias*. In particular, though, he indwells every faithful soul who truly loves God, as a bridegroom in a wedding chamber.[115] Such a soul is the truest, most intimate "house of God."[116] The difficulty, though, is that, as a result of the Fall, the soul must be re-constructed in order adequately to accommodate the divine Spouse. "Let us build [His dwelling]," exhorts Hugh, "for, if we have prepared a place for Him, He will gladly come to us, He who made us that He might indwell us, even Jesus Christ our Lord."[117] How does the soul become again a place of divine indwelling? "By knowledge and by love,"[118] but, again, Hugh emphasizes the first, since love will follow spontaneously. He relates these to one another, characteristically, in architectural terms: "knowledge erects the structure of faith by knowing, whereas love, like an adorning color, embellishes the building by its virtue."[119]

Hugh is now poised to introduce the titular theme of the treatise. The remedy, which the remainder of the treatise explains at length, is to build this house of God in the soul in the manner of an ark: "Now therefore, enter your own inmost heart, and make a dwelling place for God. Make Him a temple, make Him a house, make Him a pavilion, make Him an ark of the covenant, make Him an ark of the flood; no matter what you call it, it is all one house of God."[120] The final item in this list of biblical structures is the first "salvific structure" recorded in Scripture: Noah's ark, conceived by divine providence as a means of human salvation, but constructed by Noah himself. That in one breath Hugh includes it with various other biblical edifices suggests that, while he has chosen to symbolize this "skill or practice" with Noah's vessel, the soul-constructing activity itself is far more significant than its symbolization. The same impression emerges later in the work, when Hugh says:

He who requires [that you build an ark within yourself] is a skillful builder, and He chooses others to be builders too. We have learnt of many who were trained by Him from the testimony of Holy Scripture. He taught Noah to build the ark.

[113] *Archa Noe*, 1.2 (Sicard 7.28–30; CSMV 48). [114] *Archa Noe*, 1.2 (Sicard 7.35–36; CSMV 49).
[115] *Archa Noe*, 1.2 (Sicard 8.47–48; CSMV 49).
[116] *Archa Noe*, 1.2 (Sicard 8.54; CSMV 49); see Chapter 5 above.
[117] *Archa Noe*, 1.2 (Sicard 8.71; CSMV 50). [118] *Archa Noe*, 1.3 (Sicard 9.1–2; CSMV 50).
[119] *Archa Noe*, 1.3 (Sicard 9.4–7; CSMV 50). [120] *Archa Noe*, 1.3 (Sicard 9.18; CSMV 51).

He showed Moses the pattern on which he was to build the ark [of the covenant]. He taught Bezaleel. He enlightened Solomon with wisdom, that he might build a temple to His name. Paul the apostle too He made a builder.[121]

All these examples are meant to inspire: like them "you will build a house for the Lord your God *in and of yourself*" (emphasis added).[122]

But what does this mean, that "we must build [an ark] within ourselves" by "an unseen process of construction"?[123] Hugh's twofold answer corresponds to the two modes of divine indwelling noted above, through knowledge and love. There is both an ark "which wisdom builds daily in our hearts *through meditation* [emphasis added]," which is "realized in knowledge," and an ark which "grace effects in us by joining together many virtues in a single charity," which is "realized in virtue."[124] These are clear references to allegorical and tropological interpretation, respectively; the "ark of wisdom" corresponds to the first; the "ark of virtue" to the second. But again Hugh clarifies his present concern: "the special subject we have undertaken to discuss is the ark of wisdom."[125] Meditation, then, aligned with allegorical exposition, is the practice by which this "ark of wisdom" is constructed within.[126]

What exactly is the "ark of wisdom"? As in the *Didascalicon* above, it is the interiorized, personally appropriated, mental construct derived from the salvation-historical realities ("works of restoration") through allegorical exposition. What allegory uncovers "in the sphere of existence" is to be constructed into an ark of wisdom "in the sphere of thought."[127] "Let us therefore have right thoughts … for of such matter we shall build our ark";[128] and "the matter is pure thoughts"[129] and "reasonable thoughts."[130] Hugh's platonic metaphysics undergirds his point:

For things have their own kind of being in the mind of man, where even those which, in themselves, are past can coexist with those yet to come. And in this respect the rational soul bears a certain resemblance to its Maker. For as in the mind of God the causes of all things exist eternally without change or temporal differentiation, so also in our minds things past, things present, and things future exist together *by means of thought* [emphasis added].[131]

[121] *Archa Noe*, 4.1 (Sicard 87.35–40; CSMV 123).
[122] *Archa Noe*, 4.1 (Sicard 87.30–31; CSMV 123).
[123] *Archa Noe*, 1.3 (Sicard 17.221–33; CSMV 59).
[124] *Archa Noe*, 1.3 (Sicard 17.236–39; CSMV 59).
[125] *Archa Noe*, 1.3 (Sicard 17.247; CSMV 60).
[126] The tropological ark of virtue will be treated in the next chapter.
[127] *Archa Noe*, 2.1 (Sicard 33.4–5; CSMV 73).
[128] *Archa Noe*, 2.1 (Sicard 33.19–20; CSMV 73).
[129] *Archa Noe*, 4.1 (Sicard 86.9; CSMV 122).
[130] *Archa Noe*, 4.1 (Sicard 88.63; CSMV 124).
[131] *Archa Noe*, 2.1 (Sicard 33.11; CSMV 73).

Hugh can stress so realistically the soul-forming nature of theological meditation because he assumes a kind of realist or semi-realist existence of platonic forms. These have an actual existence in the human mind and can thus actually form it. Moreover, to be formed thus is to participate in the divine mind in some fashion. Here is the link with Hugh's exemplarism, noted earlier (see Chapters 1, 4), which Hugh makes explicit with an appeal to divine Wisdom, the master-Architect:

He is Himself the Wisdom whereof it is said, "Wisdom hath builded her house," and in another place the selfsame wisdom shows where and out of what material the house has been made, saying, 'I, wisdom, dwell in counsel and am present in reasonable thoughts …' it is clear, therefore, that wisdom builds herself a house in the heart of man out of reasonable thoughts.[132]

The "ark of wisdom" is ultimately the structure built by Wisdom itself out of thought.

While the *Didascalicon* employed a generic construction metaphor, here Hugh adopts the particular structure of Noah's ark to symbolize meditation's act of interiorization and appropriation. "Let us consider the measurements of the ark and how they may be realized in us."[133] To range in thought over the length of salvation history is to make "the lengthwise measure of your heart three hundred cubits," that is, the length of the literal ark. And, "if you review the Church in thought and, having contemplated the believer's way of life, adopt it as your pattern (*exemplum*), you stretch your heart to fifty cubits wide." And, "if you have acquired the knowledge of Scripture, which is comprised in thirty books, you build up your heart to the height of thirty cubits." "This," in short, "is the ark that you must build."[134] The dimensions of the ark are to become the dimensions of a structure built up in the soul. "For what is expressed visibly in a figure in this house is exhibited entirely through invisible truth in the human soul."[135] "Ponder and meditate unceasingly upon the mysteries of your restoration," says Hugh in a related treatise, "and you have entered into the ark."[136]

The significance of the ark-symbol is that in Hugh's hands it is a theological construction, depicting a theological interpretation of all of reality, especially salvation history, and a visual principle, as it were, for organizing and inter-relating theological claims, a visual patterning of theological

[132] *Archa Noe*, 4.1 (Sicard 88.58–64; CSMV 124). [133] *Archa Noe*, 2.1 (Sicard 34.32–33; CSMV 74).
[134] *Archa Noe*, 2.1 (Sicard 34.38–43; CSMV 74). [135] *Sacr.*, 2.5.1 (*PL* 176. 439B–C; Deferrari 279).
[136] *Vanitate*, 2.3 (*PL* 176.717B; CSMV 177). *PL* reference is followed by CSMV's translation in *Selected Spiritual Writings*.

data. It is not simply an elaborate memory-storage and retrieval device. Hugh already assumes that salvation-historical information is ready to hand in *memoria*; rather, its very structure makes constructive, theological claims about reality. More precisely, with the ark-symbol, Hugh synthetically represents a sapiential conception of Christ's salvific work as the structural center of reality (see Chapter 4), a corresponding view of the church and its sacramental efficacy (see Chapter 5), as well as Scripture's deep structure (see Chapter 6), and a theological anthropology, all within an overarching theology of history and cosmos. In it:

> All the works of restoration are contained in all their fullness, from the world's beginning to its end; therein is represented the condition of the universal Church. Into it is woven the story of events, in it are found the mysteries of the sacraments, and there are set out the stages of the affections, thoughts, meditations, contemplations, good works, virtues, and rewards. There we are shown what we ought to believe, and do, and hope. There, the form of man's living and the sum total of perfection are contained. There that which is hidden comes to light, there burdensome tasks seem easy, and matters which might in isolation seem unfortunate are seen to be appropriate. There the sum of things is displayed, and the harmony of its elements explained. … There the present does not follow on the past, nor the does the future supervene upon the present, but whatsoever is there, is there as in the present.[137]

In short, the ark-symbol is a synthetic, constructive symbolization of the "works of restoration." By comparison with the "works of creation," which are myriad and nearly unlimited, the "works of restoration" are few (though still varied, to relieve tedium). From one people, in one place, came one Savior – yet for the whole world. This intimates the desired unity toward which salvation moves. Accordingly, the ark-symbol gathers together those "works of restoration" into a single whole, so that they may become the focus of salvific theological meditation.[138] A divinely instituted "order of things," it generates an "order of our thoughts," whereby they "can be reintegrated," so that "a spiritual house of wisdom could be built in us (*spiritualis domus sapientiae in nobis aedificari possit*)."[139] The ark sets out visually the "order and arrangement there should be in our thoughts, so that a house for God may be built out of them."[140]

To build the ark of wisdom within is to appropriate and interiorize mentally, through meditative *allegoresis*, those realities thus symbolized,

[137] *Archa Noe*, 4.9 (Sicard 115.135–116.150; CSMV 152).
[138] See *Archa Noe*, 4.10 (Sicard 98.1–101.75; CSMV 134–37).
[139] *Archa Noe*, 4.8 (Sicard 110.153f.; CSMV 146) (Rorem's translation).
[140] *Archa Noe*, 4.1 (Sicard 89.84–86; CSMV 125).

to re-structure the soul with these particular theological claims, with this constructive synthesis. "Now the figure of this spiritual building which I am going to present to you is Noah's Ark. This your eye shall see outwardly, so that your soul may be fashioned to its likeness inwardly."[141] With this "ark of wisdom" constructed in the soul, the desired *stabilitas* is recovered. Through meditative *allegoresis*, "we may finally arrive at true, God-like *stabilitas*."[142] And, "through meditation" the soul is "converted" to the likeness of God.[143]

The ark-symbol appears thus as a paradigmatic instance of Hugh's theory of meditative *allegoresis*, reflecting its synthetic, constructive, personally appropriated character. On display here is his platonic conception of reality, undergirding the symbolic, theo-aesthetic orientation of his conception of theology, as well as the profound "architectural intuition" that governs much of it. Ultimately, such theological thought is receptive, inventive, and constructive. It is *receptive* in that the arrangement of the doctrinal "stone courses" essentially corresponds to the logic of salvation history, conforming to the sacramental "order of things" or "works of restoration" found in salvation history, mediated through Scripture, and to the creedal fundamentals of the church's faith. It is *inventive* in that the exegetical activity of uncovering the deeper meanings of the *sacramenta* through *allegoresis* requires intellectual ingenuity and skill, as well as well-formed theological sensibilities. It is *constructive*, in that the symbolized synthesis of theological thought requires the creative ability of the theologian to "put it all together" within himself, as the very act of mental symbolization is an act of personal appropriation. In some sense it is an actual, interior, construction process. Yet, it is also clear that Hugh does not posit the ark-symbol as the only way such theological meditation can or should proceed. It is but one example; presumably, others could and even should be employed.

MEDITATING ON THE VANITY, BEAUTY, AND MORAL SIGNIFICANCE OF CREATION

An additional dimension of the ark-symbol as an image of the theologically re-structured mind is that it not only lends itself to imaging the personally appropriated nature of theological thought, but also allows Hugh

[141] *Archa Noe*, 1.3 (Sicard 10.35–37; CSMV 52). [142] *Archa Noe*, 4.2 (Sicard 90.34–35; CSMV 126).
[143] *In hierarchiam* (*PL* 175.1078B). Fassler aptly says: "Hugh's art is meant to initiate transformation, to help remake the observer in God's image" (*Gothic Song*, 218).

to integrate other meditative acts and objects into a coherent framework. That is, stabilized as an "ark of wisdom," the soul can now meditate on other things, especially those very external things, the "works of creation," which had before threatened to dissipate and disintegrate it.

Noah's literal ark had a window at the top, from which Noah released a dove to see whether the flood waters had resided (cf. Gen. 8:8–11). In *De archa Noe*, this movement of the dove symbolizes three additional acts of meditation. Hugh stresses that these forms of "going out" into meditation on external things prompt the soul ultimately to return within. Like the dove that Noah released from the window, the soul does not linger in these "external" acts of meditation, but always returns to the ark. Yet, the dove always brings something back with her, symbolized by the olive branch, which is then internalized or assimilated in the interior meditation within the ark.[144]

First, there is meditation on created things in themselves, which focuses on the vanity, the ephemeral emptiness of created things: "all things are vanity because, just as each creature comes into being out of nothing, so too its daily changes show that of itself it also tends to nothing."[145] Hugh pursues this kind of meditation at length in his *De vanitate mundi*. That work fairly drips with a poignant ambivalence about the love-worthiness of creation, which colors his meditative enjoyment of its beauty. The wonders of the visible world, marvelous though they are, are fleeting, ephemeral, and transient. Their mutability makes them ultimately incapable of offering a stable object to the soul's knowledge (and ultimately its love). This mutability of created things is captured repeatedly in the image of flowing water. "While this life lasts, you should think of this entire world, because of the mutability of everything, as if it were a flood of down-coursing waters."[146] These dissipate both themselves and the souls of those whose loving attention to such things provokes an inappropriate attachment. If "the soul through cupidity immerses itself in all that is borne down in the flood, it is forthwith torn by countless distractions, and, being somehow divided from itself, it is dispersed abroad."[147] Perceiving

[144] *Archa Noe*, 2.3–4 (Sicard 38.39–39.1–21; CSMV 79–80). In the following discussion, Hugh consistently uses the word "contemplation" to refer to these different forms of meditation. He clearly does not mean contemplation in the sense noted above in this chapter, of interior and direct knowledge of God. The ambiguity is clarified in his first sermon *On Ecclesiastes*, where Hugh distinguishes between two different types of contemplation: one related to God, and another to creatures. The second is virtually indistinguishable from, and falls under the larger category of, meditation.

[145] *Archa Noe*, 2.2 (Sicard 36.47–50; CSMV 77). [146] *Vanitate*, 2.2 (*PL* 176.713B; CSMV 174).

[147] *Vanitate*, 2.2 (*PL* 176.713D; CSMV 175).

"the mutability of present things" the soul feels "contempt for the world"[148] and loses its "esteem for all that seems fair in the world." Visible beauty now prods the minds of human persons to seek *within* "the loveliness of their Creator all the more ardently."[149] This desire is the olive branch in leaf which the dove brings back.[150] This return shifts the meditative focus back from the "works of creation" without, to the "works of restoration" within.

This shift, for Hugh, distinguishes the Christian theologian from "pagan philosophers," who investigate the nature of things with curiosity. The latter, only "inquiring into the works of creation, have become futile in their thoughts"; by contrast, "Christian sages, by meditating constantly upon the works of restoration, drive every vanity from theirs."[151] Wise Christians, accordingly, must continually "mount up *from* the works of creation, *by means of* the works of restoration, *to* the Author of creation and restoration." But this ascent is within, Hugh reminds, "inwardly, as taking place by means of steps within the heart."[152] To meditate thus mitigates against a dissipating attachment to temporal things: "if, then, we have begun to live persistently in our own heart through the practice of meditation, we have already in a manner ceased to belong to time; and, having become dead as it were to the world, we are living inwardly with God."[153]

A second kind of meditation, again symbolized by the dove departing and returning with an olive branch in leaf, sees in created things reflections of the divine nature, since "the temporal work mirrors the immutability of the eternal Author of the work."[154] In the treatise on Noah's ark, Hugh mentions how "God's unseen power and wisdom"[155] may be discerned in visible things. This reference to "power and wisdom" is telling, for it establishes a clear link to another of Hugh's works, *On the Three Days*, and provides a clue to its interpretation. This complex theological masterpiece contains an extended reflection on the visible creation, wherein Hugh sees in the immensity, beauty, and utility of creatures a reflection, respectively, of divine power, wisdom, and kindness, which in turn he appropriates, respectively, to the Father, Son, and Holy Spirit.

148 *Archa Noe*, 2.4 (Sicard 39.22–23; CSMV 80). 149 *Archa Noe*, 2.4 (Sicard 39.8–11; CSMV 79).
150 *Archa Noe*, 2.4 (Sicard 39.4; CSMV 79). 151 *Archa Noe*, 4.6 (Sicard 101.9–11; CSMV 137–38).
152 *Archa Noe*, 4.6 (Sicard 102.25–26; CSMV 138).
153 *Archa Noe*, 2.1 (Sicard 33.12–15; CSMV 73). Contrary to first impressions, Hugh is not so much disparaging history and temporality or fleeing from it, as containing it and giving it theological significance by, in some sense, standing above it in order to interpret it as a whole, embracing past, present, and future.
154 *Archa Noe*, 2.2 (Sicard 37.55–56; CSMV 77). 155 *Archa Noe*, 2.4 (Sicard 39.15–17; CSMV 79).

Here, a patently more positive appreciation of the "works of creation" than in *De vanitate mundi* leads Hugh to linger over the myriad ways in which the visible beauty of creation reflects the invisible wisdom of God (cf. Rom. 1:20). In an oft-cited passage, Hugh compares the beauty of the whole universe, the beauty of each individual part of it, to a beautifully illuminated manuscript: "For this whole sensible world is a kind of book written by the finger of God, that is, created by divine power, and each creature is a kind of figure, not invented by human convention, but established by the divine will to manifest and in some way signify the invisible wisdom of God." Not all read this "book" rightly, however. Some, "foolish and carnal," remain fixated on the beautiful appearances and do not penetrate to "the deeper intent of the divine wisdom." So, "it is good to contemplate carefully and wonder at the divine works," Hugh observes, but only if one "knows how to turn the beauty of physical things to spiritual use."[156] Such "spiritual use" means returning to contemplate the "works of restoration" within the ark of wisdom within. For "as often as we learn to marvel at God's unseen power and wisdom in things visible, we bring back, as it were, the olive branches from the waters to the ark," prompting us to "love God within ourselves."[157] So, the wise person "is afraid to be away for long from the safeguard of inward meditation."[158]

Lastly, in *On Noah's Ark* the dove represents a third type of meditation that finds in Scripture and in created things an admonition to render to the Creator an obedience befitting a rational creature, that is, in love, and to flee the consequences of failure to do so, that is, in fear.[159] Returning to the ark admonished thus, the dove-soul is "renewed inwardly by His fear and love."[160] This corresponds to the "meditation on morals," which the *Didascalicon* and *On Meditation* list among the three basic types. The latter offers this description:

Meditation in tropology operates on that which the sayings bring forward, asking about what they insinuate should be done, or what they teach is to be avoided; what is for erudition, what is for exhortation, what is for consolation, what the reading of Scripture proposes for terror, what illuminates for the understanding

[156] *Tribus diebus*, 4 (Poirel, 9–10.94–104): "Universus enim mundus iste sensibilis quasi quidam liber est scriptus digito Dei ... et singulae creaturae quasi figurae quaedam sunt, non humano placito inventae, sed divino arbitrio institutae ad manifestandam et quodammodo significandum invisibilem Dei sapientiam ... Qui autem spiritualis est et omnia diiudicare potest, in eo quidem quod foris considerat pulcritudinem operis, intus concipit quam miranda sit sapientia creatoris." (My translation.)

[157] *Archa Noe*, 2.4 (Sicard 39.19; CSMV 80). [158] *Archa Noe*, 4.13 (Sicard 108.81–82; CSMV 144).

[159] *Archa Noe*, 2.2 (Sicard 37.57–64; CSMV 77) and *Archa Noe*, 2.4 (Sicard 39.20–21; CSMV 80).

[160] *Archa Noe*, 2.4 (Sicard 40.24; CSMV 80).

of virtue, what nourishes the affection, what teaches the form of living (*formam vivendi*) for the journey of virtue.[161]

This reflects Hugh's interest, not only in rightly structured thought, but also in well-formed moral life. We recall from above that, while Hugh's primary focus in the ark treatises was the "ark of wisdom," constructed in the heart through *allegoresis-ad-meditatio*, he gestures as well at an ark which "grace effects in us by joining together many virtues in a single charity," which is "realized in virtue."[162] For, by meditation is gathered together also "whatever is ... instructive of good morals,"[163] and while "knowledge erects the structure of faith by knowing," love, "like an adorning color, embellishes the building by its virtue."[164] As will be seen in the next chapter, this is in fact the immediate goal of rightly structured theological thought. In this way, the "ark of wisdom" will become an "ark of counsel," that is, not a different ark, but the ark of wisdom as it leads to morality:

> If, therefore, you are studying and you have understanding and you already know what must be done, this is the beginning of the good for you, but it is not yet enough; you are not yet perfect. And so, mount into the ark of counsel (*arcem consilii*) and meditate on how you may be able to fulfill what you have learned must be done. For there are many who have knowledge, but few who know in the way it behooves them to know.[165]

Re-structured and stabilized by the doctrinal edifice of faith, built up within through meditative practices, the soul is now able in fear and love to pursue the moral practices that will adorn and beautify the ark-edifice in the soul.

CONCLUSION

For Hugh of St. Victor, the human recovery of contemplative intimacy with God requires a restoration of both the knowledge and love of God lost in the Fall. He conceives of this intimacy as divine indwelling of the human, which corresponds (whether as cause or effect matters

[161] *Meditatione* (Baron 48.57–63): "In tropologia meditatio operatur quem fructum dicta afferant, exquirens quid faciendum insinuent, vel quid doceant esse vitandum; quid ad eruditionem, quid ad exhortationem, quid ad consolationem, quid ad terrorem scripturae lectio proponat, quid ad intelligentiam virtutis illuminet, quid nutriat affectionem, quid formam vivendi ad iter virtutis edoceat."

[162] *Archa Noe*, 1.3 (Sicard 17.236–39; CSMV 59).

[163] *Script.*, 5 (*PL* 175.14A; adapted from Turner's trans.): "postmodum meditando colligas quod vel ad fidei aedificationem, vel ad instructionem bonorum morum per similitudinem adducas."

[164] *Archa Noe*, 1.3 (Sicard 9.4–7; CSMV 50).

[165] *Didasc.*, 5.9 (Buttimer 109.25–110.2; Taylor 132).

ponders in Scripture "the virtues of the saints" and "whatever else there is that serves to improve my conduct and stimulate my spirit." But this is not sufficient. For there is no profit in such knowledge unless the reader begins "to imitate" such virtues and to take these examples as "a pattern for living." This is the second story, where the exegete is "to perform good and profitable actions." Yet, profitable though they are, virtuous actions must lead further to the interior acquisition of the virtues themselves: "to possess within myself the virtue which I show in outward works." This is to ascend into the final story of the ark. Hugh labels these stories, respectively, knowledge, works, and virtue, or, similarly, knowledge (*scientia*), discipline (*disciplina*), and goodness (*bonitas*).[32] They constitute and encompass tropology, the moral life and its practices, and in their ordered sequence chart a process of moral re-formation.

Better integrated into the larger framework of his thought is the notion that *moralia* is a means of more deeply indwelling the "ark of wisdom." In a short treatise on the nature of love,[33] Hugh puts it thus: "let us build an ark so that we might have sound faith, then, let us indwell the ark of faith through charity, so that we may believe what we ought to love and love what we believe. And so let both the law of God be in our hearts through the cognition of right faith and our hearts be in the law of God through love."[34] Indeed, for Hugh, "the perfect man" is he "who loves what he believes."[35]

Third, perhaps most typically, Hugh thinks of *moralia* as the aesthetic finish (intimated above) to the entire process of construction that began with a litero-historical foundation laid down in memory and upon which was then built a doctrinal framework or structure in "the ark of wisdom." After laying the foundation and constructing the building, one ought, "through the loveliness of morality, to paint the structure over as with the most beautiful of colors."[36] Hugh can evoke this aesthetic *telos* variously, pastorally, for example, as when he compares Scripture to a flowery meadow

[32] *Archa Noe*, 2.5 (Sicard 41.36–40; CSMV 82) and also *Archa Noe*, 4.9 (Sicard 115.112–13; CSMV 151).

[33] Hugh of St. Victor, *Quid vere diligendum sit, in Six opuscules spirituels*. Introduction, critical text, French translation, and notes by Roger Baron. SC 155 (Paris: Editions du Cerf, 1969), 94–99. Cited as *Quid vere*. Translations are mine.

[34] *Quid vere* (Baron, 98:49–55): "Primum ergo si hoc mare magnum illaesi pertransire volumus, fabricemus navem, ut fidem integram habeamus. Deinde navem fidei inhabitemus per charitatem, ut et credamus quod diligere debemus, et diligamus quod credimus. Sicque et lex Dei in corde nostro sit per rectae fidei cognitionem, et cor nostrum in lege Dei sit per dilectionem."

[35] *Archa Noe*, 4.8 (Sicard 106.41; CSMV 142).

[36] *Didasc.*, 6.3 (Buttimer 116.24–25; Taylor 138) quoting Gregory the Great. See Taylor, *The Didascalicon of Hugh of St. Victor*, 223, n. 9.

in which "the animals of God are fed, in which are found the diverse precepts of the virtues, like flowers for decorating souls." Hugh explains: "We run in this field when we read divine Scripture; we gather flowers, when we learn the precepts; we adorn our clothes, when we decorate our souls with the virtues by fulfilling the commands. For patience is in the rose, chastity in the lily, charity in the crocus, humility in the violet, purity in the sapphire."[37] More commonly, though, the architectural imagery comes to the fore, as love, "like an adorning color, embellishes the building by its virtue"[38] and the student acquires "virtue to adorn your soul."[39] Such a one "embraces the beauty of morality (*moralitatis gratiam*)."[40]

In the end, these strategies are mutually compatible and one need not choose exclusively between them, since, "while the truth remains the same, the exposition of [the ark] may be multiplied."[41] What they compositely affirm is that *moralia* is the culmination of the re-forming process. Those who love God alone "build upon a foundation of gold, silver, and precious stones. In the love of virtue is gold; in the understanding of truth, silver; in the consummation of good works, precious stones."[42] This *finale* (Rorem's apt term) is represented by the constructive completion of the entire structure, both as the architectural form reaches its apex, narrowing as it does to a single square cubit, and as it is adorned by the application of color and decoration. When this is accomplished, the ark–house–temple will be ready for habitation, both divine and human, and will ultimately become a bridal chamber of intimacy.

KNOWLEDGE: READING SCRIPTURE FOR TROPOLOGICAL *SCIENTIA*

As just noted, Hugh's third and final level of meaning in scriptural exposition is the tropological or moral. Hugh offers various

[37] *Misc.*, 1.174 (*PL* 177.572C–D): "Ager est sacra Scriptura, ubi pascuntur animalia Dei, in qua inveniuntur diversarum praecepta virtutum, quasi flores quidam ad decorandas animas, et cardui quoque corruptionum ad depectenda superflua. In hoc agro currimus, quando divinam Scripturam legimus; flores colligimus, quando praecepta discimus; pannos coloramus, quando praecepta implendo virtutibus animas nostras decoramus. Patientia est in rosa, castitas in lilio, charitas in croco, humilitas in viola, puritas in saphiro."

[38] *Archa Noe*, 1.3 (Sicard 9.4–7; CSMV 50). [39] *Archa Noe*, 1.3 (Sicard 10.39–40; CSMV 52).

[40] *Didasc.*, 5.7 (Buttimer 105.4; Taylor 128). The phrase is from Gregory the Great. See Taylor, *The Didascalicon of Hugh of St. Victor*, 220, n. 23.

[41] *Archa Noe*, 4.9 (Sicard 113.75; CSMV 149).

[42] *Misc.*, 1.44 (*PL* 177.495A–B): Hugh continues: In those who love God along with something else "the foundation remains," yet "they build with wood, hay, and stubble." In those who love something instead of God, "the foundation is altogether destroyed, since the love of God cannot exist

descriptions: "Tropology is when in that action we hear was done, we recognize what we should be doing ... for without a doubt we turn the word of story about others to our own instruction when, having read of the deeds of others, we conform our living to their example."[43] Such moral exemplars reflect the very nature of God: "you have ... in morality," that is, in tropological exposition, "the means through which to imitate [God's] perfection."[44] Again, tropology "adorns [the mind] with morals"[45] and offers guidance to the one "who seeks in it the correction of his morals and a form of living (*forma vivendi*)."[46] Through it, one gains "knowledge of the virtues" and finds a "form of living (*forma vivendi*)."[47]

Like allegory but unlike litero-historical exegesis, tropology pertains more "to the meaning of things than the meaning of words."[48] "For in the meaning of things lies natural justice, out of which the discipline of our own morals, that is, positive justice, arises." By considering "what God has made we realize what we ourselves ought to do. Every nature tells of God; every nature teaches man; every nature reproduces its essential form, and nothing in the universe is unfecund."[49] Accordingly, also like allegory, tropology "is served by knowledge of arithmetic, music, geometry, astronomy, and physics"[50] – the quadrivium. Tropology seeks knowledge (*scientia*) of the deeper, moral import of created natures or essential forms of scriptural things/entities (*res*). This is a different kind of *scientia* than the doctrinal *scientia* sought in meditative *allegoresis*. Hugh alludes to this moral *scientia* elsewhere: "When finally by zeal and application you come to understand the knowledge of Holy Scripture, then you lift your heart to thirty cubits' height."[51] Such moral knowledge, he clarifies, is obtained "in two ways, namely by example and by instruction: by example, when we read the deeds of the saints, by instruction when we learn what they have said that pertains to our disciplining."[52]

where it is not the sole or the highest [love]. [Sunt qui amant solum Deum, hi aedificant super fundamentum aurum, argentum et lapides pretiosos. In amore virtutis aurum; in cognitione veritatis, argentum; in consummatione boni operis, lapides pretiosos. Sunt alii qui amant aliud praeter Deum, tamen nihil contra Deum, neque aliquid plusquam Deum. In his fundamentum quidem manet, quia amor Dei non destruitur; sed tamen ex [495B] affectu eorum quae pariter amantur, quia quaedam corruptio contrahitur, ligna et fenum et stipula superaedificantur. In ligno peccatum illiciti operis; in feno, sine opere peccatum pravae delectationis; in stipula, illicitae culpa cogitationis. Sunt alii qui amant quaedam contra Deum, et in his fundamentum omnino destruitur, quia amor Dei esse non potest, ubi non est vel solus vel summus.]"

43 *Chronicon* (Green 490–91). 44 *Didasc.*, 6.3 (Buttimer 116.27; Taylor 138).

45 *Didasc.*, 5.6 (Buttimer 104.21–22; Taylor 127). 46 *Didasc.*, Pref. (Buttimer 3.7; Taylor 45).

47 *Didasc.*, 5.7 (Buttimer 105.8–9; Taylor 128).

48 *Didasc.*, 6.5 (Buttimer 122.27–123.1; Taylor 144–45).

49 *Didasc.*, 6.5 (Buttimer 123.2–6; Taylor 145). 50 *Sacr.*, 1.Prol.6 (*PL* 176.185C–D; Deferrari 5).

51 *Vanitate*, 2.3 (*PL* 176.717C; CSMV 177). 52 *Didasc.*, 5.7 (Buttimer 105.18–21; Taylor 128).

But this knowledge of "deeds and sayings"[53] is sought through a continuation of the meditative practices begun at the previous stage of *allegoresis*. The prior chapter noted how Hugh's various definitions of *meditatio* consistently included a "meditation on morals" and that he also sub-divided *scriptural* meditation into three foci, including not only history and allegory, but also tropology.[54] So, tropology involves meditative scrutiny and investigation of the moral significance of scriptural realities, which leads to moral practices. For "through reading Holy Scripture [tropologically] we are prepared for doing good works."[55]

What should be read for tropology? The one "who seeks knowledge of the virtues and a way of life from the Sacred Word ought to study especially those books which urge contempt for this world and inflame the mind with love for its creator; which teach the straight road of life and show how virtues may be acquired and vices turned aside."[56] What biblical books does Hugh have in mind? Curiously, he mentions explicitly only "those marvelously written down by blessed Gregory," as most inspiring here.[57] Such knowledge of moral paragons produces by its beauty "a desire to imitate the virtues set forth."[58]

DISCIPLINES: AN ORDERED FORM OF LIVING (*DE INSTITUTIONE NOVITIORUM*)

Possessing moral *scientia* derived from Scripture, the subsequent tropological task is to put such knowledge into practice. Hugh addresses this at length in an important work, *On the Formation of Novices* (*De institutione novitiorum*),[59] a kind of organizational manual for new members of

[53] *Didasc.*, 5.7 (Buttimer 105.21; Taylor 128). [54] See Chapter 8 above.

[55] *Archa Noe*, 1.3 (Sicard 15.180; CSMV 17). [56] *Didasc.*, 5.7 (Buttimer 105.8–12; Taylor 128).

[57] *Didasc.*, 5.7 (Buttimer 105.21–23; Taylor 128). In *Didasc.*, 4.2 (Buttimer 72.6ff.; Taylor 104) Hugh places the writings of the Fathers within the scriptural canon. See Rainer Berndt, "Gehören die Kirchenväter zur Heiligen Schrift? Zur Kanontheorie des Hugo von St Viktor," *Zum Problem des biblischen Kanons*, Jahrbuch für biblische Theologie, vol. III (Neukirchen-Vluyn: Neukirchener Verlag, 1988), 191–99. It is perhaps surprising that Hugh does not mention the biblical book of Ecclesiastes, on which he wrote a commentary containing much tropological exegesis.

[58] *Didasc.*, 5.7 (Buttimer 105.25–26; Taylor 128). To seek this kind of moral knowledge is to be a "Christian philosopher," a lover of Christian wisdom (*Didasc.*, 5.7 [Buttimer 106.5f.; Taylor 129]). Taylor (*The Didascalicon of Hugh of St. Victor*, 220–21, n. 27) observes that Hugh's use of this term "represents a traditional Christian extension of the Socratic emphasis on moral uprightness in the philosopher and derives from the identification of the 'wisdom' sought with Christ, Wisdom of the Father."

[59] *OHSV* I.18–114. Cited hereafter as *Inst.*, followed by page and line number. All translations are mine. See Zinn, "*Vestigia victorina*" on the later medieval influence of this work.

the community at St.-Victor.[60] It delineates the daily routines, communal customs, and individual behaviors required of abbey canons. Rehearsing in the Prologue the above-noted progression from "knowledge to discipline to goodness (*scientia*, *disciplina*, *bonitas*)," which "paves the way to beatitude," Hugh narrows in on the middle term: "one can only arrive at beatitude through virtue, and virtue cannot be truly apprehended unless the discipline (*disciplina*) of virtue is not negligently guarded."[61] *Disciplina* pertains to exterior matters, to bodily comportment or manners (*mores*) – how to walk, talk, gesture, eat, drink, and dress[62] – and the work considers these extensively, in turn.[63] It has been called a quasi-"finishing institution"[64] approach to discipline and a carry-over into the cathedral schools of a monastic view of education as "a process of formation."[65]

Specifics matter less here than the underlying rationale. Hugh provides copious instruction, with minute specificity, about how to walk, talk, eat, gesture, etc.; but his deeper concern is to direct his readers' attention to exemplary individuals, holy people or saints, who exemplify the desired behaviors, as models for imitation. This reflects tropology's orientation toward the exemplary "deeds of the saints" noted above. An oft-cited passage invokes the analogy of a seal impressed upon wax to describe the impact of such imitation:[66]

> Why do you think, my brothers, we are enjoined to imitate the life and conduct of good men, except that by imitating them we are reformed (*reformemur*) to the likeness of a new life? For in them the form (*forma*) of the likeness of God is engraved, and when through the process of imitation we are pressed against that likeness, then we too are shaped according to the image of that same likeness.

[60] Jaeger has highlighted some of the dominant mores found at St.-Victor, attending in particular to Hugh's writings and especially to *De institutione* (*Envy of Angels*, 246). What has not been sufficiently noted, though, is how these ideals and practices are situated squarely within Hugh's larger program of re-formation and are best appreciated from that perspective.

[61] *Inst.*, Prol. (*OHSV* 1.18:9–11): "Ad beatitudinem autem nemo venire potest, nisi per virtutem, et virtus non alio modo veraciter apprehenditur, nisi disciplina virtutis non negligenter custodiatur."

[62] Jaeger notes that *disciplina* is central to Hugh's *De institutione*, and that Hugh gives it a unique content and definition. It describes the process of learning virtue, as well as the content that is learned. It was a kind of training in courtesy and traditional court behavior (*Envy of Angels*, 257, n. 62).

[63] Swanson seems to refer to Jaeger's work when he notes: "it has been claimed that [the cathedral school's] function was instruction in *mores*, teaching the pupil to model himself on the master in behavior and personal deportment, as well as transmitting the intellectual inheritance" (*Twelfth-Century Renaissance*, 15).

[64] In reference to Jaeger's claims regarding the nature of cathedral school education, Swanson uses the phrase "finishing institution" (ibid.).

[65] Ibid., 13–14.

[66] See Jaeger, *Envy of Angels*, 258–59 and Constable, "Renewal and Reform," 46.

> But you must know that unless the wax is first softened, it cannot receive the form (*forma*), and thus also a man cannot be kneaded to the form (*forma*) of virtue through the hand of another's action unless he is softened by humility ... What else, therefore, is indicated to us in this except that we who seek to be formed (*informari*) by the example of good men, as through some marvelously sculpted seal, perceive in them the traces of actions ... [which should be imitated] ... When saintly men act in such a way as to arouse the admiration of human minds, then they appear as exquisite sculptures. What stands out in them should be recreated inwardly in us ...[67]

Here, Hugh describes a process of being re-formed into the likeness of God through con-formity to saintly exemplars brought about by imitation of them.[68]

Several things should be noted in this text. First, Hugh's predilection for the notion of *forma* is manifest. Like soft wax, the disciple receives the stamp or seal of the exemplar as matter receives form. But this does not happen all at once; there is a gradual process of formation, as humility and obedience facilitate ever greater reception of the form through imitation. Not only the process, though, but also the goal of this exterior *disciplina* is construed in terms of *forma*. The ultimate goal is the *forma* of the divine likeness; the intermediate goal is the interior *forma* of virtue. Above all, this text makes patent the particular role that *disciplina* has in Hugh's overall program of re-formation, namely, that which facilitates the acquisition of interior virtue, that is, "goodness (*bonitas*)." "Gradually the same form of virtue (*virtutis forma*) is imprinted on the mind through habitual practice, which is observed externally through discipline (*per disciplinam*) in the habits of the body."[69] Not that Hugh considers *disciplina* merely a temporary expediency on the road to virtue. Rather, increasingly, the exterior and the interior affect and reflect each other. "Gradually the mind is inwardly composed to peace, since through the custody of discipline, the mind's evil desires are not allowed to flow out." The result is the *integritas* of the whole. "There is, therefore, integrity of virtue, when the members of the body are ruled in an orderly way through internal custody of the mind." Hugh likens this *integritas* to "a kind of republic

[67] *Inst.*, 7 (*OHSV* I.40:340–42:378).

[68] Jaeger comments: "this became the theological grounding of moral training at St. Victor" (*Envy of Angels*, 260). Bynum quotes the same passage to emphasize the twelfth-century tendency to seek out models to imitate in the spiritual life (*Jesus as Mother*, 90). Jaeger also observes helpfully: "By claiming that the image of God constitutes that principle of imitability, he created a great scale of discipline beginning in the training of the body and ending in similitude to God" (*Envy of Angels*, 259).

[69] *Inst.*, 10 (*OHSV* I.50:483–85).

of the human body, in which individual members are distributed in their offices." If this ideal state is disrupted by inordinate bodily actions, "the concord of the whole (*concordiam universitatis*)"[70] is lost. As Jaeger puts it: "the first step on the path to God is governance of the body: the mastery of external things leads to mastery of the inner world, and the composed and mastered body gives testimony to the virtuous soul."[71] This link between inner and outer, between visible and invisible is, as Jaeger goes on to suggest, "a conceptual unity underlying the life of St. Victor" and "Hugh's ethical thought" in particular.[72]

This notion of *integritas* (to be explored further below), of body/soul or exterior/interior synchronization, of ordered harmony between inner disposition and outer acts, is evident in the specific instructions Hugh offers. Here, the language of measure, of balance, of composure, evident in Hugh's descriptions of the initial state of human beings as well as what was lost in the Fall (see Chapters 2–3), returns, along with its subtle aesthetic overtones. "In those things which are right, he tells the canons, "maintain mode and measure (*mensuram et modum*)."[73] Everything, he continues, should be done "in that mode and measure in which it ought to be done," that is, "no more and no less and not otherwise than is necessary." No act should "exceed the limit of temperance (*temperantiae limitem*) or decorous form (*formam honestatis*)," such as laughing with one's teeth apart.[74] When eating, one should "maintain mode and measure (*modum et mensura*)" so as to eat "slowly and not with too much haste."[75] After fasting, there should not be "an immoderate desire for eating," such that "measure is not maintained (*mensura non tenetur*)."[76] Good actions are "neither contrary to decorum nor beyond necessity (*neque contra honestatem neque supra necessitatem*)."[77] The sense here is of moral poise, of maintaining a pose, of holding a note with perfect modulation and control, of disciplined execution (*mensuram et modum tenere, rationis moderamen*), all of which reflect rigorous training and practice.[78] Re-formation in virtue thus begins with the pursuit of "good form" in discipline:

> The one who does good, works the matter (*materia*) in good works, but if he does not do the good well (*bene*), the good matter is deformed (*deformatur*) through a bad form (*malam formam*). The good is the form (*forma*), [and] where it is neither more nor less it is just. If it is more than just it is sin [by commission]; if it is

[70] *Inst.*, 12 (*OHSV* 1.72:822–26). [71] Jaeger, *Envy of Angels*, 261.
[72] Ibid. [73] *Inst.*, 6 (*OHSV* 1.38:312–13).
[74] *Inst.*, 12 (*OHSV* 1.74:839). [75] *Inst.*, 21 (*OHSV* 1.98:1220–30).
[76] *Meditatione* (Baron 54.139). [77] *Inst.*, 20 (*OHSV* 1.96:1193–1204).
[78] See Jaeger, *Envy of Angels*, 259.

less than just it is [sin by] omission. Thus, he who does the good well, in a sense imprints a good form upon good matter.[79]

Fittingly, the French translation of the *De institutione* is entitled, "*De la formation des novices*."

Moral formation through imitation of others also reflects the distinctive ethos of the twelfth-century canonical movement. Bynum's classic characterization of the canons regular as distinguished in their ideal of teaching "by word and example" relies in part on Hugh's *De institutione* for supporting evidence.[80] She notes how "canonical authors assume that canons are not only learners who grow toward God but also pattern (*forma*) and example (*exemplum*) to those who encounter them."[81] Bynum also links this characteristic to the canonical reform programs: "twelfth-century religion was characterized by a strong concern for conforming the behavior of members of a group to a very precise pattern, that the existence of such an articulated pattern for the group helped to make it a group, and that explicit theories of reformation by imitation (in the outer as well as the inner man) bolstered the importance of models."[82] As Hugh says, "having contemplated the believers' way of life, adopt it as your pattern."[83]

In sum, *disciplina* is a crucial aspect of tropology, initiating a process that leads ultimately to beatitude: "For the discipline of God refashions [us] into the end, since, fully and perfectly *reforming* the human person, it leads through virtue to beatitude."[84] The *De institutione* focuses on the *disciplina* of mores and of behavior (*morum disciplina*), taught in the school of discipline (*schola disciplinae*), whose overarching goal is to instill in the novices the form of discipline (*forma disciplinae*).[85] This Victorine interest in decorum in table manners, speech, gesture, and dress, this exquisite attention to all aspects of behavior, what Jaeger calls "courtesy,"

79 *Misc.*, 1.97 (*PL* 177.536C). 80 Bynum, "Spirituality of Regular Canons," 37.

81 Ibid., 43.

82 Bynum, *Jesus as Mother*, 105. Bynum observes further: "For twelfth-century religion did not emphasize the individual personality at the expense of corporate awareness. Nor did it develop a new sense of spiritual and psychological change, of intention, and of personal responsibility by escaping from an earlier concern with types, patterns, and examples. Rather twelfth-century religious writing and behavior show a great concern with how groups are formed and differentiated from each other, how roles are defined and evaluated, how behavior is conformed to models. If the religious writing, the religious practice, and the religious orders of the twelfth century are characterized by a new concern of the 'inner man,' it is because of a new concern for the group, for types and examples, for the 'outer man'" (ibid., 85).

83 *Archa Noe*, 2.2 (Sicard 34.39; CSMV 74).

84 *Inst.*, Prol. (*OHSV* 1.18:19–21): "Disciplina namque Dei in finem corrigit, quia, plene et perfecte hominem reformans, per virtutem, ad beatitudinem perducit."

85 Jaeger, *Envy of Angels*, 256.

is the distinctly Victorine pursuit of "good form" in this communal regimen.[86] This discipline both fosters and will ultimately reflect interior virtue. There is a deep and reciprocal relationship between this "discipline of manners" (*morum disciplina*) and the interior state of the virtuous soul. By contrast, the one who lacks such discipline is like the changing appearance of the moon in its phases, reflecting an underlying instability in its nature: a foolish person "now weeping, now laughing, now sad, now happy, as if waxing and waning and passing from one [state] to another, reveals vacillating forms (*formas*) in a single man."[87]

Evident in all of this is the importance of *forma*. In as much as it retains a platonic sense of *ratio* and ideality, that which gives essential shape and organizing structure to things, formation, as the gradual reception of *forma*, is the goal that *disciplina* intends and is the ontological basis for the *integritas* that is its fruit. For, as Hugh indicates elsewhere, it is the interior *forma* that is expressed externally, made visible as the specific appearance of any particular thing.[88]

VIRTUE: THE BEAUTY OF THE FORM OF JUSTICE WITHIN THE SOUL

As noted above, both moral *scientia*, derived from tropological exposition of Scripture, and exterior *disciplina*, practiced in the customs of daily life at St.-Victor, facilitate the formation of interior *bonitas*, goodness within the soul through the acquisition and possession of virtue. The "good form" practiced in external *disciplina* produces a corresponding form of virtue within the soul, which is the immediate goal of the entire reforming process. This progression is evident where Hugh says: "when I have begun to do the works of the virtues, I should labor to have the virtues themselves – that is to say, that I should possess within myself the virtue that I show in outward works."[89] But Hugh does not posit an automatic, immediate, or even directly causal production of virtue through

[86] Ibid., 249.

[87] *Misc.*, 1.4 (*PL* 177.481C–D): "Sicut una est luna, et dicitur prima, et secunda, et tertia, et quarta, et quinta, etc., et fiunt multae varietates in uno corpore, sic stultus modo [481D] plorans, modo ridens, modo tristis, modo hilaris, quasi crescens et deficiens et de alio ad aliud transiens, multas ostendit formas in uno homine."

[88] *Tribus diebus*, 26 (Poirel 35.565–71) indicates the connection between interior *forma* and exterior appearance: "Likewise the beauty of creatures deriving from their natural form (*formam*) pertains to something habitual ... But what pertains to habit is more proper and more certain than what pertains to act, because nature is connected to habit ..." Accordingly, "the representation of beauty [linked to *forma*] precedes both immensity and utility in cognition."

[89] *Archa Noe*, 2.5 (Sicard 41.24–26; CSMV 81).

the cultivation of external disciplines. For this, the interior work of grace through the action of the Holy Spirit is required. But before pursuing this further, his conception of virtue in general must be sketched.

The *De sacramentis* contains an important discussion of virtue in relation both to pre- and especially to post-lapsarian humanity. To begin, Hugh famously defines virtue (*virtus*) as "an affection of the mind (*affectus mentis*) ordered according to reason."[90] The "organ" of these affections is the will (*voluntas*), which is their "root and origin." They are "in one will" and collectively "are one will." Such affections, moreover, are as numerous as the various objects toward which the will can tend by its desires or appetites. In fact, the will "forms various affections" by an appetitive act *vis à vis* any object.[91]

Anticipating (and influencing) later scholastic discussions, Hugh distinguishes between natural and supernatural virtue. The first consisted of "certain goods implanted in created nature" by "creating grace (*gratia creatrix*)," which were "ordered according to nature" (*secundum naturam*) and by which the rational creature willed "naturally" (*ex natura*)."[92] Hugh does not give specific examples, but notes simply that these were implanted "according to justice" and that by them the first man sought out goodness and justice by natural desire, his nature having been "formed and instructed (*formata et instructa*) by these virtues from the beginning."[93] The Fall entailed some kind of forfeiture of these natural virtues. Accordingly, "saving grace (*gratia salvatrix*)" needs to restore "the goods which nature, when first corrupted, lost." But, crucially, that is not all. It also needs to restore "those goods, to which nature, when it was imperfect and had not yet received them, aspired."[94] The first act of saving grace begins to re-establish the integrity of vitiated human nature by restoring free will (*liberum arbitrium reparatur*);[95] through the second act of saving grace, the restored will begins to cooperate in acts that exceed its nature. In this state, the will begins to move, not "according to nature only," but also "according to God," and it now operates "above nature."

90 *Sacr.*, 1.6.17 (*PL* 176.273B–C; Deferrari 105): "nihil aliud est quam affectus mentis secundum rationem ordinatus."

91 *Sacr.*, 1.6.17 (*PL* 176.273C; Deferrari 105).

92 *Sacr.*, 1.6.17 (*PL* 176.274A; Deferrari 106).

93 *Sacr.*, 1.6.17 (*PL* 176.274D; Deferrari 106–7).

94 *Sacr.*, 1.6.17 (*PL* 176.273C–D; Deferrari 105; trans. assistance by Hugh Feiss).

95 On Hugh's conception of freedom, with a comparison to that of Anselm of Canterbury, see Baron, "L'Idée de liberté." While Anselm defines freedom as the ability to maintain justice for its own sake, for his part Hugh seems to stress the will's irreducible freedom: "*liberum arbitrium* is said of the will," and again: "[it is] in the power to choose (*potestate eligere*) and the freedom to judge (*libertate judicare*) in which the *liberum arbitrium* consists" (*Sacr.* 1.5.21 [*PL* 176.255C; Deferrari 83]).

He first effects good will in man, Himself alone operates, but in that afterwards He operates through the good will, He Himself does not operate alone, but the will too [operates] through which He operates."[109] Or again: "The Holy Spirit first instils (*aspirat*) a good will so that it may exist, and He then inspires (*inspirat*) so that it may move and work lest it be idle. The Holy Spirit first works it, then He works through it."[110] In this present time, in the "period of grace," there are those who, "breathed upon by the inspiration of the Holy Spirit are illumined to recognize the good which must be done, and are inflamed as they love and are strengthened to accomplish the good."[111]

For Hugh, ultimately, saving grace is a function of the active presence of the Holy Spirit at the deepest level of the human spirit, namely, the will, the seat of its desires, affections, loves – the heart. As a result of the Fall, the will's freedom was so enfeebled as to be effectively lost in relation to sin: "there is in it power to sin and not power not to sin."[112] With the advent of the Spirit's grace this situation begins gradually to be changed. Prior to and independently of any human movement, operatively, as an unmerited gift, the Spirit first brings about a change in the will, making it both fragilely good and incipiently free. Subsequently, the will can now begin to move itself toward the good, yet requires the on-going cooperation of grace. Such grace-enabled, yet free, movement of the will merits the gift of more grace, "grace for grace." These further graces are "God's through gift, and man's through merit." In this way, grace not only "restores the goods which nature … lost," but also "in-spirates the goods which nature … has not yet received."[113]

It is not insignificant that Hugh uses the same term, *artifex*, to describe God's primordial act of creation, or more precisely, of formation, that he uses here in relation to the restoration of virtue: Through divine goodness, wisdom, and power, "God, the Artifex, gave form (*forma*) to His work."[114] And when the Spirit hovered over the waters of creation, "it heralded the divine intention of forming the work in the manner of an Artifex."[115] Nor is it surprising that, in his discussion of

[109] *Sacr.*, 1.6.17 (*PL* 176.274C; Deferrari 106). On this theme, see also *Sacr.* 1.5.27 (*PL* 176.258C); *Sacr.* 1.8.11 (*PL* 176.313A); Hugues de Saint-Victor *De septem donis Spiritus Sancti* 2.3 (*Six opuscules spirituels*, SC 155, ed. Roger Baron [Paris: Cerf, 1969], 120–32, at 124; 126); to be cited as *Septem donis*; *Archa Noe*, Prol. (Sicard 3–4); *Archa Noe*, 3.3 (Sicard 57); *Archa Noe*, 3.6 (Sicard, 67); *Libellus* 5 (Sicard 134–35); *Misc.* 2.5 (*PL* 177.590A); *Meditatione* 3.3 (Baron 52).

[110] *Sacr.*, 1.6.17 (*PL* 176.274B; Deferrari 106).

[111] *Sacr.*, 1.8.11 (*PL* 176.313A; Deferrari 149).

[112] *Sacr.*, 1.6.16 (*PL* 176.273A; Deferrari 104–5).

[113] *Sacr.*, 1.6.17 (*PL* 176.273C–D; Deferrari 105).

[114] *Sacr.*, 1.2.11 (*PL* 176.210D–211A; Deferrari 34).

[115] *In Pent.* (*PL* 175.36A): "Spiritum Dei vocat ejus intentionem, qui quasi artifex operi formando praecerat."

creation, Hugh could not resist anticipating its tropological significance for fallen humanity. Just as God illumined the creation by separating light from darkness, so the rational creature "must be illumined to see its evils, and to distinguish light from darkness, that is, virtues from vices"[116] and "see itself and recognize the horror and shamefulness of its confusion."[117] Just as God gathered the primordial waters into one place, so "the whole man, being recalled to the status of his nature and disposed according to the order of reason, may collect into one place every desire to the end that the flesh may be subject to the spirit and the spirit to the Creator."[118] Or, regarding the reason why God divided the waters above and below, let not the rational creature "seek outside himself, who believes that these things were made for his sake. For there is in that world which has been fashioned interiorly a certain something possessing the form and examplar of this work."[119] Always pairing the "works of creation" and the "works of restoration," Hugh makes clea that the recovery of justice and virtue is a kind of moral re-formation patterned on the original formation of creation, which instructs the rational creature how it should "dispose itself to order and conform to truth"[120] and "fit itself to that rational disposition and order of truth … according to the exemplar of reason and form of wisdom."[121]

As adverted to in Chapter 4, the "exemplar of reason and form of wisdom" is an allusion to Christ, who is at work with the Spirit in both formation and re-formation.

In a pregnant image, Hugh likens this recovery of virtue to the soul being re-cast by the forging heat of the Spirit's fire into a pre-formed mold. The Holy Spirit "inflames the soul with the desire for eternal goods," and "in a way liquefies it through the fire of love." So, "just as a liquefied mass is poured into a mould through a pipe and receives a form, so the mind, dissolved by the fire of love, flows … into the image of the divine likeness."[122] This mold is, of course, Christ, as will be clear below from the ark-symbol. At the same time, Christ himself sends the liquefying fire of the Spirit in the first place: "The Lord Jesus sent the good fire [i.e., the Holy Spirit] into the earth, and wills that the world be inflamed thereby

[116] *Sacr.*, 1.1.12 (*PL* 176.195C–D; Deferrari 16). [117] *Sacr.*, 1.1.12 (*PL* 176.195D; Deferrari 17).
[118] *Sacr.*, 1.1.12 (*PL* 176.196D; Deferrari 18). [119] *Sacr.*, 1.1.19 (*PL* 176.200C–D; Deferrari 22).
[120] *Sacr.*, 1.1.12 (*PL* 176.195C–D; Deferrari 16). [121] *Sacr.*, 1.1.12 (*PL* 176.195D; Deferrari 17).
[122] *Misc.*, 1.173 (*PL* 177.572A): "… opus sancti Spiritus … eam desiderio aeternorum bonorum accendit, et quodammodo per amoris ignem liquefacit … Et sicut massa liquefacta per fistulam in monetam funditur et formam accipit, ita mens, amoris igne soluta … in imaginem divinae similitudinis currit."

(Luke 12)."[123] Indeed, Hugh consistently gives a Christological orientation to the tropological formation described thus far:

Our purpose in reading Scripture is that, by gaining knowledge of what He did and said and commended, we may be enabled to do what He told us and receive what He has promised. Growing in this way both in the knowledge of the truth and in the merit of virtue, spiritually we strive towards *conformity* (*conformitatem*) with Him and "the measure of the age of His fullness" (Eph. 4:13) [emphasis added].[124]

In short, the progression from exterior practices to interior virtue is a process of increasing con-formity of the human person with Christ.

The recovery of integritas

As described in Chapter 3, Hugh conceives of vice as having a disintegrating, de-forming impact on the human person. Not surprisingly, then, he thinks of the virtues not only as the opposite of vices, but also as a remedy to their devastating effects. Accordingly, he defines virtue, not only as an *affectus mentis*, but also as "a kind of wholeness (*sanitas*) and integrity (*integritas*) of the rational soul."[125] In Hugh's corpus, *integritas* appears as an umbrella term, encompassing others, including justice, unity, peace, concord, and ultimately beauty, which together describe the dimensions of re-formed *humanitas*. Ultimately, integrity is a kind of proper structuring and right ordering of the whole person, body and soul. The original "cloister/structure of integrity[126] (*integritatis claustra*)" within the soul and the "integrity of uprightness"[127] between body and soul were ruptured by disordered desire or concupiscence. Sin vitiated human nature, removing "its integrity (*integritatem*)."[128] In restoration, "the integrity of the virtues is truly repaired,"[129] as is "the integrity of the flesh (*integritatem carnis*), by which the soul is clothed."[130] This extends even to "the integrity of good works (*bonorum operum integritatem*)."[131] So, "there is integrity of virtue (*integritas virtutis*) when the members of the body are ruled in an orderly fashion through the internal custody of the mind."[132]

[123] *Misc.*, 1.173 (*PL* 177.571A): "Ignem bonum Dominus Jesus misit in terram, et voluit ut accenderetur (Luke 12)."
[124] *Archa Noe*, 2.7 (Sicard 46.90–95; CSMV 86).
[125] *Sacr.*, 2.13.2 (*PL* 176.526C–D; Deferrari 376).
[126] *In Eccl.* (*PL* 175.165B).
[127] *Lament.* (*PL* 175.291B): "quasi plagae quaedam integritatem rectitudinis earum corrumpunt."
[128] *Sacr.*, 1.7.10 (*PL* 176.291B; Deferrari 125).
[129] *Misc.*, 1.77 (*PL* 177.511D): "neque ad virtutis integritatem veraciter reparatur."
[130] *Lament.* (*PL* 175.272C). [131] *Lament.* (*PL* 175.317B).
[132] *Inst.*, 10 (*OHSV* 1.48:464–66).

Under the notion of integrity, and closely linked to justice, is the notion of measure, which delimits the proper boundary of human nature, "so that it neither flows beyond itself, presuming what it ought not, nor falls short within itself, shrinking away from what is required,"[133] thus compromising its integrity. Sin entailed the forfeiture of measure. So, the virtues must be "guarded and held together, lest in their expansion they are relaxed beyond the measure of justice and flow away."[134] Hugh glosses the Dionysian notion of hierarchy as that in which nothing trespasses its "assigned mode, measure, and proper order," thus ensuring that no member "go beyond or fall short of the divine likeness."[135] His concern with interior measure mirrors his above-noted interest in proper poise, modulation, and balance in exterior actions and customs: "... to be ordered and moved such that one does not exceed the limit of temperance and the form of moral comeliness (*formam honestatis*),"[136] that is, to "transgress the measure of temperance (*temperantiae metas transierit*)" and so be thrust into "superfluity" (*superfluitatem*).[137]

This recovery of integrity is also a movement from exterior multiplicity to interior unity, from external self-dispersion to internal self-possession. Concupiscence "divided the human person and alienated him from himself." Now he journeys "so that he might return to himself, and become one from many, and then proceed unto Him who is above him. The first one is from many to a manifold one. The second one is from one to a simple unity. The first one is from vice to virtue; the second one is from truth to beatitude."[138] For "the more we draw near to God by fleeing the world, the more we are gathered together into one."[139] Or again, "the habit of the virtues congregates those virtues into one, lest they flow away or

[133] *Misc.*, 1.119 (*PL* 177.544D): "ut nec extra illam effluat praesumens ea quae non debet; nec infra illam subsistat, torpens ab iis quae debet."

[134] *In hierarchiam* (*PL* 175.1145D): "quae custodia ipsas virtutes ambit, et custodit, vel constringit, ne in sua multiplicatione extra metas justitiae relaxentur, aut diffluant."

[135] *In hierarchiam* (*PL* 175.994C): "so that nothing might presume to go beyond the modum, and measure assigned by it, and its proper order (*ut praeter modum, et mensuram ab ipso assignatam et ordini suo debitam*) ... so that in nothing does it deviate or fall short of that similitude, in which it has been placed (*ut in nullo deviet vel declinet ab ipsius similitudine*) ..."

[136] *Inst.*, 12 (*OHSV* 1.74:837–39).

[137] *Inst.*, 20 (*OHSV* 1.96:1201–3).

[138] *Misc.*, 1.55 (*PL* 177.502A): "Concupiscentia divisit hominem, iniquitas abalienavit, mortalitas debilitavit. Nunc ergo prima via est, ut ad semetipsum redeat, et de multis unus fiat, deinde pergat ad ipsum qui est super ipsum. Prima una est de multis ad unum multiplex. Secunda una est de uno ad unitatem simplex. Prima una est de vitiis ad virtutem; secunda una est de veritate ad beatitudinem."

[139] *De amore sponsi ad sponsam* (*PL* 176.994A): "quia quanto magis mundum fugiendo Deo appropinquare incipimus, tanto magis in unum congregamur."

recede from the concord of unity."[140] Like integrity and justice, unity extends to the whole person, so that a state of concord and peace obtains throughout. "When the [human] spirit has become fully subject to God, then grace will *reform* to a state of peace that contradiction which it carried in its flesh, so that man will be wholly pacified, externally with his neighbor through fraternal charity, within through a good conscience, above through divine grace" (emphasis added).[141] When the human "spirit returns to peace," it "composes to peace" the other parts. For, "if the spirit is zealous to exhibit both the owed subjection to God and the just regimen to the flesh, perfected and completed justice will follow, and thus *reformed* in justice, perfect peace and concord will be repaired" (emphasis added).[142]

This progressive recovery of virtue is nicely illustrated in a short treatise entitled *On the Five Sevens*. Paired over against the seven capital vices (pride, envy, etc.), Hugh posits the following seven virtues: humility, gentleness, mental sorrow, desire for justice, mercy, purity of heart, and internal, mental peace.[143] Not the traditional seven (i.e., the three theological virtues of faith, hope, and love, added to the four cardinal virtues of fortitude, prudence, etc.); rather, Hugh seems to have derived his septet from the Beatitudes found in the Sermon on the Mount. He then correlates three other septets (petitions in the Lord's Prayer,[144] gifts of the Holy Spirit,[145] and beatitudes[146]) with these seven virtues and coordinates their overall, remedial effect:[147] "The gifts of the Holy Spirit are antidotes; the virtues are sanities; the beatitudes are joys."[148] The treatise charts a progressive re-formation of the dis-integrated soul, moving from exterior to interior, as the soul recovers interior peace and contemplative, loving

140 *In hierarchiam* (*PL* 175.1145D): "quod habitus virtutum ipsas virtutes in unum congregans, ne diffluant sive ab unitate concordiae recedant."

141 *Misc.*, 1.6 (*PL* 177.482B): "Cum autem spiritus Deo plene subjectus fuerit, tunc et illam quam in carne sua portat contradictionem, gratia ad pacem reformabit pacatus sit totus, ut homo, et extra se cum proximo per charitatem fraternam, et in se per conscientiam bonam, et supra se per gratiam divinam."

142 *Misc.*, 1.20 (*PL* 177.489A): "Hujus autem discordiae, quia solus spiritus auctor est, necesse est ut ipse prior ad pacem redeat, et caetera post se subsequenter ad pacem componat. Si enim ipse et Creatori debitam subjectionem, et carni justum regimen exhibere studuerit, perfecta et consummata justitia subsequitur, et reformata justitia, concordia quoque et pax perfecta reparatur."

143 *Sacr.*, 2.13.2 (*PL* 176.526D; Deferrari 376): "Prima est humilitas, secunda mansuetudo, tertia mentis compunctio, quarta desiderium justitiae, quinta misericordia, sexta cordis munditia, septima pax mentis interna."

144 *Quinque sept.* (Baron 100.9–19).

145 *Quinque sept.* (Baron 102.19–23).

146 *Quinque sept.* (Baron 102.29–32).

147 See *Sacr.*, 2.13.2 (*PL* 176.527A–B; Deferrari 376–77) for a similar scheme, though minus a septet.

148 *Sacr.*, 2.13.2 (*PL* 176.527A; Deferrari 376).

concentration on God.[149] Gradually, thereby, the soul regains the integrity of its nature, as "the human person is fully and perfectly reformed in the image of God."[150] As Hugh says elsewhere: "the progress of the virtues is ... the reparation of nature."[151]

PRAYER AND PERFORMANCE

As noted at the outset of this chapter, Hugh can construe the Christian life in successive steps, moving from study or instruction and then meditation to "prayer and performance."[152] Implicit in this sequence is a movement (described in the preceding paragraphs) from moral *scientia* and exterior *disciplina* to interior *virtus* and *affectus*. This progress is nicely illustrated in a short treatise that Hugh devotes explicity to the topic of prayer, *De virtute orandi*.[153] Moderns are perhaps not used to thinking of prayer as central to ethics or the moral life as it is for our Victorine.

While in one sense it is a practical manual delineating and classifying the diverse types of prayer, the deeper burden of the treatise is to exhort the reader to use the practices of prayer as tools for cultivating the appropriate affections and dispositions of the virtuous life. Beginning with the kind of moral *meditatio* defined above, here on human misery and divine compassion,[154] Hugh "forms his readers/hearers toward an inner disposition of their affection and love for God."[155] In their turn, the diverse forms of prayer cultivate humility, sorrow for sin, hatred of the world, but also love for and delight in God. The operative category here is *devotio*: "a turning to God with pious and humble affection."[156] But such devotion is for

[149] For a fuller discussion of the entire treatise, see my "Hugh of St Victor," in *The Sermon on the Mount through the Centuries*, eds. Jeffrey P. Greenman, Timothy Larsen, and Stephen Spencer (Grand Rapids: Brazos Press, 2007), 72–102.

[150] *Quinque sept.* (Baron 118.265–68): "plene ac perfecte homo ad imaginem Dei reformetur."

[151] *In hierarchiam* (*PL* 175.1146A): "Virtutum enim progressio ... sed reparatio est naturae." Elsewhere (*Misc.*, 1.77 [*PL* 177.512A]), Hugh describes a similar, though less elaborate, process: "Thus vain delight disperses the soul, but the sorrow of confusion collects it, the joy of consolation composes (*componit*) it, the sorrow of discipline binds it up, the joy of felicity makes it whole (*sanat*)."

[152] See page 194, n. 21 above.

[153] *OHSV* 1.126–71. Cited hereafter as *Virtute orandi*, followed by page and line number. All translations are mine.

[154] *Virtute orandi*, 2 (*OHSV* 1.128:36–40).

[155] Rorem, *Hugh of St. Victor*, 122. *Virtute Orandi*, 5 (*OHSV* 1.132:86–89): "Assiduous meditation produces knowledge; knowledge thus derived expels ignorance and produces compunction; compunction thus produced flees indolence and produces devotion; and devotion completes prayer."

[156] *Virtute orandi* 5 (*OHSV* 1.132:97): "Devotio igitur est conversio in Deum pio et humili affectu." See also *Virtute orandi*, 5 (*OHSV* 1.132:91–92): "Devotion is a pious and humble *affectus* unto God, which is born of compunction."

Hugh not vacuous and vague sentiment, but virtue-laden intentionality. Devotion "has in itself the three principal virtues: faith, hope, love," since it believes and hopes in divine salvation and loves God more than evil.[157] In short, "prayer, therefore, is nothing other than devotion of mind (*mentis devotio*), that is, a conversion unto God through pious and humble affection (*pium et humilem affectum*), relying on faith, hope and love."[158]

Typically Hugonian, and of direct relevance here, is the fact that Hugh's treatment is not haphazard, but has a clear "pedagogical progression."[159] That is to say, it is formative. Gradually, in an orderly fashion, prayer, especially the Psalter and the prayers of the liturgy, form the *affectus*. As Rorem aptly notes: "Through the literal words and the knowledge built upon this textual foundation comes the spiritual finale of an affection that is aflame for God, a fervent love that goes beyond all words, even the words of prayer."[160]

While Hugh consistently constructs formative processes that move from exteriority to interiority, he also recognizes that virtue within expresses itself in words and actions without. Here is performance: "Let us show outwardly by words that we have an affection of devotion toward God within us."[161] Internal virtue produces virtuous, more precisely, just, acts: "a work of justice is in the movement of the rational mind (*motu mentis rationalis*) that moves in accord with God, arising from a conception of the heart (*cordis conceptione*) and extends externally all the way to the completion of the corporeal act."[162] External actions reflect "the movements of the internal soul," while "the inner movements of the affections (*affectionum motus*) bring external actions to completion."[163] Again: "Good works are living, when they occur through right intention."[164] In particular, Hugh has in mind the six so-called "works of mercy": to feed the hungry; give drink to the thirsty; take in the stranger; clothe the naked; and visit the sick and imprisoned.[165] Ever the ecclesial reformer, though, Hugh has pointed admonitions for the clergy in particular: Those placed in authority ought first to be "taken up by grace toward excellence in virtue," before

[157] *Virtute orandi*, 5 (*OHSV* 1.132:99–104). [158] *Virtute Orandi*, 5 (*OHSV* 1.132:105–7).

[159] See Poirel's presentation (*OHSV* 1.123) of the plan or outline of the treatise along with its principal themes, including his expression "progression pédagogique" (cited in Rorem, *Hugh of St. Victor*, 121, n. 7).

[160] Rorem, *Hugh of St. Victor*, 121. E.g., *Virtute orandi*, 12 (*OHSV* 1.148:331–38).

[161] *Virtute orandi*, 13 (*OHSV* 1.150:360): "Ostendamus foris verbis habere nos intus erga Deum affectum devotionis" (cited in Rorem, ibid.).

[162] *Sacr.*, 2.13.2 (*PL* 176.526D; Deferrari 376). [163] *Lament.* (*PL* 175.284C–D).

[164] *Lament.* (*PL* 175.273C): "Vivunt bona opera, quando recta intentione fiunt."

[165] *Sacr.*, 2.13.2 (*PL* 176.527A–B; Deferrari 376–77).

they are "externally called through obedience to excellence in dignity."[166] This is the ideal state of affairs: to have one's affections rightly ordered within and to be of service to one's neighbor without.[167] To desire inwardly "to be dissolved and to be with Christ," but outwardly, "to remain in the flesh" out of necessity in service of others (cf. Philippians 2).[168]

In one place, Hugh provides a lapidary summary of the progressive formation in virtue that is the moral life, for those whose "salvation grows by steps and virtue increases."[169] This also entails a subtle Trinitarian dimension. In the words of the prophet Malachi (6:8), he says: "It is necessary, therefore, first for you 'to do justice' so that, what you discern rightly, you may fulfill in work." This is moral *scientia* that is put into practice, *disciplina*. "Then," he continues, "'love mercy,' so that the good you do, you do from love not fear." Here is the *affectus* of love within. "Then take care to inflame [your love]," lest you fail to make progress in this goodness. To do all this is "to cooperate with the work of the Trinity in you." For "wisdom illuminates you unto the understanding of truth, charity inflames you unto the desire of goodness, paternity guards in you what it effects, lest it be lost." In this way, he concludes, "you effect the image of the Trinity; and then you offer the true sacrifice yourself, when you are *reformed* according to its likeness" (emphasis added).[170]

THE BEAUTY OF MORALITY

These various dimensions of tropology, of the moral life in the broad Hugonian sense, converge in a notion of beauty. Hugh's interest in

166 *Verbo* 6.1 (Baron 76.264–73).

167 Apparently the most accurate way to characterize the distinctive ideals of the canonical movement in the early twelfth century, at least as it was pursued at St.-Victor, is (1) a conviction that the mixed life (contemplation and active service) is superior to the contemplative life; (2) a new emphasis on preaching; and (3) a new emphasis on sacraments and history (Bynum, "Spirituality of Regular Canons," 33–34).

168 *Misc.*, 1.93 (*PL* 177.524A): "Intus *cupio dissolvi, et esse cum Christo* (Philippians 2). Foris *manere in carne necessarium propter vos* (ibid.)."

169 *Misc.*, 1.13 (*PL* 177.484D): "Sic gradibus suis crescit salus, et virtus proficit."

170 *Misc.*, 1.99 (*PL* 177.532A–B): "Oportet ergo te primum facere judicium ut quod recte discernis, opere compleas; deinde diligere misericordiam, ut bonum quod agis non ex timore, sed ex amore facias. Postremo sollicitum incedere, ne vel bonum, quod necdum habes, non merearis accipere, vel bonum quod habes amittas. Porro in his tribus trinitati in te operanti cooperaris. Sapientia enim te ad agnitionem veritatis illuminat, charitas te ad desiderium bonitatis inflammat, paternitas in te custodit quod creavit, ne pereat. Per illuminantem ergo sapientiam tibi collucentem, rectum discernis; per inflammantem charitatem, tibi coardentem, misereris; per providentem [532B] paternitatem, tibi contuentem, temetipsum custodis. Per trinitatem itaque cooperando trinitati, trinitatis imago efficeris; verumque tunc sacrificium teipsum Deo offeris, cum ad ejus similitudinem reformaris."

aesthetic themes has already been discussed at various points. Beauty for him is ultimately a sapiential notion – reflecting the wisdom and indeed beauty of God himself. He was deeply sensitive to beauty in various manifestations, for example, in the visible beauty of creation and of a disciplined manner of life. Above all, though, he was most concerned with the spiritual beauty of the soul – a beauty that surpasses "the loveliness and beauty of all visible things."[171] For him, such beauty compasses and consummates the other aspects of the soul's re-formed *integritas*; indeed, it is the consummation of the entire re-forming process which this study charts, the tropological *finale*,[172] which "adorns with morals (*moribus ornat*)"[173] and yields "the beauty of morality."[174]

There is for Hugh an exterior beauty in a well-ordered and disciplined manner of life. He consistently describes *disciplina* thus: Moral knowledge "pertains to the institution of living rightly and becomingly (*recte et honeste*)."[175] "Discipline is good and becoming (*bona et honesta*) behavior,"[176] as well as "the ordered movement (*motus ordinatus*) of all the members, and a fitting disposition (*dispositio decens*) in all habits and actions."[177] A "good act" has "external beauty (*decorem*)."[178] The literal walls of Jerusalem stand tropologically for the "discipline and beauty (*disciplinam et decorem*) of external good works."[179] Only with difficulty do the obdurate receive "the form of discipline (*formam disciplinae*) and the appearance of loveliness (*speciem honestatis*)."[180] One should pursue "the beauty of chastity (*decora castitate*)."[181] There is even "adornment of beauty and integrity of wholeness" that pertains to the body itself.[182]

But such external decorum corresponds to a more profound loveliness of soul and "beauty of the spiritual life (*spiritualis vitae honestas*)."[183] There is "both beauty without and beauty within, and wholeness without and wholeness within, and when beauty is removed, ugliness and turpitude

171 *Arrha* (*OHSV* 1.230:76–77; Herbert 15). 172 Rorem's apt term, *Hugh of St. Victor*, 117.

173 *Script.*, 13 (*PL* 175.20C). See *Didasc.*, 5.6 (Buttimer 104.21–22; Taylor 127).

174 Hugh's aesthetic finds expression in a wide array of terms, including *pulchritudo*, *decor*, *honestas*, *formosa*, as well as *temperantia* and *harmonia*, whose meanings seem to overlap with each other rather diffusely (and for which exact English equivalents are often lacking), as if he was grasping for something multifaceted that ultimately eluded precise conceptualization.

175 *Inst.*, 1 (*OHSV* 1.22:62–63). 176 *Inst.*, 10 (*OHSV* 1.48:451).

177 *Inst.*, 10 (*OHSV* 1.48:451–55). 178 *Lament.* (*PL* 175.276A).

179 *Lament.* (*PL* 175.273C). 180 *Inst.*, 12 (*OHSV* 1.74:859–63).

181 *Arrha* (*OHSV* 1.238:184; Herbert 18).

182 *Misc.*, 1.186 (*PL* 177.582D): "bonum vero corporeae naturae est decor pulchritudinis et integritas sanitatis."

183 *Sacr.*, 2.3.18 (*PL* 176.433A; Deferrari 272).

ensue."[184] Before the Fall, man was "most beautiful (*speciosus*) through the innocence of his conscience," until guilt rendered him "most dark and equally ugly (*foedam*)."[185] For "every soul is turned either away from or toward God." To be turned away is to be removed from God, and the greater the distance of separation, the greater the ugliness of soul. Conversely, to be "near to" (*propinqua*) God is to be "beautiful (*speciosa*)," though not yet totally; but to be "next to" (*proxima*) God is to be "totally beautiful (*tota speciosa*)."[186] This reflects Hugh's view that the divine intent in giving *esse* to human beings was that they might attain *pulchrum esse* through a turning to the Creator in love,[187] and harks back to charity, the source of all other human virtue. The whole moral life, indeed the whole re-forming process, leads to this turning of the creature in love to the Creator, which is simultaneously beautifying and beatifying. As Jaeger notes, "Hugh clearly thought of spiritual formation in terms of the model of human handicraft ... The finished man, reformed to the image of a new life, is the work of art."[188]

This spiritual beauty of the soul pertains to both dimensions of the spiritual nature, the intellectual and the volitional. Hugh's *On the Three Days* argues that rational activity is the most manifest likeness of the beauty of divine wisdom, "because that which *knows* shows forth invisible wisdom more clearly than anything else."[189] Or again: "cognition of truth is a kind of beauty of the spiritual nature"[190] and "the faculty of wisdom within is like the natural beauty of your face."[191] More typically, though, Hugh stresses the beauty of virtue that accrues to the will: "the holy Church of the elect is beautifully adorned with a variety of virtues and good morals."[192] And "the love of virtue is like a certain kind of wholeness."[193]

[184] *Misc.*, 1.186 (*PL* 177.582D–583A): "est pulchritudo foris et pulchritudo intus, et sanitas foris et sanitas intus. Et cum pulchritudo tollitur, succedit foeditas et turpitude."

[185] *Lament.* (*PL* 175.271B).

[186] *De amore sponsi ad sponsam* (*PL* 176.989D): "Omnis anima vel aversa est a Deo, vel conversa ad Deum. Aversarum autem alia est remota, alia remotissima. Conversarum vero alia propinqua, alia proxima. Quae remota est, turpis quidem est, sed non tota. Quae remotissima est, tota turpis est. Item quae propinqua est, speciosa est, sed adhuc non tota; quae proxima est, tota speciosa est."

[187] *Sacr.*, 1.1.3 (*PL* 176.189A; Deferrari 9). [188] Jaeger, *Envy of Angels*, 258.

[189] *Tribus diebus*, 16 (Poirel 36.591–93).

[190] *Misc.*, 1.186 (*PL* 177.582D): "Est enim quasi pulchritudo quaedam spiritualis naturae ipsa cognitio veritatis."

[191] *Arrha* (*OHSV* 1.254–56:448f.; Herbert 24f.): "sapientia quasi naturali pulchritudine faciem vultus tui decorans intus."

[192] *Sacr.*, 2.Prol. (*PL* 176.363; Deferrari 205): "Sicut enim sancta electorum Ecclesia morum bonorum ac virtutum varietate pulchre adornatur."

[193] *Misc.*, 1.186 (*PL* 177.582D): "quasi sanitas quaedam est amor virtutis."

In the end, Hugh is concerned with the integral beauty of the whole person, of which Mary, the Mother of God, is the paradigm of the chaste, virgin soul: "This is total beauty: beauty in body, beauty in mind. In the body, the integrity of virginity makes you beautiful; in the mind the virtue of humility exhibits beauty … For in you beauty lacks nothing which it does not possess: *decor* obtains over all; *formositas* holds over all, *honestas* rules over all."[194] As Rorem notes, following Bernadette Jollès, Hugh's description here is "about Mary as an exemplar for all the faithful." Fassler notes the extension of moral beauty to all: "for Hugh, beauty … is found … in human beings. Hugh's church … is beautiful for its saints."[195]

All this receives its most sublime treatment from Hugh in his spiritual masterpiece, *De arrha animae*. Construed as a dialogue with himself, a central theme is the soul's need for recovering its lost beauty, of arriving at *pulchrum* and *formosum esse*,[196] which had been granted it in creation but was lost in the Fall. That beautiful soul surpassed "nothingness through its existence" and surpassed "the merely existing" because it possessed "form (*formam*)."[197] "He gave us being and beautiful being (*pulchrum esse*); he also gave us an existence that excels through essence what does not exist, [excels] through form (*formam*) what is disordered or uncomposed, and [excels] through life what is inanimate."[198] But in sinning, Hugh tells his soul, "you have corrupted your integrity (*integritatem*), made ugly your beauty (*pulchritudinem*), dispersed your adornment (*ornatum*)."[199] This deformed state is the primary obstacle to divine–human intimacy. For "it is not fitting to join deformed things (*deformia*) to beautiful ones."[200] The divine activity in creating beauty pre-figures the divine activity in re-creation – as ever, Hugh finding parallels between creation and salvation.

By his gift you had been made beautiful, but you were made ugly through your own iniquity. Yet again you have been purified and made most lovely (*formosa*) through his compassion, his charity operating in both cases. When you did not exist, he loved you so that you would; afterward, when you became ugly, he loved you so as to restore you to beauty (*pulchram*).[201]

[194] *Pro assumptione Virginis* (*OHSV* II.118:87–94; *PL* 177.1211D): "*Tota pulchra es, amica mea, et macula non est in te.* Tota pulchra res. Pulchra in corpore, pulchra in mente. In corpore pulchram te facit integritas virginitatis, in mente pulchram exhibet virtus humilitatis. Tota ergo pulchra es, corpore nivea, mente sincera. Tota pulchra es: nihil enim in te pulchritudo reliquit quod non possideat; totum decor obtinet, formositas tenet, regit honestas."

[195] Fassler, *Gothic Song*, 222.

[196] *Arrha* (*OHSV* I.252:414f.; Herbert 23).

[197] *Arrha* (*OHSV* I.252:415f.; Herbert 23).

[198] *Arrha* (*OHSV* I.254:423f.; Herbert 24).

[199] *Arrha* (*OHSV* I.256:448f.; Herbert 24).

[200] *Arrha* (*OHSV* I.232:103; Herbert 16).

[201] *Arrha* (*OHSV* I.258:498ff.; Herbert 26ff.).

In fact, though, this text states as completed what is a process that is still under way, and the burden of the treatise is to exhort the soul to pursue it with zeal. For divine–human intimacy, here construed in bridal terms, cannot be achieved until human beauty is restored. So, the whole spiritual life for Hugh is here construed in terms of the recovery of the form of the beautiful. "How can you therefore seek to go so quickly into that chamber of modesty and chasteness, unless by some care and zeal you first regain your former comeliness (*decorem*)?"[202] The soul thus begs to know "what those remedies are by which I ought to reform the beautiful appearance of my features (*decorem reformare*)"[203] so as to be worthy of the Bridegroom's love. The answer? "Be zealous to improve your form (*formam*), to adorn your face, to compose your deportment, to wipe away your guilt, to repair your purity, to correct your morals, to follow discipline, and being changed for the better (*in melius*) in all things, present yourself as a worthy lover of a most excellent spouse."[204] Specifically:

> Put on the vestment of good works, and the fruit of almsgiving, with fasts and prayers, with holy vigils and other deeds of piety, as if decorated with various adornments (*ornatu decoraris*). Finally there follows the fragrance of the virtues, the sweet odor of which breathing forth dispels the stench of past filth, so that somehow you seem wholly changed (*mutari*) and transformed (*transformari*) into someone else.[205]

As above, the "engine" driving this regimen of re-form is charity. "That is the force of love," that "somehow by the association of love you are transformed (*transformaris*) to the likeness of the very one to whom you are joined by affection (*affectum*)."[206] Hence, the crux of Hugh's spirituality is the process of re-form that ultimately beautifies the soul. The whole success of the spiritual life hinges on the recovery of beautiful form through patient practices of tropology: "Your perfection (*perfectio*) is patiently awaited by Him."[207]

THE SOUL AS ARK: RE-FORMED *INTEGRITAS* AS RETURN TO CHRISTOLOGICAL *FORMA*

As noted above, Hugh finds various layers of tropological meaning in the ark-symbol. Indeed, its deepest meaning lies in these, by providing graphic illustration of the process and results of the re-formation in virtue described above.

[202] *Arrha* (*OHSV* 1.262:565ff.; Herbert 28ff.).
[203] *Arrha* (*OHSV* 1.268:647f.; Herbert 30f.).
[204] *Arrha* (*OHSV* 1.264:575f.; Herbert 28f.).
[205] *Arrha* (*OHSV* 1.270:680f.; Herbert 31f.).
[206] *Arrha* (*OHSV* 1.232:109f.; Herbert 16f.).
[207] *Arrha* (*OHSV* 1.280:829–30; Herbert 35).

To begin, the formal nature of the ark-symbol merits emphasis. Just as justice is the "form" imprinted on the "matter" of the soul's affections, so the ark is a "form" received by the heart: "We put before you the pattern (*exemplar*) of our ark … and when you have impressed the form (*forma*) of this pattern on your heart, you may rejoice that the house of God has been built in you."[208] And, God's salvific actions are "producing in our hearts the form (*formam*) of an invisible ark."[209] More precisely, though, this is an architectural *forma*, constructed by the divine Artisan – "[The Holy Spirit] will come to you, in order to build a mansion in you. For He will not find it when He comes, but He will come in order to build."[210] But not by Him alone: "You will build a house (*fabricabis domum*) for the Lord your God in and of yourself. He will be the craftsman (*artifex*)," but "He chooses other builders (*artifices*) too."[211] So "there are two artificers" at work: "God and the man himself."[212] At the same time, according to the sapiential Christology described in Chapter 4, Christ too is the wise Architect: "For in truth [Christ] is Himself the wisdom whereof it is said, 'Wisdom hath builded her house.'"[213]

Quite clearly, the ark-symbol represents the soul's emerging integrity and unity, which is constructed gradually, in stages of increasing virtue, like an emerging edifice: "Let us picture to ourselves a human soul rising out of this world towards God and, as it rises, gathering itself ever more and more into a unity." This is the deep significance of "the form (*forma*) of our ark, which was broad at the bottom, and narrowed gradually as it rose, till at the peak it came to measure a single cubit only." For we too "grow steadily in the virtues as by certain ordered stages in our hearts, and we are gradually drawn towards a unity, until we attain even to that simple oneness, that true simplicity and eternal stability, that is in God."[214] Again, such an ark, wide at the bottom, narrower at the top, symbolizes the soul "gathering itself together" so that it is increasingly "integrated and drawn up to a point."[215] This God-like *stabilitas* is a signal characteristic of the soul's structural wholeness and formal integrity.

[208] *Archa Noe*, 4.17 (Sicard 117.168–72; CSMV 153).
[209] *Archa Noe*, 4.5 (Sicard 100.60–64; CSMV 137).
[210] *Septem donis*, 1 (Baron 122.27–29): "Veniet ad te, ut mansionem faciat in te. Non enim inveniet quando veniet, sed veniet ut faciat. Prius aedificabit, postea habitabit."
[211] *Archa Noe*, 4.1 (Sicard 87.30–34; CSMV 123).
[212] *Archa Noe*, 4.1 (Sicard 88.66–67; CSMV 124).
[213] *Archa Noe*, 4.1 (Sicard 88.58–59; CSMV 124).
[214] *Archa Noe*, 4.4 (Sicard 90.35–91.49; CSMV 126–27).
[215] *Vanitate*, 2.3 (*PL* 176.714B; CSMV 176).

At the same time, the Christological center of the moral life is manifest in the structure of the ark-symbol. As just noted, Hugh's ark narrows as it ascends until finally arriving at "the measure of a single cubit at the top." This cubit, which is the topmost point of a "pillar set up in the middle of the ark," represents Christ incarnate,[216] who as such is not only "the Head of His Church," but is also "the Saint of saints," and "like to other men in all respects in nature, but in the uniqueness of His virtue He is above them all."[217] Christ is the exemplary form and true measure of ideal humanity: "[Christ] was at once perfect, and yet never overflowed. In His body, He did not desert patience; in His soul, His compassion never exceeded the measure of justice." In that sense, His is the holiness and virtue to be imitated; but because the soul is to receive this as a *forma*, imitation is more precisely participatory con-formation. In short, insofar as the ark represents a process of moral formation, it is always Christo-formation. This gives Hugh's use of the language of Ephesians special resonance: "thirty [cubits denotes] 'the measure of the age of the fullness of Christ' (Eph. 4:13)."[218] Again: "we strive towards conformity with [Christ] and 'the measure of the age of His fullness' (Eph. 4:13)."[219]

The aesthetic signature of the tropological is also readily apparent in the ark-symbol:

I give you the ark of Noah as a model of a spiritual building, which your eye may see outwardly so that your soul may be built inwardly in its likeness. You will see the colors, shapes, and figures which please the eye; but know that they are set there to teach you wisdom, understanding, and virtue, to adorn your soul.[220]

This is the beauty that the prophets of old longed to see.[221] This is the *pulchrum esse*, wrought first in the visible creation of the world in six days, as a sacramental symbol of what God intended to bring about in the rational creature over six ages of salvation history (see Chapter 2). Indeed, in the ark treatises, Hugh offers hope to his readers on this basis:

He created everything you see from nothing. He it was who fashioned the marvellous framework of the world. He contrived the shapes and forms that were to be assumed by every single thing, and gave all things their beauty. You may well judge, then, what He can do in things invisible, who has disposed visible things so marvelously.[222]

216 *Archa Noe*, 2.5 (Sicard 41.33–35; CSMV 82): "That is why the ark is gathered into one at the top, that even now we should be thinking of the One, looking for the One, desiring the One, even our Lord Jesus Christ."

217 *Archa Noe*, 1.5 (Sicard 24.26–30; CSMV 65).

218 *Archa Noe*, 1.5 (Sicard 27.85–86; CSMV 67).

219 *Archa Noe*, 2.7 (Sicard 46.90–95; CSMV 86).

220 *Archa Noe*, 1.3 (Sicard 10.39–40; CSMV 52).

221 *Archa Noe*, 1.2 (Sicard 8.65; CSMV 50).

222 *Archa Noe*, 4.1 (Sicard 87.44–49; CSMV 123).

If God's creation is thus, *a fortiori* what will the beauty be of His re-forming artisanship within the invisible soul itself?

Finally, as noted, Hugh can describe the whole of tropology as the "ark of charity," indicating the centrality of love in the moral–spiritual life. For "among all these [virtues] there is one that is supremely necessary, namely, charity, which unites us to God."[223] Love is the root, ground, and source of all the other virtues and so of the overarching integrity that ensues from them. In the architectural imagery of the ark, charity's role is depicted as the apex and architectural climax of the re-structured soul. The third and highest story of the ark, after faith and hope, corresponds to charity.[224] Grace gradually constructs the "ark of charity" by building up "many virtues in a single charity."[225] Charity is also imaged as a fire (ignited by the Spirit) that liquefies the soul so that it can be re-cast in the Christological form atop the ark. "So the mind, dissolved by the fire of love, flows … into the image of the divine likeness."[226] The integrity of virtue is ultimately a re-establishment of the soul's love: sin and vice disintegrate and destabilize the soul by dissipating its affection toward illicit and inferior objects "outside" and "beneath" it. Virtue, by contrast, makes the soul "one in the love of the One."[227] The immediate goal of the moral life is to re-orient affection Godward, which is simultaneously its re-integration, imaged as re-structuring. The re-constructed *stabilitas* of the ark represents the restored integrity of the soul. The cubit atop the ark represents the ultimate unity of re-integration: Let us attain the love of God, "for He will integrate and stabilize our hearts" and "restore our peace."[228]

By charity, the soul comes to indwell itself more fully, the "heart" becomes "more at one with itself."[229] Through the preceding practices of *memoria* and *meditatio*, the soul lays a foundation and constructs an edifice of faith (see Chapters 7–8). Now, through the practices of *moralia*, it comes to inhabit that structure by loving what it knows and believes:

> What good does it do them to have faith, and not abide therein? … The true believers are not of this sort … Hear, then, what is said of him. "The law of his God is in his heart" (Ps. 37:31) – that is, he has an ark inside. And, in case this should not be enough, listen also to this. "His will is in the law of the Lord" (Ps. 1:2) – that is, he lives in the ark. He is the perfect man, who loves what he believes, so that his faith is that which works by love.[230]

223 *Archa Noe*, 2.5 (Sicard 41.32–33; CSMV 82). 224 *Archa Noe*, 4.9 (Sicard 115.109; CSMV 151).
225 *Archa Noe*, 1.3 (Sicard 17.236–39; CSMV 59–60).
226 *Misc.*, 1.173 (*PL* 177.572A). 227 *Archa Noe*, 1.1 (Sicard 5.47–48; CSMV 47).
228 *Archa Noe*, 1.2 (Sicard 7.24; CSMV 48). 229 *Archa Noe*, 2.5 (Sicard 41.22; CSMV 81).
230 *Archa Noe*, 4.8 (Sicard 106.31–42; CSMV 142).

This too reflects Hugh's overarching concern with *integritas*, or integration.[231] Moral practices are not "tacked on" to the preceding intellectual practices of historical study and theological meditation, as some pious afterthought or accidental by-product; rather, the tropological is the personal, even "existential" appropriation and consummation of the preceding practices of Hugh's re-forming program. The soul becomes an edifice in two ways, he says, "by knowledge and by love." But there is the difference between them: "knowledge erects the structure of faith by its knowing, whereas love like an adorning color embellishes the building by its virtue." But the integrity of the soul requires both: "each is thus seen to be essential to the other, for the building could not be glorious if had never come to be, nor could it give delight were it not glorious."[232] Just as, for the Augustinian Hugh, God cannot be known without being loved, nor loved without being known, so too doctrine and devotion, theology and spirituality are inextricably and essentially inter-connected: "This is what is said in the Gospel: 'Where your treasure is, there is your heart' (Matthew 6). As if it had said … Such is your affection, such also is your cogitation."[233] Or again: "to believe" is a "property of the heart," which receives "the character" of that which it loves and knows.[234]

CONCLUSION: *AD CONTEMPLATIO*

This for Hugh is tropology: virtue as a re-structuring of the human person, an inflaming of the heart with charity, a right ordering of the will and its desires and affections, the establishment of peace and concord within the whole person, body and soul. Virtue is re-formed affectivity and integrity, accomplished by the Holy Spirit in conformity with Christ. It is the culmination of a re-forming process by which the soul acquires its true beauty (*pulchrum esse*). But the soul's beauty is not an end in itself; rather, it draws the divine Bridegroom into the soul. The ultimate goal is divine indwelling:

> Indwell us, therefore, O sweet and suave charity, dilate our hearts, expand our desires, enlarge the cavity (*sinus*) of our mind, amplify the dwelling place of our heart, so that it may be capable of being a host and tabernacle for God. Inflow and diffuse yourself into our hearts through the Holy Spirit of our only

[231] *Archa Noe*, 4.2 (Sicard 91.48–49; CSMV 127): ark-building is the "manner of our reintegration (*reparationis*)." *Archa Noe*, 4.2 (Sicard 92.68–69; CSMV 127) "reintegrated (*colligatur*) after being scattered abroad."

[232] *Archa Noe*, 1.3 (Sicard 9.7–9; CSMV 50). [233] *Lament.* (*PL* 175.290D).

[234] *Archa Noe*, 4.7 (Sicard 103.24–25; CSMV 139).

Redeemer and Savior, Jesus Christ the Son of God, so that with the Father He might deign to come to us and make in us a dwelling place.[235]

It is in this loving indwelling that Hugh locates, as it were, the final and consummating human practice, namely, *contemplatio.*[236] Returning to the progression, noted at the outset of this chapter, to "study or doctrine, meditation, prayer and performance," Hugh appends a fifth and final step: "contemplation, in which as by a sort of fruit of the preceding steps, one has a foretaste, even in this life, of what the future reward of good works is."[237]

[235] *Laude* (*OHSV* 1.200:281–87): "Illabere igitur nobis, o dulcis et suavis charitas, dilata cor nostrum, expande desiderium, distende mentis nostrae sinum, amplifica cordis nostri habitaculum, ut capere possit hospitem et mansorem Deum. Infundat et diffundat te in cordibus nostris per Spiritum sanctum suum Redemptor noster unicus et Salvator Jesus Christus Filius Dei, ut ipse cum Patre ad nos venire dignetur, et mansionem in nobis facere."

[236] Rorem, *Hugh of St. Victor*, 32: "In particular, contemplation will remain an important category in Hugh's works, correlated to tropology ..."

[237] *Didasc.*, 5.9 (Buttimer 109.16–17; Taylor 132): "quinta deinde sequitur, contemplatio, in qua, quasi quodam praecedentium fructu, in hac vita etiam quae sit boni operis merces futura praegustatur."

Conclusion

CONTEMPLATION

As noted at the conclusion of the preceding chapter, the overriding goal, not only of tropology, but indeed of the entire re-forming process (including the memorial and meditative practices associated with literal and allegorical exegesis), is contemplation[1] – "the highest degree of perfection."[2] Though the term can at times have a wider sense for Hugh, *contemplatio* has here the narrow meaning of a direct and immediate "loving knowledge" of God. For this, God created humanity in the first place: "God made humankind for Himself, not because He needed humankind, but so that humankind could enjoy Him, for He could give nothing better."[3] This, pre-lapsarian humanity enjoyed, delighting in God "by cognition" and "by love."[4] This, post-lapsarian humanity needs to recover, and to do so is to arrive at beatitude: "There are two things by which the whole nature of the rational soul is disposed, namely, cognition and affection … If the soul completely obtains these and genuinely disposes [itself] with these, it is blessed."[5] Such beatific "loving knowledge" is wisdom (*sapientia*), which is itself a participation in divine Wisdom: The rational creature was made "through (*per*) the wisdom of God, so that he might exist (*esset*)." But mere existence was not the goal. Rather, humanity was also made "for" or "toward (*ad*)" the wisdom of God, so that it "might exist blessedly (*beate esset*)." Standing within the ancient tradition of the spiritual senses of the soul, Hugh's contemplative beatitude is an experiential

[1] For a discussion, see Dominique Poirel, *Hugues de Saint-Victor,* Initiations au Moyen-Age (Paris: Cerf, 1998), 123ff.

[2] *Archa Noe,* 3.15 (Sicard 82.18; CSMV 119).

[3] *Tribus diebus,* 11 (Poirel 30.483f.).

[4] *Sacr.*, 1.6.5 (*PL* 176.266D; Deferrari 97).

[5] *In Eccl.* (*PL* 177.141B–C): "Duo quippe sunt, quibus animae rationalis natura tota disponitur, videlicet cognitio et affectus, id est sapientia et amor. Quae duo si anima perfecte obtineat et legitime disponat, beata est."

and "intimate taste of wisdom."[6] "For charity itself is wisdom, since by charity we taste God, and tasting we know him."[7] Contemplation, moreover, is the means by which the rational creature experiences the "presence of God": "By always seeing Him he would thus always have loved Him, by always loving Him he would always have cleaved to Him, and, by always cleaving to Him who is immortal he too would have possessed in Him life without end."[8]

Contemplative beatitude is thus constantly present in Hugh's thought as the horizon within which the "work of restoration" occurs, even though he does not typically discuss it at length.[9] Indeed, he maintains a fairly consistent eschatological reservation regarding contemplation. "The cognition of all those things that we learn in the present with the zeal of reading or meditation … is only a kind of image of that full and perfect cognition which afterwards we will drink up in contemplation. Hence the Apostle said: 'Now we see through a glass darkly, but then face to face' (1 Cor. 13)."[10] Full contemplation is for the next life, and in the present there are only hints and intimations. Sometimes, "by a secret and familiar visitation" from God, the soul "*in a fashion* begins to possess Him present through contemplation …" (emphasis added).[11]

HOW LOVELY IS YOUR DWELLING PLACE: DIVINE INDWELLING OF THE SOUL AS BRIDAL CHAMBER

Despite this eschatological reserve, Hugh sees crucial continuity between the labor of this present life and the contemplative rest of the next. This can be construed in terms of reward: "for those to whom the love of God is the cause in work, the presence of God is the reward in requital."[12] But more typically the practices of this present life – both intellectual and moral, as described in the preceding chapters – are preparatory in the sense of a

6 *Lament.* (*PL* 175.291B): "dum vaga mens eas ad internam quietem non colligit, usque ad gustum intimi saporis non pertingunt."

7 *Archa Noe*, 3.1 (Sicard 55.6–7; CSMV 94): "quia per charitatem Deum gustamus, gustando autem cognoscimus."

8 *Archa Noe*, 1.2 (Sicard 4.31–33; CSMV 46).

9 But see the extended discussion in *In Eccl.* (*PL* 177.116D–118D).

10 *In hierarchiam* (175.950C–D): "Omnis enim illa cognitio, quam … studio lectionis vel meditationis discimus, quasi imago tantum est illius plenae [950D] ac perfectae cognitionis, quam postmodum ex praesenti contemplatione hauriemus. Unde et Apostolus ait: 'Videmus nunc per speculum in aenigmate; tunc autem facie ad faciem' (1 Corinthians 13)."

11 *Sacr.*, 1.10.4 (*PL* 176.333C–D; Deferrari 171).

12 *Sacr.*, 1.6.17 (*PL* 176.274B; Deferrari 106): "ut quibus amor Dei causa est in opere, praesentia Dei praemium sit in retributione."

"capacitation" of the soul, both cognitively and affectively, for contemplative intimacy with God, that the soul "may rise up strengthened to that supreme stability, the contemplation of God."[13] In Hugh's preferred terminology, the soul needs to be formed again, re-formed, in order to enjoy the presence of God. This is the significance of the structural or architectural intuition governing so much of his thought. Re-formation facilitates the recovery of contemplation by re-structuring, re-constructing the soul so that it can be a fitting place for divine inhabitation: "He will come to you in order to make a dwelling place in you. For He does not find [it] when He comes; rather He comes in order to build. First He constructs, afterward He indwells."[14] Again: "the Lover of pure hearts cannot abide in us, unless He has first made Himself a dwelling in us."[15]

As noted in the Introduction, Hugh primarily conceives of *forma* in this structural-architectural fashion. This allows him to envision *re-formatio* in distinctive ways. First, the architectural *forma* enables him to conceive of Christ, church, and Scripture symbolically as so many concentric and overlapping structures to which the soul is simultaneously con-formed. Second, the associated process of construction enables him to conceive of the Christian life in a very practice-oriented way, and to coordinate these practices in a specific, structured progression. Here, the simple Gregorian image of a foundation, a scaffolding, and an adorning cover facilitates the coordination of various intellectual and moral practices with one another within a coherent process leading to a particular end.[16] Finally, the architectural image allows Hugh to conceive of the result of these re-forming practices as having both structural integrity and pleasing form. Re-formation restores wholeness of the self – the discipline of the body and a right relation to visible creation without; genuine knowledge of God and virtuous affectivity within – and thus its beauty. Most precisely, this is the "work of restoration (*opus restaurationis*)."

[13] *Archa Noe,* 4.2 (Sicard 92.73–74; CSMV 128).

[14] *Septem donis* 1 (Baron 122.27–29): "Veniet ad te, ut mansionem faciat in te. Non enim inveniet quando veniet, sed veniet ut faciat. Prius aedificabit, postea habitabit."

[15] *Archa Noe,* 4.1 (Sicard 88.56–58; CSMV 124).

[16] While the coordination of these various practices within the architectural image sheds helpful light on Hugh's theology, such a schematization cannot avoid a certain artificial separation, compartmentalization, and sequencing of practices that in the actual lived experience of the Abbey of St.-Victor would have occurred simultaneously and have been bound up together to one degree or another. Reading-for-memory, for example, would not cease once the practice of meditative *allegoresis* had begun, nor would the practices of the moral life only have begun after the completion of intellectual practices. What does seem to be the case, though, is that Hugh conceived of a certain overall progression in the Christian life and a certain logical (not necessarily chronological) and structural relation between various intellectual and moral practices.

Indulging the structural image one final time for the contemplative consummation, Hugh conceives of the re-formed soul as a bridal chamber, a place of the greatest divine–human intimacy. The soul's re-formed beauty draws God into it as a bridegroom to a bride: God "would not have been captivated by you unless a singular comeliness (*singularis decor*) in you, admirable beyond that of others, had attracted him."[17] What does your beauty – "so sublime, so decorus"[18] – signify, "but that he who clothed you has been preparing you as his spouse for his bridal chamber?"[19] "God is in the world as ruler of his kingdom; He is in the Church as head of the family in His own home; He is in the soul as the bridegroom in the wedding-chamber."[20] This is the goal of Hugh of St. Victor's theology of re-formation.

HUGH: A DISTINCTIVE THEOLOGICAL VISION

Approaching Hugh's theology from this perspective highlights several of its distinctive features.

(1) Early twelfth-century thinkers were keenly aware of themselves, both as indebted to their patristic (especially Augustinian) inheritance and as pioneering new theological territory. For his part, the "second Augustine" drew deeply from the bishop of Hippo, but he also introduced his own emphases and even novel elements. Where, for Augustine, the fallen wayfarer must reverse the gravitational pull of sin toward non-being, and ascend toward being itself, and terminate its homeless wandering there *in patria*, its true homeland, for the "second Augustine," the homeless sinner must rather re-construct a place within for divine indwelling.[21] For Hugh, the solution to the threat of non-being is not ascent but construction; the basic human ailment is dis-integration and de-formity, and the solution is a re-structuring re-form of the soul. Where Augustine turns "inward" in order to ascend "upward," Hugh turns inward, not so much to ascend a ladder, as in order to construct a house, a *templum Dei*. Where Augustine's spiritual exercises refurbish the *imago trinitatis* within the soul, enabling greater and higher participation in the Trinity, Hugh's reforming practices gradually restore the *forma sapientiae* within the soul, enabling divine descent and indwelling.

[17] *Arrha* (*OHSV* 1.234:126–29; Herbert 16).
[18] *Arrha* (*OHSV* 1.254:440; Herbert 24): "Quam sublimis, et quam decora."
[19] *Arrha* (*OHSV* 1.254:441f.; Herbert 24f.).
[20] *Archa Noe*, 1.2 (Sicard 7.46–8.48; CSMV 49).
[21] See F. Ohly, "*Cora mantis non angustum*," in *Schriften zur mittelalterlichen Bedeutungsforschung* (Darmstadt: Wissenschaftliche Buchgesellschaft, 1983), 128–55.

(2) Hugh's architectural intuition also assimilates and transforms the Dionysian approach to symbols. For the Areopagite, biblical symbols are illuminating and anagogic, while for Hugh they are not primarily meant to uplift or enlighten, but to trans-form; less tools for ascent or instruments for insight, and more structures with which to be formed so as to restore the soul's integrity. As Zinn has argued, medieval symbols were "not simply intellectual constructs which augment or ornament arguments," but were rather "agents of transformation."[22] In Hugh's hands, under the biblical and incarnational impulse of divine *descent* – the Word's indwelling of, and presence with, created realities – this traditional itinerary is given new orientation and emphasis.[23] The upward, ascending thrust receives a *terminus*, not in God *above* the soul, but, in light of the architectural framework, at the Christological apex *within* the soul, such that the upward thrusting tendency is turned into soul-forming scaffolds, restoring the soul's integrity and constructing a *templum Dei*.

(3) Hugh's tendency to harness the ascent for purposes of construction allows him to remain grounded in the creaturely world. Perhaps more than his patristic forebears, he can accommodate the material aspect of the human being within this framework. The human creature straddles the material and immaterial worlds, a divinely intended position not negated by the soul-structuring re-formation. The contemplative remains grounded in the earth, even as the structured soul rises above in contemplation. The foundation is not negated; nor are material things transcended as so many symbolic ladders to be climbed and then kicked away.

(4) Hugh's "theology of re-formation" entails a profoundly integrated notion of theological formation, one that unites theological speculation and practical application. For Hugh, theological practices are deeply linked to Christology, ecclesiology, and scriptural exegesis, and in the end find their deepest significance and meaning within that context. Conversely, speculative theology is never divorced from a practical orientation and is always conceived with an eye toward soteriological formation.

(5) Another distinctive feature of Hugh's theology might be termed a "dynamic essentialism." From his synthesis of a neoplatonic ontology of timeless, essential "forms" and a biblical "ontology" of dynamic, historical progression toward an eschatological goal comes a conception of

[22] Zinn, "Mandala Symbolism," 318.

[23] See Zinn, "Book and Word," 146, on Hugh's "ability to absorb and synthesize traditions to which he is debtor, while also advancing his own insights."

nature – especially human nature – as possessing simultaneously a particular, divinely intended structure or essence that is also in some sense open to novelty, capable of change "for the better (*in melius*)". This is more than a developmental essentialism, as in a seed that "becomes" a flower. As noted, salvation for Hugh is not a return to Eden; his soteriology is more forward looking than backward, which is why the term "restoration" (*restauratio*), taken casually, can be misleading. Rather, without spelling it out completely, Hugh's anthropology attempts a "middle way" between a fixed, timeless, essential human nature, on the one hand, and a (modern) absolutely unhindered, self-positing subjectivity, on the other.

(6) For Hugh, accordingly, the necessity of traversing the distance between fallen "de-formation" and eschatologically realized "re-formation for the better" implies a human subject that is always "on the way" (*in via*), always undergoing formation, always moving toward, but never arriving at, fully formed subjectivity.

(7) This historically emerging *forma* of the self is received gradually, historically by participation in the *Forma* of all forms, namely, Christ. He is the ultimate *Forma*, which is *antecedently* present in and to creation and history, but not yet fully revealed there and only gradually being realized in individuals. This is conceived of as a gradually intensifying participation in the *forma Christi*, mediated by the forming structures of church and Scripture derived from it. This is depicted in the ark-symbol, where Christ simultaneously embraces as Alpha and Omega and informs as Center: cosmos, history, church, and individuals.

(8) Finally, the human person is simultaneously receptive of the preestablished Christological *forma*, while also invited – indeed summoned! – to active, participatory, "self-construction." As Hugh quips: "God would have us work with him." While the "*forma* is one," and comes from without, from "above," and must be received from divine Wisdom, who herself "builds her house" in soul and church, the "matter is different." That is, the *forma* is actively appropriated in each person uniquely and individually.

Bibliography

I PRIMARY WORKS BY HUGH OF ST. VICTOR

Adnotationes elucidatoriae in libros regum
PL 175.95–114.

Adnotationes elucidatoriae in Pentateuchon
PL 175.29–86.

Adnotatiunculae elucidatoriae in threnos Jeremiae
PL 175.255–322.

Chronicon vel De tribus maximis circumstantiis gestorum (*The Chronicles*)
Green, William. "Hugo of St. Victor: *De tribus maximis circumstantiis gestorum*." *Speculum* 18 (1943), 484–93.
Carruthers, Mary, trans. "The Three Best Memory Aids." In *The Medieval Craft of Memory: An Anthology of Texts and Pictures*, eds. Mary Carruthers and Jan M. Ziolkowski. Philadelphia, 2002, 32–40. A revision of Mary Carruthers, *The Book of Memory*, Cambridge, 1990, 261–66.

Commentaria in hierarchiam coelestem s. dionysii areopagitae (*Commentary on the Celestial Hierarchy*)
PL 175.923–1154.
Poirel, Dominique. *Hugonis de Sancto Victore Opera iii: Super Ierarchiam Dionysii*. CCCM 178, Turnhout, forthcoming.

De amore sponsi ad sponsam/Eulogium sponsi ad sponsam (*On the Love of the Bridegroom toward the Bride*)
PL 176.987–94.
Norris Jr., Richard A. 2003. In *The Song of Songs Interpreted by Early Christian and Medieval Commentators*, ed. and trans. Richard A. Norris Jr. Grand Rapids, Mich., 2003, 167–72.

De archa Noe (*Noah's Ark*)
PL 176.617–80 (*De arca Noe morali*).
Sicard, Patrice. *Hugonis de Sancto Victore: De archa Noe, Libellus de formatione arche*. CCCM 176, Turnhout, 2001.
"Noah's Ark: 1." In *Hugh of St. Victor: Selected Spiritual Writings*, trans. by a Religious of The Community of St. Mary the Virgin, intr. by Aelred Squire. Classics of the Contemplative Life. London, 1962, 45–153.

De arrha anime (*Soliloquy on the Earnest Money of the Soul*)
PL 176.703–40.
OHSV I.209–300.
Herbert, Kevin. *Soliloquy on the Earnest Money of the Soul.* Milwaukee, 1956.

De beatae Mariae virginitate (*On the Virginity of the Blessed Mary*)
PL 176.857–76.
OHSV II.182–252.

De grammatica
Baron, Roger. 1966. *Hugonis de Sancto Victore Opera Propaedeutica.* Notre Dame, Ind., 1966, 75–156.

De institutione novitiorum (*On the Formation of Novices*)
PL 176.925–52.
OHSV I.18–114.

De laude caritatis (*On Praise of Charity*)
PL 176.970–76.
OHSV I.173–207.

De meditatione (*On Meditation*)
Baron, Roger. 1969. In *Six opuscules spirituels.* SC 155, 1969, 44–58.

De quatuor voluntatibus in Christo (*On the Four Wills in Christ*)
PL 176.841B–846C.

De quinque septenis (*On the Five Sevens*)
PL 175.405–11.
Baron, Roger. 1969. In *Six opuscules spirituels.* SC 155, 1969, 100–18.

De sacramentis christianae fidei (*On the Sacraments of the Christian Faith*)
PL 176.173–618.
Deferrari, Roy, J. *On the Sacraments of the Christian Faith* (*De sacramentis*). Medieval Academy of America 58. Cambridge, Mass., 1951.

De sacramentis legis naturalis
PL 176. 17–42.

De sapientia Christi (*On the Wisdom of Christ*)
PL 176.845–56.

Descriptio mappe mundi (*A Description of the Map of the World*)
Dalché, Patrick Gautier. *La "Descriptio mappe mundi" de Hugues de Saint-Victor: Texte inédit avec introduction et commentaire.* Paris, 1988.

De scripturis et scriptoribus sacris (*On the Scriptures*)
PL 175.9–28
Stammberger, Ralf. "*Diligens scutator sacri eloquii*: An Introduction to Scriptural Exegesis by Hugh of St. Victor Preserved at Admont Library (MS 672)." In *Manuscripts and Monastic Culture*, ed. Alison I. Beach. Turnhout, 2007, 241–83.
Turner, Denys. *Eros and Allegory: Medieval Exegesis of the Song of Songs.* Kalamazoo, Mich., 1995, 265–74 (partial trans.).

De septem donis Spiritus Sancti (*On the Seven Gifts of the Holy Spirit*)
PL 175.401–14.
Baron, Roger. In *Six opuscules spirituels*. SC 155, 1969, 120–32.

De substantia dilectionis (*On the Nature of Love*)
PL 176.15–18.
Baron, Roger. In *Six opuscules spirituels*. SC 155, 1969, 82–92.
Squire, Aelred. In *Hugh of Saint-Victor: Selected Spiritual Writings*. London, 1962, 187–91.

De tribus diebus (*On the Three Days*)
PL 176.811–38.
Poirel, Dominque. *Hugonis de Sancto Victore: De tribus diebus*. CCCM 177, 2002.
van Zwieten, J. *Hugh van St. Victor, De drie dagen*. Kampen, 1996.

De vanitate mundi (*On the Vanity of the World*)
PL 176.703–40.
Squire, Aelred. 1962. In *Hugh of St. Victor: Selected Spiritual Writings*. London, 1962, 157–82.

De Verbo incarnato (*On the Word Incarnate*)
PL 177.315D–324A

De Verbo Dei (*On the Word of God*)
PL 177.289–94.
Baron, Roger. In *Six opuscules spirituels*. SC 155, 1969, 60–80.

De virtute orandi (*On the Power of Prayer*)
PL 176.977–84.
OHSV 1.126–71.

Didascalicon
PL 176.741–812.
Buttimer, C. H. *Didascalicon de studio legendi: A Critical Text*. The Catholic University of America Studies in Medieval and Renaissance Latin 10. Washington, D.C., 1939.
The Didascalicon of Hugh of St. Victor: A Medieval Guide to the Arts, ed. and trans. with introduction and notes Jerome Taylor. Records of Western Civilization: Sources and Studies 64. New York, 1961 and 1991.

Egredietur virga
OHSV 11.270–80.

In salomonis Ecclesiastes
PL 175.113–256.
Squire, Aelred. In *Hugh of St. Victor: Selected Spiritual Writings*. London, 1962, 183–87.

Libellus de formatione arche (*The Making of the Ark*)
PL 176.681–704 (*De arca Noe mystica*).
Sicard, Patrice. *Hugonis de Sancto Victore: "De arche Noe, Libellus de formatione arche."* CCCM 176, Turnhout, 2001.

Weiss, Jessica, trans. "Little Book." In *The Medieval Craft of Memory: An Anthology of Texts and Pictures*, eds. Mary Carruthers and Jan W. Ziolkowski. Philadelphia, 2002, 45–70.

Maria porta
OHSV II.282.

Miscellanea I
PL 177.469–77.

Practica geometriae (*Practical Geometry*)
Baron, Roger. In *Hugonis de Sancto Victore Opera Propaedeutica*. University of Notre Dame Publications in Mediaeval Studies 20. Notre Dame, Ind., 1966, 15–64.
Homann, Frederick A. *A Practical Geometry*. Milwaukee, Wisc., 1991.

Pro assumptione Virginis
PL 177.1209–22.
OHSV II.112–60.

Quid vere diligendum sit (*What Should Be Truly Loved*)
PL 177.564–65.
Baron, Roger. 1969. In *Six opuscules spirituels*. SC 155, 1969, 94–99.

Sententiae de divinitate (*Sentences on Divinity*)
Piazzoni, A. M. "Ugo di San Vittore 'auctor' delle *Sententiae de divinitate*." *Studi Medievali*, 3rd series, 23.2 (1982), 861–955.

Super canticum Mariae
PL 175.413–32.
OHSV II.16–99.

II OTHER PRIMARY WORKS

Pseudo-Hugh of St. Victor. *Expositio in regulam beati Augustini* (*Explanation of the Rule of St. Augustine*)
PL 176.881–924.
Smith, Aloysius. *Explanation of the Rule of St. Augustine*. London, 1911.

Summa sententiarum
PL 176.41–174.

III SECONDARY WORKS

Baron, Roger. *Hugues de Saint-Victor. La Contemplation et ses espèces*. Desclée, 1955.
"L'Idée de liberté chez S. Anselme et Hugues de Saint-Victor." *RTAM* 32 (1965), 117–21.
"Notes biographiques sur Hugues de Saint-Victor." *Revue d'histoire ecclésiastique* 51 (1956), 920–34.
Science et sagesse chez Hugues de Saint-Victor. Paris, 1957.

Bauerschmidt, Frederick Christian. "Order, Freedom, and 'Kindness': Julian of Norwich on the Edge of Modernity." *Theology Today* 60 (2003), 63–81.
Bautier, Robert-Henri. "Les Origines et les premiers développements de l'abbaye Saint-Victor de Paris." In *APS-V*, 1991, 23–52.
Benson, Robert L., and Giles Constable, with Carol D. Lanham, eds. *Renaissance and Renewal in the Twelfth Century*. Medieval Academy Reprints for Teaching 26. Toronto, 1991.
Berndt, Rainer. "Gehören die Kirchenväter zur Heiligen Schrift? Zur Kanontheorie des Hugo von St Viktor." In *Zum Problem des biblischen Kanons*. Jahrbuch für biblische Theologie, vol. III. Neukirchen-Vluyn, 1988, 191–99.
Bruyne, Edgar de . *Etudes d'esthétique médiévale*. 3 vols. Bruges, 1946.
Bynum, Carolyn Walker. *Docere Verbo et Exemplo: An Aspect of Twelfth-Century Spirituality*. Harvard Theological Studies 31. Missoula, 1979.
Jesus as Mother: Studies in the Spirituality of the High Middle Ages. Berkeley, 1982.
"The Spirituality of Regular Canons in the Twelfth Century." In *Jesus as Mother: Studies in the Spirituality of the High Middle Ages*. Berkeley, 1982, 22–58.
Carruthers, Mary J. *The Book of Memory: A Study of Memory in Medieval Culture*. Cambridge, 1990.
The Craft of Thought: Meditation, Rhetoric, and the Making of Images, 400–1200. Cambridge, 1998.
Carruthers, Mary J., and Jan M. Ziolkowski, eds. *The Medieval Craft of Memory: An Anthology of Texts and Pictures*. Philadelphia, 2002.
Charry, Ellen. *By the Renewing of Your Minds*. New York, 1997.
Châtillon, Jean. "La Bible dans les écoles du XIIe siècle." In *Le Moyen âge et la Bible*, eds. Pierre Riché and Guy Lobrichon. Paris, 1984, 163–97.
Le Mouvement canonial au moyen âge: réforme de l'église, spiritualité et culture. Bibliotheca Victorina 3. Paris/Turnhout, 1992.
Chenu, Marie-Dominique. *Nature, Man, and Society in the Twelfth Century: Essays on New Theological Perspectives in the Latin West*, ed. and trans. Jerome Taylor and Lester K. Little. Chicago and London, 1968.
"Civilisation urbaine et théologie. L'Ecole de Saint-Victor au XIIe siècle." *Annales: Economies, sociétés, civilisations* 29 (1974), 1253–63.
Cizewski, Wanda. "Reading the World as Scripture: Hugh of St. Victor's *DE TRIBUS DIEBUS*." *Florilegium* 9 (1987), 65–88.
Clark, William W. "Context, Continuity, and the Creation of National Memory in Paris, 1130–1160: A Critical Commentary." *Gesta* 45 (2006), 161–75.
Colish, Marcia. *Peter Lombard*. 2 vols. Leiden, 1994.
Constable, Giles. *The Reformation of the Twelfth Century*. Cambridge, 1996.
"Renewal and Reform in Religious Life: Concepts and Realities." In *Renaissance and Renewal in the Twelfth Century*, eds. Robert L. Benson and Giles Constable with Carol D. Lanham. Medieval Academy Reprints for Teaching 26. Cambridge, Mass., 1982, 37–67.
Coolman, Boyd Taylor. "Hugh of St Victor." In *The Sermon on the Mount through the Centuries*, eds. Jeffrey P. Greenman, Timothy Larsen, and Stephen Spencer. Grand Rapids, 2007, 72–102.

"Hugh of St. Victor on 'Jesus Wept': Compassion as Ideal *humanitas*." *Theological Studies* 69 (2008), 528–56.

"*Pulchrum Esse*: The Beauty of Scripture, the Beauty of the Soul, and the Art of Exegesis in the Theology of Hugh of St. Victor." *Traditio: Studies in Ancient and Medieval Thought, History, and Religion* 58 (2003), 175–200.

Croydon, E. "Notes on the Life of Hugh of St. Victor." *Journal of Theological Studies* 40 (1939), 232–53.

Dickinson, John C. *The Origins of the Austin Canons and Their Introduction into England*. London, 1950.

Duprè, Louis. *Passage to Modernity: An Essay in the Hermeneutics of Nature and Culture*. New Haven, 1993.

Eynde, Damien van den. 1960. *Essai sur la succession et la date des écrits de Hugues de Saint-Victor*. Spicilegium pontificii athenaei antoniani 13. Rome, 1960.

Fassler, Margot. *Gothic Song: Victorine Sequences and Augustinian Reform in Twelfth-Century Paris*. Cambridge, 1993.

Feiss, Hugh. "*Bernardus Scholasticus*: The Correspondence of Bernard of Clairvaux and Hugh of Saint Victor on Baptism." In *Bernardus Magister: Papers presented at the nonacentenary celebration of the birth of Saint Bernard of Clairvaux, Kalamazoo, Michigan, sponsored by the Institute of Cistercian Studies, Western Michigan University, 10–13 May 1990*, ed. John Sommerfeldt. Cistercian Studies 135. Spencer, Mass., 1992, 349–78.

Gemeinhardt, Peter. "Logic, Tradition, and Ecumenics: Developments of Latin Trinitarian Theology between c. 1075 and c. 1160." In *Trinitarian Theology in the Medieval West*, ed. Pekka Kärkkäinen. Vaajakoski, 2008, 10–68.

Green, William. "Hugo of St. Victor: *De tribus maximis circumstantiis gestorum*." *Speculum* 18 (1943), 484–93.

Hadot, Pierre. *Philosophy as a Way of Life: Spiritual Exercises from Socrates to Foucault*. Oxford/New York, 1995.

Harkins, Franklin. "Victorine Christology." *The Thomist* 72 (2008), 595–624.

Hofmeier, Johann. *Die Trinitätslehre des Hugo von St. Viktor dargestellt im Zusammenhang mit den trinitarischen Strömungen seiner Zeit*. Munich, 1963.

Howe, John. "The Nobility's Reform of the Church." *American Historical Review* 93.2 (1988), 317–39.

Illich, Ivan. *In the Vineyard of the Text: A Commentary on Hugh's Didascalicon*. Chicago, 1993.

Jaeger, C. Stephen. *The Envy of Angels: Cathedral Schools and Social Ideals in Medieval Europe*. Philadelphia, 1994.

Javelet, Robert. *Image et ressemblance au douzième siècle: de Saint Anselme à Alain de Lille*. 2 vols. Paris, 1967.

Jeffery, David Lyle, ed. *A Dictionary of Biblical Tradition in English Literature*. Grand Rapids, 1992.

Johnson, Luke Timothy. *The Creed: What Christians Believe and Why It Matters*. New York, 2003.

Karfíková, Lenka. *"De esse ad pulchrum esse." Schönheit in der Theologie Hugos von St. Viktor*. Bibliotheca Victorina 8. Turnhout, 1998.

Ladner, Gerhart H. *The Idea of Reform: Its Impact on Christian Thought and Action in the Age of the Fathers*. Cambridge, Mass., 1954.

Lasić, Dionysius. *Hugonis de S. Victore theologia perfectiva: eius fundamentum philosophicum ac theologicum*. Studia Antoniana 7. Rome, 1956.

Longère, Jean ed. *L'Abbaye parisienne de Saint-Victor au moyen-âge. Communications présentées au XIIIe colloque d'humanisme médiéval de Paris (1986–88)*. Bibliotheca Victorina 1. Turnhout, 1991.

Lubac, Henri de. *Exégèse médiévale: les quatre sens de l'écriture*. 4 vols. in 2 parts, 2 vols. each. Paris, 1959–64.

Corpus Mysticum: The Eucharist and the Church in the Middle Ages. Notre Dame, 2007.

Luscombe, David. "Thought and Learning." In *The New Cambridge Medieval History, vol. iv c.1024–c.1198*, eds. David Luscombe and J. Riley-Smith. Cambridge, 2004.

Luscombe, David, and J. Riley-Smith. "Introduction." In *The New Cambridge Medieval History, vol. iv c.1024–c.1198*, eds. David Luscombe and J. Riley-Smith. Cambridge, 2004.

McGinn, Bernard. *The Growth of Mysticism: Gregory the Great through the 12th Century*. New York, 1996.

The Essential Writings of Christian Mysticism. New York, 2006.

McGonigle, Thomas Declan. "Hugh of St. Victor's Understanding of the Relationship between the Sacramental and Contemplative Dimensions of Christian Life." Ph.D. dissertation, Harvard University, 1977.

Mews, Constant. "The World as Text." In *Scripture and Pluralism: Reading the Bible in the Religiously Plural Worlds of the Middle Ages and Renaissance*, eds. T. J. Heffernan and T. E. Burman. Studies in the History of Christian Traditions. Leiden, 2005.

Ohly, F. 1983. "*Cora mantis non angustum*." In *Schriften zur mittelalterlichen Bedeutungsforschung*, 128–55. Darmstadt, 1983.

Piazzoni, A. M. 1982. "Ugo di San Vittore 'auctor' delle 'Sententiae de divinitate." *Studi medievali* 23.2 (1982), 861–955.

Poirel, Dominique. "'Alter Augustinus – Der Zweite Augustinus': Hugo von Sankt Viktor und die Väter der Kirche." In *Väter der Kirche: Ekklesiales Denken von den Anfängen bis in die Neuzeit: Festgabe für Hermann Josef Sieben SJ zum 70. Geburtstag*, eds. Johannes Arnold, Rainer Berndt, and Ralf M. W. Stammberger. Munich, 2004, 643–68.

"*Hugo Saxo*. Les origines germaniques de la pensée d'Hugues de Saint-Victor." *Francia. Forschungen zur westeuropäischen Geschichte* 33.1 (2006), 163–69.

Hugues de Saint-Victor. Initiations au Moyen-Age. Paris, 1998.

Livre de la nature et débat trinitaire au XIIe siècle: le "De tribus diebus" de Hugues de Saint-Victor. Bibliotheca Victorina 14. Turnhout, 2002.

"Symbolice et anagogice: l'école de Saint-Victor et la naissance du style gothique." In *L'Abbé Suger, le manifeste gothique de Saint-Denis et la pensée victorine, colloque organisé à la Fondation Singer-Polignac le mardi 21 novembre 2000 par Rencontres médiévales européennes*, ed. Dominique Poirel. Rencontres médiévales européennes 1. Turnhout, 2001, 141–70.

Pollitt, H. J. "Some Considerations on the Structure and Sources of Hugh of St. Victor's Notes on the Octateuch." *Recherches de théologie ancienne et médiévale* 33 (1966), 5–38.

Poppenberg, Eberhard. *Die Christologie des Hugo von St. Viktor.* Hiltrup/ Münster, 1937.

Robert, G. *Les Ecoles et l'enseignement de la théologie pendant la première moitié du XIIe siècle.* Paris, 1909.

Robinson, I. S. "Reform and the Church, 1073–1122." In *The New Cambridge Medieval History, vol. iv c.1024–c.1198*, eds. David Luscombe and J. Riley-Smith. Cambridge, 2004, 268–334.

Rorem, Paul E. *Hugh of St. Victor.* Oxford, 2009.

Rudolph, Conrad. *"First, I Find the Center Point": Reading the Text of Hugh of Saint Victor's* The Mystic Ark. Transactions of the American Philosophical Society 94, pt. 4. Philadelphia, 2004.

Schlette, H. R. "Die Eucharistielehre Hugos von St. Viktor." *Zeitschrift fur katholische Theologie* 81 (1959), 67–100; 163–210.

Sicard, Patrice. *Hugues de Saint-Victor et son école: introduction, choix de texte, traduction et commentaires.* Témoins de Notre Histoire. Turnhout, 1991.

Diagrammes médiévaux et exégèse visuelle: Le Libellus de formatione arche de Hugues de Saint-Victor. Paris/Turnhout, 1993.

Smalley, Beryl. *The Study of the Bible in the Middle Ages.* Oxford, 1952.

Southern, Richard. W. "Presidential Address: Aspects of the European Tradition of Historical Writing: 2. Hugh of St. Victor and the Idea of Historical Development." *Transactions of the Royal Historical Society*, 5th series, 21 (1971), 149–79.

Scholastic Humanism and the Unification of Europe. Vol. II: *The Heroic Age.* Oxford, 2001.

Standaert, Maur. "La doctrine de l'image chez saint Bernard," *Ephemerides Theologiae Lovanienses* 23 (1947), 70–129.

Stiegman, Emero. "Three Theologians in Debate: Saint Bernard's Tract on Baptism." In *Bernard of Clairvaux: On Baptism and the Office of Bishops, on the Conduct and Office of Bishops, on Baptism and Other Questions: Two Letter-treatises*, trans. Pauline Matarasso. Cistercian Fathers Series 67. Kalamazoo, Mich., 2004, 85–147.

Stump, P. H. "The Influence of Gerhard Ladner's *The Idea of Reform.*" In *Reform and Renewal in the Middle Ages and the Renaissance: Studies in Honor of Louis Pascoe, S.J.*, eds. Thomas M. Izbicki and Christopher M. Bellitto. Studies in the History of Christian Thought 96. Leiden, 2000, 3–17.

Swanson, R. N. *The Twelfth Century Renaissance.* New York, 1999.

Taylor, Jerome. *The Origin and Early Life of Hugh of St. Victor: An Evaluation of the Tradition.* Texts and Studies in the History of Medieval Education 5. Notre Dame, Ind., 1957.

van den Eynde, Damien. *Essai sur la succession et la date des écrits de Hugues de Saint-Victor.* Spicilegium Pontificii Athenae Antoniani 13. Rome, 1960.

Van Engen, John H. "Images and Ideas: The Achievements of Gerhart Burian Ladner, with a Bibliography of his Published Works." *Viator* 20 (1989), 85–115.

van Zwieten, J. W. M. "The Preparation to Allegory: Hugh of St. Victor's *De Sacramentis* and His Notes on the Octateuch." *Nederlands archief voor kerkgeschiedenis* 68 (1988), 17–22.

Zinn, Grover A., Jr. "Book and Word: The Victorine Background of Bonaventure's Use of Symbols." In *S. Bonaventura 1274–1974*, ed. Jacques Guy Bougerol Vol. II. Rome, 1974, 143–69.

"*De gradibus ascensionum*: The Stages of Contemplative Ascent in Two Treatises on Noah's Ark by Hugh of St. Victor." In *Studies in Medieval Culture*, ed. J. R. Sommerfeldt, vol. v. Kalamazoo, Mich., 1975, 61–79.

"Exile, the Abbey of St-Victor at Paris, and Hugh of Saint Victor." In *Medieval Paradigms: Essays in honor of Jeremy du Quesnay Adams*, ed. Stephanie Hayes-Healy, vol. II. New York, 2005, 83–111.

"*Historia fundamentum est*: The Role of History in the Contemplative Life According to Hugh of St. Victor." In *Contemporary Reflections on the Medieval Christian Tradition: Essays in Honor of Ray C. Petry*, ed. George H. Shriver. Durham, NC, 1974, 135–58.

"History and Contemplation: The Dimensions of the Restoration of Man in Two Treatises on Noah's Ark by Hugh of St. Victor." Unpublished doctoral dissertation, Duke University, 1969.

"History and Interpretation: 'Hebrew Truth,' Judaism, and the Victorine Exegetical Tradition." In *Jews and Christians: Exploring the Past, Present, and Future*, ed. James H. Charlesworth. New York, 1990, 100–23.

"Hugh of St. Victor and the Ark of Noah: A New Look." *Church History* 40 (1971), 261–72.

"Hugh of St. Victor and the Art of Memory." *Viator* 5 (1974), 211–34.

"Hugh of St. Victor, Isaiah's Vision, and *De Arca Noe*." In *The Church and the Arts: Papers read at the 1990 Summer Meeting and the 1991 Winter Meeting of the Ecclesiastical History Society*, ed. Diana Wood. Oxford, 1992, 99–116.

"Hugh of St. Victor's *De scripturis et scriptoribus sacris* as an *Accessus* Treatise for the Study of the Bible." *Traditio: Studies in Ancient and Medieval Thought, History, and Religion* 52 (1997), 111–34.

"The Influence of Augustine's *De doctrina christiana* upon the Writings of Hugh of St. Victor." In *Reading and Wisdom: The De doctrina christiana of Augustine in the Middle Ages*. Notre Dame, 1995, 48–60.

"Mandala Symbolism and Use in the Mysticism of Hugh of St. Victor." *History of Religions* 12 (1972), 317–41.

"Personification Allegory and Visions of Light in Richard of St. Victor's Teaching on Contemplation." *University of Toronto Quarterly* 46 (1977), 190–214.

"Suger, Theology, and the Pseudo-Dionysian Tradition." In *Abbot Suger and Saint-Denis: A Symposium*, ed. Paula Lieber. New York, 1986, 33–40.

"Texts Within Texts: The Song of Songs in the Exegesis of Gregory the Great and Hugh of St. Victor." *Studia Patristica* 25, Leuven, 1993, 209–15.

"*Vestigia victorina*: Victorine Influence on the Spiritual Life in the Middle Ages with Special Reference to Hugh of Saint-Victor's *De Institutione novitiorum*." Unpublished paper, 2009.

Index

Page numbers in bold indicate topic discussed more thoroughly.

CPSIA information can be obtained at www.ICGtesting.com
Printed in the USA
LVOW06s2145010714

392552LV00001B/400/P

9 781107 612259